# BURKSEY

## THE AUTOBIOGRAPHY
## OF A FOOTBALL GOD

# PETER MORFOOT

# BURKSEY

## THE AUTOBIOGRAPHY
## OF A FOOTBALL GOD

## PETER MORFOOT

Know The Score Books Limited
www.knowthescorebooks.com

First published in the United Kingdom
by Know The Score Books Limited, 2006

First published in the United Kingdom
by Know The Score Books Limited, 2006

Know The Score Books Limited
The College Business Centre
Uttoxeter New Road
Derby
DE22 3WZ

www.knowthescorebooks.com

A CIP catalogue record is available for this book from the British Library
ISBN 1-905449-49-6

Cover Photography by Anthony Brown
Artwork by Marc Jones, D2E design and print
Book design by Lisa David

Printed and bound in Great Britain
By Cromwell Press, Trowbridge, Wiltshire

# ACKNOWLEDGEMENTS

Special Thanks to Gareth Edwards and Simon Lowe

Thanks to my ever supportive wife and family: Liz, Rob, Kate and Clare Morfoot

For other invaluable help, thanks to: Stephen Allard, Rick Glanvill, David Hatcher, Lisa Hitch, Neil Maynard, Helen Reed, Katherine Roddwell, The Scott Family, Harry Harris, Peter Smith, the PFA, Chris Lowe, Jonathan Lowe, Le Meridien Hotel, Piccadilly, AFC Wimbledon & Paul Zannetti

*Cover Photograph*
Stephen Burkes, football's most famous celebrity, acknowledges the crowd after scoring yet another goal for England

# PUBLISHER'S DISCLAIMER

To clarify, Stephen Burkes does not exist, has never existed and hopefully, never will exist. Accordingly, accounts of his involvement with real or imaginary personalities from the worlds of football, popular culture, celebrity, the arts, the media and politics within these pages are also totally fictional.

But if Burksey's story rings true to you, we wouldn't be surprised.

Finally, if anything intended to raise a laugh within these pages offends you, we're sorry. Really, we are.


# BURKSEY'S DISCLAIMER

If I've misremembered, misquoted or just plain made up stuff about the players, managers, clubs, matches, tournaments, media people, celebs, wives, girlfriends and even fans I talk about in this book, I hope you – and they – will forgive me. But think twice before you condemn me for the numerous inaccuracies and fictions that no doubt litter these pages. Instead, blame all the booze, drugs and other problems that for a while threatened my very existence on what I now regard as this lovely planet of ours. I would especially like to say that if I've offended anyone – however rich and powerful – I'm truly sorry.

Steve Burkes, April 2006

FOR ANDY MERRIMAN AND SUSAN HILL

# CONTENTS

# FOREWORD

Football? It's in my blood. I was conceived on World Cup Winning night – July 30th 1966 – not because my parents were football fans, but because my Grandma, who'd been living with them for the past seven years, had died in a freak stair-lift accident the previous day and my parents had felt like celebrating. Once they'd patched-up the hole in the landing ceiling.

The rest, as they say, is history. Almost.

At various times in my life, I've been dubbed a "clown", a "work-shy tosser," a "c*** on legs", a "pile of human garbage". I tell you, they don't write school-leaving reports like that any more. Later, fans and journalists have been even more outspoken – and divided. For some, I've been the best thing since mobile phones. After my last minute thirty yard back-heeled free kick sent Wolves crashing out of the FA Cup quarter final in '94, *The Mirror's* top soccer scribe Larry Harrison wrote: "Steve Burkes' reverse rocket through the Wolves wall will go down in history as one of the greatest – and certainly the cheekiest – goals ever scored. At times like these, Burksey doesn't just walk on water – he waltzes on it!"

*The Times'* Bryan Gonville was equally enthusiastic: "Burkes may be a little too much of the riddle wrapped in a mystery inside an enigma to command the total *rispetto** of manager and supporters alike, but there are moments in every game when what is called for is precisely the kind of *genio strano*** that he so abundantly possesses. His goal was as audacious as it was brilliant." You can't say fairer than that – or so my friend, the great Gianluca Vialli tells me, anyway.

But for every "yea" I've earned over the years, there have been at least as many "nays". Abuse, hate mail, mock executions and worse – I've been subjected to them all. And not only by referees.

So what am I – Saint or sinner? W***er or winner?

In short, who is the real Steve Burkes?

---

*Just to check, I typed this into one of those free translation services on the interweb and it came up with 'respect'. I couldn't agree more, Bryan.

**This one, however, must have been mistranslated as it came up with 'weird genius'. 'Genius' I can understand, but 'weird'? 'Out of this world,' yes.

2

So much has been written about me over the years that you probably think you know all about me. You don't. But here's a promise: by the time you've finished this book, you will know more about me – and not just some old boozer journo's lies about me – than even some of my wives know.

You want true revelations? You'll get them here. You want exclusive inside stories on some of the biggest players, matches and tournaments over the last twenty plus years? You'll get them here. You want the low-down on some of the biggest happenings away from the world of football? You'll get them here. You want a blow by blow-job account of all of my sexploits as a serial superstud? You can f*** off. No, okay, I might drop the pants on just a few of them for you.

But here's a warning. As you read this book, some of my words may surprise you. They may shock you. They may horrify you. But at least there's one thing you can be sure of. They are my words (as shared with Jim Felch, Rob Calderwood, Kevin Graham, Paulo Ciarliero, John French, Tim Sterne, Beth Stallings, and Ray Collins).

So, who is the real Steve Burkes?

If you think you're hard enough, read on.

Steve Burkes, April 2006

‾ ‾ ‾ ‾ ‾ ‾ ‾ ‾ ‾ ‾ ‾ ‾ ‾
| CHAPTER ONE |
‾ ‾ ‾ ‾ ‾ ‾ ‾ ‾ ‾ ‾ ‾ ‾ ‾

# PARADISE REGAINED

I've seen some big nights in my time. And I've been blind for quite a few others; blind drunk. Or smashed on crazy cocktails of drugs that could have flattened a charging rhino.

But not for this one. It was special – the first ever final of the Champions Champions Cup, the new League and Knockout competition for Europe's super elite clubs sponsored by Oiloco International in association with Stelsat TV. Yes, the evening of Wednesday 17th May 2006 was a good one for firsts. The game was the first football match ever to be screened as a P.P.V.B.I. (Pay Per View By Incident) event on TV.

And it wasn't a bad night for lasts, either. After sixty England caps and more than four hundred senior league appearances here and abroad, The European Champions Champions Cup Final was going to be my last ever game of professional football. You wanted revelations? How's that for starters? Yes, Steve Burkes is now an ex-footballer.

You won't need me to tell you that it was against all the odds that my club – Sporting Meriden – made it all the way through to the final. Do I hear fans moaning about how the club bought its way to the top? Alright, nobody knows better than me that it would never have happened without the vision and generosity of our owner, Canadian gas billionaire, Grady Speerman. Not for the first time, prime time pundit Alan Hansen had it about right when he said: "The team's a hobby for Mister Speerman, right? A pet project. If he'd decided to use his pocket money on something else – say buying Finland – Sporting Meriden would still be languishing in non-league obscurity."

As I say, the former Liverpool ace had it "about right." An open cheque book can buy you players, a manager, a stadium, fans, tame press and much, much more; but it can't buy success. That's down to how the players perform on the pitch. And *what* players Mister Speerman brought to the club! Players who were brave enough to slot into an untried set-up, who were prepared to roll their sleeves up and get their hands dirty, who were desperate to give their fans what supporters everywhere want to see: newly won silverware being paraded around their home pitch.

Of course, if you listen to the Terribloids and the Trash Tops, they'll try to convince you it was the promise of £100+k a week and other juicy incentives that lured us all to the Can Gas Heart of England Stadium. Don't believe it. Ask any top pro – in any walk of life – and they will tell you that they like to be paid what they are worth. But there isn't a superstar footballer alive who doesn't love playing the game just for the fun of it. From Rio to Rio Ferdinand, we would all play football for nothing*. And that's the truth.

Before I get on to just which players Mister Speerman attracted to William Shakespeare Way, I'd just like to say a few words about the man himself. People often ask me what sort of a bloke he is. Most folk have swallowed a load of media garbage about his "shady past," the "layers of secrecy" surrounding him and that he knows nothing about football. Some even claim that the "Mystery Man from Moose Jaw" is a recluse. I wouldn't know – I've never met the feller. But what I do know is that he's put more than just money into Sporting Meriden. He's also put his son, Grady Speerman Jnr, into it as Chief Executive. And from the Alberta Prairie Dogs to the Yukon Goldpanners, that boy knows his soccer.

Just in case you've been living on a different planet for the last few years, here's a quick recap on Sporting's rapid rise to glory. As you know, mega-rich businessmen have bankrolled a lot of clubs in recent years. As a case in point, one of my old clubs, Chelsea, have never had it so good thanks to the input of Mister Abramovich. And at another, Man United, Mister Glazer has unselfishly risked his own fortune and that of his three likeable sons to rescue a club who were almost on their knees after winning only one trophy in the previous two seasons – and that a poxy victory over minnows Millwall in the FA Cup. After a dodgy start, everyone at Old Trafford now appreciates just what the man, and his many businesses, have done for the wellbeing and the reputation of "the World's most famous football club".

And everyone at Stamford Bridge is thankful to Mister Abramovich and his oil. At my club, Sporting Meriden, fans thank God for Mister Speerman's gas.

But consider this. Most of the clubs we're talking about were fairly successful outfits before their Fairy Godfathers came on the scene. Sporting weren't even in the football league when Mister Speerman blew his "wind of change" into the club. Always investing just enough to take the club on to the next level, his money fuelled

---

*Apart from many kick-arounds with my son, Frank, I have played for nothing in charity games on many other occasions. It's not my fault they've been highly publicised events and "sharpened my profile as a humanitarian."

a season-by-season rise that eventually climaxed in promotion to the Premiership. But would that climax be premature? The answer was a deafening "no f\*\*\*ing way!" The club won the thing in its first season. And why? Because Mister Speerman, taking advice from top footer brainboxes like Franz Beckenbauer, Johann Cruyff and Chris Kamara, went out and bought class. He bought Luis Figo. He bought Ashley Cole. He bought Iker Casillas. He bought Ledley King. He bought Xavi Alonso. He bought Freddie Ljungberg. He bought Stewart Downing. He bought Peter Crouch. And late in the piece, he bought an ageing but still gifted striker by the name of Tristan Stephen Burkes. Tristan? There's another revelation for you.

And the new Gaffer? After undergoing in excess of five thousand hours of coun-selling, Ron Atkinson, "the manager who came in from the cold", was appointed. And what a brilliant appointment he was, by the way. Starved of involvement in the game he loves for years, the man has given his new job everything he's got. And what he's got is plenty.

Alright, let's get it out of the way here and now. Is Ron a racist? Let's face it, what he said about one of our friends of colour was about as PC as that joke about the blind Irish paedophile sh\*\*\*ing his guide dog. But in my experience Ron isn't a racist in the nasty meaning of the word. He just let his mouth run away with him when he was off his guard. They say talk is cheap. Oh really – tell that to Big Ron. Or to anyone who's been sued for talking out of turn for that matter. But in any case, it's not what a guy says that matters. It's what he does. Ask former Liverpool great, John Barnes – he'll tell you what Ron actually did for the many black players he employed at his various clubs: The Three Degrees at West Brom; Remi Moses and Viv Anderson at Man Utd. He even gave Dalian Atkinson a contract at Aston Villa. Get it straight – Ron Atkinson loves black people. If you still don't believe me, check out the man's suntan. He's practically burnt himself to a crisp trying to look like one of them.

Right, so Sporting went from nowhere to the Premiership title in seven short years. But as most of you know – only just. Winning it in the final seconds of the final day of the 2004/05 season – relegating Chelsea to play in the less lucra-tive UEFA Champions League the following year – certainly was cutting it fine. Although I've done literally millions of things I'm proud of in the game, I have to say that grabbing that last gasp goal to beat my other old club Spurs to clinch the title was a little bit special. And now as a result, here we were on a steamy May evening in the Estadio Santiago Bernabeu, Madrid, ready to do battle against one of my former Serie A adversaries, SSC Napoli, for the right to be crowned the true Kings of European football. What a story. You couldn't make it up, could you?

It was a night of what John Motson would call "contrasting emotions." Even before we got out onto the pitch, Ron's team talk concentrated on "setting our stall out early doors," "playing in little triangles," and (looking me in the eye) not "overdoing the lollipops." If we just let our basic quality shine through ... "we might just be in with a shout, here you know."

Our skipper, the magnificent Luis Figo, was a tad more optimistic.

'Napoli stink, no? We'll kill them!'

We headed out for the tunnel with our hopes and our heads high. Now I'll tell you something. You could write an entire book about what goes on in tunnels before, during (slice of pizza anybody?) and after a big game. Technically, the tunnel area is the first Z.O.P. (Zone Of Pressure) any player encounters in a match. The pre-match tunnel experience that evening in Madrid turned out to be a dandy. Like most of our guys, I was expecting the usual routine – exchange the odd pleasantry with our opponents as we lined up, maybe high-five or hug one or two of the more familiar ones, then link up with our assigned mascots before walking out hand-in-hand with them on to the pitch.

Nowadays mascots come in many shapes and sizes. Sometimes they surprise you. I remember playing in one game in Eastern Europe where the kids were bigger than most of us players. The fresh-faced young sprog I got lumbered with sported an impressive moustache and had a handshake like a steam hammer to go with it. And the boy mascots weren't much better.

For the ECCC Final at the Bernabeu, we had the opposite problem. Under the terms of a deal with a baby milk manufacturer, players of both teams were contracted to march on to the pitch cradling new-born babes in their arms. Aah, bless – what a sweet idea? No, it bloody wasn't. It was a nightmare – one of the crappest ideas in the history of the game. Of course, the Latin types on both sides took to it just like that – stroking the little cherubs' foreheads, marvelling at the size of their little noses, the whole bit. Cuddling babies? No problemo.

For us English lads, it was a different story. It's not that we are reserved – you only have to look at the behaviour of our football hooligans over the years – it's just that we're not what my second wife, supermodel Cinzia Pifferi, used to call "compatico" when it comes to things like babies and stuff. Me, Ash, Stewie, Ledders and Crouchy felt right nanas standing there clutching our bundles. And worse, it turned us into nervous wrecks. We were all convinced we were going to drop the little mites on their heads. Now, ask any sports psychologist and they'll tell you that if you worry about making a mistake, the next thing that happens is that you make that very mistake. And I had another reason for being nervous with the little blighter I was carrying that night. But I'll get to that later.

I shall now reveal – for the first time by somebody who actually took part in it – exactly what happened next. Straight away, I have to put my hand up and say that I started it. But it wasn't my fault. The prototype hyper-bladed boots I was going to use in a competitive match for the first time were brilliant on grass – I wouldn't have allowed those good people at Avatak Sports to put my name on them if they weren't. But they were crap on bone-hard surfaces*. As we mooched around in the tunnel waiting for the pre-match entertainment (Julio Iglesias and Monseratte Caballe duetting the European Champions Champions League anthem, *Give Me Everything You've Got – and More*) to finish, I slipped on the concrete, chucking my innocent young charge into the air. Opposite me, Francesco Totti's bronzed features went white as he saw my babe loop-the-loop with nothing between it and the tunnel floor beneath. Quick as a flash, the star striker's tossed his own bambino to the team-mate standing immediately behind him and launched himself to save mine.

Good job he'd put plenty of diving practice in over the years. But behind him, his mate drops the pass. Then in making a grab for the rebound, he succeeds in dropping his own babe. The next second, babies are flying all over the shop as players on both sides try to catch the falling infant I.M.V.P. (In the Most Vulnerable Position) near them. It was bonkers – like a speeded up version of pass the parcel.

Thankfully, none of the babies were damaged, but it was an unsettling incident for us. And of course, the excitement made all the babies start crying, wetting themselves and worse. Fortunately, there were no flies on the milk people – there's something you weren't expecting to read today – and they immediately swapped the real babies for identically kitted-out plastic dolls. It was the first time most of us had ever touched a doll – ones you don't have to blow up anyway – and of course, because it didn't matter if we dropped them, nobody did. We should have been issued with them in the first place. After we had no more than a few moments to get our heads together, we walked onto the pitch trying to look as if nothing had happened. Nobody in the stadium twigged a thing.

But some of those watching at home got a right eyeful. Why only some? Because like I said, the match was being screened as a P.P.V.B.I. event. Just in case you don't know how Stelsat works, customers pay nothing to receive their brand new football

---

*This performance issue refers only to the design prototype of the Avatak Burksey Netbusta and has been resolved subsequently. The production model of the Netbusta is now the fastest selling soccer shoe in markets worldwide.*

Note: "Avatak" is a brand of the Stelsat Corporation of America. All rights reserved.

channel and also pay nothing to view the first half of any game shown. Aside from that, you pay-as-you-go only for what you want to see – the second half of the match, pre-match build up, replays, interviews or whatever. So anyone who pressed the "Buy Tunnel?" button on their home handsets that night clocked the whole sorry business.

And that business backfired big style on the Better Than Breast's Best Baby Milk Corporation. Trying to hush up the incident afterwards only made matters worse for them. The press, as so often, had a field day and the "Babygate Cover-Up" was born. But before you start getting all "Disgusted of Doncaster" about it, just remember two things. One – no baby was hurt in any way during the incident. Two – in the court case that followed, we footballers were rightly found not guilty of any wrongdoing whatsoever. Not only that, most of us were later awarded medals by a range of national welfare organizations and other bodies. I will always wear my Silver Hyena medallion – awarded by the Order of the Sisters of Excruciating Sorrows – with pride. What makes it particularly special is that it had only ever been bestowed on two Brits previously – Rod Hull and Emu.

Back to Sporting v Napoli and the on-pitch pre-match ceremonies. Both teams lined up to be introduced to the dignitaries and unlike some other finals I could name, they weren't all a bunch of nobodies. Guest of honour was a gentleman by the name of Edson Arantes do Nascimento. Never heard of him? How about Pelé? What can you say about this legendary giant of our game? Plenty. But that's for another time.

Anyway, there was a great moment when skipper Luis, introducing the great man to our team, got to my place in the line – I always stand seventh, I don't know why – and before he could introduce me, Pelé said; 'No need to introduce the great Burksey!'

Let me just say this. I have got the greatest respect for Peter Crouch as a human being. He's a smashing lad who has done remarkably well considering. But needless to say, when Luis got to him, a full intro was necessary. It boils down to this. At the very highest level, only the very highest quality counts. Sorry Crouchy. Mutual respect is a two-way street. It's something you can't buy, beg, steal or borrow. It has to be earned. I knew at the moment that I shook hands with Pelé that whatever was about to happen in my final game – not that anybody knew that but me – I would go out on the biggest high possible. Me, a simple lad from Huddersfield, had just been called "great" by the greatest player ever to play the game; a man who also went on to do great things after his playing career; a man whose tireless work for a number of causes has made a difference to so many people. Take fronting that campaign to fight impotency – the scientific name for not being able to get a hard-on – and think about what it took to do it. I'll tell you what it took – balls. Big hairy ones. What a guy. If there was ever a poll to decide the Man Of The Millennium, would anyone think of voting vote for Pelé? I would.

Off went the dignitaries and David Mellor, and at last, both sides were ready to join together in the centre circle for the obligatory minute's silence to mark the latest tragedy that had hit the world. I'm one of those players who always pays maximum respect during such moments. In an odd way, I even enjoy them. It's not that I revel in death and disaster. Far from it. But there is something very stirring about it – especially at these European Champions Champions Cup games where the Memorial Minute Slot is sponsored by Krispy Korn Krunchies PLC\*. I find it very touching to stand shoulder to shoulder with my fellow pros in the centre circle, all of us gazing up at the big screen as the film comes on. Watching that family sharing a fun breakfast in slow motion together always chokes me. A fun breakfast that the people whose passing we were honouring would never be able to enjoy again. Those watching the telecast at home who didn't press the "Buy Silence?" buttons on their hand sets really missed out on a moving experience. And there's another tick in the box for the Memorial Minute. That sixty seconds of calm before the storm really helps to focus your thoughts on the battle to come.

And what a battle it turned out to be.

For a while, it didn't go to plan. Maybe we didn't set out our stall properly as Ron had asked us to because our passing game was way off for the first half-hour. And to be fair, maybe Napoli had done their homework on us because they kept disrupting the little triangles we liked to play in. Deployed in the withdrawn striker's role behind Crouchy, I kept finding that my little knock-ons, dinks and chips to him were being blocked off. And so were my lay-offs to Figs and Freddie. So I resorted to Plan B – my Plan B not the Gaffer's – trying as many lollipops as I could pull off. Drag-backs, spin-ons, nutmegs, double twisting somersaults with pike – I went for the lot. The only reward I got for my efforts was a tight left hamstring and an earful of spittle from iron-hard Napoli centre-back Gianluca Sporco. After one failed trick too many, I risked a glance at the bench. Ron indicated that he wanted me to stop pulling the lollipops. I think that's what his hand gesture meant at any rate.

And then just as the ref was about to blow for half-time – every side's worst nightmare – the opposition scored. Hard working young midfielder Fabio Gatti clipped a through ball to the slippery Roberto Cani and the Argentinean hit-man's exocet of a shot blasted high and wide past Ike's despairing dive.

Now I don't need to tell you that I am a bit on the temperamental side. Hell, my rattle's been thrown out of the pram so many times, it's practically got air miles. I'm also a very bad loser. And I'm proud of it. I always say, "show me a good loser and I'll show you a loser." But as true as I lie here, when that goal went in, I hardly reacted.

How could I be so unfeeling? How could I be so unprofessional? How could I not care? Because just at that second, my thoughts were elsewhere. They were turned to a maternity home back in West London, where my fourth wife – TV Presenter Iona McHardie – was due to have our first child at any minute. Talk about bad timing. Now you'll understand why the Babygate incident before kick off got to me so much. It was all too close to home. Oh, just to set the record straight, the maternity home in question – The Clarendon – is not the "exclusive" establishment you may have read about in the press. Anyone who can fork out thirty grand a pop can book the place.

There was no live webcam picture from Iona's delivery suite on my mobile when we got back to the changing room. No news was good news? No way. I learned later that so many punters had logged on to watch what was going to be the first live P.P.V.B.I. birth in history (free for the initial period of labour, then priced in a rising scale right up to the "Buy Afterbirth?" moment at the end) that it had crashed the system. Still, I consoled myself with the thought that the million-dollar deal my agent, Dave Green, and Io's agent, Rebecca Charrington, had struck with Stelsat would help keep Burksey Junior in disposable nappies for a while. You parents out there will know just how quickly the little tinkers get through them!

I sent Io a quick text and then sat there trying to listen to Ron's half-time team talk. I tell you one thing. After 45 minutes of hard running and lollipops, my entire body ached; including my ears when the Gaffer finished having a go at me. What did he want – blood? At one stage in my career, I would have nipped off to the bog and had a few slugs, or dropped a few tabs of something to pep me up and to keep the demons at bay. But now all I had to fall back on was myself. And it was a hard landing. So I decided to use a technique I'd been taught at a therapy centre in California by a young lady who was to become my third wife, Brandee Wavedance-Ebelficker. Concentrating on my own personal secret word (I chose "football"), my happy place ("football pitch") and an activity that makes me happy ("playing football"), I completely blotted out what was going on around me – what therapists call "the now."

Let's face it, a lot of this new age healing stuff – ever had your aura balanced and polished? – is a right load of old w***. I'll tell you about some of my experiences in that area later. But there's no doubt about it – some of it works.

I tell you what also works. Having a player as great as Luis Figo putting his arm around you and telling you that you're still the best number nine on the planet. And despite what you may have read, it was that moment with Figs that turned me round for the second half – not the call that came in from Mister Speerman Senior promising "a million dollar bonus to each player" if we went on to win the thing.

It must have been a good game. Stelsat say that over 90% of the fans that watched the first half for nothing pressed their "Buy Second Half?" buttons at half-time. Some of those punters would be suffering from repetitive strain injury come the final whistle but hey – that's football.

We were all over Napoli after the break. Ash and Stewie really got hold of the left-hand side of the pitch and their overlapping runs and sheer work rate rattled the Italian lads. Then Figs, Freddie and Chav (Xavi Alonso) started working their magic in midfield and soon holes started appearing in the Azzurri's defence. With twenty minutes to go, it was through one of these holes that I threaded an inch perfect return ball to Freddie and the flamboyant, yet quietly-spoken Swede lashed in the equaliser. Joy... Excitement... No, I'll stop there because you can't describe what it feels like to have set up a goal as important as that. Only one thing is better – scoring yourself.

Numerous chances came and went. Crouchy was especially unlucky with a header from the sort of cross only he or a low-flying aircraft can reach and I had a right foot screamer hit the woodwork late on. At full time we were on top, but you get nothing for that. We had to keep it going in extra time. I was really knackered now and worried that Ron might think of giving me the hook. Groggy genius versus lively lesser legs – that was his dilemma.

'You alright, Burksey?'

'F***ing A!' I lied. Whether the boss bought it or not, he decided to keep me on. It turned out to be one of the best decisions of his career.

How exciting was extra time? 99% of the viewers at home stayed with it until the end, buying the action in five-minute chunks until the last five minutes (priced in a rising scale per minute). In England, if you watched the entire game, the extra incidents, all the replays and the interviews, it wound up costing you £49.50. Damn good value when you think what the tickets cost in the stadium.

The match was still level with seconds to go when Ledders headed a Napoli cross out of defence almost to the half-way line. Chav won the knock down and whipped a ball out to Figs, who set off on a powerful mazey run that ended with a perfectly weighted ball into the box. Ghosting in on a great angle, I beat Sporco to it and was just about to pull the trigger when the bastard took my legs from behind. I felt as if a truck had hit me. But who cared? Like a modern day Adolf Hitler, the German referee, Dieter Pimmel, raised his arm emphatically and pointed to the spot.

Although I'd been crocked, I was desperate to take that pen. And I was gutted when Figs walked slowly forward and picked the ball up theatrically, milking the moment for all it was worth. However much money, however much fame and however much glory some players have had in their overlong careers, you'll always find one who wants more. But then Figs looked over to me, winked – and tossed me the ball. What a gesture. And what a display of class from one of the game's true gentlemen.

All around the World, fingers frantically pressed the "Buy Penalty?" buttons on their handsets. As I set down the ball, keeper Imbroglione came out to offer me some advice, but I took no notice of what he said. It was easy – I couldn't understand a single word of it. Although a decade before I'd played three entire seasons in Serie A, I'd made a point of not learning Italian during my stay. Why? I was worried that it might interfere with something very precious to me – my sense of who I was. As far as I was concerned, my self image – my very identity – was written in stone: I was a down-to-earth Yorkshireman and I would never do anything to compromise that. I'd set fire to my Gucci loafers first. And then run over the ashes in my Maserati.

Finally returned to his line, I walked back and waited for the ref's whistle to take the kick. He seemed to wait for ever whilst Stelsat ran another brilliantly entertaining advert but finally, he gets the word in his earpiece; and blows his whistle.

Everything and everyone was riding on me. So many things came into my mind: my childhood, my parents, my first club Huddersfield Town, Bernie The Goat, Gazza crying at Italia 90, pilchards, severed pig-heads and the surf breaking at Malibu... Yes for everything I had been and for everything I was and could ever be; for all the people who had supported, believed and loved me, for my agent, the sponsors and the fans, the kids and even my wives, I knew that it was essential I didn't balls-up this chance. Safety first. Pick a side, aim low and wide and quietly side-foot the ball there. But then I thought f*** it, shut my eyes and tried to smash the cover off the thing. The result? As they say in South America, gooooooooooooooooooooooooooooooooal!!!!!!!!!!

To complete an amazing night for the Burkes clan, at the precise moment that I went into my world-renowned goal celebration for the last time in my career, my son Diego Tarquin Burkes was born. Double whammy!

Sporting Meriden had become the first winners of the European Champions Champions Cup. And yet again, Steve Burkes had been the Go-To Guy, the Star – or as Larry Harrison dubbed me the next morning in *The Mirror;* "The Football God."

It had been quite a day. Quite a night. Quite a career.

But how on earth did my extraordinary rollercoaster of a life arrive at this dizzy height? There's only one man on the planet who knows the whole story. So let me take you right back to the beginning. Are you sitting comfortably? Once upon a time...

CHAPTER TWO

# SUMMONED BY BALLS

**A**sk any player and they'll tell you when *it* happened: the moment when they knew beyond a shadow-stripe of a doubt that they were going to dedicate their lives to football. For the great Sir Bobby Charlton, the moment came when as a wide-eyed youngster, he first saw his Uncle – Geordie Goal Giant Jackie Milburn – playing for Newcastle United. One look at "Wor Jackie" performing one of his top tricks – sliding into a tackle and then sprinting away with the ball in one continuous motion – was all it took. The kids today? They are just as susceptible to the lure of The Beautiful Game. I know one young International who knew where his destiny lay before he saw a ball even being kicked. Whilst an apprentice at Portman Road, clocking a brand new Rolex glinting on an Ipswich Town player's wrist did it for him.

And for Tristan Stephen Burkes? I can remember it as if it was yesterday. The time: late on a wet and windy winter's afternoon in early 1975. The place: Sandringham Avenue, Crosland Moor, Huddersfield. Picture a mischievous eight year-old being driven home from his weekly ballet class. Like any young tyke, I was "being a handful", testing my Dad's patience with a range of antics: staring idly out of the window; picking my nose; sucking the laces of the dancing shoes that were knotted around my neck – I did the lot. I was a rebel, even then.

And thanks to undiagnosed Attention Deficit Disorder, I was also bored out of my infant skull. And getting zero sympathy. But as we neared home, I suddenly saw something that grabbed my attention. Grabbed it and wouldn't let go. A bunch of kids from the council estate were messing about on the big grassed-over roundabout that stood at the bottom of our road. Using a battered old Space Hopper for a ball, they were playing what I later came to know as "Three And In". I couldn't take my eyes off their game as we circled round them and then continued on our way to our semi at the Belmont Park end of the street.

As we got out of the car, I looked back and asked my Dad what the kids were doing.

'They're being a damn nuisance. Now come in – you'll catch cold.'

But I didn't go in straight away. I stood and watched. And as I did, something inexplicable stirred deep within me. For reasons I couldn't understand at the time, kicking a ball, even a big mis-shapen one with ears, suddenly looked like the most wonderful thing in the world. I spat out the lace of my ballet shoe.

The Beautiful Game had gained another convert.

And it was a conversion of religious proportions. God, the Big Talent Scout In The Sky, must have been hovering over Crosland Moor that day. I thank Him, and Aquilino Cosani, the Italian inventor of the Space Hopper, for calling me to the cause.

An Italian, eh? It's enough to make you believe in fate, isn't it?

Anyway, from that moment on, I lived, slept and breathed football. But there was a snag. And it was a big one. I had to keep my new passion a secret from my parents. Why? Because I knew that my librarian Dad, Brian, and my music teacher Mum, Evelyn, wouldn't approve. They had very different ideas about what was good for me and my fifteen year-old brother, Tarquin. It didn't help matters that he had already given them a gutful of grief over his choice of future career. The head-bangers amongst you won't need reminding what path Tarka chose. "Orange Microdot", the outfit he started with a bunch of mates from school, went on to cut seven albums (including the famous – some say infamous – *Pizzle Drizzle*) and, although they never made it as mega big as the Floyd or Zep, each of the guys eventually made a pretty good living playing the music they loved.

To avoid the kind of aggro Tarka was getting, I decided to keep my new found love of football to myself and pretended I was still going to dance classes when I was really going off to play football. Mum and Dad could never understand why I used to come home covered in bruises. I had a range of stock excuses:

'That Corps de Ballet were mental, I'm telling you. Especially in the second act.'

'The Sugar Plum Fairy caught me late.'

And so on. I'm not proud of it, but I found that lying came easily to me and Mum and Dad never suspected what I was really doing. Even when I asked for a pair of Huddersfield Town "leg warmers" for Christmas. And didn't cut the feet off.

To understand why I had to go through this elaborate charade, you have to understand where my parents came from. They came from Outland. Where? Exactly. It pulls my chain that some people see Outland as a quaint rural backwater standing at the gateway to the majestic moorland that lies to the west of Huddersfield. Crap. To me, it's a grim, windswept p***hole of a place on the edge of nowhere. A place whose sole claim to fame is that yonks ago, its inhabitants stoned superstar preacher John Wesley* out of town. I've been stoned in Outland a few times myself – especially with my old mate Honley Dave** – but not in the same way. And definitely not for the same

*Top American folk singer Bob Dylan wrote a song about John Wesley's sad experience. "A Hard Rain's Gonna Fall", I think it's called.

**Now a senior Air Traffic Controller. Makes you think, doesn't it?

reason. Anyway, it was growing up in obscure poverty in Outland that made Mum and Dad determined to rise above the common herd. And by talent and sheer hard work, rise they did. By the time I came along, everything was set fair for we Burkes.

Where we lived said it all about our status. Sandringham Avenue is a street of two halves: cheap and not so cheerful council houses at the "poor end", leafy semis and larger homes at the posh, or "nob end" as we used to call it. The house I grew up in, "Manderley", was right on the half-way line, the very first of the better houses. That location showed we had arrived as a family. And our brand new Rover 2000 showed we were going places to boot. Onward and upward was our motto. A "common" pursuit like football just didn't fit in to my parents' vision of the good life that they were buying into. Football was something the poor end of the street was interested in. Of course, that didn't stop me.

Do I ever feel gutted that I didn't learn the game at my father's bootlaces – like Becks and so many other top pros? Not really. Was I bitter about my parents' initial lack of support?

No way*. Alright, what they stood for didn't make life easy for me as a young footballer, but it taught me something valuable. It taught me to aim high. It taught me never to settle for anything less than the best. And it taught me that if I really got stuck in, anything was possible. I don't suppose I would have understood these things with such total certainty if I hadn't come from a family of "Nob Ends".

I'll tell you one thing. It's a good job I had what it took to become a superstar footballer because I was strictly non-league standard at schoolwork. Not that it was my fault. A whole raft of learning disorders and other difficulties slowed my progress from the kick-off. Nowadays, teachers understand about the effects of hyperactivity disorder, disruptive behaviour syndrome, dyslexia and the various other problems I suffered from. Back then, teachers like flat-chested frump Miss Hardman understood nothing – they just punished you for being "naughty" and "thick". At my school, punishment meant "fire drill" – being made to stand in the corner with a four-gallon bucket full of sand on your head. Most kids couldn't take more than a few seconds of it. Being a Burkes, I used to keep the thing up there for hours at a time. And I got the last laugh out of it as the effort hugely developed my neck muscles, laying the foundations for the celebrated heading ability I was to develop later. So I was already "Bull Neck Burksey" even as a kid was I? You'd better believe it. In my school leaving photo, I make Wayne Rooney look like Kate Moss.

*Later on, it was a different story.

As a final thought on my childhood, I'd just like to say to all the teachers who said I would never amount to anything – go f*** yourselves, you losers. Especially the ones who have had the nerve to ask me back to present prizes and the like over the years. Or – like "No Tits" Hardman* – try to tap me up for tickets.

The day after I left school, 10th July 1983, was momentous for me in more ways than one. Apart from starting as an apprentice grinder at the Lockwood Gear And Tool Company, I outed myself. Yes, to my parents' horror, I told them about the double life I had been leading for eight, secretive years. Wondering where they had "gone wrong", they cried, wailed and gnashed their teeth. But I explained I was just the same lad they had always known and if they loved me, they would have to accept what I was. From that moment on, living a lie was out of the question. When the new season started in late August, I was going to play football in a proper team and that was all there was to it.

Mum and Dad listened, but they didn't really change their minds about things until a couple of months later. What did the trick? A phone call from the legendary ex-Huddersfield and England striker, Frank Worthington. In words of one syllable, he spelled out to them just how talented I was. And how much money I was likely to earn in the game. They perked up considerably at Frank's kind words.

Frank Worthington, a genius of a footballer and a Prince among men. But how did he get involved in my story?

*Miss Hardman's bosom – and therefore her whole life – was obviously a source of constant disappointment to the woman. If only she had known about Pamperwell Breast Augmentation Clinics. May I take this opportunity of recommending them to you? With literally years of experience behind them, Pamperwell lead the way in providing a range of unrivalled breast enlarging and re-contouring procedures at affordable prices. Ladies – why be embarrassed by your meagre, unfeminine bosom when a happy solution is just a phone call away? Yes, if you want your man to sample something ample – take the plunge and choose Pamperwell Augmentation Clinics. Pamperwell – the breast just got breaster.

Note: Pamperwell is a brand of Stelsat Corporation of America.

All rights reserved.

## CHAPTER THREE

# PREMATURE EJACULATION

**1983** was going to be quite some year for Steve Burkes. The climate – I'm not talking about the weather – was perfect for talented and thrusting youngsters like myself to kick down the door to the Promised Land. And who did we young movers and shakers have to thank for making us believe we could hit the heights? – our Prime Minister Margaret Thatcher. What's this – a little bit of politics from Burksey? Yeh, why not!

Thanks to a brilliant away win in the Falklands War the previous year, The Iron Lady's popularity was riding as high as a nipple on a fake tittie at the time. And rightly so. On the back of it, the '83 general election was over before it began, with Gaffer Mags leading the Tories to a well deserved victory.

Surprised I'm more of a Seven than an Eleven on the political park? You shouldn't be. When you think about it, anyone who strives to be the best, who gets a kick out of coming first, and who thinks they should be rewarded big style for doing it – is a "Mag Hag" whether they realise it or not. "Greed is good"? Of course it is. Without it, nothing happens. Do you think Kick Arse Tycoon Rupert Murdoch would have built up his hugely successful business empire if he'd just sat on his backside and twiddled with his privates? Course he wouldn't. And I bet all the thousands of people who earn good money working for him are glad he got stuck in as well. Yes, they benefit from his genius too. The "Trickle Down Effect", my mate Tony Blair calls it. Just in case you've never heard of it, I think it may have been old Spurs supremo Alan Sugar* who had a great way of explaining the idea: "What's good for the Dictator is good for the dictated-to." And he should know – he's trickled down on loads of people over the years.

No, I'm not afraid to say it – Thatcher's Britain was a Great Britain to live in. Our motto was: "If it's out there, go grab a piece of it. Even if it belongs to somebody else."

I tell you who summed up the feeling we all had in those heady days best – my favourite TV character of all time, Derek "Del Boy" Trotter: "This time next year we'll all be millionaires!" And he was right if you remember – he and lovable old Rodney

---

*Actually, I don't think it was Sir Alan now I think about it. It was some Chairman, anyway.*

did become millionaires in the end. If they could do it, anybody could. As long as you worked hard. And you had their kind of talent.

Besides – what's the alternative? Equal shares for all? Sorry, it's not natural. Remember all those do-good social worker types – the corduroy jacket and specs brigade – who thought that kids should play only non-competitive games so there would be no winners and losers? Yeh – that's a great way forward. If you want to breed a nation of Also Rans. Let's go for gay "marriages" and women "priests" as well.

I see it like this. It's not just on the pitch or in bed that I am an animal. I am an animal everywhere. I have an animal's instinct. Duncan Ferguson, Einstein, Delia Smith – we're all animals. And what law do animals live by? The law of the jungle. The strong don't just survive, they win and keep winning. The weak get their arses kicked. That's the way of the world and it always will be. Here's a thought for you. In the days when you got your milk in bottles, you could see that cream always rises to the top. Just because they put it in blind cardboard cartons now (who's responsible for that by the way?), doesn't mean that it's stopped doing it. Put it this way. Am I sitting here reading your book? No, you're sitting there reading my book. Would you have paid good money to read about the life of a useless tosser? I don't think so.

But back to the football. Later on, you will read about my life with top managers like Sir Alex Ferguson, Bobby Robson, Graham Taylor, Sven Göran Eriksson and others.

However, my professional playing career started under a slightly less illustrious gaffer – Mister Mick Buxton, manager of my home town club Huddersfield Town. Not that he was any slouch. He had enjoyed success with a club as big as Sunderland and he was a near god at Huddersfield at the time, having steered us from Fourth Division obscurity to Second Division respectability in only four seasons. His style? He was a no-nonsense disciplinarian, a workaholic who expected nothing less than total commitment from his players and staff. So what did he think about signing one of England's greatest players-to-be as a sixteen year-old apprentice? Nothing. He didn't realise he'd done it. Until I'd left, become an overnight success elsewhere and it was too late to get me back.

But I'm still getting ahead of myself.

My various learning difficulties meant that I left school without any qualifications. Nowadays, from sports journos to clever people like Melvyn Bragg, I am regarded as one of the best wordsmiths who's ever played football. Where did I learn all those big words? In school? No, it was playing tenner a point Scrabble, Boggle and Balderdash with hardened wordos like Norman Whiteside and Paul McGrath.

That's where I learned words like "vulva" (33 points on a triple word score) and "comatose" (36pts).

And it showed. The first proper interview I did at Man United was after we'd played Liverpool and I'd snatched a late winner with a trademark bullet header. The much missed Barry Davies was wielding the mike. Apparently some kind of technical hitch meant the interview wasn't broadcast, but I can remember exactly what I said.

Barry: 'I think it could be said that you left it a little late there, Burksey.'

Me:  'Just a bit, yeh. But it went in eventual so that's all that matters.'

Barry: 'An old cliché, but it was something of a game of two halves for you.'

Me:  'Yeh. I played like a bit of a comatose vulva early doors. But I got my cranium on it when it mattered.'

Thanks Nasty. And thanks Macca. You taught me more than any English teacher I ever had.

So I left school without any paper qualifications, but I was qualified in other matters alright. If I say so myself, I was a perfect physical specimen at the age of sixteen. At five-foot nine I wasn't the tallest but like the immortal Diego Maradona, I was big where it mattered. I was really the ideal build for the kind of player I was going to become.

But there was one area that was undeveloped. Because I'd had to play and practise mainly in secret, my football hadn't come on like it would have done under normal circumstances. So although I looked the part, I was neither game savvy nor match hardened. It was – to use my mate, Sir Clive Woodward's favourite word – a "huge" disadvantage. I had played no games for the school team to hone my skills. Or for the district or county. And with nowhere to showcase my talents, no league club knew anything about me. And as for the dizzy heights of the England youth set-up – forget it.

I tell you, by the time their balls have dropped, some kids have had hundreds of hours of professional coaching. Not me. All I'd ever been taught in a coaching situation was the difference between "good toes" and "naughty toes" in my ballet lessons.

As you know, Steve Burkes is a rare beast in many ways. By the time you've finished this book, you'll know just how rare. But how's this for starters? I never had a second's football coaching in my life until I was nearly seventeen. I'm a virtually self-taught footballer. How many other international stars can claim that?

There's another down side to my enforced absence from the game as a youngster. I didn't grow up in the company of any of the players I would later do battle with or play alongside. It made me an outsider. In the autobiographies of some of my peers, you'll read funny stories about stuff that went off in junior training camps and on tours. Cute little stories about unknown young herberts who later went on to become household names. Things like: "the first time I ever saw X, he was crying 'cos someone had nicked his jelly babies!" You won't read stories like that in my book. By the time I got to know people like X, they were already crying over their tax returns.

Football changed for ever for me when I played my first really serious organised game – as a sixteen year-old centre-forward for my works team, Lockwood Gear And Tool. Everything about that Sunday afternoon is etched in my mind. You've no idea what it felt like to walk into that dressing room before the match and change into a pukka playing kit for the first time. To be honest, it wasn't the most inspiring – faded yellow shirts, shorts, and socks – but to me it was the most wonderful strip in the world. And my shirt had a big black number nine on the back. Overcome? Excited? Hyped up? As I tore off my civvies, I didn't know whether to cry, get a hard-on or kick holes out of the changing room wall. So I did all three for good measure. My show of naked emotion impressed my new team mates. Especially those nearest to me. Exchanging amazed looks, they cleared their stuff away immediately, letting me have one side of the changing room completely to myself. Respect. And I hadn't even set foot on to the pitch yet.

The match was against "Collegians," an old boys side who play their home matches in an area of West Huddersfield known as Salendine Nook. Sounds cosy, doesn't it? And so it is – if you like playing on the edge of a cliff with a freezing force ten blowing up your chuff. But it didn't matter to me. Nor did I care that most of the Collegians weren't exactly the scholars and gentlemen that their club name suggested. At least two of them looked as if they had escaped from a locked ward somewhere. Especially the skipper, a big flame-haired centre half whose role it was to mark me. And mark me he did. Both my shins, groin, nose and right ear all came in for a right hammering. And that was just in the first tackle. At least he had the decency to ask if I was alright as he trotted away.

'How did you like that, you thick f***ing yellow c***?'

I replied in the best way possible. Although I could barely stand and had to be subbed seconds later, I blasted in the resulting free kick from fully thirty-five yards. It was the first time I'd ever scored a goal in a proper net. I'll never forget the way it bulged out or the fizzing sound the ball made as it boomeranged viciously around the knotted twine. It was such a powerful strike that their goalkeeper, Hugh "Fat" Bastard, I think his name was, never even moved. Scoring a goal like that in my first proper match was one thing. Doing it under the nose of Mister Frank Stewart Worthington was another. Why was he attending such a lowly fixture? The answer is he wasn't. Or he hadn't intended to. Then 35 and enjoying a less than stellar season with south coast strugglers Southampton, the great man was cutting across the playing fields on his way back to a mate's house after an all-night party when he clocked my wonder strike.

Thanks to Frank, a week later I was sitting in the office of Huddersfield Town Manager Mick Buxton. With a pen in my hand. And a big grin on my face. I was in Dreamland. Can you imagine my feelings? No, of course you can't. Yet over the years, many fans – even people in wheelchairs, bless 'em – have tried to tell me where I went wrong at various times in my career as a top international sportsman. And one of the things the punters always bring up is me signing that first contract. "You should have gone to a big club!" they bleat. But what did I know at sixteen years of age? Besides, to me, Huddersfield Town was a big club. One of the biggest clubs of all time. Weren't they the first team in history to win the forerunner of the Premiership – the old First Division – three times in a row? And then go on to finish second in the next two seasons? Alright, it happened more or less at the same time old John Wesley was leaving town in a hail of pebbles – but that's not the point. Once great –always great. And as a future wife of mine would say about the mysteries of history and time: "Don't diss yesterday – it's just a tomorrow that's already happened?'*

I couldn't get over how far I'd come in such a short time. As Bryan Gonville has pointed out, one minute football was for me "the love that dare not speak its name", the next minute, there's Burksey right in the middle of it "with the world literally at his feet." Nevertheless, there's an element of truth in what the fans say about my first contract. It stank. Signing it showed my total inexperience in the game. And in the ways of the world. If only agents, one of the greatest things to happen to football in the last thirty years, had been as thick on the ground back then as they are now! You see, I should have been treated as a superstar in the making from the off. I don't mean I should have been given special privileges. But I should have been handled with kid gloves and given some reward for being – how did the great José Mourinho put it? – "not just from the bottle." A good agent would have sorted me out a much better contract – in all respects – than the one I signed.

Take the money. If you're wearing a hat, hold on to it. My wage as an apprentice footballer with Huddersfield Town, a mid-table Second Division side – the equivalent

---

*My third wife, philosopher, friction therapist and interior designer, Brandee Wavedance-Ebelficker-Burkes. By the way, this American fondness for double barrelled names is a game, isn't it? Good job Jane Fonda never married David Seaman. Boo-boom.

of The Championship today – was LESS than I was getting as an apprentice grinder at Lockwood G and T! Think I'm exaggerating? I've still got my first wage packet to prove it. Actually, I've kept a lot of souvenirs and stuff from my time in football. My film director mate Spike Lee calls it my "shit". Shit indeed, Homey – that wage packet shows I was paid the princely sum of £70. For a MONTH'S work. Alright, I was still living with my parents, but even so.

Maggie T's Promised Land was looking a long way off at this point let me tell you. My cream was definitely in the milk bottle – but it still had a long way to rise to the top. Hey, nobody said it was going to be easy.

Some of you may be thinking, "well, being paid seventy pound a month as a 16 year-old just for booting a ball around doesn't sound bad." Yeh, well let me tell you what we juniors had to do to earn that pittance. Most punters know that apprentices clean players' boots. But it doesn't stop there. We sorted and packed kit for away matches, we cleaned the showers, dressing rooms, helped the groundsman, swept the stadium. By the way, you wouldn't believe the stuff we used to find in the stands – betting slips, used condoms, false teeth. And that was just in the Directors' Box. We found a partially sacrificed goat under a seat once. I guess Town were promoting an initiative to entice more of our ethnic friends into the ground at the time.

But putting the terraces in order was a stroll along the prom compared with every apprentice's nightmare job – cleaning the ground's toilets. Don't forget, we're not talking Town's new home here – Sir Alfred McAlpine's magnificent Galpharm Stadium – where the punters' enjoy a range of top line facilities. We're talking the manky old Leeds Road Ground. After a match, the toilets behind the Cowshed End had to be smelled to be believed. On my very first day at the club – I hadn't even set foot on the training pitch yet – I was detailed over there with my bucket and mop. The fuming reek coming off the bogs didn't just act like an invisible wall, it forced my head back so fast, I suffered a bad whiplash injury. My neck muscles being over-developed meant that the area of damage was colossal. If I'd been a giraffe neck, I would have been okay within a week. But the club doctor estimated that I would be in a neck brace for eight. Eight whole weeks! The news put me in solid with Town Supremo, Mick Buxton 'I don't know what to make of you, lad', he said. Of course, I should have replied, 'What you can make of me is a top-flight international footballer'. But we can't all be Gordon Strachan, can we? Instead, I threw up on his shoes.

The day didn't get much better after that. Picking up a bad neck knock didn't stop the other young players from introducing me to the delights of "arse banging." Sounds more like the sort of thing some of the lads used to get up to after my ballet classes, doesn't it?

To my new mates, the words had a slightly different meaning. It was the name given to Town's famed initiation ceremony for new boys.

Now some people might enjoy having their arse whitewashed and then jammed into a car tyre. They might continue to enjoy it as said tyre is then hoisted on to the goal posts thereby exposing their blanched rubber-encased bum to the world. I know I did. But that was before Riggy, Bonce, Flippo and Twatters started pinging balls at it for a spot of target practice. Every bull's eye jarred my injured neck something rotten. And made the damage worse. At one point I nearly blacked out, but my shrieks of agony did nothing but pep the lads up for more of the same. I tell you, I felt like a tart at a pre-season training camp. After a while though, my tormentors got bored and left me there dangling. Whilst a stadium tour was just beginning.

'There's summat you don't see every day', I heard one of the punters say.

They're a dry lot, my fellow Tykes.

I had already prepared myself for the nightmare hell of eight weeks out. After my new team mates got through with me, just eight weeks would have been a godsend.

So my time at Town hadn't begun well. And it continued like that. It felt like I had been given a brilliant opportunity, but the more I tried to take advantage of it, the more I couldn't. It was like getting a brilliant bird into bed and then not being able to get a hard-on. Or so they tell me. Speaking of that – here's a revelation for you: despite having a right handful in the tadger department, I had never had a girlfriend or even had sex before I joined Town. I suppose it was another thing that alienated me from the rest of the lads who were all much more experienced than me. All in all – and not for the last time in my life – I felt excited by what was going off around me but I also felt alone, confused and frustrated. But I just got on with life at Leeds Road and told myself that things had to improve.

I've told you about the worst job we apprentices had to do. The best? Cleaning the players' cars. There were a few big Mercs and the odd Jag around, but they didn't really do it for me at the time. My top motor? It was a Ford Escort.

"F*** off Burksey," I hear you cry. "You've been smoking your funny fags again." No, I'm dead serious. But I'm not talking entry level stuff here – I'm talking a classic marque that rolled off the production line for the first time in that very year of 1983 – the Ford Escort XR3i. And thanks to a Town-friendly dealer, the club had six of them on a special promo deal. Six! And that wasn't all. One of them was earmarked for use by the apprentice who was putting in the best all-round performance on the pitch and around the stadium. What a carrot. As if I needed one. I was mad for that motor – Go-Faster stripes, 7 inch wheel rims, front grill like a floodlight pylon – magic. But best of all, the beast had a top speed of 150 mph and went 0-60 in 8.5 secs.

I wanted use of that car so badly I used to dream about it at night. And what I might – at last – be able to get up to in it.

A full five months after I'd sustained my injury – three months later than it should have been – my neck brace was removed and I was finally cleared to start doing what I'd been sent to this planet to do. My first match was for Town 'A' away at Leeds United 'A' played at Harrogate Town. You remember how I reacted to putting on humble Lockwood G & T's naff yellow strip? Then just maybe you can imagine what it felt like to get off the minibus, walk into the changing room and see the famous Terriers kit – blue-and-white striped shirt, white shorts, blue-and-white socks – folded in neat piles under everyone's peg. It sends a shiver down my spine when I think of it even now. The moment affected me much more than it had at The Nook, and I was soon prancing round in the nuddy like a mad thing, too overcome with it all to get my kit on.

Frank Worthington had succeeded in persuading Mick Buxton to make the trip to Harrogate to see me in action and the sceptical first team boss chose that moment to enter the changing room. I suppose it could have gone one of two ways. He could have had a bit of a laugh about it and thought: "Crikey, I've heard of getting up for a match but this is ridiculous." Or he could have thought, "What's this jibbering lunatic up to?" He went for the latter.

'Burkes?'

'Yes boss?'

'Apart from owt else, what are you doing with a boner on, lad?'

'Oh, sorry boss. I'm just excited', I said, practically sticking the thing in his face.

With that, my new team mates have collapsed in a heap. Of laughter.

'I don't know what to make of you, son. But I know one thing, you're not playing tonight. Get dressed.'

My hard-on went down quicker than a mill chimney with Blaster Bates on its case.

I felt cheated, robbed of the chance of a lifetime. And I told the boss how I felt about it in the language that I was picking up from the other lads. The language of football.

'Not playing? F*** off! I've hardly kicked a f***ing ball yet!'

Silence.

'My office, nine o'clock tomorrow morning.'

With that, he turned on his heel and left. I shed a few more tears, kicked a few more lumps out of the changing room wall and finally got back into my civvies. I watched the game from the bench without taking in a single thing.

The next morning, I went in to see Mister Buxton and he gave me the bollocking of my life. And suspended me for another two months from taking part in matches, training or anything that involved kicking a ball. All my other duties were stepped up. That news was bad enough, but the worst part was when he told me I'd let him, the club, my team mates, and – the real choker – Frank Worthington down. The message was simple – no more "funny business" or I was out.

I was determined not to stuff up again. I tried to think of anything and everything that would help me in my mission. I even bought a gas mask to use when cleaning the toilets.

Nothing was going to stop me proving myself as an apprentice footballer – and "winning" that XR3i. I was down to take my Test on my 17th birthday in April and knew I would pass. That little blue and white baby was just sitting there waiting for me.

Tuesday 26th April 1984 was a day I won't forget in a hurry. I walked my driving test in the morning and – wait for it – I was finally allowed on to the training pitch in the afternoon. Now, at last, was my chance to dazzle. I still wasn't up to speed with some aspects of the game – like passing – but my talent must have shone through because come the weekend, I was back in the 'A' side. The match was a tricky home fixture against a club you may just have heard of – Manchester United. Over the moon, made-up with it – whatever you want to call it, I was it. Now, I would be able to show what I was really made of.

Or that was my goal. Now, for the first time ever, I can reveal that when it came to it, my shot at goal was blocked. Why? Because something got in my way that week that was going to get in my way hundreds of times in the future. And it was no small thing. It was a monster. A monster that takes no prisoners. A monster that can shaft you, give you the shakes and give you the shits all at the same time. And I don't mean Roy Keane, Stuart Pearce or Anne Robinson.

That monster is booze.

How did I get my first taste? How does anybody get their first taste – they get drunk with their mates. As I said, I felt like an outsider* – I see now that my efforts to become "one of the lads" was really responsible for what happened. Besides, I didn't even know I was drinking alcohol. To start with.

I'm sure that not everyone reading this book is a couch cabbage. Some of you have probably had a go at some sport or other and know about the importance of liquid intake. You've probably knocked back the odd bottle of Energade during a marathon run or whatever. It's good stuff that does exactly what it says on the tin.

---

*French goalkeeper Albert Camus wrote a book about being an outsider. "The Plague," I think it's called.

Ever had an E. T. – an Energade Tops? It consists of half a pint of the isotonic health drink mixed with beer. The only problem is that it also contains double slugs of vodka, scotch and white rum. I don't know how many of these lethal buggers I got down my neck that night but let's just cut to the chase – by the time the Police picked me up in Huddersfield's noted central thoroughfare – St George's Square – I didn't have my pants on and had no idea of what I was doing. What I was doing, according to the Boys In Blue, was "attempting actual or simulated sex" with one "Bernie M".

Wot – Burksey a bender? No way, mate. Not that Bernie was a bird either, mind you.

Bernie was the name me and the lads had given to that seriously singed goat I was telling you about – the one we found on the terraces. We called him Bernie because we thought he was a dead ringer for our fave comedian at the time – Bernard Manning – and we had adopted him as a sort of unofficial Apprentice's Mascot. He went all over the place with us hidden in kit bags, disguised as this, that and the other. He had just one problem. He stank like the kind of stuff I used to have to clean up behind the Cowshed. Still, it was a right laugh messing about with him. Until that night. And, of course, Burksey was the only one they caught.

Let's be honest, we've all done crazy things. How many people haven't tried to s*** a dead goat at one time or another? In biker gangs, some army regiments and among Reality TV programme devisers, it's practically everyday behaviour. But you've guessed it, Mister Buxton didn't see it that way and once the club had straightened the thing out with the Police, he called me into his office once more. I cried so much, I barely heard what he said, but the gist of it was that I had disgraced my club, my species, and, yes, Frank Worthington.

I was "let go". Nooooooooo! My career looked as if it might be over before it had begun. All those years of practising my football in secret and now I was being ejaculated from the club I loved. I hadn't played a single second in a Huddersfield Town Youth or 'A' Team shirt. And as for the first team – I had hardly even spoken to most of them. Players like Steve Doyle, Dave Sutton and my near namesake, full back David Burke, may as well have played for the Dark Side of the Moon XI for all I'd had to do with them.

How did I feel about being sacked without being given a fair shout? I was gutted. Gutted with the biggest and most gut wrenching de-gutter thing ever dreamed up in the dark dregs of an evil genius' mind. Or a Dream Team scriptwriter's.

Regrets? I've had a few.

I might have been gutted. But I wasn't put off. Not for a second. I still knew I would make it as a top professional footballer. I didn't just have conviction. I had evidence.

There used to be a target set up at one end of the Leeds Road car park – remember it Town fans? – and after training, players would often go and use it to sharpen up their shooting skills. This particular morning I was busy re-pointing a wall outside the players' entrance when some of the forwards came out and started strutting their stuff. I couldn't take my eyes off likeable hit man Kevin Stonehouse's efforts. Some have said that the hard-working striker couldn't hit a barn door with a banjo and, as I watched balls flying off his foot here, there and everywhere, you could be forgiven for believing them.

Why was I so mesmerised by his performance? Because before anybody had arrived at Leeds Road that morning, I had taken a bag of balls into the car park and for a solid half-hour had peppered the dead centre of that target. From all parts. With both feet.

Yes, I knew I would make it eventually. But what to do next? I was dead set on one thing – I couldn't carry on living with my parents. I was an up-and-coming mover and shaker who had just suffered a temporary setback – not some kid tied to his folks' apron strings.

So, really worried about how they would take it, I went back home that afternoon and told them how I felt. I thought it was to their undying credit that they didn't try to talk me into staying. Dad even volunteered to take me anywhere I wanted to go as long as we went immediately. I supposed they must have had an inkling of how I was feeling as they had already packed my stuff up whilst I was still in custody.

I had decided to go and live with my brother, Tarquin. His band were doing pretty well and he had always said that I could stay with him for as long as I liked. The attic room he had going in his Brighton pad wasn't big, but it would do for me until I found my feet. And finding my feet was exactly what I intended to do. My football feet.

Before I left Manderley for the last time as a home team player, I made my parents a sacred pledge. I vowed that despite my bad luck with Town, I knew I would still make it as a professional footballer and that before very long, they wouldn't be living half-way along Sandringham Avenue. They would be living in The Elms, the mansion that overlooks Belmont Park itself. And I was going to put them in it. I'll never forget my mother's words,

'Tristan, you've already put us in it.'

There's a mum's confidence for you, I thought. She must have understood instinctively what I knew for a fact: I knew I could make a football talk. And what it said to me was, "You're a winner! Fame, money and fun are yours for the taking!"

I only took the bare minimum with me from my old room. But two things I didn't leave behind were my signed photo of Frank Worthington. And my Hot Motor Magazine poster of the Ford XR3i.

I was determined to be worthy of them both.

CHAPTER FOUR

# HARD TIMES

E ver been to Brighton? Ever been to Huddersfield? Not very similar are they? And living apart from my parents was obviously a new thing for me as well. Although as my future wife, Brandee once pointed out: 'Stephen, I'm getting a sense here that you were always, like, living apart from your parents?' She was always saying things like that. The tosser.

I spent the whole first week at my brother's place writing to every Football League club in existence. Except Leeds United, of course. I might have been desperate, but I wasn't that desperate. Just kidding, Elland Roaders. For obvious reasons, Town were the one club who didn't get a letter. So all in all, I wrote ninety-one of the buggers. Ninety-one! And wrote them all by hand mind you – not many people had home computers back then. And imagine how much it took out of a lad with dyslexia to pen all those notes without a spell-checker to help him?

Here's another first for you. I never usually talk about the many charities and other good causes to which I give sparingly of my time and money, but it was partly because of my experience of writing those letters that The International Dyslexia Foundation got added to my donation list when I became a top-earning star. "Giving it away, eh Burksey? – that doesn't sound like you." I hear you. And I also warn you. The *Daily Spew's* Darren Snape is just one jerk-off who has learned that it's a bad call to suggest publicly that my donation programme "is all about earning Burksey sizable tax breaks and deductions." Still paying for that, aren't you Darren? It's like my Auntie Vi used to say, "some people are just born evil."

Wanna know how many replies I got to my ninety-one letters? I'll tell you. I got zilch. Nowt. Not one club was interested. They must have heard on the grapevine that Steve Burkes was injury prone, that he was a trainee drunk, and that he was a hyperactive pervert who enjoyed interfering with dead goats. And people complain there are no characters in the game any more.

By a weird twist of fate, Frank Worthington signed for Brighton & Hove Albion for the 1984/5 season. But as soon as I twigged that my Guru was going to be a neighbour, I instantly made up my mind about something. I decided not to re-introduce myself and tell him I was living locally. I knew if I did, there was a slight risk I could become one of the saddest kind of bastards who walk the face of the earth. It's a type everyone in the public eye knows only too well – the hanger-on. I respected us both too much for that.

I've had a lot of nerdy toe rags hang around me over the years and I want to tell you that it's not funny. I've lost count of the restraining orders, injunctions and other stuff I've had to slap on these people at various times. During my days at Chelsea, there was one young kid who came from out Croatia way or somewhere and he used to drive me mental. He was everywhere. "Can I carry your bag?" "Can I clean your boots?" "Can I sleep under your car?" It was fun at first, but I soon got tired of it and when the authorities finally deported him, it was probably the best thing that could have happened. I was determined I wasn't going to become a similar nuisance to Frank.

Yes, I didn't want to be a pain, but I didn't think it would hurt if I got Frank up to speed with the nightmare hell I was going through. So I poured my heart out to him on a postcard and waited eagerly for the reply. None came. I suppose it must have pissed me off and it showed. As he "built" his fifth joint of the day — I know that won't shock anyone — my brother Tarka asked me what was wrong.

'Oh nothing — I wrote to Frank Worthington about nobody being interested in me and he hasn't replied either.'

Although Tarks has never been interested in sport or sportsmen, he knew about Frank. He was a well known figure around Huddersfield and Tark had once come across the rock-and-roll mad striker in Wood's Music Shop buying a couple of Elvis albums.

Tarka was gutted that my hero hadn't replied.

'Bummer man', he said.

I needn't have worried. By the very next post, I got my reply. Frank apologised for not writing sooner, but explained that he'd been busy moving house. His advice about my situation inspired me through the difficult — no difficult doesn't say it — f***ing shit days that lay ahead. Here's what he wrote:

> "Taking all those suspicious minds to heart will only ensure that your stay at the heartbreak hotel will continue. Don't get all shook up! Clubs won't always be cruel to a heart that's true. It's not now or never! Don't get all bummed out and may the force go with you, man."

Amongst my "shit", I still have the brick red Rizla fag papers packet that these kind words were written on. Written, oddly enough, in the same green ink Tarka always used.

The little money I had been given by my parents was running out so I signed on the dole. What a shocking experience that turned out to be. I was called in to a meeting with a "woman" whose name I'll never forget — Ms Y Killmartin. I don't know about killing Martin, but she certainly wanted to kill me. Not that the fat ugly bitch made it obvious. Just the opposite — she smiled and pretended to be sympathetic. But she didn't fool me. I decided to keep what had happened at Town to myself. She would never have understood it in a month of Sun Jihai's.

'I see you have no qualifications?'

'So?' Who did she think she was? Stephen Fry?

'And what sort of job are you seeking?'

'I want to be a professional footballer.'

'Uh-huh. I don't think I can help you there, Mister Burkes. But I'm hopeful that there may be openings for you elsewhere. I know they were hiring at one of the local building sites yesterday and I'm fairly sure they would...'

'I want to be a professional footballer.'

'I really do think that a more realistic approach...'

I'm not proud of it, but at that moment I wanted to smash my fist right into her big grinning gob. But then I thought of the example of former Wolves and England skipper, Billy Wright*. Despite being in the thick of all the aggro going, the "Man of Ironbridge" was never sent off or even booked in nearly 650 senior games. Now there was a gentleman who stuck to principles of decency and right-mindedness.

'I want to be a professional footballer, you fat f***er,' I said, keeping my fists to myself.

For that – can you believe it? – I was red-carded. And after a couple of similar interviews, a suspension followed. A suspension of benefit. They wouldn't give me a penny. I protested, pointing out that I wasn't some no-hope vagrant loser from a bad background, I was Tristan Stephen Burkes, a true "Nob End". I saw them making a note of it, but the bastards still wouldn't give me anything.

It was a real good job that I was living with Tark or I don't know what I would have done. One night, after he had treated me to a slap-up Indian, we went back to the flat and got talking about things. As he knocked back rum and limes, I sipped straight Energade – I was determined not to lose the high fitness level I had worked so hard to build up. Tark understood the employment situation perfectly.

'Yeh, it's a bad scene if you haven't got a job at the moment, Tris.'

'You telling me!' I replied.

'There may be a few "Haves" around. But there's a shit load more "Have Nots". Makes you think, doesn't it?'

It certainly did. It made me think that the sooner I was picked up by a club, the better. Tarka lit up a joint, took a sip of his drink and continued his argument.

'It's like this "Me Generation" bollocks everybody's into now. I don't believe in it.'

'Tell that to Ms Shit Features at the dole. She had no interest in me at all. I'm just a number to her.'

---

*For those of you who are not scholars of The Beautiful Game, think of Billy as the Gary Lineker of his day. But without the dosh, the tan, the TV programmes, the endorsements...

'Yeh, take a ticket, wait for the number to come up. "Desk number three, please!" Fancy a hit on this?' he said, offering me a toke on the joint. Whoa! Some of the smoke went up my nose as I stared at it like a rabbi caught in Kieron Dyer's headlights. I can smell it now – the "sickly sweet stench of temptation" as I think BBC weather man Michael Fish calls such moments.

We've all been there, haven't we? These P.M.I.T.G (Pivotal Moment In The Game) situations. You know what I mean – having to make a judgement call that you know could decide the outcome of the game you're playing. Or the life you're living. Stay wide or tuck in? Press up or drop off? And especially – pass or shoot?

So – what to do? Now you've heard all the rumours about my "bottomless" appetites for this, that and especially the other thing. You know the documented facts – the famous "Three Loins In The Fountain" incident in Madrid for starters. And you've heard the stories – my "speed and coke-fuelled" appearance on *Blue Peter* is one most people know. And don't forget the jokes:

Q: "How did Burksey make the Spurs cheerleaders drop their pom-poms?"

A: "He took 'em up the Arsenal."

Laugh? I thought I'd never start.

But of course, people don't just talk. They write. A scandal sheet journo I know in The States – Clyde Tater of the *National Requirer* – wrote : "It seems 'Gland Boy' just can't help himself. He demonstrates about as much self-control as a star-struck nympho in a Jacuzzi full of Pro Jocks." Why nymphos should find Scotsmen sexy, I'm not right sure. But the point the Yank muckraker is making is that yours truly can resist anything except temptation. Really? Cop this, Stars And Tripe – I said "no" to that toke on Tarka's joint.

And later on in my six-month stay in Brighton, I said "no" to booze, acid, speed, smack, ecstasy, angel dust and coke. With or without the cola. Why? Because of the two pictures I had on my little attic room wall. Did Frank Worthington get where he got by abusing his body and his mind? Is that how he had dazzled crowds all over the country?

So it just wasn't an issue for me. Booze and drugs were out. And as for the cruder stuff – no way. Sniffing solvents solves nothing, believe me. Glue? – you can stick it.

I was keeping myself as pure as I believed Frank had, so that when the call from on high came, I would be ready to shine; ready to take the sports world apart, ready to realise my destiny as what God had intended me to be – a superstar footballer.

But before that, I got a job flogging "Vegetable Patch" dolls in a department store in Brighton. They were all the rage at the time even though they looked like a bunch of spanners. I think the kids liked the gimmick that each one came with its own "birth certificate."

"Care In The Community Bears" went one better – each carried a personalised case file including everything from employment records to psychiatric assessments. These fluffy fellahs looked really cute in their shiny suit jackets and baseball caps and I actually preferred them to their vinyl-bonced Veggie brethren. I still have one in my "shit". Trevor, he's called.

My stint at Cannington's lasted two whole weeks which gave me a bit of much needed dosh. I spent some of it on one of the hand-held video games that were really starting to take off at the time. In Tindonto's *Tutty Hump* you controlled Boy King Tutankhamen as he tried to shore up a collapsing pyramid with scaffolding. Sounds easy? They've never had a go, have they game fans? Whilst Tut's doing his stuff with his scaffolding poles, Hump, the Evil Camel, keeps nicking his clamp podgers. Every one he gets goes into his hump which can only be got back by squirting him in the eye with the embalming potion Blah the Mummy Maker keeps in his scorpion-guarded tool chest.

Here's another revelation – in twenty years of playing *Tutty Hump*, I've only ever successfully shored up that pyramid three times. Fellow Game Fan Ian Dowie tells me he had exactly the same trouble with Crystal Palace's defence in the 2004/5 season. Too right, Dow.

Back on the dole, times were grim. And looking on helplessly as the nice family next door – the Turners – had their house repossessed didn't do me any favours either. All that shouting, screaming and crying really put me off my lunch. Why? 'Cos as anyone who really knows me will tell you, I'm an old softie at heart. And just because I believe in the law of the jungle doesn't mean I get any jollies from watching a bunch of leopards chasing down a family of koalas and then ripping them to shreds. Why did it go tits-up for the Turners? It seems that the father, who worked as some sort of track inspector on the railway, had lost his job over something or other – I think all his mates on his gang lost theirs as well – catapulting them into a downward spiral of hopelessness and debt. Of course, Mister Turner's problem was that – unlike me – he was not one of the chosen few. Despite my many setbacks, I knew I would be more than comfortable eventually. He stood no chance. After all, who needs rail track inspectors? So how did Mister Turner's story turn out in the end? Badly – the wheels came off for everyone concerned. Very sad.

I don't know about you, but the thing that will always stick in my mind about the year I lived in Brighton – 1984 (apart from my future mate Arnie Schwarzenegger's brilliant movie *Terminator* coming out) – was the staging of the XXIII Olympiad in Los Angeles. Do you remember – I'm sure you do – our Superhero Supreme Steve Redgrave winning the first of his umpteen boating medals? Now I'm not knocking the man in any way – how could you, he's one of the greatest sportsman who's ever lived – but let's face it: how many people do you know row boats? And how many do it worldwide? I've no idea how many it is but it's probably about the same as the number of people who play Horse Polo, Real Tennis, or Wellie Chucking. Now think about how many people run. Unless you're unlucky enough to have no legs, every bugger on the planet does it, don't they? I think becoming an Olympic Champion in a running event is a far greater achievement. And for me, one moment stands out above all others in the L.A. '84 Games. It was watching Sheffield steel carving up the opposition in the 1500 metres. Yes, Hallamshire Harriers' very own Sebastian Coe won gold. And he did it for the second time in succession.

But who would have thought that, as I sat there watching him triumph on Tark's shitty little portable TV – there was so much snow on the picture, I thought I was watching the Winter Olympics – that twenty-one years later, I would be standing shoulder to shoulder with Seb as between us, we brought the Olympic Games to London.

But more of that later.

I've told you about some of the things I said "no!" to in my six months enforced holiday in Brighton. I'll tell you another thing I said "no!" to and this is going to have you falling on the floor in disbelief. I said "no!" to sex. And first time, virginity-breaking sex at that. I could have s***ged any number of my brother's band's groupies and hangers on. But I didn't f*** one of them. Why? Because they were all riddled with the clap, chlam and/or worse? No, that wasn't the reason. Besides, there were a couple of fit fifth formers from Roedean who had hardly anything. No, I didn't want to do it because I knew that once I started up that slippery slope, there'd be no coming down. At the age I was, sex would have taken my wind, it would have taken my mind, and as for my legs – well, they would literally have exploded. There would be plenty of time to play hide the salami once I'd got my foot into a pair of boots somewhere. I needed to be in prime condition to strut my stuff on the pitch when my chance came.

And on 12th October 1984, that chance finally arrived. Or the possibility of it did.

A mate of Tark's who knew soccer mad songster Rod Stewart had heard from his roadie's cousin that a certain North London football club were about to advertise for an assistant groundsman. I'd done a fair bit of pitch work at Leeds Road as part of my apprentice duties there and I knew I would stand a good chance of landing the job if I got an interview. The pay wasn't much good, but that wasn't the point. Once I was actually at the football club, I figured that eventually, I would be able to impress the Boss and his staff with both my skills – getting silkier every day – and my strong, physical playing potential. As long as they didn't find out that I had been Huddersfield's Junior Hellraiser of the Year before I had the chance to shine, I thought I stood every chance. Once I had shone, I reckoned it wouldn't matter to them who I was – Jack The Ripper, Alan Partridge, the future Lee Bowyer – I would be in.

So I was going to take no chances to start with. Looking back, one of the things that did the most damage to me at Town was my tendency towards P.M.B.A. (Pre Match Boner Activity). I just couldn't get my kit on without Mister Willie wanting to stand up and see what was going off. I found the whole experience of playing football such a mental and physical turn on that I couldn't help but show it in the only way a 17 year-old knows how. I needed to stop it. But how? As with so many problems in life, there was no easy, quick fix solution. So I asked Tarka for a loan.

'I'll pay you back, Tark, honest. Soon as I can.'

'Hey, no need to do that man. Just take it, okay?'

I did as my brother asked and went out and bought a full playing kit for every side in the top division. For hour after punishing hour, I practised getting undressed and putting on some of the most famous strips in football. How did it go? Let's just say that for the first few weeks, I practised long and hard. But then I made a sensational breakthrough. I found, like many an Englishman before me, that by singing the National Anthem, every ounce of vitality and inspiration went right out of my system. Yes! It worked brilliantly. Soon I was able to strip off and put on any kit of my choosing without even a sniff of a hard-on. Every kit except one. And that kit was.... Watford's. No, that's just a rib-tickler for my old England Mentor and Tormentor, Graham Taylor. The anthem-proof kit was actually Man United's. But, hey, they weren't likely to come calling just yet. I'd cross that bridge if I ever came to it.

The day of the interview arrived. After borrowing the fare from Tark, I went to Brighton station and bought a single ticket to London. I was that confident in my own ability – and I also didn't have enough cash for a return. Which club was I off to? I don't really need to tell you, do I?

But before I get on to that, I want to give you a couple of interesting little sidebars on that time. Remember two of Orange Microdot's most popular live numbers – *We Generation* and *Serving Number Seven*? Tarka was inspired to write them after that evening we talked about the waking death that is living on the dole. Cool, eh? Although, to be honest, The Dots' winning blend of blues, rock and punk didn't do much for me – I'm more of a Belinda Carlisle man – I always love hearing those two numbers.

The other thing? In the early hours of the very morning I set off to London for my interview, terrorists tried to blow up Maggie Thatcher and some of her colleagues at the Grand Hotel, only about a mile or so from where I was staying with Tarka.

That someone had tried to blow up my heroine was the worst possible omen for me and I got to the venue for my interview fearing the worst for my chances. The result? I walked it. I got the job. Life? It's a funny old game isn't it!

## CHAPTER FIVE

# THE PROMISED LAND

**A**nd so what was the identity of the North London club I headed off to that day? No prizes for the correct answer, but just in case you suffer from Alzheimer's or something, it was the mighty and majestic Tottenham Hotspur FC.

But before I get on to what happened in my first few months at White Hart Lane, I have to sound what Motty calls a "serious note".

I said at the start of this book that I was going to reveal a lot of things that have never been revealed before. What I am about to tell you is one of the most terrible. It's something that will shock you to what Bryan Gonville calls "the very core of one's being". I have actually been warned not to say anything about it by a number of people – including my agent, Dave Green – but sometimes you have to just stick your courage to the sticking plaster and stand up for what is right. So if you want to know something filthy and horrible about one of the game's most beloved characters – read on. If you don't – and I respect that view – I suggest you skip a page or two.

Let me start by saying just quite straightforwardly that I love Gary Mabbutt. Not in a weird crack-packing way of course. I mean just in a normal bear-huggy bloke way. Everything you've ever heard about this man – his cheerfulness, his generosity, his hilariously misplaced affection for Swindon – is true.

What is also true is that, whilst he was a practising professional footballer, Gary "Poppins" Mabbutt was a heavy performance-enhancing drug user.

How do I know? Because I saw him at it.

My suspicions were aroused the first time I noticed him nipping into the changing rooms at The Lane and then coming back out wearing a slightly different look on his face. Whatever he was doing in there was making him feel good and I just had to find out what it was. So one day, I got in there before him, hid in an empty locker and waited. I wish I hadn't. A few hours later, I watched as Gary, a man his fellow professionals admired and respected, a man children all over England preferred to their own fathers, sneaked in, took a syringe full of junk out of his kitbag – and injected himself.

No! Not Gary! Of course at the time, I was a drug virgin and didn't know exactly what he was shooting up, but after years of doing everything from snorting Thai Wang Dust to popping Miami Kick Boxers – I'm sorry kids – I can tell you that what he was mainlining was really heavy stuff. Judging by its devilishly harmless appearance, I think it was probably White Knuckle Ride. Or maybe Bristol Scream Candy.

I tell you, peeping at Gary through the grill of that locker, I nearly cried with disbelief. Of course, it was also a warning sign to me if I'd only realised it. If Gary Mabbs had become a junkie, anybody could become one. Why didn't I think on? Why didn't I vow there and then never to go down that deadly route? Because I was too thick. The simple truth is that I still had a lot, some say a world, of stuff to learn. And maybe I still do. Nobody's perfect. Except José Mourinho, of course.

I was gutted at watching such an idol abusing himself. And I made up my mind there and then to do something about it. I needed to help Gary kick his filthy habit. But how?

Then it hit me. Whenever I had the chance, I resolved to rummage through his stuff, find his fix – and then lose it.* Because of my assistant groundsman's duties, I wouldn't always be in a position to put my plan into action, but if I found myself in the right place at the right time – bingo!

I'll tell you how I got on with my one-man re-hab scheme later. But let's back up a little. I think it was brainy crosspatch Jeremy Paxman who said that the first few months of my three-year stint at Tottenham Hotspur Football Club were a bit like Cinderella's life in the well known panto. What did he mean? He meant that, whilst the Ugly Sisters in the shape of Mark Falco etcetera were out enjoying themselves on the pitch, innocent little Stevie "Cinders" Burkes was flogging his guts out in the basement.

Not that I minded – just the opposite. Like I say, I wanted to blend into the woodwork without anybody noticing me. To start with. I'd been too visible at Town from the off, getting far too much up manager Mick Buxton's nose – almost literally – to ever get settled in. I was determined not to blow it now I had the opportunity of a lifetime.

I knew that my whole future career might depend on that first few months at Tottenham but I never expected it to have quite the effects it did. Even in odd little ways.

I've often been asked what "that little twitch you sometimes do with your head" is all about. You've all seen it at one time or another – the ball comes to me and for a brief moment my head jets to the side and then jets back again. It puts opponents off brilliantly and buys me time and space to show off my silky skills on the ball. For the first time, I will reveal how I got that twitch. I don't know how I carried it off, but when I first went to the Lane, I was so determined not to do anything that would

---

*I learned some years later that the junk was actually called "Ince Yellin!" – celebrating the supersonic vocal power of my future club-mate – mega-gifted midfielder Paul. See p 244.

draw attention to myself that I wouldn't so much as look at a football. If one ever came into my eye line, I would quickly look the other way so as not to be tempted. Tempted to start showing off with it. That was how it began. After a while, the move became second nature. Of course, "the twitch" has often been misinterpreted. Several brainbox pundits have had a go at me for "overdoing the eyes" over the years. Clueless as usual. They pay these people good money for coming out with all this garbage, you know. Anybody who has ever watched a tape of a TV preview show after the game they're previewing knows that ninety percent of what most of the "experts" predict turns out to be wrong. You know the ones I'm talking about.

If I want to avoid the usual suspects – the puddin'-headed pundits we so often have to put up with on TV – I turn over to Stelsat's excellent coverage. From Stevie Claridge to Stan Collymore, Niall Quinn to Antony Worrall Thompson, the quality of their experts' analysis always stands out. And if I was asked to cast a vote for the Top TV Sports Anchor Person at the moment, I would give it to Stelsat's "astute and cute" Clare Tomlinson. I dare say you'd give her one as well lads, wouldn't you?

But back to my early days at Spurs. Although my almost uncontainable excitement at being at such a magnificent football club made it difficult for me to keep my head down, I just about managed it. And my plan began to work. Gradually, I earned a reputation as an honest kid who turned up, carried out his assistant groundsman's duties – which I thoroughly enjoyed, by the way – and then went home. Not that I had far to go. Although nobody knew it, for most of the week, "home" was a cramped space behind the hot water pipes in the stadium's furnace room. Yes, for four months I slept on a bed made from the cardboard delivery cartons thrown away by one of the ground's many fast food outlets. To this day, just thinking about cream cheese bagels is enough to send me soundly off to sleep.

One difference between me and Cinderella was that whilst she was beavering away at her chores, she had no idea that one day, she would go to the ball. I did know. And I knew when – Shrove Tuesday, February 19th 1985. Pancake Day. What's so special about that? My old Lord's Taverners mate, Mike Gatting, has just had a seizure at that question, but seriously, it's special because it's the day always set aside for the annual match between Spurs' First XI and the White Hart Lane Ground Staff. About a week before the Big Day, I was putting the gang mower away when the game's organiser – kit man Johnny Wallis – approached me. 'Alright, Stevie?'

'Not three bad', I replied. Although I was, still am, and always will be a proud middle class Yorkshireman, I was getting the Cockney working class lingo thing down pat. It was a good ploy because it stopped anybody connecting me with the events of my recent past. And, looking back, I can also see that it was another cry for help, really. You see, I was desperate to fit in. Be part of things.

'Do you fancy playing in our little game, then?' asked Johnny.

'Playing? Blimey guv'nor, I dunno. Oh go on, why not?' I tell you, I should have been nominated for an Oscar for this performance.

'Good stuff – I'll put your name down. Don't care where you play do you?'

'I f\*\*\*ing do! Centre forward! Er.... if no-one else wants to.' Whoops. One minute I'm Robert De Niro, the next I'm that bloke in *Casualty*.

'Nah, should be alright. Be in the changing rooms next Tuesday – half-ten.'

'Okay, yeh. Sweet.'

'It's always a good laugh. See you then!'

As soon as Mister Wallis was out of sight, I was punching the air like a demented boxer. I almost felt like going into the goal celebration that I had been rehearsing in my spare time. You've all seen it. Seen it 319 times if you've followed my entire career. I've been asked almost as often where I got the idea for the intricate series of moves that I was shortly to reveal to the world and twelve years later, would copyright – the first goal celebration ever to be copyrighted in world football.

So now I can reveal exclusively to you, dear reader, where it came from. The first part – the four bounding hops – was inspired by my favourite TV programme as a kid – *Skippy The Bush Kangaroo*. The middle phase – the pirouette into splits – was a nod to my roots; a reprise of one of my more spectacular ballet moves, and the final phase – forward hand spring on to my head for the corkscrew skull-spin climax – was inspired by a young breakdancer I saw busking outside my Dad's library in Hudders. I guess he didn't copyright his move as I've never been taken to court over it.\*

Just another word on Johnny Wallis. If you ask your average Spurs fan this question: "which one man in history deserves the accolade 'Mister Tottenham?'" – there would only be one answer: Bill Nicholson. But I tell you what – Johnny would get a good few votes from those in the know. He started at the Lane in the thirties and did every backroom job going. Including first team trainer. Johnny Wallis – a diamond geezer and a true Tottenham Hotspur.

*\*Some of you will have read that in 2002, I sued a 19 year-old South African named Glorious Takeleh for performing an unauthorised replica of my goal celebration at a televised Inter Township Tournament held the previous year. And so I did. It was nothing against the lad, it was just a matter of principle. What the Daily Arsehole forgot to tell you is that I also paid for the building of TWO new temporary classrooms at the Special Needs School which Mister Takeleh attended.*

But back to the Spurs v Ground Staff game. It would be a bit of fun would it? A good laugh. Not for me it wouldn't. For me it would be one of the most important games I would ever play in. I would be able to demonstrate what I had to offer against some of the best opposition imaginable. Let's face it, as fine a bunch of players as Brian Cox, Brian Stanton and the other guys I'd encountered at Leeds Road were, we're talking a different league at Spurs. We're talking big stars like goal monster, Clive Allen. We're talking World Cup Winner Ossie Ardiles; lightning quick Garth Crooks; big-hearted workhorse Steve Perryman; 100% committed Graham Roberts. And in my future Chelsea and England boss Glenn Hoddle, we are talking simply one of the greatest artists who ever stepped on to a football pitch. Anywhere. Anytime.

Was I in awe of these people? You bet your bloody life I was. And I got all their autographs to prove it. Impressing the manager would be no easy task. Although in one way it would – new Boss Peter Shreeves would be playing right behind me in midfield!

Apart from a smattering of contracted apprentices and other back room staff, our side also featured a few old Spurs players like Terry Naylor and Ralph Coates. I knew I needed to play well in that game to catch the eye. And there would be no better way of doing it than scoring a goal or two. The more spectacular the better. To start with, as the Spurs first team players arrived for the match, there was good news on that front. England's top shot stopper Ray Clemence wasn't going to play in goal. The bad news was that Tony Parks was. Who? Shame on you! He was the kiddie who had stepped in and saved two of Anderlecht's penalty shoot-out spot-kicks to win the UEFA Cup the previous season.

And I had another challenge. Before I could do anything, I had to get into my kit first.

And just to make matters worse, our opponents insisted that we had the privilege of playing in Spurs' sacred first team strip whilst they opted to turn out in an assortment of tops with matching bibs. Did I say it would be a challenge?

Johnny handed me the white shirt with its famous insignia, the white shorts (the club had temporarily abandoned its usual navy blue ones) and socks and looked at my face for the expected delighted reaction. He could see I was touched and left me to it. As I anxiously stripped off, I heard someone behind me – one of the turnstile operators I think it was – comment on what putting on that famous shirt meant to him. At least, I hoped that's what he meant because what he actually said put the fear of Vinnie Jones up me.

'Look at that cock, mate. F***ing massive to me, that is!'

No!!!!!! I wasn't at it again, was I? And Boss Shreeves was getting changed right next to me. I looked down at my wanton willie, but thankfully, it was still on the dangle. Just. But I knew I needed to put what Brandee used to call my "like coping strategy" into operation immediately, so as I peeled the number nine shirt over my torso,

I launched loudly into a rousing rendition of God Save The Queen. It worked – the fast train from Salami City to Bonersville stalled in the depot. And stayed there. Yes, I will always be grateful to the composer of our national anthem – Dr Henry Carey – for his dismal efforts.

And not only that, my rendition got a laugh. Not a "what the bloody hell is this toerag doing?" sort of laugh – the lads thought I was being deliberately funny. That relaxed me even more. And for the first time in my life, it gave me a sense that I was starting to belong to something. I was bonding with mates. By the time you were nearly eighteen, you'd probably done that thousands of times. Apart from my big brother Tarka, I'd never had a real friend. Or any kind of friend, really. It was a magical moment.

Remember my sacred mission to wean Gary Mabbutt off his mainlining habit by hiding his rocket juice? The day of The Match put me in the perfect P.O.M.O. (Position Of Maximum Opportunity) to nab his stash. I took it – and squirted the gunk down the bog. Gary would have to play without the drug-fuelled high he was used to.

And boy did it show in the match that followed. Without his Ince Yellin', Mabbs was deprived of that extra 20% that made him a top class defender and England international. Time and time again, I shimmied past him, nutmegged him, went right through him. In short, I made him look a right donkey – a breathless, pale and sweating no-hoper like you seeing playing at Hackney Marshes every weekend.

Any other first team star – what did the match matter to the likes of him and Ossie Ardiles? – would have gone off and had a lie down, but Gary kept going to the end. "I didn't want to disappoint the lads", I heard him wheeze to Johnny W. afterwards. Gary, you had already disappointed the lads. This lad, anyway. Forever. Of course later, I was to follow a similar path to blissful happiness. Wrongly, I should add.

How did I perform against Spurs' top stars overall? Considering I found the experience totally daunting, I did brilliant. Apart from Gary's lacklustre display, the level of his team's play was massively different from anything I'd encountered before. Even though, with two exceptions, they weren't really trying that hard.

Who do you reckon the two exceptions were? I'll tell you. The first was Graham Roberts. The bloke played as if his life depended on it. I used my physique to knock him off the ball early in the first half and I thought he was going to kill me when he climbed back on to the pitch. We became mates eventually, but at the time I thought my number was up. The second guy to give it his all was none other than Mister Glenn Hoddle. Not in a Robbo tearing around the pitch kind of way, of course. He impressed by pulling off a series of killer tricks and by passing the ball all over the pitch with radar-like accuracy. At one point, Glenn's taken the ball off keeper Parks, flicked it up onto his head and then, with his eyes closed, kept it there whilst he's

41

jogged eighty yards through our team before dropping the thing on to his foot and then blasting it past our keeper. Still with his eyes closed! Don't believe that? I was there. I saw it. And as I did, I realised I hadn't even begun to put in the hours of practice necessary to live out my dream.

It goes without saying that I was easily the best player on the Ground Staff team – Ralph Coates might argue with me on that but I'm bigger than him, so can it, Coatesy! – and I kept getting little cheers, odd words of encouragement and pats on the back from everybody on the pitch; including from Mister Hoddle, although I don't think he liked it when, from a corner, I won a round of applause for lashing a brilliant bicycle kick past Tony Parks. What makes me think he didn't like it? Because Glenn spent the next fifteen minutes doing nothing but launching bicycle kicks off in all directions, every one of them sweeter struck and more accurately placed than mine. He was making a point. Fair enough, Glenn.

At the final whistle, we'd lost seven-three. But I'd scored one goal, made another and played well in general. As we shook hands all round, I realised that some of the game's great players were giving me a funny look. "Who is this lad?" you could see they were thinking. But to a man – including Glenn – they all said "well done, mate", "well played," "magic", "brilliant" and stuff like that. Ossie Ardiles, who I'd skinned a couple of times in the game, said "You do that again and I'll cut chor knackers off!" But then the lovable Argie – we were all friends with our South American cousins now – gave me a big wink. I was on Cloud Nine! But a big wink from a world star is one thing – it's what Manager Peter Shreeves wanted to give me that really had my attention. I looked over expectantly, but I couldn't see him clearly because Gary Mabbutt was having a word in his ear. I learned later that, before he collapsed, Mabbo said something along the lines of "you've got to sign this lad, boss."

The manager came over to me and told me to come to his office at nine in the morning. The last time I'd heard that phrase, I was given the bollocking of my life when I showed up for the meeting. This time, I had a feeling the outcome was going to be slightly different.

In an interview years later, Glenn Hoddle recalled that kick-about game, the game that changed everything for me.

"Yeh, as soon as Burksey's run on to the pitch with them legs, I knew he was the business. He reminded me of Gerd Müller or Diego Maradona. I don't mean he was the same class – not then – but he was the same type. Powerful. Low slung, and with a bit of something about him. As the game went on he done too many tricks, but apart from that I thought, yeh, let's get this lad into the squad."

'Too many tricks?' You tell 'em, Glenn.

Most of you know what happened at the meeting with Mister Shreeves the following morning. The Boss told me everybody had been impressed by me in the match and that my record on the groundstaff had been exemplary – Mick Buxton would have had a fit if he'd heard that – and he offered me terms. I don't mind admitting it, I think his words made me wet myself. I was ecstatic. He suggested that I may as well wait a couple of months – until my 18th birthday – before signing as a professional player proper but got me to put my name on a document holding me to the club until then. They were worried I might go elsewhere! In April I would get a small signing-on fee and my first £400 per week pay cheque. It was more money than I could have dreamed of. In the meantime, he said that I was to start immediate training with the senior squad – yes! – but he also asked me if I minded serving out my notice on the ground staff and grooming the new lad who would be appointed to take over from me. I said I would be happy to. See how reasonable I was compared to some of the stories you've heard about me? He asked me where I was living. I could hardly say "the furnace room", so I said I was still in Brighton.

'That's no good. Go and see Maureen in the office and she'll fix you up with some digs nearby.'

No more hot water pipes. No more bagel box beds. No more dreaming about what it would be like to be a professional footballer. Now I was one. Nearly. I went off to see Maureen without a care in the world. After a few phone calls she fixed me up with a Mrs Daggs of Edmonton.

My life was changing. But by Crikey, as I moved my stuff into Doyle Villas, London N18, I didn't know by just how much.

---
# CHAPTER SIX
---

## GETTING MY ROX OFF

At the start of this book, I promised to pull back the covers on just a few of my supercharged sexploits for you. Feeling a bit short-changed so far? In this chapter you'll get your first whiff of the Burksey sex machine in action.

But before that, have a guess at the first thing I did after I left Mister Shreeves' office on the day he offered me terms? Went out and got p***ed maybe? No, I rang Mum and Dad. Yes, Bad Boy Burksey – the "unthinking woman's crumpet"* – strikes again. They were out as it happens, but I left a message on their answer phone. Then I rang Tarka. He hadn't got up yet, but I left a message on his answer phone. Next, I dropped a line to Margaret Thatcher, thanking her for everything she had done to make my deserved entry into The Promised Land possible. Penning another postcard to Frank Worthington was my next task. This time, it was a happy one.

But then I had a slightly different message to deliver. I went and bought a big padded envelope, took a dump in it and sealed it with this note inside: "Whilst I'll be rolling in money, you'll still be rolling in this!" I addressed it to Ms Y Killmartin at the Brighton Dole Office and dropped it in the mail. Brutal? Maybe. Justified? You bet your life. If it had been up to that woman, Steve Burkes would never have become a professional footballer. He would probably still have been labouring on a building site somewhere. Yes, the bitch had dumped on me, I was just dumping on her back.

I think my natural feeling for revenge is one of the things that endeared me to the Italian public later. They love a good vendetta down Italy way. But before I leave the question of what did, and what almost didn't, happen to my life at this point, I want to say a word about my first real boss. Nowadays, Peter Shreeves is not thought of as one of the great winners in Spurs managerial history. That's interesting because if you actually look at the records, you'll see that in his two stints as Gaffer, he did a superior job to most other managers they've had at The Lane. I tell you why I think people don't think better of him. It's his looks. "F*** off Burksey, you've been sucking your Harrogate

---

*I believe BBC Sportscaster Hazel Irvine called me that in a conversation with Scots Curling Great, Rhona Martin. You don't know me, girls. Don't know me at all. But if you'd like to, call my agent – Dave Green – and an application pack will be sent to you.*

Horse Toffee again!" I hear you cry. No, I am serious. You don't think looks matter? Seek psychiatric help because you're mental. Let's face it, Peter Shreeves looked more like a foreman in an auto parts warehouse than the manager of a top football team. You can picture him in his brown smock, can't you – two biros and a delivery docket stuck in his breast pocket. Labour Loser Neil Kinnock had a similar problem. Mind you, Old Carrot Dome would have had to have looked like George Clooney to have stood any chance of beating super classy Mrs T.

But back to Peter Shreeves. He was a nice man and a bloody good football manager. How good? He plucked me from obscurity, didn't he? On the strength of just one game. I thank him. And The World thanks him.

Mister Shreeves was also a shrewd operator. Whilst I was out there training and serving out my two-month notice on the ground staff, he was using that time to investigate who I was and where I'd come from. And there's me thinking that delaying signing a proper contract was just to do with the timing of the thing. Dave Green?! Where were you when I needed you?!

I know what you're thinking now. The Gaffer had me investigated, but he still wanted to take me as a player when push came to shove on my birthday? Yes and by then he knew all about my time at Town – the injuries, the boozing, the weird behaviour. Including the notorious "Berniegate" incident. So how come he still wanted me?

Two reasons. One: although raw and unschooled, I was dazzling everybody in training. Two: the boss set me a test and I came through it with flying colours. What was that test? One morning after training, he's marched up to me carrying a plain brown envelope. He doesn't say a word as he takes a photo out of it and without looking, shows it to me – I think he got it off a mate of his at Birmingham City or something. Anyway, keen to see what my immediate reaction to the photo would be, he looks me straight in the eyes as I take a gander at it. It was a shot of a sheep sh***er. On the job.

'What do you make of that?', he asked, stony faced.

'I prefer a longer horn myself. The hooves are kinda cute, though.'

Under the circumstances, it was rash. It was brave. It was stupid.

After a moment's silence, it also got a laugh. A doubled-up, side-splitting, tears down the face job. The Gaffer was in pieces.

Everything was alright. I was in. Peter Shreeves – a man of vision.

By the way, one of the Spurs lads who wished to remain nameless – although I can tell you it was natty net belter Clive Allen – nicked that photo and cheekily put it up on the club notice board. You wouldn't think good old housewives' choice Clive – the beloved, be-cardiganed, be-butter wouldn't melt in his mouth Mister Nice Guy – would have got up to such a stunt would you? You don't know footballers. What brought the house down even more was that later somebody – who really will remain nameless – substituted a head shot of new Arsenal supremo George Graham in place of the sheep sh\*\*\*er. And Paul Merson's in place of the sheep. A couple of the lads added brilliant speech bubbles. I can't repeat what they said, but you can check it out on that website. You know the one I mean – the one with the cartoon of the Spurs Ladies' "football" match? You've got it.

We members of the football community get a lot of stick today, but I'll tell you how great a lot of us are. Both Mister Graham and Merse nearly killed themselves with laughter when they saw that picture. George Graham a prude? In some ways, maybe. But he's a fun guy once you get to know him. I know at least three people who think that.

I want to say something now that's just come into my head. The very fact that you're reading this book means that you're a cut above the average football fan, so when I say "you" in the following remarks, I'm not referring to you at all, but to certain other people.

Right, here goes. Most of you fans work all week at some dull job and then come the weekend, what do you want? You want your jollies. You want your football. So off you all go to watch "your" team playing "their" team. You sit there, cheering your heads off for us players one minute, questioning our parentage the next – whatever – then when it's all over, you go back home happy or sad because of what "your" team has done.

Yes, you support us. You idolise us. You help to pay our comparatively modest wages... Whoa – time out! Do I hear sniggers? Alright, look at it this way – I might earn £100+k a week basic, but do you know how much I would get if I was a top American Footballer? Or baseball player? Or basketball star? I'd get several times more! We poor little monkeys get peanuts compared to those big organ grinders.

But anyway, back to the point I'm making. We players don't look at ourselves the way you lot look at us. What you all need to realise is that "your" players and "their" players have a lot more in common with each other than they do with you, their own fans. You don't like that? You want us to hate "their" players? Get real, you sad losers. Why did Spurs fans slaughter Sol Campbell for going to Arsenal? Why did Barcelona fans pelt my future club captain, the great Luis Figo, with coins, mobile phones and half the contents of a butcher's shop when he turned out for Real Madrid at the Nou Camp? Why? I'll tell you why. Because your average football fan is a sad w\*\*\*er who should get out more.

Alright, it's a documented fact that when Frank Worthington went to Leeds United, I had to be sedated and lost the will to live for a while. But I got over it. And so should you lot. And in the meantime – please keep going to matches. And if you want to feel good about yourself because of what I and my mates get up to on that pitch – why not? Go for it. It's fine with us.

All kidding aside, we players really do love our fans and realise that we would be nowhere without them. And just to prove it – do you know how many autographs I have signed in my career? More than ninety-three thousand, six-hundred and ninety-one.*

My three year contract signed that very day, I began to relax almost for the first time in my life. At last, I was part of something. And part of something big. But life's funny, isn't it? Now I was part of a distended family, I lost the need to be accepted at all costs as one of them. Don't get me wrong, I wasn't standoffish or anything – I just didn't feel the need to be everybody's best mate all the time.

Mister Shreeves thought that it was a good idea if I buddied up with a Spurs stalwart who not all that many fans talk about today, but he was a big part of things at the time.

In fact, he played a key role in one of the greatest – some say *the* greatest – goal ever scored in an FA Cup Final. It was this lad who gave the final pass to Spurs legend Ricky Villa before he went on that helter-skelter run to score the winner in the 1981 replay against Man City. And the name of that lad was... Tony Galvin. Why did Mister Shreeves put us together? Because Tony hails from Huddersfield as well.

I'm not being funny, but I have to say that that's where the similarity between us ended. We were very different people. You see Tony was a brainbox. He even had a University degree. And it wasn't in Sports Leisure Management. It was in – wait for it – Russian. Well, you can imagine how that made me feel. I didn't have a C.S.E. to my name and I'm supposed to pal up with this guy just because of an accident of birth?

What could we talk about? I did make a bit of an attempt to get to grips with the thing by pluckily buying a video of *From Russia With Love* and watching it several times. But all I got out of it was one word – "nyet". I wasn't quite sure what it meant but I started peppering our conversations with it in the hope that it would break the ice. Tony came up to me before training one day, wearing that big brainbox grin of his. He opened up with a typical ploy to make me look small:

*\*This figure refers to the number of autographs signed before I successfully underwent treatment for Obsessive Compulsive Disorder at a California Clinic in 2003. The total number of signings is therefore higher than the number stated.*
*Thirteen thousand, six-hundred and thirty seven higher to be exact.*

'Alright Burksey?'

'Nyet.'

'Really? What's up?'

'Nowt.'

'Sorry mate, I though you said there was.'

'Nyet off, Einstein!'

Tony shrugged and went off to join another one of the club's academic whizz-kids, Garth Crooks. Years later, my wife Brandee would go on at me for "acting like too defensive?" To be fair, she was right. I was often off sides with folk and it would usually come out in the form of verbal or physical aggression. Like the time I was invited on to a live TV programme presented by the glamorous Gabby Yorath – as she was then – and seconds before we went on the air I gave her a slap in the gob when she suggested that the best thing that had ever come out of Huddersfield was the A62 to Leeds. Panic stations! As her lips began to swell, the studio floor manager frantically rushed forward with the only thing he had to hand – his lip gloss – to treat the affected area.

As you all know, tragically, poor Gabby eventually became addicted to the treatment that was meant to help her. I'm so glad that becoming the first recorded victim in history of the condition known as Lip Gloss Dependency hasn't prevented Gabby from leading an almost full life. And I'm sorry, Gab, for what I did. I realised later that you were only making a joke. And whilst we're on it, I'd like to thank you for not sending future hubby Kenny Logan after me when the truth came out. Although to be fair, I know I could have taken the haggis-guzzling oval-baller if it had come to a punch-up.

Anyway, what it all boils down to is that overcoming defensiveness was another mountain I would have to climb in my life. I said I had a lot to learn.

I tell you what didn't help me much in that area. Going to live with the blowsy Mrs Daggs in Edmonton. Some have called her the "landlady from Hell". I would go along with that. Having led a sheltered middle class kind of life up until then – according to my future manager, the peerless Sir Alex Ferguson, I was brought up "not in the School of Hard Knocks, but the School of Soft Knockers" – I had just never come across a person like Mrs Daggs before. Not one who was a wife and a mother anyway. Common? She made Waynetta Slob look like Joanna Lumley.

And then there was her 20 year-old daughter, Roxanna. Compared with her mother, the little redhead had class. She was always clean, tidy and presentable. But there was something else about her. I liked the way she tied her mop of red hair back in bunches. I liked her cheeky smile. Alright, she was a bit on the plump side, but maybe that was why she had such a brilliant rack on her. There was no getting away from it, Roxanna was no Michelle Pfeiffer or anything – but she hit me right in my

Z.O.P (Zone Of Pressure). In other words, I fancied the little ginger luv ninja summat rotten. I'll never forget our first conversation together.

'Alright?'

'Alright?'

So far so good. I decided to open up a bit.

'My name's Steve. I'm a footballer. With Spurs.'

'All our lodgers are.'

W***er. I should've thought of that. Be sophisticated, I thought to myself.

'Course. So what do you do, then?' I said to her. This was more like it.

'I'm a chicken strangler.'

Jesus.

'Yeh, I work at a free range poultry place up Barnet.'

I'd no idea where Barnet was, but I decided to give the place a miss.

'Oh... that's interesting.' I said.

'Nah, when you've strangled one chicken, you've strangled 'em all. But if you're interested,' she said giving me a sly look, 'I could show you how we do it.'

Then, without any word of warning, the girl's slowly opened my fly and pulled out my tadger. I couldn't believe what was happening.

'We grab it here and pull. Sometimes, we have to do it more than once. Like this...'

I can only say that those chickens must have died happy. A minute later, we were in bed going at it for all we were worth. Sh***ing a professional chicken strangler – what a way to break your duck. Roxie was amazing. She raged over me like a madwoman. Over me, under me, upside down – you name it – we did it. Despite being no light-weight, she was as flexible as a footballer's contract and she seemed to be able to move her hips in seven different directions at once. I was rung out after fifteen minutes, I'm telling you. I defo needed to put in some heavy training at this new game. That wouldn't be difficult – my new girlfriend was right on the job to train* with me.

Roxanna Daggs – my first time. I wondered if it had been hers.

It wasn't just me that was putting it in, Spurs were getting stuck in as well and went on to finish third in the league that season behind runaway winners Everton. It was a bit of an empty feeling for me because as there was only a month or so of the

---

*Speaking of training, my worries that sex would take too much out of me turned out to be like Fulham Football Club from 2002-4. Groundless.

season to go when I signed, I didn't play in any games – not even for the reserves. But Mister Shreeves promised me I would get a start on our upcoming summer tour of the Far East.

The Far East! And getting a start! I was ecstatic, even though it meant leaving Roxie behind for a bit. I was already looking forward to making up for lost time when I got back. And I was getting paid for all this.

For the record, my first ever senior game of football for Spurs was on 23rd May 1985 in Hong Kong. Alright, our opposition wasn't the best – Seiko FC – but I can't tell you what it felt like to walk out onto that pitch. And when I scored later – from a Mark Falco cross – I was in heaven. The only downside was flattening Gary Mabbutt during my goal celebration, but hey, you can't have everything.

He can't have been that badly injured because he scored twice in our four-nil win. Later, we went out to paint the town red. How many drinks did I have? Not one. How many drugs did I take? Not one (meanwhile Gary was up to his old habits again). How many birds did I tup? Not one. Bad Boy Burksey was a thing of the past. Unfortunately, it was a thing of the future as well. But for the time being, I was determined to be a model pro.

We flew off to Australia for the second leg of the tour and I couldn't wait to see what the land of my childhood hero, Skippy the Bush Kangaroo, would be like. And what was it like? Brilliant! From the "Trouser Press", the Aussie nickname for the famous Sydney Harbour Bridge, to the Great Barrier Reefer, I loved the place. And the people. They reminded me of folk from my native Yorkshire – direct, no-nonsense, open and warm.

'Mate, you played like a wet wombat's willie', one of them said to Ossie after our first match of the tour – a disappointing one-nil loss to an Australian Federation X1.

'Up chors!', I think Ossie replied.

Our next two games pitted us against proper, hardened opponents from world famous footballing nations. I played a big part in both, but again, I was gutted with how they went for the team as a whole. In the first of these two games, I got my first bite of what would become a very familiar taste to me – the "bitter sweetness" of Italian football. Udinese were our opponents. And they beat us two-nil. They weren't that good to be honest – we were just crap on the day. In the second game, we at least managed a draw with one of the top sides in Brazil – Vasco De Gama.

The thrill of playing against Brazilian opponents was indescribable. The class, the touch, the power. But the best player on the pitch? Glenn Hoddle. By a distance. I tell you kids, if all you know of the bloke is seeing him blathering away on the box, you've missed something. He was one special footballer. And he'd be the first to tell you that.

I played pretty well in the Vasco match ("the Vasco match!" Get me! Only four games previously, I hadn't been certain to start for Lockwood G & T) and I definitely outplayed my opposite number, a hugely talented 19 year-old by the name of Romario. As great as he obviously was, I believed in my heart, brains and legs that I was greater, but there was something about the way he went about his business on the pitch that really pulled my chain. He was a winner. But he was also a whinger. And if there's anything that I can't stick – it's a moaner. I made up my mind. "I'm having you!", I said to myself. And waited. With fifteen minutes to go, they won a corner and I went back to defend it. I could run all day then, it didn't worry me. Anyway, before the ball is played in, I get tight on Romario and floor him with a sneaky kidney punch. A real hard dig that not one official spotted.

As soon as I did it, I was sorry. I may have been built like a light-heavyweight boxer, but I was really a pussy cat at heart. Cheap shots weren't my thing. None of their lot saw who'd done Romario. But three of ours did. They reacted very differently to my moment of madness. Skipper Steve Perryman gave me a look that said "Don't do that in the box, you f***ing tosser!" Graham Roberts gave me a pat and shouted "Nice one!" in my ear. And Mabbo? As the Brazilian's gone down and started rolling over like a burrito with an outboard motor, I'm already copping a right earful. His angry words made me feel like a piece of shit and rightly so. On the spot, I made my mind up never to do anything like it again. Of course I did – many times over – but it was a good thought.

The game finished one apiece with Mark Falco slotting a neat equaliser. It was the only goal we scored on the Australian leg of the tour; a disappointing tally for such a smoothly accomplished, attack-minded team. A typical Spurs team, you might say.

Afterwards in the showers, something happened which I didn't grasp the meaning of until much later. Referring to me felling cry-baby Vasco hitman Romario, one of the lads turns around to me and goes:

'Flattening a Brazilian, eh Burksey? Bet you've been doing a lot of that lately!'

Some of the other guys laughed and stifled chortles. What was he talking about? Brazilians? I'd never even seen one before. Then someone else asked me if I'd pruned Roxie's bush lately. I don't know why they thought I was into gardening, perhaps it was my assistant groundsman's background.

When I got back to Edmonton, me and Roxie didn't take long to get down to some serious b***ing and, what with the new season looming just around the corner, I was as happy as a kid in two candy stores. The only slight problem was that the owner of one of those stores, Roxie's mum, Vera, was eyeing me strangely. She even started treating me almost as if I was a human being. What was her game?

But it wasn't all Weirdsville, Arizona. One day, Rox was just going back into the house after sticking a load of chicken entrails into the wheelie bin when she hears a car draw up outside and sound its airhorn. The tune it plays – Come On You Spu-urs! – makes her look round. She sees a familiar face sitting behind the wheel. The face belongs to yours truly. The car was a brand new Ford XR3i. And "Steve" and "Rox" was etched across the top of the windscreen.

My dreams were all coming true.

I tell you, everybody should be a footballer. Just for a day. It's f***ing brilliant.

Most of you know what happened between me and Roxanna. Or think you do. She got pregnant and we got married – right? There was more to it than that. A lot more. The wedding itself, later described as "shambolic" by TV's Richard and Judy, wouldn't have been a brilliant occasion even if the two families involved had had something in common. It was like *Keeping Up Appearances* meets *Eastenders*. But ten times worse.

For the first time anywhere, I'll tell you what made it so bad. On the morning of the wedding, I received a padded envelope in the post. What was in it – a gift from some fan for a young player rapidly becoming a hero at The Lane? If only. It was a magazine featuring close-up photos of women's privates. As instructed by the stick-on note attached to the cover, I turned to page twenty-three. I nearly dropped dead with the shock. For the sake of decency, I won't describe the various shots of the faceless woman splattered over those pages – so I'll just tell you what some of the captions said: "Check out the Brazilian on this babe!", "There could be a court case – that hedge is blocking out the light!" "Wouldn't mind grabbing her by the long and curlies!" Et-f***ing-cetera. It didn't matter that the "model" in these shots was faceless. I would have known the owner of those pubes – shorn close at the sides, left shaggy in the middle – anywhere. Yes, Twat Topiary's "Minge Of The Month" belonged to none other than my blushing bride-to-be, Roxanna. "Gutted" just doesn't say it. There are no words to describe how I felt. Maybe "shafted" comes close.

I walked straight in and had it out with Roxie. She told me not be "naïve" and "didn't I realise what had happened?" "Some old boyfriend" had snapped the pix and then sold them to the mag for a few quid. Then somebody was just having a laugh by sending them to me on my wedding day. Since her face wasn't in the spread, "what did it matter?"

So Michael Douglas and Catherine Zeta Jones are not the only ones to have had problems with wedding day photos. The first thing I want to say about "Mingegate" is this: what kind of sick bastard would send something like that to someone through the post? An envelope full of hate and pain? If whoever did it is reading this, I want you to understand that if I ever find out who you are, I know people who would give your genitals more than a trim.*

The second thing I want to say is that if I behaved poorly at the wedding ceremony ...

Vicar: 'Will you take this woman...?

Me: 'Why not, pal? Everybody else has.'

and later at the reception...

Best Man, Tarka: 'And now I'd like to call upon the bridegroom to say a few words.'

Me: 'Stuff it, Tark. I can't be f***ing arsed.'

... you can understand why. The truth is that I entered into that marriage virtually under false pretences. And like another victim I have a lot in common with – our beloved Princess Diana – I knew it from Day One.

Roxie wasn't really a bad girl. She was just a sex-mad chicken strangler with an eye for the main chance. She'd heard from one of the lads that I was going to be the Next Big Thing and since we got on really well, she decided to nail me. "In every sense", as that tongue-tied old king of commentary, David Coleman, used to say.

Although she tricked me, I have to put my hand up and say that once we were married, Ro-Ro was at least faithful to me and made a "good" wife. To start with. And from my point of view, having Tottenham's Top Tup Tottie in bed with me every night made up for a lot. I decided to try and make the best of it.

My first full season in football – 1985/86 – was what the BBC's Wizard of Words, the late and severely lamented Peter Jones, called "a curate's egg". I think he meant I came out of my shell and ran all over the place. Anyway, the main thing to say about it was that I blew hot one minute, cold the next. My hot streak happened early doors. I scored my first goal in only my third appearance as a sub in a four-one home win against Chelsea. As those of you lucky enough to see it know, that goal – a 30-yard screaming bender – brought the house down. And so did my well-rehearsed goal celebration after.

My first start for the football club in a league game was something I'll never forget. It was at a legendary ground – Anfield – against a legendary football team – Liverpool.

---

*People "not unconnected" with one of my old mates from Italy days – Regional Development Officer and town mayor, Gianiago "Razor Boy" Casalupanzo.

They were flying high at that time and would go on to win the League and Cup double that season. The main reason I remember the game is for the goal I scored right in front of The Kop – a powerful diving header from a corner by our new signing, the hugely talented Chris Waddle. We wound up losing the game four-one, but as any striker will tell you – including Mister Supernice Gary Lineker – scoring a goal doesn't half take the sting out of a loss. Especially if it was a belter.

After the game, their foreign stars – Welshman Ian Rush, Scotsman Alan Hansen and Irishman Mark Lawrenson* – didn't want to know me. But African keeper Bruce Grobbelaar took time out to find me in the dressing room to congratulate me on the goal and to say that he knew there would be hundreds more. Nice, eh? But his kindness wasn't over yet. The lithe and likeable loony also gave me – completely free of charge – a selection of "sure fire" horse, greyhound and ostrich racing "bankers"**. And then, to top it off, he generously offered to sell me, at a knockdown price, "a time-share in a brand new condominium located in the Belgian Congo." But I wasn't interested in it. Why? Because I don't believe in using condominiums. Well, it's like wearing socks in the bath, isn't it? Ro-Ro and I were practising the T.I.O.B.Y.C (Take It Out Before You Come) method of contraception at the time, and although it resulted in an unwanted pregnancy, I still think it knocks cock hats into a cocked hat.

But anyway, back to Crazy Legs. The man was alright, let me tell you. If you've been told different about the guy, you've been told wrong.

As the season wore on and life with Ro got more and more difficult, I began to lose form on the pitch. "A promising beginning", according to Bearded Bard Jimmy Hill, turned into "something of a damp squid". Yeh? His squid would have been pretty damp if he'd had to put up with what I had to.

It all came to a head in January when my first child, Frank Gary Brian Burkes, was born. From that moment on, everything changed. And I mean everything. My form went downhill on the paddock. And it went downhill in the hammock. I barely existed for my wife. Know what I mean, you new Dads out there? The baby came first and last and that was all there was to it. And rumpy pumpy? Forget it – all of a sudden Roxanna was "too tired". And that went on for days – and days. Once again, I felt like an outsider. An outsider in my own family. It's not just goalkeepers who feel that way.

---

*The cheeky leprechaun was born in Preston, an outlying suburb of Dublin.
For a time, he was neighbour of that other well-known Paddy – Tony Cascarino.
**They turned out to be more w***ers than bankers, but I appreciated the gesture.

Ever had a feeling that the whole world is sitting on your shoulders? Of course you have. I want to tell you that it feels a lot worse if *you've* put the bloody thing there yourself in the first place. I'd made a massive mistake in falling for Ro and getting married at such a young age. And it was beginning to show. At least Chris Waddle was sympathetic:

'Howay Burksey! Look – yah've gorrin thah lass's knickahs and they've f***in' explurded in yah face – reet? Well divven't f***in' myther aboot it, man. If it's not f***in' workin' oot – gerrin some othah f***in' lass's!'

Wise words. Words that I would eventually understand. And follow.

Despite not being able to play as well as I knew I would have done otherwise, it was a massive buzz playing for Spurs that season. Everything about it was magic. The crack with the lads, the training, the travelling together, the crowds chanting your name, watching yourself on TV, the knowledge that what you were doing mattered to millions of people – it was all fantastic. And then, there was playing The Beautiful Game itself.

It was a huge privilege for you to have seen me doing it.

My future wife, Interior Designer Brandee Wavedance-Ebelficker, didn't know how to actually paint and decorate a room, but she understood the value of "like, preparation?" And so did I when it came to football. From the off, I made notes on my fellow strikers and especially on the defenders who would be marking me. I figured it would give me an edge. By the time I went to Sporting Meriden, I could practically have told you what all my major opponents had for breakfast. In the case of Forest and future England star, Stuart Pearce, I think that breakfast must have consisted of barbed wire washed down with petrol. You want hard? You want Stuart Pearce. In our away match at Forest – which we won one-nil thanks to a blinding Chris Hughton volley from a full yard out – I skinned Psycho a couple of times early doors and even had the balls to wink at him after I'd done it. Early in the second half, I nutmegged him. What happened next, I can't remember, but it felt as if I'd been hit by a wrecking ball. I outweighed the guy by over a stone, but I went down like a tart in a lay-by.

Luckily, I was soon conscious again and ten minutes later, I found myself in the P.O.M.O. (Position Of Maximum Opportunity) to take my revenge – a fifty-fifty ball which we would both be sliding in for. I'm sorry Jesus, Mother Teresa and Frank Worthington, but as we both went for it, I went right over the top with a big two-footed lunge. Both sets of studs crunched into Psycho's shins and gouged huge lumps out of them. By the way, you can check out those actual lumps today if you visit M.I.L.F. – Stelsat's new Museum of Interactive Living Football. Entrance to the museum is via their entertaining and informative P.P.V. half-time game show package. Just press 'Buy Milf?' on your handsets.

But back to the diabolical tackle that made Steve Burkes "a legend in his own lunge time".* The moment I'd done it, I was sorry. I knew Psycho would be injured by it, possibly even maimed for life. Mind you, with his competitive spirit, I knew he would carry on in some form or variation of sport – possibly as one of those "special athletes" – you know the ones, bless 'em – the guys 'n' gals in wheelchairs who interrupt the coverage of the proper Olympics on TV. I'll tell you something now. Big bad old Burksey always goes and make a cuppa when the "chariot races" come on. And not just because they're totally boring.** It upsets me to see the competitors' weedy little "legs" strapped to their seats. Too soft, that's my trouble.

But let's go back to my assault on Psycho. I'm thinking that I've nearly killed the guy and what does he do? He just gets up. Gets up straight away and prepares to take the free-kick as if nothing has happened. He doesn't say anything. He doesn't look at me. He doesn't look at the damage to his blood-splattered legs. It was unbelievable. I decided to steer well clear of him for the rest of the match. Burksey intimidated? You bet your life!

In conversation with The Master – Des Lynam – years later, Psycho recalled that first encounter with me on the pitch:

DL:   'And young Mister Burkes – what did you make of him?'

SP:   'For a young lad, I could only admire his great feet and his auda-cious vision, you know. I should have broken both of his legs the first time he went past me'.

DL:   'And what about his infamous tackle?'

SP:   'Yeh, he's a big old boy is Burksey.'

DL:   'I meant that terrible challenge he caught you with. 1985, I think it was. It could have ended your career.'

SP:   'Some would say that would've been a good thing. But no, these things happen, you know. Besides, my Missus has caught me with worse than that.'

How hard is Pearcey? As hard as diamond.

A footnote to the incident is worth mentioning. As I practically ran off the pitch at the final whistle – I was trying to avoid Psycho – a familiar voice called me over to the bench. 'Young man? Ger' over here!'

*The words of – who else? – my future Meriden Boss, Ron Atkinson.
**This view is emphatically not shared by Olympic Bid Director Lord Sebastian Coe or any of his team, any other team, or any other body or organisation in world sport.

Oh-oh. I don't need to tell you who that voice belonged to. My blood ran cold. I felt as if I was back at school and I'd just done something bad. I could almost feel the weight of the old fire bucket on my head as I did what I was told.

Me:    'Yes Mister Clough?'

BC:    'After you've changed into your ra-ra skirt or whatever it is you change into when you've finished playing football for the day, I want you to go into our dressing room, find Stuart Pearce, shake hands with him and all that kind of thing – and then when you've done that I want you to tell him that you're sorry.'

Me:    '"Sorry"?'

BC:    'Sorry, yes. It's not a difficult word. And then I want you to thank him for A – not getting you sent off and B – not killing you.'

Me:    'I will do.' Shit, I didn't fancy that.

BC:    'Now bugger off!'

With that, Mister Clough's given me a clip around the ear and booted me up the backside as I've walked off down the tunnel. I didn't mind, somehow. But in any case, I hadn't gone more than a couple of yards before he shouted after me:

'By the way, son. You're one of the best bloody youngsters I've seen in years. If you don't waste your talent, you just might – I said "might" – do a bit of something in this game.'

I was stoked. Talk about a boost. I have to confess that I didn't go and find Psycho in the Forest dressing room later. As a mark of respect to Mister Clough, I should have. The word "great" is overused today, isn't it? But if the now sadly late Brian Clough isn't one of the Great Men of Football – I don't know who is.

That early game against Forest turned out to be a bit of a high point for me as far as the season went. I finished it on the bench. On the pitch and at home. Funny enough, what went for me also went for the football club as a whole. That's right – 85/86 wasn't a great season for Spurs. After finishing third the previous year, we finished only tenth in the league and didn't win any silverware. I knew it wasn't good enough and things needed to change. I made a sacred vow that next term would be different. And I can remember the exact moment I made it. It was July – one of those hot, gritty summer days you only get in London. Or Tokyo, which is exactly the same. Anyway, I was bombing up Tottenham High Road in the XR3i when this great song comes on the radio. Remember *Live To Tell* by Madonna? Well, it blew my head off. And it blew the heads off most of the people shuffling along the pavement as well as I cranked the motor's 200-watt sound system up to the max. As I slowed to allow a procession of limos take for ever to pull out of the premises of Henry Shenton & Son Funeral Home and Chapel of Rest, I shouted "Live to tell! Live to tell that Steve Burkes is going to be the best f***ing striker in the league in the 1986/87 season!"

And did I turn out to be? I had a damn good go at it...

# CHAPTER SEVEN

## MONKEY BUSINESS

With Ro and little Frankie inseparable, I really got down to some serious training over the close season and come August I was fitter, sharper and silkier-skilled than ever before. August 1986 was a "momentous" month. Canadian poet, Milton Acorn died. The World Frisbee Championships were held at Essex University, Colchester. And David Pleat became the manager of Tottenham Hotspur Football Club.

I was pleased to see Mister Pleat take the helm of the Good Ship Tottenham. But there was one change to our crew that everyone onboard hated. After being at the heart of our engine room for a record-breaking 851 sailings, the great Steve Perryman took shore leave for the final time and said goodbye to the vessel he loved – and was loved by.

Would we miss him? Was Pope John Paul II an ex-member of the Hitler Youth Movement? Of course we would! Thinking of Spurs without Steve Perryman is like thinking of The Rock of Gibraltar without Moses and his tablets. Let's face it, Steve Perryman didn't just play for Spurs, Steve Perryman *was* Spurs.

Still, we all had to get on with it without him so that was all there was to it. And speaking of getting on – I got on well with new Boss David Pleat from the off. He liked me. He thought I had something. I knew I was in with a good chance of starting a lot of games, but I was over the moon when I was picked for the season's shirt-lifter – our opening game away at Aston Villa.

Pleaty targeted that game. What happened in it would "set the pattern"* for the whole season. And what happened in it was this: Hod, Ossie and Wad dominated the midfield and the flanks – me and Clive Allen ruled the roost up front. We won it three-nil with Clive netting twice and me once. It wasn't a one off. Game after game, the same thing happened. The Glory Glory Days looked to be on their way back to The Lane.

Talk about a life of two halves. My home life was a nightmare hell. My professional life was brilliant beyond belief. Don't get me wrong – I was not yet the master

---

*A phrase of Mister Pleat's. The man is as clever as that Tony Galvin any day. More clever if you ask me. Tony's a lecturer now, they tell me. Big deal, eh?

of my trade, but put it this way, by the mid-point of the season, I had started in all but four games and scored twelve goals. To be honest, when a gifted striker is on the receiving end of such quality service – threaded inch-perfect passes, gentle dead-weight dinks, cheeky reverse defence splitters – you'd have to be a goal-shy lemon like Francis Jeffers – no offence Frannie! – not to get a hatful of goals.

I suppose it was about half-way through the season that my reputation as Spurs' Practical Joker In Chief was born. You'll already know quite a bit about the sort of things I used to get up to if you've read Jim Porterstone's interesting book on the subject called A Piranha In My Pants. Sorry about that Chrissie, by the way! Yes, Waddler has never forgiven me for sticking one of the bitey little buggers in his Y-Fronts.

> CW:   'Burksey? Worrit yous put that f\*\*\*in' little f\*\*\*ah in us f\*\*\*in' kecks?'
>
> Me:   'I cannot tell a lie, Waddler. It was Steve Hodge.'
>
> CW:   'It's f\*\*\*in' nearly 'ad us nadger off, man!'
>
> Me:   'Take it up with Hodgey.'
>
> CW:   'It weren't f\*\*\*in' Hodgey. It was f\*\*\*in' yous, yah w\*\*\*ah!'

I'm not proud of it but I can now reveal – for the very first time – that Chris had to undergo years of intensive therapy because of the little prank I pulled. He dreamed about it at night. It played on his mind at times of stress – such as the final of the 1990/1 European Club Championship with his new team, Olympic Marseille, or the semi-final of the World Cup against the hated Krauts\* at Italia 90. Of course, he's completely cured now, but that doesn't take away the years of pain my moment of madness caused. Once again, sorry Chris.

At our Christmas do that year, we had a great time with a hypnotist who had us doing all sorts of crazy stuff. As I watched him putting people under, I reckoned I could do it too – and then I had a great idea for a practical joke. And it was one that would top all my previous efforts. I looked down the fixture list eagerly. We had an easy-looking away match against relegation-bound Man City in April. Yes, that would be the one. I didn't think it was possible to hypnotise the entire team – although anybody who saw us lose three-one at Luton might be forgiven for thinking that we had been – so I plumped for a single victim instead. Now who would make the ideal victim... Yes. Ossie Ardiles.

---

*\*I've been told to call our opposition on the night: "our valued European neighbours" or some such stuff. But I know what the Germans are and so do you.*

Anybody who's seen a "hypnoshow" knows that the fun part is what professionals call the "post-hypnotic suggestion." I dreamed up a belter. I was going to arrange things so that every time Ossie heard a word I got out of the dictionary – "serendipitous" – in the match at Maine Road, he would go into an immediate impression of comedian Groucho Marx. Complete with stooping walk and killer one-liners. I chose such a strange word so I would be in control of his unconscious performances. If I'd chosen the word f***, for example, the Argentinean Ace would have been going into his routine every few seconds. Another good word – "antihistamine" – would bring him out of it.

The first part of the operation was the most difficult – putting him under long enough to give him his subconscious instructions. I needed to get Ossie somewhere where neither of us stood a chance of being disturbed for a good long while. But where? Then it came to me. I tricked the midfield maestro into coming to a branch of Dixon's with me and whilst we were waiting to be served, I did my stuff.

Come the day of the match, everything was great for Spurs – and me – "footballistically," as my neighbour, the great wacky Alsatian, Arsène Wenger puts it. We were third in the League and had just destroyed Watford in the semi-final of the FA Cup. Yes, we were on our way to Wembley. Dream time! The side was okay at the back, brilliant in midfield and out wide. And up front? Put it this way – me and Clive Allen had notched up forty five goals between us. And we weren't done yet. Or so we thought...

At Maine Road, Mister Pleat went into his pre-match team talk with all the attention to detail for which he is rightly celebrated. We took the field with so much going for us, we knew we would win. My plan was to wait until we got a couple in front before giving Ossie "the word". Hey, I might have enjoyed a joke, but I was also a dedicated Pro.

That lead never came. We played well below par. And the dip in form was to continue until the end of the season. Why? I've always said that the Chernobyl nuclear disaster in the previous year was to blame.* Yes, just when we thought we were about to breathe in the sweet smell of success, Red Ken's Commie mates in Russia poisoned the air for us.

*Some eggheads with nothing better to do have pointed out that, although contamination from the site continued to turn up in odd spots all over Europe for ages afterwards, there was no pressing danger to life and limb at Maine Road that day. Yeh? Well they don't know Moss Side, that's all I can say.

I hear you saying, "well, if the atmosphere was bad, it was the same for both teams wasn't it?" No pal, it wasn't. We were artists. We were cultured. We were classy. Sucking in lungfuls of nuclear fall-out affected us in ways that didn't affect lesser teams. I tell you what those Chernobyl-affected games were like for us. Every one of them was like playing a third round FA Cup tie against non-league opposition on their sloping, frozen pitch in the middle of a rainstorm. In other words, the gulf in class between us and our opponents was taken away.

But worse was to come at Maine Road. And it had nothing to do with a lack of clean air. Struggling for an equaliser, we won a lucky free kick about thirty-five yards out. As Hod comes forward to take it, the W.C.S. (Worst Case Scenario) happens. I hear Mister Know-It-All Tony Galvin comment to Ossie:

'F***ing hell Os – this free kick's serendipitous.'

No! Straight away, Ossie's gone into a crouch, put an imaginary cigar to his lips. and drawled:

'Call that serendipitous? Wait until we all get agents!'*

With me over on the other side of the penalty area, I've no hope of stopping Os as he starts stalking around, tossing off one-liners in all directions:

'I've had a perfectly wonderful match – but this wasn't it... I wouldn't join any team that would have me as a player.... If Coisty's not in bed by two – he goes home... Marry me and I'll never look at another Geoff Horsfield...'

The crowd can't hear any of this but they're loving it anyway. Seeking to limit the damage, I leg it towards Os – gulping in deadly fall-out with every step – but before I get within earshot, he's loped within quipping range of the bench. F***.

'I never forget a face, but in your case I'll be glad to make an exception,' he opines to none other than our manager, Mister Pleat.

'Wot thah f***in' hell's up wi' Ossie?' asks Waddler as I come flying past.

'It's this air! He needs antihistamine!' I shout in the crouching comic's direction. Thankfully, the word stops Os in his tracks and after a momentary wobble, he straightens up and throws away his imaginary cigar. Then, wondering what all the fuss is about, he waves away our physio and trots off to take the free kick as if nothing had happened. Meanwhile, I've skulked back to the penalty area to hide behind the City wall. Finally, the game restarts with bemused faces all around – especially the Gaffer's.

*People in a trance often see into the future, apparently. The only problem is that what they see often turns out to be about as true as a certain pop star's "one" nose job and those pesky weapons of mass destruction!

Praying that Galvo wouldn't say the 'S' word again, I got on with playing, but a combination of radiation sickness and nervous exhaustion brought on by "Grouchogate" took my performance down to the level of an average player. Nico Claesen eventually netted for us and the game ended in a tame draw. It was a game we could, should and would have won. But the disappointment I felt as we trooped off was only the beginning. Looking unusually stern, Mister Pleat asked to see me in his office on Monday.

The rest of the weekend dragged on like a Wagner Opera, but without the laughs. Finally, the appointed hour arrived. No-one spoke or smiled at me as I made my way to Mister Pleat's office. Some people even looked away. Suddenly, I felt about as welcome around the place as an asylum seeker in a hoodie. The meeting itself started badly.

'Come in, Stephen. Sit down. Right, let's not beat around the bush ...' Chance would be a fine thing, I thought to myself. But enough of my love death. The Boss continued:

'I don't know why you did what you did on Saturday, but I know what you did.'

I told you Mister Pleat had an eye for detail. 'It was just a...'

'Joke yes? Well it's a joke that's cost you your job, son. Your association with Tottenham Hotspur Football Club is over.'

'Mister Pleat, I'll swear on a stack of bagels* that I'll never do it again.'

'As of today, you're on the list and I don't even want to see your face around here.'

No more Glory Glory for me with the lads. And the ultimate sickener – no Wembley Cup Final. I couldn't believe it. The club that had taken me in had just spat me out.

Numb with pain, I cleared out my things and walked out of the ground in a trance almost as deep as the one I'd put Ossie in. The only difference was I didn't have any one-liners to go with it. I could have done with a laugh.

I can't really remember what I did next. Where I went. Or what I did. I think I just drove round and round. I was too stunned to properly react, too stunned to take it all in.

But eventually the pieces started falling together. Looking back on it now, I can see that at least my sacking was special. I must be the only footballer in history to have been shown the door for hypnotising another player. Why had I been singled

---

*By the way, may I take this opportunity to recommend Old Mama Goldblum's Bagels to you? The best-selling bread-based product in her "Cool Shul" range of genuine home-baked Kosher goodies, they're great as a meal in itself or just as a game-time snack. I'd select them for my First 'Uneleven' any day!
Note: Old Mama Goldblum is a registered brand of the Stelsat Corporation of America. All rights reserved.

out? Why didn't they fire the guys who had hypnotised Ali Dia, Winston Bogard and John Jensen into playing like a bunch of tossers? Or Paul Ince into having a phobia about putting his shirt on in the dressing room? That's Burksey's luck for you.

Eventually, I came to and headed off home in the XR3i. My head was full of terrible images – they even included hell bitch Ms Y Killmartin rubbing her podgy little hands in glee at my disgrace. But just before I turned into Mount Road, I took a call on my new mobile – you could talk hands-on and drive at the same time then (mind you, I still do that now) – perhaps Mister Pleat had only been trying to scare me.

'Ah – Stephen. Good – this is Karen Hart at Manchester United here. I have Alex Ferguson for you. Just hold for a second.'

'Tarka, is that you?' He was always winding me up like that. But, after a brief pause, I heard that voice come on the line. I nearly mounted the pavement in shock.

'Stevie? So do you want to come and pray for us?'

'What?'

'Do you want to come and pray for us?'

'Pray?'

'Yes – would you rike to come and pray for Manchester United?'

What the hell was he on about? Nowadays, the idea that Man United might include organised religious services as part of its brand profile wouldn't raise an eyelid. Back in 1987, United was still just a football club. The biggest club in the world, mind you.

'Erm, well, I don't know.'

'Rook. I've just been speaking to David Preat and he's told me you're on the rist so how about it in principle?'

My heart missed several beats as I finally realised what he had meant by "pray". Jesus – it looked as if I was going to be out one door in the morning and in another one by the afternoon. Talent, you see. There's no substitute for it. Although United were not then the high flyers they would become – this was only Mister Ferguson's first season in charge – I was over the moon, planets, and haemorrhoids about it.

'Yes, Mister Ferguson, I'd love to came and pray – er, play – for United.'

'Just one thing, raddy. I know why you've been risted. I'm warning you now that if you ever get up to any simirar stunts in the future, I will not only rist you on the spot, I will kick your arse for you as well.'

Well, he'd be in good company. Brian Clough had done it the season before.

I assured him that I'd learned my lesson and there would be no repeat. We rang off on friendly terms, the Gaffer finishing by saying that I had the makings of a very promising forward. I could have told him that. But still – kind words.

Again looking back after almost twenty years in the game, I can see that when a football manager takes on a "bad boy" player like me at his club, it's a bit like when a woman takes on a bloke she knows is a ladies man. They always think they will be able to turn you around. Ah, bless! It's sweet, really.

But back to that car ride home. I got in and marched straight up Rox.

'We're going to be Mankers', I said. 'I'm a Red Devil now.' Cockney Roxanna had no idea what I meant. But she would soon get the message.

As a footnote to my mainly happy footballing days at Spurs, I'd just like to mention something that the respected – although not by me – Observer Journo David Aaronivitch once had the neck to say to me at an awards dinner:

'Do you realise that if Spurs had played a five-man midfield with just one up front in that 86/87 season, Clive Allen would probably have scored the forty-nine* goals you got between you all by himself?'

I ask you – Clive Allen score forty-nine goals in just one season? As if any striker could do that!

*Yes, my departure meant that Clive only scored four more goals to add to our total in the remainder of the season. Just imagine what we could have done if we'd stayed together.

## CHAPTER EIGHT

# RED DEVIL

The 1986/87 Today League Division One finished with Spurs in third spot behind Liverpool and champions Everton – exactly as it had in the Canon sponsored league two seasons before. Weird, eh? Even more weird was that after a securing a two-year deal with United, I was no longer a Tottenham Hotspur.

After I'd sailed through the medical and completed all the other formalities, I moved into my new house – 17 Avocado Grove, Altrincham – on 16th May 1987 – Cup Final Day. Obviously, I couldn't bear to watch the match that, but for my moment of madness, I would have been a big part of. Shucking off my chagrin, I sent an inspirational telegram to the lads*, but the foot is mightier than the pen and without me Spurs crashed to a three-two defeat to humdrum Coventry. Clive Allen, battling bravely without his old strike buddie, and Gary "Ince Yellin'!" Mabbutt scored for Spurs. You don't need to be a genius to work out what would have happened if I'd been in the line-up. Mister Pleat, your curly-haired hard-headedness cost Spurs the trophy. And me a cup winner's medal. But we've all passed a lot of water since then. I forgive you, Pleaty.**

Did you notice that I said *I* moved in to my new Altrincham house? Yes, Ro-Ro and Young Frankie stayed behind in Chingford whilst I got everything completely sorted. It wasn't until June that the family became genuine "Alterations" – the name given to people who live in Altrincham. I tell you one thing – it was funny living back in the north again. I'd kind of got used to soft southern ways and the mean streets of Altrincham were a bit of a shock to Roxie. She was a pure bred Cockney bird – the Mank scene was completely foreign to her. At least the new house was bigger and nicer than our Chingford gaff.

She liked that. Me? I liked the fact that her mother was no longer living just down the road. I tell you, I wish I had a pound for every time she'd turned up at Essex Rise announcing – 'Only me, dear – just popped round for five minutes' – only to find her and her big be-fagged

---

*The best bit was "Remember Waterloo! Remember Victoria! Remember Liverpool Street!" That really affected the lads, I heard later.*

**Actually – no I f***ing don't – that medal would have meant the world to me.*

gob still yakking on five or six hours later. And then Ro's mates would turn up. I should have seen the signs then: the signs that all was not right with my marriage.

I was able to buy a better house not just because of the lower property prices in the north. Another reason was that in my initial talks with United Officials at Watford Gap Services, I'd managed to secure a big hike in wages from what I'd been on at Spurs. How did I do it? By thinking of a daft number and then doubling it. The club agreed immediately which was a sure sign that I'd undersold myself. A babe in arms, I'm telling you. Still, it wasn't a bad weekly whack and a slice of the two-hundred and fifty grand transfer fee United had paid came my way as well.

I was in clover. And clover tasted good.

But soon, it didn't taste as good as ten pints of Guinness at The Red Bladder pub in nearby Hale. It didn't taste as good as the various lips of Page Three Stunna, Bobbie from Ormskirk. And it didn't taste as good as wads of notes won from betting and playing board games against my new team mates. Yes, I'd had my troubled times before, but they were nothing compared with what lay ahead – lay ahead like a sniper waiting to blow me away with an ouzo submachine gun.

Why did it happen? Why does anything happen? If we knew the answer to that question we would all be multi-millionaires. But the first thing to say is that it wasn't the fault of the lads. The team I joined weren't playing well – they finished only 11th in the league the previous season – but they were a top bunch of guys. People like determined defender Kevin Moran, acrobatic goalie Gary Walsh and Danish pastry Jesper Olsen were always great to me. And new signings Viv "Class" Anderson, and Brian "Choccy" McClair – my strike-partner to be – were also top lads. With one notable exception, I'd get close to all the guys over the season.

That exception was ginger jock jackanapes Gordon Strachan. And not just because I couldn't understand a single word he said. Nowadays, I really get on with the superbly shrewd and funny Celtic Supremo and Stelsat summariser, but when we played together, it was a different story. There was just something about him that got up my nose. Maybe it was because his springy ginger hair reminded me of Roxy's minge*. I think some of

*You may have read in The Daily Shite that I wanted to name the first racehorse I owned "Roxy's Minge" as an act of revenge on my first wife and because I thought it would sound funny coming out of legendary commentator Peter O'Sullivan's posh mouth: "And it's Roxy's Minge coming up the outside..." etc. As so often, the story is completely untrue. I wanted to name the animal "Roxy's Bush." As you know, good sense prevailed in the end and I called it, "Wotta Brazilian!"

the other lads must have cottoned-on to that link as well, because a few of them used a related nickname for him when he helped Leeds pip United to the title in 1992.

Everybody knows that the players I really got close to at United were Bryan "Captain Marvel" Robson, Norman "Nasty" Whiteside, and Paul "Silk N' Steel" McGrath. Let's face it – you could put "Mine's A Pint" in place of those other nicknames, couldn't you? I bet they would say that themselves. Now if you're young or just plain ignorant, you might not know as much as you should about these legends. Here goes: he won 90 caps; he was United's longest-serving skipper in history; and at his best was one of the most potent attacking midfielders in world football. Unlike that other magician I'd left at The Lane – Glenn Hoddle – Robbo's ball skill levels might not have been the very best, but in every other way, he was a champion. First name on the team sheet. No messing. Some mental pygmies and Liverpool fans have dissed Robbo for his "corporeal fragility". Alright – he broke twenty-four bones in his body throughout his career. To me, that makes Bryan Robson a hero, not some accident-prone spanner.

Apart from top pace, "Nasty" had everything a top pro should have and then some. But his big frame was weaker than it looked because his joints were crap. He should have had a word with my brother, Tarka. No, seriously, Normo claims a medico gave him the wrong exercises to do when he was a kid and it almost b***ered him for life. It didn't stop him becoming a top player, though. Ask Neville Southall – he's still looking for Normo's extra-time winner against Everton in the '85 Cup Final.

Macca was a skilful, domineering defender, but the thing about him that I spotted straight away was that he was a naturally gifted athlete. One of the most gifted to have taken up football as a career. I'm sure that if he'd gone in for something else – boating, say – he would have p***ed all over that Sir Steve Redgrave – no offence.

So that's Robbo, Nasty and Macca for you. Three great footballers and three great lads. And three to avoid if you ever see them down the pub.

Spurs is a big club. United is bigger. Playing in that red shirt at Old Trafford in front of over forty-thousand fans* was an unforgettable experience. Mister

---

*Yes, attendances back in the eighties were nowhere near what they were to become. More dosh being chucked at the game changed things. Also, the BBC's Saturday afternoon Grandstand programme was worth watching back then. Now all they show is horse-jumping, bowls and ping-pong.

Ferguson wanted us to play a vigorous high-tempo game and that suited me down to the ground. I sensed the season ahead was going to be a belter and knuckled down to training to do everything I could to become part of the Big Red Machine. A big part – the crankshaft, say. And there was another thing I loved about being a Man United player. They say it's "not a club, it's a family." Yeh? It was better than your average family by a mile. All its members seemed to really care for you. The Gaffer was like a father to me. All the more because my real Dad, Brian, didn't understand football or what being a top professional footballer was all about. I didn't realise just how much until later, but we'll let that go for now. Yes, all the United staff – chairman Martin "Who Made All The Pies?" Edwards; Mr Ferguson's assistant Archie "Opportunity" Knox; coaches like Jim "Rhino" Ryan; "phantastic" physio Jim McGregor – even Alice, the jolly old gimmer who helped make our lunches at The Cliff Training Ground – treated us like their own.

And how did I repay all these people's openly given trust and care? I shat all over them. I didn't mean to. And it wasn't my fault. But that didn't make life any easier for those caught under the flight path of my falling faeces.

Not that they got splattered to start with. At first, it went brilliantly. In that first season at the club, me and "Choccy" McClair netted over forty times between us as United bagged twenty more goals then they had in the previous campaign. And overall, the team played well. Steve Bruce's arrival from Norwich in December greatly strengthened us at the back and, what with Robbo and wee Gordon weaving their magic going forward, it was no surprise when we finished as high as second in the league. That made it twenty years without a title for Man United, but it was a good effort because winners Liverpool were in their pomp, narrowly missing doing the double for the second year running.

And my old club? Spurs finished a dismal thirteenth. What can I tell you? I have to say that playing against them felt weird, especially at The Lane where the fans gave me a mixed reception – some called me a pr***, others a c***. So taking three points out of four against them felt good. Maybe if I'd whispered "serendipitous" into Ossie's ear, we would have got all four.

Off the pitch, my life was crap. Roxanna never took to living in Altrincham and kept spending more and more of the week in London with her mother and her old friends. We had some real rucks over it. That girl could give as good as she got, believe me. One time, I threw a Waterford Crystal bowl containing Monster Munch at her mother's photo. Roxanna reacted by Jonesing* me so hard I sounded like Barry Gibb doing *Stayin' Alive* for about a week afterwards.

Eventually, we stopped rowing. But only because we practically stopped talking altogether. Soon after, she and little Frankie, the boy I hardly knew, were never at home. As Tark used to say – 'bummer, man'.

Then one Monday in October, me and the lads are doing a promo event in Manchester for something or other and I meet this amazing-looking blonde. Eyes like saucers and, lower down, jugs to match. A real hot tomali. I decided to talk to her.

'Hi I'm...'

'I know who you are. I'm Bobbie.'

I was off to a good start. But at that moment, Robbo pulled me aside:

'I wouldn't go anywhere near that if I were you, Burksey. You don't know where it's been, man.'

Of course, I didn't listen and an hour or so later, me and Bobbie have checked in to the Mabington Hotel where we were soon going at it like there was no tomorrow. That bronzed beauty really got me W.I.M.M. (Where It Matters Most) and I was soon showing her what sex with a superstar footballer was all about – except there were only the two of us and we were indoors. Tall and blonde, Bobbie was a very different kettle of fish from chunky little redhead Roxie. She had legs right up to her arse and her arms were as long and slender as a swan's. I was narked when I discovered her jugs weren't real, but there was nothing fake about her f****. Although she wasn't as supersonically sexcharged as Roxie had once been, she knew how to ride the stallion alright and by the time we reached Squirt City Arizona for the fifth time – a personal best – I was well happy.

Remember Dinah Washington's great old smash hit *What A Difference A Day Makes*?

Yeh, well twenty-fours hours after me and Bobbie had banged each other's brains out, the Daily Scum's front page featured two stories: "Black Monday – Man Jumps From Fourteenth Floor As World Stock Market Crashes!" And the main one: "Burksey's my Five Goal Hero!" I was gutted. Yes friends, "blonde and bountiful Bobbie," who turned out to be a page three model, had sold the story for cash – and stitched me up tighter than a sparrow's chuff. And there's me thinking that it could have been the start of a really meaningful relationship. That guy who jumped from the fourteenth

---

*In case you live in the Shetland Islands or something; to "Jones" means to grab a bloke's bollocks – Gazza's say – and squeeze. The move was named after that street scrapper turned screen star, business guru Sir John Harvey Jones

floor? I felt like following him from the fifteenth. Anyway, I've no sooner read the article than the phone rings. Roxanna's solicitor – I didn't even know she had one – informed me that she wanted a divorce.

In quick time she got it – settlement, sorting out my visiting rights on the kid, the whole deal. Me? The "Love-Tug Dud?" I got taken to the cleaners. I held on to the Altrincham house and my beloved XR3i, but that was about it. I felt shafted. I felt raped. I felt I needed a shoulder to cry on. So I jumped into the car and shot over to Hale where Robbo, Nasty and Macca lived. I would get to know that road pretty well over the next few months.

But I'll never forget that first time. It was raining hard and every time I stopped at a red light, it looked as if red tears – tears of blood – were flooding down from the "Steve" and "Rox" etchings on the XR3i's windscreen. I tell you, I was in bits. Tammy Wynette could have written a song about that moment. In fact, a couple of seasons later, after I'd been inspired by the work of that great player, manager and poet John Toshack, I penned a few lines of verse about it myself. United were on our way to a Rumbelows Cup encounter with Portsmouth at the time. Luckily, I still have a copy of it in my "shit".

> Roxie, you didn't stand by your man
> But The Force was with you like Solo, Han.
> So I just watched the rain run down that screen
> Wondering what could have been.
> But you were just a common slag
>
> That come out of a right old bag.
> So, though I splattered you with everything I had
> Now the rain it falls on this lad.
> And all I'm left with is a question that's this...
> Were you for real or just taking the piss?*

Anyway, I somehow made it to Hale that night and knocked up the lads. Trying to console me, they took me to a local pub where the landlord's discretion meant that we could behave as we liked without the press – or anyone else – knowing. How we behaved I'm not right sure. I was blind drunk in less than an hour.

*I have to thank Big Gary Pallister for coming up with that last line.

The next day at The Cliff was something else. How I drove there in the first place, I'll never know. Anyway I got stripped and pluckily managed a slow jog out onto the training pitches. Here's a tip for you Sunday League footballers out there. If you ever get the sort of hangover that feels as if a road gang are trying to drill their way into your skull at the same time as a tree-felling crew are trying to chain-saw their way out – don't put your head in the way of a driven Viv Anderson cross. I didn't think it was possible to feel worse than when I'd come out of the changing rooms. I was wrong.

And it was the last straw for our trainer, Jim Ryan. Furious, Rhino's pulled me off and sent me straight to the showers. And how did my drinking partners fare the morning after? Nasty and Macca were maybe a tad sluggish, but no more. Robbo? He was like a spring chicken. Running, tackling, shooting. Unbelievable. In its way, it was as heroic a performance as Pearcey getting up as if nothing had happened after I'd tried to put him in hospital.

I'd just finished throwing up in the changing rooms when Mister Ferguson's come in. At first, he didn't see me, but I saw him. He was – to borrow a phrase from the then *Telegraph's* top soccer scribe Paul Wayward – "incandescent with rage". Talk about red in the face, the Boss looked like a burst blood vessel on a turkey's neck. I did the only thing I could do. I hid behind Liam O'Brien, but unusually, the boy's moved quickly and exposed me. So Fergie comes roaring up to me like a charging rhino closes in on an exhausted gazette. Hair dryer? I'm expecting the Govan-born Gaffer to rip into me like a shipwright's rivet gun. But he doesn't even shout. He puts his arm around me instead.

'Rook, I know your wife's just reft you and that's rough. But this is not the way to deal with it. Drinking only makes things worse.'

I don't mind admitting it – I cried as the Boss continued:

'Besides, if you ask me, you're better off without the wee hooer.'

Wiser words were never spoken and I cheered up on the spot. Mister Ferguson reminded me that whilst players were in training, no alcohol at all was permitted and he fined me two weeks wages. I wondered if he knew about Robbo, Nasty, Macca, and one or two of the others. I got my answer at the end of the next season. Nasty and Macca were transferred out. And Robbo? Well, you couldn't sack Captain Marvel, could you?

I took Mister Ferguson's words on board, but there was just one problem – I was starting to get a taste for alcohol. And another major vice soon began to rear its ugly head and I'm not talking about my tadger. I'm talking betting. Once again, it wasn't my fault. I was led into it by the Three Musketeers. I think it all started in October '88 when we were on our way to take on Wimbledon's

"Crazy Gang"* at their characterful if rubbish Plough Lane stadium. Yes, little did we know that we were about to spawn a craze that would sweep through the nation's footballers like Sudoku through the Middle Classes years later.

The lads were entertaining themselves in all the usual ways on the coach to the ground: some listening to music – Gloria Estafan's *Anything For You* was everybody's fave rave at the time; some playing cards – usually Pontoon or Cheat; some reading the paper – mainly The Bun.

Me? I was playing *Tutty Hump Three*. Then from behind the pages of his Vogue International, Wee Gordon's piped up.

'Eh, Robbo?'

'Yes Big Man?'

'Them breeks o'yoornuh f***in' taier thana na'sarse, by the way'**

'F*** off!'

'Mine are tighter,' I said, as Hump's nabbed a podger. Damn that delinquent dromedary.

'Bet they aren't,' says Robbo.

'Bet they are,' I said, managing to nick some embalming fluid from Blah the mummy maker. Squirt that gunk, baby! I suddenly thought of Gary Mabbs, I don't know why.

'Bet they f***in' aren't man!'

By the way, this is typical of the level of debate footballers engage in on their way to matches. And they say we're a bunch of dummies. We hadn't gone many more yards before Nasty's joined in with...

'Care to make it interesting?'

I didn't know what he meant to be honest, but I soon got the message when everybody's wads started coming out. Who wore the tightest shorts? That's how it all began. A Ton to the winner. When we got to the stadium, getting changed took on a whole new fun level. You see, that's what's so great about gambling. Like taking drugs, it makes even the most boring things interesting.

Who won that ton? Me. How? I cheated.

Nabbing a spare pair of Gordon's kecks out of his kitbag did the trick. By the way, it turns out I wasn't the only one who resorted to the dark arts to get a result. Years later, our eagle-eyed physio Jim McGregor told me that he'd spotted all the other

---

*Although I seriously rated my future team-mate Dennis Wise as a player, I could never bring myself to call him and his brotherly band of buffoons, The Crazy Gang. I called them the Pathetic Twats; when they were well out of earshot.

**Translation: "Those shorts of yours are tighter than a gnat's arse, by the way."

players trying on something similar. Literally. How Gordon found a smaller pair, I'm not sure. Maybe the Krankies had played the stadium the day before.

Anyway, how did our match against Dennis and the other Wise Men turn out? Barely able to move, we scraped a one-all draw with me scoring with a scrappy tap-in. It was a really poor match. On what happened next, I can only say sorry to all those who were there – the mums and dads, the kids and the more sensitive members of The Crazy Gang.

Under the circumstances, I should never have attempted the goal celebration that split Gordon's shorts, causing the old crown jewels to boing out into plain sight. But look at it this way – at least it meant that there were a couple of decent balls on view that afternoon.

Eventually, the craze of footballers betting on who could play in the tightest shorts spread like crabs at a rock festival. At its height, we were practically playing in bikini bottoms. Mental.

Still, the style did have its advantages. It was a wow with female fans everywhere. Despite what some of them say, they like a bit of lunchbox work do the ladies. Picnic hampers they like even more. And short shorts were also great for showing off the arse department. Cheek Peek Magazine voted my buns Rear of The Year twice during the late 80's. Contrary to what you might have read by the way, I didn't walk out of an interview with its editors when I realised they were fragrant homosexuals. I legged it because I was worried they might try to drug me with amyl nitrate gas and have their filthy way with me when I was unconscious. Like they did with that crown green bowler from Batley. Hasn't rolled a decent wood since, they tell me. Poor sod.

The 88/89 season turned out to be a real disappointment for everybody connected to the football club. After finishing second in the league the previous term, we only came eleventh. True, there was still too much booze and stuff going on in the background, but the main reason we didn't progress was a surfeit (good word, that – 30 pts on a triple word score) of injuries. Ace defender Viv Anderson spent more time on his back than a two-penny trick and having to use 23 players in 24 games ruined our rhythm. I didn't escape the catastrophic catalogue of cripplement myself. In the run up to Christmas, an away fixture at Highbury saw me and Arsenal's top defender Tony Adams going at it from the off. Just before half-time, I'm trying to get on the end of a Mike Phelan cross when TA's come flying in and tried to take my knee cap off with his nose. Pain? My lights nearly went out, I'm telling you. And then I really didn't appreciate it when Tone's picked himself up, come across to me and said:

'Sorry, mate. Alright?'

'F*** off!' I replied. I knew the bastard had deliberately nosed me. Of course, the ref hasn't seen it that way, cautioning me for a dangerous challenge. Tony gets off

Scot free. I was determined to get the f***er back, but my revenge would have to wait as I was stretchered off. Naturally, we went on to lose the game one-nil.

A lot has been made of the fact that TA, who became a great mate and mentor of mine in the end, played on with a broken nose when I went off with what turned out to be just a bruised panatela. Yeh? Physios will tell you that it's often less painful – and easier on the body – to suffer a break. If Tony had pulled a muscle in his conk, he would have gone off alright, believe me. Years later, by the way, there was an interesting little footnote to this story. It occurred during a romantic gondola ride around Venice with my second wife-to-be, Italian supermodel Cinzia Pifferi. After a late supper at The Gritti Palace (I don't know why they call it that – it's quite nice there really), we were lying back looking at the stars, whispering sweet nothings to each other about life, love and the merits of the flat back four system, when I mentioned Tony and the brutal nosing he subjected me to on that December afternoon back in London. Taking a sip of Dom Perignon, Cinzia's remarked that according to a friend of a friend of a friend, my injury would've been a lot worse... "if he'd caught you with his cazzo". I don't know about that, but I tell you one thing – his chopper could have re-arranged my furniture, big style. But that's another story.

By a funny coincidence, the 89/90 league season began with us "entertaining" none other than the self same Arsenal at Old Trafford. How did we entertain them? We stuffed them four-one with me netting twice – both strikes brilliantly audacious efforts. The second, a screaming volley from a Clayton Blackmore cross brought this classic moment of commentary from *Match Of The Day* Great, John Motson:

'Burkes isn't going to volley it, is he? He is you know! What a goal! What a goal!*'

After I finished my goal celebration, the guys were all waiting to hug me, but the thing that will always stick in my mind is the Gaffer's reaction in the dugout. He's jumping up and down, as happy as a kid with a new toy. If you notice, he's still reacting like that today. Sir Alex loves to win – no doubt about it. But he also loves to see great football. And if it's his boys that are playing it, he loves it to bits. Four-one against The Arse – what a great start! This was going to be our season, surely.

*That wonderstrike won me my first 'Goal Of The Month' award. And by the end of term, no less than four others – a record that still stands – had joined them for the award of Goal Of The Season. When I pressed him later, presenter Des Lynam admitted that these five were better than the eventual winner. Sorry about the damage to the suit by the way, Des. And I'm glad to see you're still wearing it.*

Just one thing cast a doubt in the players' minds. It unsettled us to witness the prospective buyer of Manchester United Football Club – Mister Michael Knighton – performing a vigorous display of keepy uppy in front of the Stretford End before the match. It looked all wrong somehow – like a vicar on a skateboard. We needn't have worried. Mister K. couldn't seem to juggle his finances as well as a football and the deal fell through almost immediately. We heard later that he'd consoled himself with a spot of retail therapy. He went out and bought Carlisle United. And a UFO Spotter's outfit – if the stories are true. Shall I just say 'shades of David Icke' and have done with it? We were well out of it, I reckon.

But back to our new season. Although it was weird not to have Nasty, Macca and Wee Gordon on deck with us, we piped aboard some real talent in their wake – Able Seaman Paul Ince, Midshipman Gary Pallister*, and returning Gunnery Officer, Sparky Hughes. So – it was "all ahead full" for the good ship Manchester United, was it? You'd think so, wouldn't you. But as my Auntie Vi used to say – "there's nowt so queer as Queers". She could have added football teams to that list.

Despite everything, things just didn't work out for us in the league. Take our two-nil loss against a moderate Charlton side at The Valley in November. Yes, take it and chuck it in the rubbish. It was all too typical of what went off that season. A two-one home loss to Derby County in January was even worse. We ended the season in a dismal thirteenth place. Did I say dismal? F***ing bollocks is more like it. Still, at least communism came to an end in Europe, so it wasn't a complete dead loss.

I'll tell you what was also on the up – my own personal standing in the game. The team may have been pants in the league, but my own form didn't drop for a second. It wasn't just that I scored goals. It was how I scored them that was making me a legend around Old Trafford and beyond. Far beyond, as we'll see later. Like I said before, come May time, half of *Match Of The Day's* Goal Of The Season entries were Burksey efforts. Half! No other player had more than one. Remember the old saying that winning is everything and coming second is a total pisser? Try coming second, third, fourth, fifth and sixth and see how you feel. In the same competition. Still, it's counter productive to be, like, bitter? So let's move on. My star was rising and rising fast – that's the main point. I loved scoring spectacular goals, but one of the most

*Here's one for you quiz addicts out there. Who's the "winning-est" United player of all time? Answer – Gary P. And another good one about him concerns his birthplace. Where do you think he was born – somewhere near Pallister Park in Middlesbrough? Wrong. Ironguts Pally's a man of soft southern county, Kent! Ramsgate, to be exact.

memorable I netted in 89/90 was a simple, routine header – the solitary score in our Third Round FA Cup victory at Forest. Why does that goal stick out? Because it saved Alex Ferguson's job as Manager of Manchester United Football Club, that's why. It wasn't just the crowd that were on the Govanator's back at the time. The man was within minutes of picking up his P45 from the pay office when I nodded Mark Robins' searching cross between the sticks. Just think – had we crashed out of The Cup that day, one of the greatest periods of stewardship in football history would never have happened. It might have stalled there and then. I tell you – take Burksey out of football over the last couple of decades and you would hardly recognise it. Scary.

That FA Cup win at The City Ground began a run for us that would take us all the way to Wembley. As the rounds went by, securing a winner's medal – after what had happened at Spurs – became an obsession for me. And it would go a long way to saving United's season, further safeguarding the Gaffer's bacon. Oh yes, Mister Alex Ferguson still had his doubters back in the Spring of 1990. And he was literally light years away from becoming *Sir* Alex, believe me.

It was about this time that something I would eventually become known for – my trendsetting looks and styles – began to establish itself. For really the first time, I began spending on designer haircuts, clothes, shoes and stuff. Why was I pampering myself? Because I was worth it. And how did I know that? Because I now had an agent looking after my interests. Yes, when my initial two-year deal with United was nearing renewal at the end of the previous season, I took a phone call from a man who would change my life for good. For very good. A man who would become like a father to me. And later, a man who would literally save my life. That man's name was Dave Green. It's a simple as this: I wouldn't be the man I am today if East End Kid Dave had decided to continue raking it in as a stock jobber in The City and not run away to join the circus – the circus of Personal Management and Promotion. Dave's made even more of a killing in his new field. And that's good. As I've said before, folk who make money make money for everybody. The company he founded – Get Real! – is simply the best and I thank him with all my heart for everything that he and his staff have done for me.

It's funny to look back now and think that I never wanted an agent originally. I just didn't like the idea of anybody taking a slice of what I was earning with the sweat of my feet and forehead. Paying tax was bad enough. But what I hadn't twigged was that it's a lot better to give away fifteen percent of a shed load of dosh than hang on to all of a small stash. Signing on to Dave's ever-growing client list changed everything for me. Suddenly, doors opened to a world I never knew existed. In short, Dave took my already exciting life and made it ten times more exciting. And ten times more lucrative. Of course, at that stage, I wasn't one of the game's top earners – but at least my foot was on the ladder. True to my family's motto, I was heading "onward and upward!" alright.

Now, you fans don't mind paying for all that with your season tickets and stuff, do you? If I seemed to suggest earlier that you people are a bunch of gullible tossers for keeping us superstar footballers in a style to which we have all become accustomed, I didn't mean it. You get your money's worth and we get your money's worth – so the whole thing's fair. For example, I love the loyal fans who – every season – spend forty quid or so on a replica shirt. I especially love those who pay that bit extra to have a player's name stuck on the back. I see so many "Burkes" around – it's brilliant. And there's loads of other fun stuff to buy. I've lost count of the number of times I've come across a Burksey T-shirt, beach towel or car seat cover. It's alright – they're all washable!

By the way, just whilst we're on this, I'd like to set you straight on a load of garbage that was reported in *The Daily Gutter* recently. It was about my contract with Avatak International, the world's leading sportswear manufacturer. I do not earn £1.5 million a year just for endorsing their fine products. The figure is a lot higher than that. What do you think I am – some kind of loser?

But back to the 89/90 season at Old Trafford.

If I ended up taking my foot off the gas in league games on the pitch – just a little – I was ramming my pedal to the metal off it. Yes, I started running around town a bit. Drinking a bit more booze. And tupping a lot more birds. What about dope, coke or pills, I hear you ask? No, I wasn't interested. Well done me, eh? Actually I had anotheraddiction to deal with. And it was a big one: one that had begun as an innocent punt on the size of shorts.

Of all the things I'm sharing with you for the first time in these pages, the next revelation is probably the most shocking. There's no getting round it – I come out of it badly. Never mind that medical experts have constantly backed my assertion that being a world class athlete stresses a person in ways that ordinary people can only imagine. Never mind that mega celeb-dom makes you do things that you would never do if you were a mere say, doctor, teacher or probation officer. You see, there are just too many calls on our time, too many voices screaming out of the darkness at us. And if we heroes listen to these voices – what my future wife Brandee called "listening to your, like, outer child?" – we become vulnerable. And when you add "listening to your, like, inner child?" into the mix as well, it's no wonder we go off the rails sometimes. I'm not making excuses, but what it boils down to this: me and my fellow superstar footballers are never really responsible for anything we do. So, knockers of Kieron Dyer, Jermaine Pennant, Lee Bowyer, and the most misunderstood of all, the mega-gifted Stan Collymore – think on.

That said, I have to put my hand up and say that what happened four seconds into our FA Cup semi-final replay against Oldham Athletic at Maine Road on 11th April 1990 was basically down to me.

You'd think I would have learned from the disappointment of Grouchogate that keeping your nose clean around FA Cup Final time is a good idea. But oh no, that's too easy for me. Once again, I was drawn to go the other way. But understand this – it was only because I was so totally confident that we'd win through to Wembley by beating Second Division Oldham – and we did eventually win two-one – that I did what I did. So what was my "crime"? I put a bet on a match that I was playing in. Sorry, United fans. Sorry, Sir Alex Ferguson. Sorry, my former team mates. Sorry, Frank Worthington.

And sorry to the Beautiful Game itself. If I've left anybody out, see my agent.

How it went down was like this. As the bet was strictly illegal, I needed the services of a bookie who would ask no questions and keep his mouth shut if push came to shove. In short, I needed "Mister G", a figure well known in Mank crime circles. Understandably, getting in contact with him was about as difficult as getting somebody to pick up the phone at MFI, but eventually, I met a bunch of young lads known collectively as "The Salford Keys", a network of shadowy go-betweens who agreed to unlock the doors that led to the hookie bookie – for a small consideration, of course. Through The Keys – whose real names were Con McCornachie, Denny Sharfe, Wayne Blatt and Joey Spool* – I put a range of wagers on the match, the main two being special spread bets. The spread on a first Oldham goal was 60–75 minutes. Now, even though we'd conceded three in the first game, I was confident we could shut them out completely in the second. So my first bet was a "buy" on an Oldham goal at five grand a minute. Taking up the no-score bonus option meant that if the Latics failed to score at all, I would pocket a cool seventy-five grand. The second was my banker – a "sell" on the first corner of the match coming between 6–10 minutes at ten grand a minute. That meant that if there was a corner in the first few seconds, I would pouch a sweet sixty grand. If all my bets came in, I stood to pick up over two-hundred thousand pounds. And I needed it. Why? Because the previous weekend, I'd lost over a hundred grand playing Balderdash with Steve Bruce.

*Having served "five and dimes" (five to ten year prison sentences) for the crimes of obtaining money with menaces, extortion and fraud, it was great to see the chaps resurface in society as chart-topping boy band 'Dimples'. Hope you don't mind me mentioning your colourful past, lads.

In fact, what with the divorce and loads of other outgoings, my personal finances were becoming a real source of worry to me in general. True, Dave Green's negotiating skills had secured me a deal that should have given me more than enough to deal with my money problems, but that brought problems of its own. Soon I began to panic* that I was using my money in the wrong way. If you've never had a lot of money to handle, you can't know what that feels like. But help was on its way. The Spread Betting Cavalry was coming on over the hill to save me.

I know what you're thinking now. How could I possibly "bank" on something as haphazard as the timing of a first corner in a football match ? You're forgetting that I was in a position to influence how the game went. Especially if we won the toss – which we did. "Choccy" McClair taps the ball to me straight from the kick-off, I turn to face our line and, pretending to slip, boot the ball straight out for a corner. Brilliant! Sixty-grand for me! And how about fifteen grand a second as a rate of pay, by the way?

If only it had turned out that way. What happened was this. As I was almost horizontal when I've made contact with the ball, it's imparted a wicked – what we professionals call "spin" – on it and it's gone fizzing off over centre-backs Brucie and Pally's heads like a Catherine Wheel on steroids. Unprepared, our agile jock goalie Jim Leighton nevertheless gets himself into a great position to take the ball on the bounce. But as the thing's pitched, it's done a Shane Warne and completely googly-ed the hapless keeper, leaving him stranded on one post and Mike Phelan on the other. Meanwhile, Andy Ritchie, Oldham's goalgrabber supreme, laughed uproariously as he watches the ball fizz between them and then bounce tamely toward our net. I look back in anger and horror from the centre circle. No! Don't go in! It does. Manchester United nil, Oldham Athletic one. After four seconds.

If the ground had opened up and swallowed me, I would have been grateful. I didn't know where to put myself. My plan to make some easy money had backfired in the worst possible way. As the ecstatic Latics' fans go into a rousing chorus of "Burksey From The Halfway Line!" Choccy looks me in the eye and says:

'Dinna worry, mon. Coulda happened tay anybody. We'll still stuff 'em.'

I felt about an inch tall, totally ashamed. I tell you another thing – I didn't need to look across at the bench to clock Mister Ferguson's reaction – I could feel the heat blazing off his chops from the centre circle. Then, of course, we have to kick-off all over

---

*Panic that inspired my great mates Morrissey and Marr, both huge Mankers, to pen a song eventually featured on The Smiths' Rank album. "Vicar In A Tutu", I think it's called.

again. As the Latics fans go into "Come on Burksey, give us a goal," and "Let's have another one," I turn and calmly push the ball safely back to Paul "Call Me Guv'nor" Ince.

It was only then that the full impact of what I'd done hit me. By scoring for Oldham in the first minute of the game, I'd lost three-hundred thousand pounds on the first of my bets. Three hundred grand! I've feinted in a lot of games – feinted left as I've jerked my head to the right before spinning off in the same or opposite direction, and I've feinted right and done the thing in reverse. But this time I didn't feint. I fainted. Spark out. And was replaced by Danny Wallace. I came round soon after and was rushed to hospital for tests. A scan on my brain showed that there was nothing there. Concerned staff, fans and my fellow players all breathed a sigh of relief. Now I felt about half an inch tall.

Speaking afterwards, respected Manchester journo David Strong described my contribution to the Oldham match as: "probably the least effective ever made by a Manchester United player." I had to wait nine years for goal "keeper" Massimo Taibi's four performances for the club to take my unofficial title. Thanks, Massimo.

By the way, my future team-mate and mentor, Graeme LeSaux tells me that *Times* man Bryan Gonville once had everyone in stitches at a literary dinner when he said of Signor Taibi: "He reminds me of Coleridge's *Ancient Mariner* – he stoppeth one of three. On a good day." I don't know exactly what he meant by that, but the punch line's clear enough. But for my money, the best gag about the Italian Scallion was made by ex-Liverpool great, Mark Lawrenson:

"I tell you what, Ray – if he's Massimo Taibi, I'd hate to see what Minimo Taibi's like."

Staying on goalkeepers, I now come to a sad postscript to my moment of madness. Our top class custodian, Jim Leighton was so "like, traumatised?" by conceding my o.g. after just four seconds that he completely lost his confidence. And it showed. His performance in the first game of the Final against Crystal Palace has gone down in history as a Wembley Trembly of the first water and Mister Ferguson chose to drop him for the replay. United won it with a goal from an unlikely source – defender Lee Martin – and so there was no winner's medal for the gallant Scots stop scotcher. Thanks to me.

And as I'm sure you all know, I missed out on both games as well. For the second time, I was robbed of my Wembley dream. Robbed of a chance to play on that sacred pitch. Robbed of my chance to tread where all our nation's great heroes – Bobby Charlton, Bobby Moore, Bobby Gould – have trod. Gutted? You could say that.

Watching Robbo lift that trophy – the first skipper ever to do it three times – brought tears to my eyes. For so many reasons.

I'd had a few run-ins with Mister Ferguson through the season, but none compared with what happened a few days after the win against Oldham. I was sitting in the changing room at The Cliff when in storms The Gaffer. Despite the look on his face, I'm hoping for the same fatherly reaction he gave me after Roxanna left me. Why? Because I had only just come out of hospital after the blackout. No Grandad, not *that* blackout – the blackout I suffered at Maine Road. As he comes up, I lean forward so he can get his arm round me. I needn't have bothered. He didn't go there. Instead, Mister Ferguson's grabbed my training top and chucked it high into the air. Just one thing – I was still wearing it at the time.

Was I scared? No. Petrified? Yes*. When discussing the incident with my wife Brandee years later, the noted therapist opined that "Sir Ferguson appears to have some, like, anger management issues?" No kidding. Why was he blowing a gasket? Because he'd found out I'd had a crafty bet on the game. He'd got the tip-off from his own dense network of local spies known as 'Alex Ferguson's Own Dense Network Of Local Spies'. He knew the type of bets I'd made and for how much. That was bad enough, but there was plenty more. He knew about my growing obsession with gaming and gambling of all kinds; he knew about the women I was "seeing to" and where they lived; he knew what I'd had for breakfast that morning and off whose 'roins'** I'd eaten it. In short, Mister Ferguson had learned quite a lot about me. And much of what he had learned sickened him. Sickened him almost as much as it sickened me.

'You could've been one of the best f***in' prayers we've ever had at this crub!' he yelled right in my face. 'You've got crass, you're brave, you score brirriant goals. But that's not enough for you, is it? Too easy. And now you've gone bad. Aye, you're nothing more than a rying, cheating, rousy heap of garbage!'

---

*I'd experienced the hairdryer treatment many times, so knew what was coming my way. The worst occasion was when I ran my beautiful XR3i into the 'HALE WELCOMES CARE-FUL DRIVERS' sign after a night of Scrabble and Sam Smith's with the lads. Pictures of what remained of the mangled sign – appropriately only the letters ALE were still read-able – were splashed all over the press. I was banned from driving for three months. The Magistrate was a City fan and a woman, it was later revealed, by the way. I still think that verdict should be overturned. But worse was that my beloved XR3i was written off in the accident. I should have hung on to her as a garden feature or something, but instead I let her go to a garage down the road. I'm told that she's played a key roll in so many armed robberies, ram raids and other crimes since, that in 1994 she was voted Moss Side's Motor Of The Year. Pride, I'm telling you!

**Ever chased Trail Mix round a bimbo's belly button? With your tongue? Try it sometime. You'll be lucky not to lose your nuts. At least once.

'We did win the game', I spluttered in my defence, barely able to even speak as he continued to hold me high up against the wall. It was the wrong thing to say. To be fair, anything I said would have gone down like a lead balloon at that precise moment.

'Win?! Well it was nay thanks to you, raddie! I'm suspendin' you! Indefinitery!'

Mister Ferguson had every right to be angry, but I can't forgive him for what happened next. In throwing me across the changing room into an open kit hamper, he damaged my haircut. Way ahead of its time, the style – by Simon of Stalybridge – utilised a prototype wax serum which created that casual yet sculpted look that's still so popular today.

When I realised what had happened, I went mental. Worried that I might do something I would regret, I stormed out of the dressing room, jumped in my new Jag and drove straight home without saying a word to anyone. Later, I spent a quiet evening nightclubbing with my mates Frank McAvennie, Patsy Kensit, Chris Eubank, Carol Vorderman and a couple of stars from the cast of local soap Coronation Street. Some muckrakers have suggested that I hastily arranged that evening so that I could show off my injury to the posse of paparazzi and gossip columnists I knew would be hanging around. That is a total lie. Besides, to protect the unstable state of my hair and to make sure that nobody – especially the press – could see what Mister Ferguson had done to me, I hid the disaster under a discreet hat. My plan backfired. You'd think people had never seen a pith helmet before. Even so, several camera and note-book-toting scumbags noticed that something was different about me and the next day, my picture was splattered all over the Terribloids – "Bull's-eye Burksey takes the pith!" – and on TV.

As a result, Mister Ferguson had to explain himself at a press conference at Old Trafford. Looking sick, he got away with the scandalous destruction of my hairstyle by coming out with a mixture of hard words and weak jokes. But never once did he mention my spread bet nightmare hell. Surprised he didn't grass me up as by rights he should have done? No, it's an unwritten law in the football community that we don't dob each other in. We just don't do it.

As the season drew to a close, I didn't realise that I was living on borrowed time at the football club. Like Normo and Macca, who had fallen foul of the supersensitive Glasgow Gaffer the season before, the simple truth was that, although he rated me hugely, Mister Ferguson had had enough of me. And that could only mean one thing. Yes, despite my increasingly recognised brilliance – I finished the season just one vote shy of beating John Barnes to the coveted

Footballer of the Year title* – Fergie was already looking to replace me for the following season of 1990/91. I was on my way out of Ol dTrafford.

Can you blame him? Yes, of course you can. If he'd stuck with me, I could have contributed to the most successful decade in United's history. Alright, without me they still copped the European Cup, the UEFA Cup, seven League titles, four FA Cups and the League Cup. But with me onboard, they could have gone to the next level. And imagine me and Eric Cantona in the same team. Not to mention me and Keano, Becks, Scholsey, Giggsy and Gary Neville. Make your heart miss a beat? It does mine.

But just as I was thinking that the 89/90 season was ending on an iffy note for me, things were about to take a turn. I was watching the first of the week's *Countdown* shows** when I got a phone call right in the middle of the conundrum. The caller? Mister Bobby Robson. Ah-hah! Now what did he want me for as if I didn't know?

'Steve Butcher?'

'Steve Burkes, Mister Robson.'

'That's right. Now listen, how would you like to come down to Bolton Abbey?'

Maybe I didn't know, after all. 'Why not? 'Lovely, yes. Used to go there on holiday with my Mum and Dad.'

'Your parents used to go to Burnham Beeches on holiday?'

'I thought you said Bolton Abbey?'

Blimey. Anyway, to cut a long story short, Mister Robson was calling to inform me that I'd been called in to train with the national squad. Yeeeeeees! Get in, Burksey. At last! I'd always known that one day I would play for England and I'd never been able to understand why nobody had given me a chance before. Not even at Under 21 or 23 level. That was about to change. Big style. Soon, I would be able to show the whole World what I could do.

---

*Barnsey had already won it once. You'd think they could have shared the thing around a bit. Especially as it was my performances for United that spurred him on to such great heights for Liverpool.

**A lady called Mrs Larkin or Larkham or Laker or Blakeman it might have been, anyway whatever her name was, she was an inmate of the Hope Springs Retirement Home in Cheadle. Without fail, she used to tape a week's worth of Countdown shows for me and send them recorded delivery to my home address. It was a real nuisance having to get up and answer the door, but you've got to keep your fans happy. You see, these are some of the nice things we footballers do that never get a mention.

I immediately called Tarka with the news. And then got out my not so little black book. If ever there was a time to celebrate, this was it.

As a postscript, those of you with plenty of R.A.M. (Random Access Memory) in your bonces will have noticed that I never mentioned whether I got my revenge on TA for his nose job on me at Highbury the previous season. Personally on the pitch – I didn't. But thanks to the events of the next few weeks, I got the sweetest revenge imaginable. I was picked to represent my country at the World Cup in Italy. Tony wasn't.

God works in mysterious ways, eh?

```
CHAPTER NINE
```

# ANY QUESTIONS?

**A**s I was preparing myself for Italia 90, I accepted a request to meet a girl from *Soccer Steam Magazine* who wanted to do a piece on me and get me to answer their popular questionnaire. I invited her up to my new place in Hale for the interview. It didn't go well from the off. I couldn't have been nicer as I greeted the pert little skirt at the door and invited her in. She had other ideas.

'Hi there, nice to see you. Come in.' I was so easy around women by this time, it wasn't true. It didn't worry me that under my Pierre Lépine towelling robe, I was stark naked. It didn't seem to worry the girl either. To start with.

'Thanks. Great to meet you. And great place!'

I looked her straight in the eyes. 'Yeh. Listen – Laura? – how would you like to do it in my Jacuzzi?' I asked, slowly undoing the belt of my robe – before tying it again a bit looser than before*.

'Do what in your Jacuzzi?'

'That's up to you babe,' I said, my hand hovering over the knot. Of course, I meant just to do the interview there, but Ms Killjoy has taken it wrong and spins me a load of crap about keeping everything on a professional basis, etcetera. As so often before, the negative attitude of another person toward me made me feel small and it brought out my defensiveness. I think it shows in my answers to the questionnaire, which is reprinted below. What I would have replied if me and Laura had got it on is shown in brackets.

*Several plonkers have written that I learned the move at a Robe Work session on a weekend course called "Lovely Ladies – How To Get Them And What To Do With Them". Apparently, I've attended the course – taught by superstud club owner Peter Stringfellow – "several times". The story is bulls\*\*\*. The Robe Trick was actually given to me as a tip – totally free of charge – by that other supercharged sex god, Peter Beardsley. The Press got their Peter's mixed up.*

Soccer Steam Questionnaire

*Name and D.O.B?*

Stephen Burkes. Born Huddersfield, 26th April 1967

*Are You A Typical Taurus?*

I'm not a typical anything (Well, I'm hung like a bull so maybe I am!)

*Clubs?*

Huddersfield 1983 –1984, Spurs 1985 –1987, Man United 1987–)

*Most Feared Opponent?*

I don't fear opponents. They fear me (Stuart Pearce, Tony Adams, Ms Y Killmartin)

*Best Game?*

*Tutty Hump Three* (The Five-one home win against Millwall in September '89)

*Best Goal?*

The one at The Stretford End (My thirty-yard bullet header against Southampton at The Dell in March)

*Favourite Player?*

Gary (Frank Worthington, Glenn Hoddle, Bryan Robson)

*Favourite Musician?*

Haven't got one (My brother Tarka Burkes, Belinda Carlisle, Madonna)

*Favourite Song?*

The National Anthem (Blue Heaven Is A Place On Earth by Belinda Carlisle, Live To Tell by Madonna, I Drove All Night by Cindi Lauper, Heart Of Glass by Blondie, Serving Number Seven by Orange Microdot)

*Favourite Film?*

Kodak (Terminator, Beverley Hills Cop, Airplane, The Great Escape)

*Favourite Actor?*

Romario (Arnold Schwarzenegger, Mel Gibson, Eddie Murphy, David Jason, Nicholas Lyndhurst, and the bloke who plays Trigger)

*Favourite Actress?*

My ex-wife (Michelle Pfeiffer, Kim Basinger, Pamela Anderson)

*Favourite Book?*

My little Black one (The three books that make up J.R.R. Tolkien's Lord Of The Rings. I haven't actually read it, but I know it backwards. How come? It's my brother's favourite book and as his Christmas present to me one year, he gave me a box containing forty 60-minute cassettes of the entire work. He recorded them at

**87**

his home studio, reading aloud every word of the three books himself. And using a different voice for each character)

*In the event of a fire, what would be the first thing you would rescue from your house?*

My little black book (The letter of sympathy and encouragement Frank Worthington sent to me when I was staying with Tarka in Brighton)

*Favourite Comedian?*

You're coming pretty close (Bernard Manning, Lenny Henry, French and Saunders)

*Favourite Cartoon Character?*

Dennis Wise (Scooby-Doo)

*Hero?*

Haven't got one (Frank Worthington, Nelson Mandela, Albert Einstein, Alex Ferguson, God)

*Heroine?*

No thanks, I never touch it (Maragaret Thatcher, Mother Teresa, Princess Diana)

*Hope For The Future?*

World peace and to get rid of you (To be the best player who ever lived and to be a credit to my Mum and Dad)

See how much more co-operative I would have been if Laura had just gone with the flow and opted for a spot of bubble and squeak in the Jacuzzi?

A sidelight: after reading the interview, Dave Green insisted on vetting all my future written work for the media. I agreed. All except for this book. This one's for real.

And that brings me on to something. I want to talk about some of the lies that have seeped out of the woodwork about the writing of this autobiography. You may have noticed that in my foreword, I quote the names of eight individuals who were retained to help me remember all the stuff that you now have the privilege of reading. Some half-wits have suggested that as many as eight were needed because none of them could stand working with me for any length of time.

Take it from me – that is bollocks. In fact you'll have to take it from me because, under the terms of a restraining order, the people I employed to help me write this book are legally prohibited from making any written or spoken comment about any aspect of the collaboration process itself, nor about any other aspect of their contact with me during the contracted period of their employment. And for a further period of thirty-five years thereafter. So there's nothing I can do but assure you that every single one of my helpers found working with me a free, easy and joyous experience.

Others have suggested that the "authorial voice" of the book is "uneven" with the result that "the narrator doesn't sound like the same person from one section to the next" and that "half the time that person doesn't sound like Burksey". Yet more experts have "discovered deliberate mistakes left in the text" by "disgruntled" helpers trying to get their own back on me by "exposing Burksey's amazing ignorance". That is also bollocks. To take the first point, if – say on recalling a great Cyrille Regis goal – I've written "O to see thee prance once more, thou still unravaged hart of Albion", then that is exactly what I said at the f***ing time, alright? And on the second point, I've read through the entire book and I couldn't find one single mistake in it. So ram that up your pipes and smoke it.

## CHAPTER TEN

# ENGLAND EXPECTS

urnham Beeches was going to be a testing time for me and I was fired up from the off. The carrot at the end of it – playing in the legendary white shirts of the game's inventors in the World Cup – made my mouth and every other orifice I had water. I knew if I made the final squad, I would be part of something big and historical – like a St Paul's Cathedral on legs. Twenty-two of them.

How did it go for me? It went great. I really showed football connoisseur Bobby Robson and his staff what I could do on the training pitches, in the gym and in the classroom. Here's one for you. I think it disappointed them in a way. Why? Because it meant they were going to have take onboard a player whose reputation as a bad boy had gone before him. If I'd been less than outstanding in training, they could have just said "thanks but no thanks" and forgotten all about me – no problem. But I'd shone so it was game on for them.

But there was really no reason for Mister Robson and his staff to be wary of me. I was no bad boy. Seeking to put the Boss straight, I requested a meeting with him on the night before our final sessions. When it came to it, I knocked on the door of his suite with some trepidation.

Off duty, Mister Robson was far from being the tracksuited dynamo I'd been drilled by all week. And I mean drilled. As everybody knows, the Gaffer is a really kind-hearted, pleasant sort of guy – but when he's working, he's as tough and as demanding as they come. It was weird to catch him in his dressing gown and slippers.

'Come in Stuart, I'm just having a cocoa if you want one.'

Once I'd realised that Mister R. got everybody's names wrong, I'd stopped correcting him. 'No, thanks.' I followed him into a spacious if small sitting area where my eye was immediately taken by a large bag full of needles and threads propped against a chair. A large piece of brightly coloured material was draped over its arm.

'Just my hobby, my pastime, my passion. I'm not that good at it.'

Hobby? I'd always thought that Mister Robson's horizons went no further than the white lines that enclose a football pitch. I was wrong. I looked as what he was working on with interest. As you know, I later became one of the biggest collectors and patrons of artists like Damien Hirst and Tracey Emin – skippers of the so-called "Britart" team that took on the world a few years later and stuffed it. Stuffed it, pickled it and stuck it in a glass tank in the boy Hirst's case. But back in 1990, my taste was different. I still thought that art had to look like something. Duh! In fact, my naïve young eyes were hugely impressed by the amazingly lifelike quality Mister Robson had got into his work – a traditional Scottish Highland scene done in thousands of coloured threads.

'What's it called?'

'The title of the piece? I've called it "Stag At Bay With Arnold Mühren Lurking". I'm going through a bit of a Dutch Master phase at the moment.'

"Dutch phase", eh? Makes you think, doesn't it? The Boss was soon to stir up a hornet's nest of controversy by announcing his decision to quit England immediately after the World Cup and take up Gafferdom at PVC Eindhoven, the Dutch club owned by the country's leading plastics Company, Plashtik Alsho.

I examined the Boss's work more closely. 'I think it's fantastic.' I meant it.

'Family thing – learned it from my mother. It's a great tradition in the North East, you know – embroidery, tapestry, crochet work. You remember Malcolm Macdonald?'

Did I ever. Some have flattered me by comparing my barrel-chested physique and bullet-fast pace to Supermac's. 'Sure – he was one of the best number nine's of all time.'

The Boss took a sip of cocoa. 'Brilliant at needlepoint, that lad.'

'Really.'

'Oh yes. You see Arnie here?' Grimacing, the Boss pointed to the crouching figure of his former Portman Road star. 'See how the light's bouncing off his bazooka? It's a sloppy effort, a tired effort, a poor effort. Now if Malcolm had done that, it would have been perfect. Anyway, you haven't come to see me about embroidery, have you?' With that, Mister Robson's put down his work, taken another sip of cocoa, sat back in his recliner and fixed me with a look as sharp as one of his needles. I couldn't return his gaze and looked down at the floor as I went into my spiel.

'Well, I just wanted to reassure you about some of the bad boy stories you might have heard about me.'

'Such as?'

I hadn't intended to list some of the moments of madness I had been unfortunate enough to be the victim of, but I could see a way around the problem. I would just say that they were all exaggerated. Or made up completely – whatever.

'Such as? Well, things like... the changing room boners, sh\*\*\*ing dead goats, the boozing, the Samantha Fox sex scandal, supergluing Alan Titchmarsh to his wheelbarrow, the drink driving, the business with the electrified door handle, the crop dusting incident, the women's sprint relay team sex scandal, putting a piranha in Chris Waddle's pants, turning up sober at the Brit Awards, hypnotising Ossie Ardiles, the cattle painting incident, the all-night Boggle parties, the Dagenham Girl Pipers sex scandal, the punch-up with Dennis Wise, the punch-up with Vinnie

Jones, the punch-up with Razor Ruddock, the punch-up with Incey, the Michelle Pfeiffer sex scandal...'

'Michelle Pfeiffer?'

'Not *the* Michelle Pfeiffer, of course.'

'Oh.'

I've carried on with the list of everything I thought Mister Robson might have heard about me. And then explained it was all a misunderstanding. By the time I finally looked up from the floor – the England manager was asleep. Brilliant. How much had he heard? I'd have to worry about that later. Gently removing the cocoa cup from his hand, I tucked him up in his tapestry and, hoping that he'd still been awake when I got to the bit where I explained that my crimes weren't as bad as they seemed, I padded quietly out of the room. Some hopes, you might say.

But my hopes were answered shortly afterwards when my name was included in the squad of players going to the World Cup. So Mister Robson had heard my explanation, right? Wrong. Brandee later explained that "the, like, Gaffer was probably asleep when you got to the part with the excuses in it? He heard your words, like, subliminally?" They know bloody everything, the Americans, don't they? Buggers. Anyway, however it happened, I was in. Italia 90, here I come! I can't tell you the happiness I felt.

Five minutes after the call from The FA, I was in pieces. Shattering news from the North had me on the floor with grief. Me and Tarka's beloved Auntie Vi, the little lady known to all in our family as Shrinking Violet, had died. She had been helping a blind man cross the road when his guide dog had a sudden seizure and pushed her under an oncoming ice cream van. She died as she lived – covered in raspberry sauce and with a chocolate flake stuck in her mouth. I wish I could get my hands on the journo who headlined the tragedy: "Sixty-Nine Year Old Ninety-Nined!" Cheap shot, scumbag.

Naturally, me and Tarka went up for the funeral and stayed with Mum and Dad in The Elms, the large detached house I'd bought for them overlooking Belmont Park. Yes, I'd kept the promise I'd made to them six years before.

The burial service, undertaken by none other than World Cup Winning England full-back turned funeral director, Ray Wilson, went beautiful and we had a great tea afterwards at the George Hotel in town. Then it was back to the house for just the family. And more stories about one of the most amazing people you could ever wish to meet.

After we were all Auntie Vi-ed out and everybody had gone, me and Tarka took a couple of nightcaps upstairs and got into our jim-jams.

'Let's stay up and talk, Tark.'

'Great idea, man.'

In between slugs, we chewed the fat off every topic we could think of. And then we got on to our own lives. We talked about how far we'd come, where we were at currently, and where we were going in the future.

And then it happened. It was whilst Tarka was trying to remember where he'd stowed his dope stash, that he opened the door to a walk-in closet and wandered in.

'Find it?' I asked, lying on his bed. I still wasn't interested in joining him in a hit. I was just being, like, supportive?

A moment later, Tarka's appeared in the closet doorway looking white as a sheet and on the verge of tears. It wasn't like him.

'What's the matter?'

'In here,' he said. That was all.

I joined him. At the back of the closet was a wicker basket that had been hidden under a pile of bedding. Tarka had glanced into it and got no further. He went and sat on the bed as I checked it out. Have you ever heard that phrase; "my blood ran cold"? I've always thought it was just one of those things that characters say in books – for effect, you know. Well, as I reached in and took out the first of the envelopes that were stored in that wicker basket, my blood ran cold. As cold as ice. The envelope was addressed to my parents. As were all the other envelopes and small packages in the chest. What did they contain? Videotapes of every televised match I'd played in, newspaper clippings of every match in which I'd done well, important match day programmes, magazine articles – in short, everything a lad in my position would send to his Mum and Dad if he thought they might not see them otherwise. There was just one snag. My proud parents hadn't bothered opening them. I started examining the packages addressed in Tarka's handwriting as well. Once they'd twigged they contained his band's records, CDs, and a lot more of the same kind of press stuff that was in mine, they hadn't bothered opening his, either.

Too stunned to cry, I walked back into the bedroom and sat next to my brother on the bed. We didn't say anything for what seemed like an age. Then we hugged each other.

Some time later, Tark found his dope and rolled a big fat spliff. I joined him in it, the first time in my life I'd sampled a proper drug. For me it could only mean one thing – addiction was just around the corner.

The following day, Tarka went back to Brighton and I drove back to Hale. From that day on, neither of us have said a single word to the parents we'd tried to include in our success – and who hadn't want to know. We were an embarrassment to them.

Yeh? They hadn't seen anything yet.

## CHAPTER ELEVEN

# THE ITALIAN JOB

Discovering that wicker basket changed me. My parents might just as well have taken a sledgehammer to my kneecaps for the all the pain it's caused me over the years.

My brother feels the same. But we've carried on, trying to put it to the back of our minds. We don't always succeed. Tarka has a great way of explaining what it's like.

'It's like somebody's played a note on an organ and kept their finger pressed down on the key so that the sound never goes away, never fades. You get so used to hearing it that eventually, you stop being aware of it – just like you're not usually aware of your own skin. But it's there alright. It's part of you. And it always will be, man.'

Tell it like it is, brother. I can't express myself in words like Tarka. But that doesn't mean I feel things any less than he does. But enough said. On to Italia 90.

Do you know how many guys – and bless 'em, gals – play football every weekend in the season in England? In proper games for clubs, I mean. Guess. Ten thousand? A hundred thousand? Two? Try two million. Yes. I'm not joking. Unbelievable, isn't it? So just imagine what it felt like to be regarded by one of the game's great figures – Bobby Robson – as one of the nation's top twenty-two footballers. Nowadays, some regard me as one of the best twenty-two players in the world. Fifteen years ago, England was my yardstick and I was absolutely made-up to the eyeballs to be included in the party.

In fact, I felt so proud to be representing my country at Italia 90 that when we gathered at Heathrow to fly off to Sardinia – where we were going to play our three first-round games – I think my chest puffed out to double its normal size. And I was chuffed to see the rest of the squad were reacting as I was. Maybe that's why we all looked a bit naff in our officially supplied "Mister Savile" branded suits. Then I realised it was just the suits. My style rival, John Barnes was quick off the mark:

'Saville? I can tell you one thing – they're more Jimmy than Row.'

Too right. And I must say, I didn't enjoy looking less than chic. As the great Peter Shilton quipped, 'They ought to pay us for wearing this gear.' It was a cracker because, of course, the Mister Saville people *were* paying us. Every company sponsoring England had to pay for the privilege. And where did a lot of that dosh end up? It went into a kitty. When everything was totted up at the end of the tournament, we players, the manager and certain key members of the backroom staff split a cool million between us. Not bad for just being given a load of stuff is it, eh?

The guy who had sorted these deals out – I didn't catch his name even though he was always hanging around – was just about the most savvy financial whiz kid I've ever come across. He could have sold sand to the Arabs, that guy. Or Ali Dia to a football club. He was really ahead of his time. One of his ideas was to "through-franchise" a certain blue jeans manufacturer into the sponsorship mix and get FIFA to rename the tournament "Italia 901". But the Suits wouldn't wear it. I tell you, this guy was so hot that I dallied with the idea of ditching Dave Green. I didn't because I was too loyal. And not because I was contractually forbidden to at the time as some have suggested. W***ers.

As with most players, I'm a bit of a one for omens and the like – so I was delighted that Sardinia would be our first home in the competition. Why? Because I'd always loved eating sardines. In fact, I worshipped all members of the Sardine family – especially their big cousins, the Pilchards – and looked forward to sampling as many of them as possible in those first few weeks. Unfortunately, the one and only Paul Gascoigne got wind of my yen for the be-finned beauties and – for reasons known only to him – bet me he could eat more of them than I could at one sitting. You reckon, Gazza? Bring it on! The bet was bound to have what my fourth wife – TV's Iona McHardie – would call "hilarious consequences." But first, we needed to sort out the stake.

'How much?' I said, spotting some easy money ahead. It was a mental thought. There's no such thing as easy money, as everybody knows. Ask nurses. Ask doctors. Ask footballers.

Gazza's come up with a figure. 'A ton?'

'Chicken.'

'I thought it was f***in' pilchahds, like?'

'It is, you wassock. Alright – a ton each.' Gary "The Bookie" Lineker agreed to hold the £200 purse. I had to laugh, really. For all Gazza's love of a wager – horses, football matches, pigeon racing, anything you can think of – he wasn't exactly a high roller like me. He would have shat himself for a week if he'd lost what I had on the Oldham semi. Not that he would have been thick enough to have put a bet on a match he was playing in. "F*** off, Burksey," I hear you cry. "Gazza not thick? You've been on the old banyan bark again."

Stop right there, Buster. Alright, so Gazza's no Einstein in everyday life – who is but the old e = mc squarer* himself? But at his job, Gazza is every bit as big a genius. Probably more so if the latest developments in string theory** are taken into account.

---

*Thanks to my old mate, Stephen Hawking for helping me out with that one.

**Thanks to Peter Stringfellow.

Yes, I would place Gazza right alongside Glenn Hoddle in the genius department. Maybe even slightly ahead of him. And I'll tell you another thing, he's probably the most likeable, the most approachable, the most soft-hearted genius who's ever lived. Can you see old Albert taking his test tubes and shit down on to the street, or the beach, or the park, to do a load of experiments with the local kids? You can't, can you? Well that's what Gazza does everywhere he goes – he shares his genius with everybody.

And it was partly because we had Gazza that I felt good about our chances of doing well in the competition – the football, not the pilchard eating. I tell you something – our centre-backs had to be the best in the world because neither Pally nor Brucey had been picked and they were brilliant. But back to the party that was selected. Apart from yours truly, there were the huge talents of Bryan Robson, Peter Beardsley, Chris Waddle, John Barnes and Gary Lineker. And then there were the hearts, muscles and studs of Stuart Pearce, Terry Butcher, Mark Wright and Steve McMahon. And then there was.... on and on. I tell you, the England squad was f***ing magic when you looked at it on paper.

But you don't play football on paper. You play it on a mixture of bents, fescues and ryes.* And at the start of the tournament, there were some worries that Manager Bobby Robson might not have been getting the best out of his top squad. What system to play – that was the question. Personally, I had only ever played 4-4-2. It was simple and I understood it. But what a lot of the senior guys were calling for was a sweeper and a strengthened midfield: 3-5-1, 3-4-3 or even 5-4-1. The idea was to prevent us being outnumbered and outrun in the middle of the park – which had happened in some of the qualifying games – which in turn would allow us to release our two world class wingers forward instead of sentencing them to more or less constant back tracking and defending.

But there was a downside for me. Playing a sweeper might be great for wingers Barnsey and Chrissie Waddle. But if we were going into battle with just one up, it halved my chances of starting in games. Still, people could get injured. Even in training. Yes, not even the Golden Boot winner at the previous World Cup, the great Gary Lineker, was squibbsy from knocks. Was he?

Just a word on Misters Barnes and Waddle, by the way. It was great teaming up with my old Spurs team mate Chrissie again. For me it was anyway. And Chris? I seemed to be his worst nightmare come to life. Put it this way, when me and the

---

*Grass to you. I learned all about it in my Groundsman's days at Spurs.
Six years later, I learned all about another type of it from Tarka. Unfortunately.

other Laner in the party – Stevie Hodge – saw each other, we went straight into the usual banter and crack that footballers the world over go in for. Chrissie? He's dodged out of the way and tried to hide behind Des Walker. When I've surprised him by getting on his blindside and saying "boo!" he's jumped higher than a field event athlete on drugs. Actually – let's face it, just the word "athlete" would have done there, wouldn't it*? Why was Chrissie behaving like a wet nelly? Because he was still scarred – mentally and physically – by a dumb practical joke I'd pulled at the Lane. I couldn't have been more sorry and Waddler knew that. But it didn't do any good. Of course, we all know what lay ahead. A mere two weeks after our participation in the tournament came to an end on that sad evening in Turin, Chris Waddle was completely cured of Pygobacaephobia**.

Two weeks too late for English football. The therapist he employed should have been shot for having taken time out to have a baby earlier in the season. Some people have no sense of priorities. Mind you, I partly blame Chrissie for the timing of the thing. If he'd gone to one of the FA's own therapists at their excellent T.F.T.V.O.F.P.J.C. (Treatment For The Victims Of Footballers' Practical Jokes Centre)*** in Wantage, they would have sorted him out long before. And what a difference *that* would have made.

*Because of my heroic efforts to bring the Olympics to London, certain individuals, groups and organisations have tried to stop me from making statements like that, but I stand by them. What these people don't understand is that I don't care if athletes do take drugs. To me, it makes sense. You want to see athletes go "higher, further, faster?" Right, let them take whatever they want. I'd personally love to see a lass with a backside like a couple of footballs clocking eight seconds for the hundred metres. And just imagine how high her pants would be riding up those twin globes going at that speed! It would be one of the great sights in sport. Or take the blokes. Be fun to see some geezer pole-vaulting fifty feet, wouldn't it? Course it would. But it's not going to happen as often as it should. Too many killjoys running sport, I'm telling you.

**The fear of finding a piranha fish in your underpants.

***Centre Head, Dr Karl Gleadle has said: "The tell-tale sign that a player has become a victim is a sudden unexplained drop in form – sometimes to sub-moronic levels. We cure 100% of the players who come to us. Of course, we cannot force the others."
The 'others', eh? No need to name and shame. You all know who they are.

Again, if you're a kid and only know Chrissie from his excellent commentary work on telly and on the radio, you've missed something special. Waddler was brilliant, a player whose mesmerising dribbling skills were all the more effective because he often looked a bit shuffling and off-balance when he was working his mazey magic. And he was intelligent with it – on and off the field – and knew how to really hurt his opponents with his tellingly teasing crosses and cannon-fire shooting. It wasn't a surprise to me that he did particularly well at his new club – Marseilles – where rightly, the Garlic Guzzlers gave him more freedom to express himself. That's what it's all about, isn't it?

Again for the kids, the Alzheimer's sufferers or the just plain ignorant, our other winger, John Barnes, was another unbelievable player. Different in style from The Wad, but like that new giant of the game, Thierry Henry (along with my club captain Luis Figo, a current player I would pay to see play), he had a quality which so few have. And I'm not talking about his laughably naff rapping style*. I'm talking grace. I'm talking balance. In short, I'm talking class. Some say the wandering Watford winger turned laid-back Liverpool lace-lasher didn't produce the goods often enough for England. Maybe the way we played our 4-4-2 system didn't help him as I've said. But he was a guy you'd want in your team. And a lovely bloke, too. In fact, our team was full of nice guys. Nice guys who could play? F*** it, we deserved to win the thing! It was only right and proper.

We checked into our not unattractive hotel near Sardinia's capital, Cagliari, with our campaign expectations sky high. The British press, of course, saw things very differently and if my agent Dave Green hadn't secured me a deal to write a column for one of The Terribloids, I would barely have given an interview to a journo during the tournament.

But in any case, there are so many calls on your time during an event of this scale that you have to watch that you didn't give too much of yourself. Like salmon paste, you can spread yourself too thinly. I knew where I was going to put my time in. I was going to train like a demon, I was going to impress on the training pitch, impress in the warm-up games, and push for a spot in the starting line-up.

---

*I refused to sing on the England Squad's World In Motion hit. Why? In protest at the way the Powers That Pee treated Tarka. Free, gratis and for nothing, he'd offered to arrange the song in a catchy rock style, to sing the lead parts and play all the instruments on the track. "Inappropriate" was the word they used. Trainee Gangsta Barnsey's effort though – that they loved. What can I tell you?

And being a model Pro would help to take my mind off certain other fish I loved to fry. Booze-shaped fish. Boggle-shaped fish. Dope-shaped fish. And especially, bird-shaped fish. Yes, I have to hold my hand up and say that more and more, I was getting to need these things. Actually need them and not just want them. I knew they weren't good for me. But hey, we all love a little bit of that, don't we?

I decided to keep my new fondness for dope under wraps – I could do it then – as I certainly didn't want a repeat of "Johnstonegate"* in 1978. Booze – although strictly regulated by the management – was again something that I could keep within reasonable, well fairly reasonable, bounds. Boggle – again, I could indulge a bit without going mental. A little sociable game for a few hundred here or there wouldn't hurt.

Birds, though. That was the one. Keeping the old p***y pleaser in my pants wouldn't be easy at all. Particularly as 'A' – we were in the land of luscious, slinky-lipped, doe-eyed Madonnas like Monica Bellucci and Cinzia Pifferri**; And 'B' we were at The World Cup.

So what did that have to do with anything? Because where there is a World Cup, there is a World Cup Promo and Sponsorship Circus that goes with it. Now, when that circus comes to town, it doesn't just pitch one tent, it pitches several. Hordes of sexy "event hostesses" and "product promo" girls lurk inside each and every tent. And I was determined to press my eager young nose against as many flaps as I could.

There's only one snag with this. Depending on the product they're promoting, you might have to chat up a girl got-up as a giant suppository ('Anusalve', Official Haemorrhoid Treatment of Italia 90), or a flea brush ('Bug-away', Official Canine Groomer of Italia 90) or maybe a conservatory ('Balmoral', Official Garden Room Manufacturer of Italia 90), but you soon get used to it. The only problem comes when things start getting interesting and you try to whip the lass's kit off. It's not always easy. One time up in Naples, I didn't know where to start with the girl who was promoting 'Cucinapura', Official Kitchen Utensil of Italia 90. Just as well, she was dressed as a giant colander.

Of course, I wasn't supposed to be getting up to any of this. And neither were the girls. But you're only young once. And I didn't hear any of my new conquests complaining. Well, maybe one. The Official Corkscrew Girl in Grappa – a city that would soon become very familiar – kicked up a bit of a fuss. But it was really her fault. She should have told me she had a left-hand thread.

*Sent home for taking a prescribed asthma treatment, Rangers' Willie "The Wheeze" Johnstone was a great loss to that tournament.

**Soon to become the second Mrs Burkes. Oh yes, get in Burksey!

I missed our opening warm-up game due to the flying cake injury I suffered during Gazza's birthday party*, but I started in the second one at the little town of Oristano. It was blindingly hot. The pitch was uneven and dusty. There were only a couple of thousand fans – and twice as many armed police – in the ramshackle little stadium. But I didn't care – I was an England player! I put the famous shirt on with such excitement that just for a second I thought you know what was going to happen, but I calmed myself with the knowledge that I would soon be hearing the National Anthem. Although when the band – who looked straight out of a bad Spaghetti Western – eventually played it, it was barely recognisable. Still, no biggie. That was the main thing.

Our opponents were a Sardinian Scratch XI made up of mainly lower league players from the Island. With one exception. And it was a huge one. Local boy Gianfranco Zola, learning his craft under Diego Maradona at Napoli at the time, agreed to play as well. It was the first time I clapped my eyes on the little maestro, a man who would go on to captivate the hearts, minds and voices of anybody with an eye, ear and nose for the Beautiful Game. Here's another brainteaser for you. How many International Caps did the Great Little Man win in his career? A hundred? Ninety? Try thirty-five. Bonkers.

Anyway, back to the game. It began with what a Bryan Gonville might call "a strange familiarity." From the whistle, Stevie McMahon's dribbled back through our ranks and slotted a deliberate own goal. I'm not joking. Look it up in the records if you don't believe me. Oh-oh. I knew it could only mean one thing. As the ball's come back to the centre-circle, I've gone up to Macca and lectured him on the evils of spread betting. A real dressing down. I'll never forget his response.

'F*** off, Burksey! It's called a diplof***ingmatic gesture, you soft bastard!'

Just like that. I was stunned. What a way to talk to a team-mate. I was just trying to be helpful and look where it got me. We became mates eventually, but I gave the poor guy a very wide berth for a while. I knew after "Maine Roadgate" that spread betting is evil and people who go in for it are asking for trouble. And those people still included me, sadly.

---

*Two days after we arrived, Gazza was 23, making me just a month older. I made the mistake of standing right behind the great daft nana at his party. Chrissie Waddle's gone to present him with the cake, but then decided to smack him in the chops with it instead. Gaz ducked and I got a marzipan goalpost in my earhole for being in the R.P.A.T.W.T. (Right Place At The Wrong Time).

Anyway, the game finished 10-2 with me netting a hat-trick. I could have slotted all ten, but I didn't want to put myself in solid with the lads. I'd already fallen foul of Macca and couldn't risk further unpopularity. I've always felt things like that very deeply.

The Pilchard Eating World Championships turned out to be brilliant fun. Most of the lads had bets down and the smart money was on Gazza. Including mine. I couldn't lose whatever happened, so I went into it relaxed. Come the day, we all sneaked off to a little spot in the far corner of the hotel's grounds that a few of the lads had got up to look like a boxing ring. They'd put ropes up and everything. In return for a ticket to the upcoming opener against Ireland, a local guy supplied two buckets of pilchards and these were placed either side of chairs placed opposite each other in the ring. First to finish his bucket would be the winner.

Then, with Survivor's *Eye Of The Tiger* blasting out of Chrissie's ever-present boom box, me and Gazza were escorted toward the ring like boxers going into a big fight. We had dressing gowns on, the lot. We larked about a bit, every move commented on Harry Carpenter-style by Stuart "The Voice Of Them All" Pearce, and then we were introduced by Emcee for the contest, David Seaman.

'In the blue corner, hailing from – where are you from, Burksey?'

'Huddersfield, you Muppet.'

'...That explains a lot – Huddersfield, England, weighing in at... too f***ing much...'

Laughs and cheers all round; shouts of 'you fat bastard!'; a few premature 'who ate all the pilchards?'; and a 'most of his weight's in his knob!' thrown in for good measure. Very funny, Mister Seaman. As you know, there wasn't an ounce of fat on me then. I just had big bones, muscles, sinews and stuff. DS continued:

'...the former Northern Area Winkle Champion, Steve "Boom Boom" Burkes!'

To a loud chorus of cheers, boos and laughs, I've come off my stool, mimed eating a few pilchards, thrown a couple of right hooks, and then gone back to my corner.

'And in the red corner...'

Gazza's already bringing the house down with a series of comic moves I just can't describe, but it was about the funniest thing I've ever seen. Ref Paul Alcock's* comedy back heel the other season doesn't come close.

'... from Gateshead, England, weighing at slightly f***ing less...'

Laughs, boos and a few choice comments.

'... Former Golden Gills Champion, Paul "Raw Prawn" Gascoigne!'

---

*Alcock by name...

Terry Butcher, our referee for the contest, calls us together to give us our instructions. We touch gloves – did I mention we were wearing boxing gloves? – somebody goes "ding!" and we sit down on our chairs. To more noise and excitement than we generated at Oristano, we got stuck in. Now I don't know if you've ever tried to eat pilchards wearing boxing gloves, but it's about as easy as trying to pee into a row of thimbles without spilling any*, drawing a picture of something with the pencil stuck up your arse**, or doing a live TV interview putting as many film titles as you can think of into your answers.***

Before we go on, thanks to my good friend, John Motson, here's a transcript of that Film Title Interview:

Motty: 'Well, Terry, after all the build-up, the Ireland game's only a couple of days away. What's the mood in the England camp?'

Terry B: 'We're feeling fairly Footloose at the minute, but ask me again in 48 Hours!'

M: 'Confident?'

TB: 'Well, we don't want to be Going Overboard. It's a Risky Business to predict Victory. But I wouldn't want to be Trading Places with any other Side Out here. We've got a lot of Goodfellas. Everywhere you look there's a Real Genius, a Lethal Weapon, a Top Gun, a Superman. We Always try to Do The Right Thing and I think we're going to make a real Splash.'

M: 'Any injury worries?'

*The hours fly by when you're on tour with England.

**The idea for this interesting pastime – it makes a great icebreaker at parties by the way – came from a slip of the tongue by me. In a conversation about Stan Bowles, I said "arsist" instead of "artist" and Gazza's picked me up on it. Then one thing led to another. To be fair, my arse-drawn effort didn't look any worse than it would have done if I'd held the pencil properly. What became of our "Bottycellis"? We presented them to the hotel manager as gifts. He had them framed, the poor sod.

***It was Terry Butcher's idea, that one. The Butch is the King of this kind of stunt, by the way. That's why I always refused to play him at Scrabble, Boggle, Balderdash – you name it. He was brilliant at limericks as well. His best one was about a bloke who'd banged a bit of local rough and caught an S.T.D. (Subscriber Trunk Dialling) entitled "Chlamydia in Sardinia". Though lacking the rough-hewn power of John Toshack's verse, it was nevertheless a fine effort.

TB:     'Psycho had a bit of Vertigo on the Airplane, but he's made of The Right Stuff so no problem there. My Left Foot was below par, but I'd give it 10 now.'

M:      'I think I'm being ribbed a bit here! If England get to the Final – who wouldn't you want to meet there?'

TB:     'Apart from Conan The Barbarian – Brazil.'

Back to Pilch Fest 90. After the first round, I don't know how many pilchards me and Gazza had got down our rude gullets, but that wasn't the only place they went. We had pilchards in our hair, pilchards up our noses, pilchards smeared all over our chests – and we could hardly breathe for laughing. A pair of plonkers and a couple of pails of pilchards – I tell you, we used to make our own fun in them days. And that fun was magic. I'd scarcely been happier in my whole life. Tarka's held-down organ note was a distant echo that evening.

Gazza won the bet. My pilchards weren't going down as quickly as his so I started craftily chucking some of the ones I had left into the trees. I was spotted. After a couple of warnings, The Butch disqualified me and Gazza was rightly crowned Champion Pilchard Chomper of Italia 90.

Everybody loved the contest. Everybody except Chrissie. I think the sight of all those fish bits splattering over our kecks was just too near the Z.O.V. (Zone Of Vulnerability) for the likable and talented pygobacaephobe.

As some of you may have guessed – although you didn't know until now – the event had an unfortunate postscript. The next day, we were scheduled to play our last warm-up match just over the water in Tunisia and as we set off to the airport, our excesses really caught up with us. Ever heard the expression "green around the gills?" Me and Gazza were greener. And we also demonstrated a range of explosive effects that didn't go down too well in the cramped confines of the bus. We'd improved in most ways by the time we got to the terminal building, but we still had terrible gas. Meriden's future owner, Mister Speerman, would have had a field day with us.

Of course, the first thing that happens as we get off the bus is that some Eye-Tie Journo – they're just the same as ours, but better turned-out – sticks a mike under my nose and asks me what I think of Sardinia. I burp out the answer and punctuate it with a couple of tommy squeakers from the other end. I couldn't help it. If the divine Mrs T herself had eaten half a bucket of pilchards the night before, she would have done just the same. Of course, nobody checks the thing out properly and the story immediately becomes prime time slime starring me – alias "Wyatt Burp, The Fartiest Gun In The West" as I "take a pop – or ten – at his Italian hosts." It was a load of crap. I loved what I'd seen of Italy. And as for disrespecting the Italians themselves – I would hardly have b***ed all that local beaver if I hadn't hugely respected the girls, would I? I tell you, if you've never had your actions misunderstood, your words twisted, or – the worst thing of all – words you've never said put in your mouth, then you can't know what it feels like.

Fast forwarding to the present day for a moment, we have a new evil in our midst now, don't we? I'm talking about these con men and sting merchants who fool Football's Glitterati into talking too freely off the record? José Antonio Reyes and Sven Göran Eriksson are just two to have fallen foul of these bastards. And in the case of Mister Eriksson, look how devastating his encounter with that Barmy Swami from the *News Of The Screws* turned out to be.

They tried to pull a similar stunt with me the other day. Yes, I got a phone call from a guy pretending to be a member of The Prince of Wales' staff. "His Royal Highness would like to speak to me," he says. "Was I available to take his call?" It all seemed so genuine. But as I'm waiting to be connected, I smell a rat. Then this voice comes on the line and I have to say it sounded exactly like the Prince.

Caller: Good morning... Burksey. Yes, this is Prince Charles, er... speaking. I was wondering...

Me: Yeh, well you can stop wondering, pal. And I'll tell you what else you can do. You can take that phone and shove it up your f\*\*\*ing arse. And if you call here again, I'll find out where you live and cut your f\*\*\*ing knackers off, you c\*\*\*!

That showed 'em. Or so I thought. Unfortunately, it turned out the call was genuine. Because the Prince is a very gracious man with a great sense of humour, me and him have had a good laugh about the misunderstanding since. But there's a serious point here. These "funny" con men are creating a climate of suspicion in which nobody can be sure of who they're talking to any more. The solution? Breach of confidence suits? No way. Execute the buggers. That would stop it straight away.

But back to Italia 90. Neither me nor Gazza got on in the Tunisia warm-up match – and neither of us much cared to be honest. For the record, we snatched a 1-1 draw in the last minute thanks to lower division goal-guzzler, Steve Bull. But that final whistle was a significant moment – it meant that at last, the whore dervs were over. Now it was time for the main course – the World Cup itself. Remember who was in Group F along with us? It was Ireland, Holland and Egypt. And we intended to eat the lot of them for breakfast.

'So Burksey, we're in the infamous Group of Eff, eh?' Gary Lineker had said to me at Heathrow before we'd flown out. See, I'm not sure Gary's as clever as people make out. Everybody in the country had known for ages what group we were in. Still, he's got a great smile, hasn't he? And he also had great legs, legs that could propel him around the box at Mach speeds. But his genius wasn't just how fast he ran. It was where he ran.

Mister Robson's called me into the classroom one day and set me down in front of the video. 'Now then, Simon, you're a special talent, an instinctive talent, a unique talent, but I want you to watch Gordon (Lineker) in these clips and see what he does with his movement.' He's pressed play and what amounted to a Gary Lineker's Greatest Hits Compilation began rolling. We were both strikers, but how different we were. Gary's one of those who has an interactive map of the box in his head at all times – a map in which all the players' positions are updated in real time as he darts first here, then there in search of space. And he always finds it. Time after time, he's the one in the P.O.M.O. Me? I'm different. As Gary once said:

'Burksey's not the brightest footballer I've ever known and he's got no tactical nous – I don't think he'd mind me saying that. In fact, he has a God-given knack for always being in the P.O.L.O. But that's where a flair player like him is dangerous. Some attempt the unexpected and the extravagant in training. But, like Alex Higgins used to do on the snooker table, Burksey has the bottle and the vision to attempt the audacious on the biggest stages – such as at Italia 90. And his technique is so good that he delivers more often than not. One helluva player. You just have to make sure he remembers to change ends at half-time.'

He forgot to mention my fabulous physique there and I'm not that chuffed with the crack about half-time, but the rest is spot-on. Watching his videos though that day didn't help me. Why? Because I can't play like that. The fact that nobody else in the world could "do a Lineker" as brilliantly as him did make me feel a bit better about it, though.

But my afternoon of instruction wasn't over. Next, I had to sit through hours of Peter Beardsley's Greatest Hits. His intelligence, his understanding, his passing.... "Enough already!" as they say up The Lane. Like I said before, Peter was a dab hand with his dressing gown cord as well, but thankfully, the Gaffer didn't have a video of those moves.

I guess Maine Roadgate was a terrible revelation to you. I know I'm a hero and a role model to so many people. Well, here's another one and I apologise to everyone in football, but especially to Gary and Peter who have done nothing but be helpful and encouraging to me throughout my career on and off the park. Here goes. I padded away from the classroom that day shamefully resolving to crock them in training. Or if that didn't work, to do them off the pitch. Secretly, of course. And nothing serious – just something that would keep one or both of them out long enough for me to prove my worth. You see, I was so desperate to play in those games, to contribute to our nation's effort, to be part of something special that I like lost the plot? Pity me. It's not nice being so tormented.

Mister Robson announced that we were going for 4-4-2 against Ireland with Peter and Gary starting up front. But I was on the bench and I contented myself – for the moment – with the knowledge that I would come on at some stage. The match would pit me against my old United buddies Kevin Moran and Paul McGrath which was no easy task, but I was confident. The game kicked off in surprisingly cool conditions at the Stadio Sant' Elia in Cagliari, but there was nothing cool about what was going off around the police-guarded terraces – or on the pitch. It was real harem-scarem stuff with the Irish running round like headless chickens and us hanging on to their coat-tails. Not that chickens wear coats, but you know what I mean. Long balls from the Emerald Islers caused us a bit of bother, but after only eight minutes, we went ahead. Waddler's whacked on a perfect ball for Gary, whose chest took it past Paki (didn't look very Asian to me) Bonner despite his attempted foul. Then the pacey number ten's slotted the shot as half of Ireland try to land on him from behind. Yes! One-nil. We were away. And I cheered louder than anybody. Don't get me wrong – I wanted to get on to that pitch by fair means or foul, but there was no way I wasn't going to go mental if one of the guys who was on there instead of me scored.

After that, Ireland's organised chaos continued to cause us problems, but we made it through to half-time with our lead intact. The Boss's team talk was a bit mystifying to my ears. I guess the other lads were used to it as they didn't seem to think it was odd.

'When we advance, we don't want to advance on all fronts like General Custard did at The Battle Of The Little Be Gone...' Or something like that. I don't remember exactly. All I know is, the lads went out for the second half full of the spirit that won us Trafalgar, the Battle Of Britain and the Eurovision Song Contest. It kept us going until 70 minutes, when off went Peter Beardsley and on came Steve McMahon to "shore-up the midfield."

Result? Macca's lost the ball almost immediately and Ireland equalise. Brilliant. Hindsight's always 20/20 isn't it? But let the record show that at the time it happened, I voiced my opposition to that substitution. I should have gone on for Beardo. If I had, the job would have been a good 'un. Simple as that.

Good penalty shouts for us came – and went – and then with a few minutes to go, I get the call to sub Gary, who'd run his legs off. Do you know, I can't remember running on to the pitch, what I did next or how. I know at one point I blazed a thirty-five yard cannonball against the crossbar with Paki as beaten as a dhobi wallah's washing. And a minute or so later, I've nearly taken Steve Staunton's bollocks off with a trademark "mistimed" lunge. Apart from that, those few minutes went by in a blur.

They were a few minutes that got me noticed, though. Replays of my vicious effort against the crossbar were shown time and time again all over the planet. Italian TV went as far as putting a speed gun on the strike. It registered 153 kilometres per hour – the hardest hit football in recorded history. Later on in the tournament, I racked up 162 kmh. Oh yes, people were beginning to notice me alright.

But it wasn't all roses. The yellow card I earned for the Staunton challenge brought me a lot of criticism. But let me just say this to my critics: F*** off. If you take that edge off my game, you take my game – full stop.

The match ended all square; a point a piece. My man of the match? Gazza. Different class. And I have to hold my hand up and say that Gary L was only a point or two behind him. He always looks so relaxed on Match Of The Day, doesn't he? Pleasant. Cheery. If I had a word to describe him in his playing days, that word would be "intense". There must be something about Alan Hansen and Lorro that just doesn't turn the amiable anchor on.

Mister Robson's call to arms at half-time in the Ireland match was only the start. Apart from our usual training, every day we did something militaristic, usually wearing full uniforms with packs. It was brilliant fun. We crawled under netting, climbed over walls, waded through mud – well, through the swimming pool, but you can't have everything – the whole bit. It all went great and it was top bonding stuff. But then came bayonet drill. We were supposed to charge a row of dummies and skewer them – no problem. Except that we had a loose cannon in our ranks by the name of Gazza. I'll never forget the scene. In full officer's uniform and with a swagger stick tucked under his arm, Mister Robson took the drill with his highly respected right-hand man, "Sergeant" Don Howe at his side.

BR:    'Now then men, it's only a few days until we take on the might of the Dutch Army – er, football team – and it's important that when Ruud Van Rental and his chaps come marching in that we give them a pretty good hiding. Isn't that so, Howe?'

DH:    'Yes, I suppose it is. Although you know, I don't think it's an awfully good idea to be larking about with bayonets and things.'

At that, the Gaffer's given Don what I think they call a "withering look" before turning to address the men once more.

BR:    'To sharpen our aggression, to hone our aggression, to put an edge on our aggression, I want each of you to rush forward at the target, ram it with your bayonet, and then give it a jolly good twist whilst shouting insults of a suitably Dutch nature at the top of your voices. Then, withdraw and form a rank on the goal line.'

"Captain" Robson blows his whistle and the first rank of bayonetters rush the targets. Private Waddle is the first to arrive at his dummy and wastes no time getting stuck in.

CW:    'Howay yah f***in' chocolate windmilling f***ah, P*** off back
        to f***in' Amsterdam, yah f***in' Daf drivin' Advocaat guzzlah!'

BR:    'Well done, Waddler!'

As the first rank of troops left the scene, the next rank, containing Gazza, prepared for action.

BR:    'Second rank.... wait for it....go!'

With that, Gazza, who's had a bet on with Platty that he would be the first man to bayonet his dummy, has picked up his rifle like a spear and whilst everybody else has sprinted off, bunged it Steve Backley-style over their heads toward the target.

Being Gazza, the rifle lands perfectly point first right in its heart.

A chorus of "f***in' 'ell, Gazza!" "f***in' w***er" and a few choice other terms of endearment rend the air from the lads who'd almost been decapitated. The Gaffer though almost looked as if he'd been expecting it.

BR:    'Gascoigne?'

PG:    'Yes sah?'

BR:    'You stupid boy.'

A bad morning for Gazza got worse when the Gaffer later confiscated his pogo stick and banned him from playing tennis when the sun was out. Which was all day, really. And when the news broke that the management had decided to stop playing soldiers in training, Gazza's day of misery was complete. He took some consolation by playing ping pong for two hours. Against himself. I tell you, it's no wonder people all over the world love Gazza. And you can put my name at the top of that list.

The meeting to discuss our tactics for the Dutch match confirmed my worst fears. We were going with a sweeper. I cursed myself for not dropping my rifle on Gary's toe when I'd had the chance. I was still on the bench, though, and when I thought about it, Gary had been up on his own for long periods in the Irish match. Maybe it wouldn't make that much difference what system we played.

When the match itself kicked off, there was a huge buzz in the Stadio Sant' Elia and what a colourful scene it was. The banks of Dutch fans looked so great in their replica kit that it inspired me to write another poem:

*The fans were all dressed in shirts of orange*
*and I was impressed ...*

I couldn't get any further, but it was a plucky effort as John Tosh later told me that there are no true rhymes for the word "shirts". But enough of that. The main thing that caught my eye from the bench was the quality of our football. It was a different game altogether than the one we'd played again Paddy O'Biff and his Bogtrotters. We weren't just stopping them playing – we looked smooth going forward, the ball being passed around in classy patterns to guys who always seemed to have space and time. Brilliant.

Pearcey and Paul Parker bombing up the flanks, Gazza and Robbo through the middle, Barnsey and Waddler free to attack – and with you-know-who at the sharp end – it all looked great. And what of Van Basten? Gullit? Koeman? We matched them. We more than matched them. We made them look ordinary. Almost.

Nil-nil at half-time. More 'battle stations', 'they don't like it up 'em' and 'Don't Panic!' from the Gaffer. Out we go for the second half. Still stalemate, but things looked good as, with a full half-hour to go, I'm told to warm up. Joy of joys! Five minutes later I'm ready to give my all for the country I love, the England of Maggie Thatcher and Rolls Royce, Harrods and Chicken Tikka Masala, Winston Churchill and Cary Grant*, Sooty And Sweep and Yorkshire pudding. Yes! I couldn't wait to get on. The Gaffer puts his arm around me outside the dugout and tells me what he wants me to do.

'I'm putting you on for Waddler.'

'F*** off – I'm not playing on the f***ing wing!'

I was outraged. Didn't Mister Robson realise who he was dealing with? Alright I was only 23, but there was no way I was going to allow him to push me around just because he had a lifetime of service to the game behind him. Besides, I didn't believe in behind – I believed in ahead. But I needn't have worried. The Boss continued:

'We're holding them, we're containing them, we're nullifying them – so I'm taking one out of midfield and putting you up just behind Garth – where Aubrey Beardsley usually plays.'

That was more like it.

'Anything you say, boss!'

'Good lad.'

---

*Bristol-born Cary is well known as the star of great movies like North By North West. But how many know that off-screen, he was a practising architect. Yes. You Gooners out there should know – he designed your lovely old Highbury Stadium. Look it up if you don't believe me.

I ran on and literally exploded into action. This was my time and I was taking it by the scrag end of neck. The first thing I do is to pick up an intended wall ball from Robbo on the half-way line. But instead of knocking it back to him, I "Cruyff" Frank Rijkaard – twice in a row – and then sprint hard toward their box. I leave my markers for dead but run into heavy traffic outside the D. No problem. The ball glued to my toe and studs, I start jinking and spinning like a crazed dodgem past my intended tacklers. Then ahead of me, I spot Gary about to lose his marker for about the fiftieth time in the match. If I release him immediately, he'll just beat the offside flag. Stopping dead, I dink a perfectly weighted through ball on to his head. He nods it goalwards...and misses by inches. Shit. Still, it was a brilliant move, one that was analysed, admired and replayed endlessly on TV screens around the world. Yes, from Alaska to Zanzibar, the name of Steve Burkes was on all footer fans' lips now. If it wasn't before.

Shortly after my explosive introduction, Robbo's been subbed by Platty, but the forward momentum we'd had didn't lessen as a result.

In the end we murdered Holland. The score? Nil f***ing nil. We even had the ball in the net twice. No justice. I was livid, but thankfully avoided a suspension by nearly getting booked again. What for? Arguing with the Yugo referee. I can't remember his name, but it was one of those that ended in "itch." I got the last laugh on him though, calling him a string of choice Yorkshire swear words that nobody but me understood.

At the final whistle, I ran over to their skipper – Ruud Gullit – as I wanted to congratulate him.

'Eh! Curly locks! Not so f***ing sharp, are you? Eh, I'm talking to you! I say you're not so f***ing clever as you think you are, you f***ing flash c***!'

He's come back with, 'Good match. You played well alsho.'

That type – trying to make you feel small by acting superior. It didn't work with me. Then, as we say up North, summat funny 'appened. As we swapped shirts, he's suddenly looked intrigued by my fine, straight hair – I'd forgotten to apply my Waxture Volumiser before kick-off – and asked if he could touch it. Too stunned to react, I let him.

'Feelsh lovely', he said.

Eh up. For a while afterwards I thought he was one of them. But it's alright – he turned out to be one of us. So why did he do it? Once again, the hairy Hollander was trying to make me look small. I vowed that if our paths ever crossed again, I would turn the tables. Little did I know that he would become my future team-mate and Boss at Chelsea!

I'd barely got into the changing room before Mister Robson's come in and given me a huge rocket for nearly getting booked again. Gratitude! I'd been a constant thorn in their side and that's all he could say. He didn't believe I could curb my temper, you see and feared I might earn a suspension, get sent off – whatever. I knew I couldn't curb my temper as well, but I knew something else even more. I knew how to get the best out of every situation I found myself in. There was no way I would stuff up with "glorious immortality"* at stake.

My heart leaped in the air with happiness when I looked at the team sheet for the all-important final group match against Egypt. With all four of the games so far having ended in draws we just had to win to qualify, so Mister Robson had picked me to start. Characteristically, he's had one of his name ricks and put Steve Bull's in place of mine, but I knew he meant me.

I was wrong. The Gaffer had gone with Bully. It was like being hit with a ten ton truck** or even a community property suit. Don't get me wrong – I had nothing against the player – Bully was a good lad and a talented footballer. But he was no Tristan Stephen Burkes. I phoned Dave Green, who immediately set a whispering campaign against Mister Robson into action. Then he set a whispering campaign in support of me into action. Then he really got going, whipping my personal sponsors into putting pressure on the England management. The result? Nowt. I suppose there's a limit to how much pressure firms like Harriet's Tea Buns of Harrogate can exert. Oh alright, my portfolio included much bigger companies as well, but it still didn't work. The fact is that I wasn't big enough – yet – to make any of the pips squeak.

Shattered, I sneaked out of the hotel wearing one of the many outfits inspired by legendary Doyenne of Disguise, Francis "Tanky" Smith*** and caught a cab into the city.

Once there, I had sex with a couple of bimbos, got pissed, stoned and had a lively colonic irrigation session – it was trendy then – all in the space of a couple of hours. And I also tried a couple of shots of the near lethal upper, "Espresso", a thick brown liquid you take from a small cup. You could get it all over Cagliari for just a few coins. Unbelievable.

---

*The phrase of – who else? – great BBC commentator Barry Davies.

**My friend Morrissey learned of this nightmare just as he went on stage in London. As a result, he dedicated probably his most famous number, Some Girls Are Bigger Than Others, to me. Thanks, mate.

***It was Gary Lineker who put me on to Tanky, a nineteenth century London policeman who went to live in Leicester – there's your connection – where he became one of the first private detectives in the country. You can check out his top sixteen disguises at Top Hat Terrace on London Road in that "lovely and fascinating" city.

Now here's a revelation which in its way is as big as some of the real blockbusters I've given you so far. After my little attempt at giving something back to myself was over, I was staggering around the back streets of Cagliari trying to find a cab back to the hotel when I knocked into someone who looked familiar. Oh-oh. This could be really bad news and I prayed that the disguise I was using would work at such close quarters.

'Hallo, Burksey', he said.

Bollocks.

Put yourself in my shoes. I know it's difficult, but try. Considering the state I was in, what kind of person would you have most wanted your victim to have been – apart from a blind match seller, that is? Whatever you chose, a journalist would come pretty close to the bottom of the list, wouldn't it? Well, that's exactly what I'd walked into. Shit. The story was going to be huge, probably the biggest to emerge out of the whole of Italia 90.

What a fool I was for thinking I could get away with behaving like that. And do you know why I thought I would get away with it? It was because I was a footballer; because I had plenty of money in my pocket; and because I was dressed as an Admiral of the Imperial Japanese Navy. Now I was really in trouble. Trouble? I was done for.

I knew the journo was the number one at his paper – the main sports writer – and he would have no trouble in running the story however he wanted. He looked me up and down and said:

'Okay, you're high, you're pissed and I'm not at all sure that you haven't had an accident in your trousers.'

As he risked an explosion by lighting a cigarette, he went on:

'Jesus, man – you've got more f***ing talent than...'

He could hardy carry on, exasperation written all over his face. But he finally gathered himself: 'Don't you realise what you're wasting? And don't you realise what you've just laid yourself open to? If the fun loving criminals you've just been with had recognised you, they could have blackmailed you, kidnapped you – anything.'

I hadn't thought of that. Looking as if it was dead against his better judgement, he continued:

'Look – don't you do anything like this again, promise to seek help and I won't file a word. Now do you make that promise?'

'I promise', I sobbed. 'Thank you. Thank you.'

'I'll be watching. And never tell a soul about this or we'll both be in trouble.'

With that, the journo's turned on his heel and disappeared into the crowd. With a great effort of will, I adjusted my braided hat, straightened my sword and followed him. Half an hour later, I was safely back at the hotel.

The name of this Guardian Angel? Even all these years later, I cannot reveal it. To do so would get him sacked on the spot. But I owe him massive. Frank Worthington made me; this journo – I'll just tell you that his surname begins with a letter from the first half of the alphabet – saved me. If you're reading this – cheers, mate. And I'm sorry that your offer to do a book with me later didn't work out. Hey, publishing – what can I tell you. Still, we did manage to get together on another project. More of that later.

That episode taught me a couple of things. It taught me that those at the top of their professions – the number ones – tend to be better people than the aptly named number twos that lurk below them. Mainly, it taught me never to be caught doing anything stupid again.

The story had a postscript which I'm even less proud of than the story itself. Much less. In fact it's so terrible that I wouldn't blame you for hating me ever after. I just ask you to bear in mind all the things that explain where I was at back then. What happened was this. When I've sneaked back into the hotel, I've walked straight into a friendly card school Shilts had organised by the pool. My outfit's raised a right laugh and, in larking about, I suddenly saw my chance. Yes, at last I was in the P.O.M.O. to do Gary Lineker. Wearing nothing but a pair of trunks, he was one of a group Gazza's press-ganged into chucking me fully clothed into the pool. As he's grabbed me, I've pressed the quick release button on my sword belt and let it drop.

The shriek and the blood stopped the horseplay immediately. I was already regretting my moment of madness when I looked down to check out the damage I'd caused. A second later, I felt roughly like I did at Maine Road after slotting that own goal. But a hundred times worse. The sword had found an unprotected toe alright – but it belonged to England skipper and my own club captain, Bryan Robson. Noooooo! What had I done? Fred Streete, one of the physios, was within earshot and we called him over sharpish. Good news – the injury wasn't serious. Bad news – Robbo would take no further part in Italia 90. I was so upset for the guy that I worshipped as a player and as a man that I broke down and sobbed for seven minutes – one for every digit of his squad number.

'Sorry, Robbo, I didn't mean to, I was trying to get Gary!'

'Trying to get Gary to stop messing about, I know, man. It's alright.'

I felt a hundredth of an inch tall. From that moment on, I vowed that no matter how desperately I wanted to play, I would never try to crock any of my team mates again. And here's one for you – I never did. Not even Fennichio Zul at Grappanese, the annoying little f***er.

The Egypt match finished one-nil to us, which meant we qualified top of the "Group of Eff", as Gary kept calling it. I came on right at the end, but I was still reeling from what I'd done to Robbo and had an off-colour few minutes. In fact, I felt as limp as the flags our fans were only allowed to drape in the stadium after the authorities had confiscated their flagpoles. But enough of that – we were through. That was the main thing. And I hadn't had a drink, a tup, an arse-loosener or a smoke since my day of shame in Cagliari.

Our home for the second round match against Belgium was a characterless business hotel near the gorgeous city of Bologna. Have you been there? With all the cheap flights they have now, I expect you might have. Those Two Towers they built in the city centre are wicked, aren't they? Although, as bookworm Terry Butcher said to me with a cheeky wink, you'd think they could have done a lot more to promote The Lord Of The Rings than that. I don't know why Tedge was winking, I agreed with him. And so would Tarka, who knew Tolkien's stories better than anyone. Where was Frodo? Where was Dildo? Where was Legless? Where were Elrond Hubbard and the Hubbardtones? See, this is where the Americans are so good. They really know how to promote stuff. If you put the Americans in charge of the Two Towers, the first thing they would do is demolish them – the one that's on the wonk looks dangerous to me in any case – and rebuild them in their own purpose-built park somewhere in the countryside. Then they would run a razor wire fence around the perimeter; fill the site with as many sets from the books as would fit; construct themed state-of-the-art rides that people would happily queue for hours to go on; build a miniature railway to link all the "experiences" together; and hire an army of out-of-work actors to dress up as the books' characters to bring the whole thing to life. Then, they would franchise several fast food outlets and other flagship service providers, add a team of ever-smiling, ever-perky Meet, Greet and Seat staff and the job's a good 'un.

Result? Everybody's happy and the local economy gets a much needed shot of dosh.

Despite the disappointment of "The Two Towers Experience", I was delighted that Bologna was our new home. I'd always loved spaghetti Bolognese and now that pasta had been scientifically proved to offer the professional sportsman the ultimate in nutrition, I was looking forward to shovelling as much of the stuff down my neck as possible. There was one disappointment though. The team doctor and physios had got wind of Pilch Fest 90 – everybody within about a square mile had to be fair – and banned any further eating competitions.

It was okay, really. We were in town on business. And now it was serious.

Pre-match preparations were going well and I thought I was in with a shout of starting against Belgium. It's ironic when I look back now. Platty was always staying behind after training to practise his ball skills and this particular day, I watched as he repeatedly tried – and failed – to bring off one of my specialities: the swivel and shoot on the volley in one continuous movement. I could see immediately what he was doing wrong in trying to copy me. Since Robbogate, I'd decided to be more expansive with my team-mates and I've gone over to Villa's would-be volley virtuoso and given him a couple of pointers. In a matter of hours, he was almost as good as me at the skill. Almost.

'Cheers, mate – I owe you one.' Did he ever.

Can you name three famous Belgians? I can – Enzo Scifo, Enzo Scifo and Enzo Scifo. "F*** off, Burksey," I hear you cry. "You've been mainlining Tasmanian Bat Shit again!" Yeh? Well, you haven't played against the bloke. I'm telling you, that night in the cute Stadio Rene and Renata in Bologna, it was almost as if there were three of him on the pitch. And it wasn't just his energy – his every touch caused us trouble. I came on for Barnsey fifteen minutes from time and up close, I was even more impressed by the future Torino and Monaco star. To keep him honest, I tried giving him a good braying a few times, but he skipped out of the way of my lunges like a cat on a hit tin poof.

Nil-nil at 90 minutes. The Boss marches on to talk us through extra time. Maybe his therapeutic embroidery work hadn't been doing its stuff as usual, because he's like a coiled spring when he comes over. Then he starts exhorting us to remember Don Kirk (whoever he is), Hagi Court (I think it's a block of flats outside Steaua Bucharest's ground), and the chain of American department stores, Marshall Field's Montgomery.

Eh? I was starting to wonder about the Gaffer but it seemed to work on the other guys almost as much as the military stuff had.

You all know what happened in extra time. With pens looming, Gazza's won a free kick and dinked it to the far post with perfect weight. With his back to goal, Platty's got on it, swivelled... and volleyed it perfectly past Belgian keeper Preudhomme for one of the most spectacular goals you could ever wish to see in such a tight situation. Watching him, I felt roughly like a diving coach must feel when his pupil executes a perfect triple barani for the first time.*

I was proud – but I wished it had been me doing it.

*You pick up all sorts of stuff if you date as many girls as I do. I don't know if you've ever had a diver, but the slippery little somersaulters are great in the sack. And so are their flick-flacking cousins, gymnasts. I had a trampolinist once. I can't remember her name, but her randy fliffis will live with me for ever.*

Sadly, Platty's never acknowledged the part I played in his career-making wonder-strike. But you will one day, won't you, David? Writing an autobiography is not as hard as you might think.

So, on we go! We said goodbye to Bologna and flew to Diego Maradona's adopted home, Naples, for a quarter-final tie against the "Brazil of Africa", Cameroon. We all loved our new hotel, perched high above the Amalfi Coast and I suppose it was about this time that I started to think what a great place Italy would be to live and to play football. The weather, the food, the girls, the clothes, the... well, just about everything I could possibly think of. As I sipped a straight Energade by the hotel's infinity pool, it crossed my mind that I might just look for a move away from Manchester United at some time in the not too distant future.

I didn't know it, but twelve hundred miles away, Mister Alex Ferguson was thinking precisely the same thing.

We were a great hit with the locals who found us approachable, friendly and fun – not what they were expecting (nor were used to with their own players, it has to be said). And of course, everybody loved Gazza. But I'll tell you something now. Just in pure football terms, the Eye Tie fans loved me every bit as much. Yes, although they were all devotees of the virtually sacred "Cat Knackers" defensive system – so called because you can barely see the gap between the buggers – it was my audacious and powerful attacking performances in the competition that was really pressing their pistachios. "Come and play for Napoli!" loads of them said to me. See – play in Italy – there it was again. Hmm.

I had other business first, though. World Cup business – for my country. And I felt confident about it. I was still off the sup and tup regime I knew wasn't good for me – well the sup part anyway – and my form was good. And our confidence as a squad was growing also. I think we all sensed big things ahead. Things as big as the trophy itself.

Now if I say the name "Wrighty" to you just like that, who's the first person you think of? I'll lay you six-to-four you thought of Arsenal's lovable livewire goal monster, Ian. I'll tell you something now – if you ask that of an Italian, a Brazilian or a German journo you might get a different answer. Why? Because quite simply, they regard the then Derby County's Mark Wright as one of the best defenders they've seen. I've already said that one of the reasons we were so successful at Italia 90 was that we played a sweeper. That would have meant diddly squat if the guy we'd used in that – for us – unfamiliar position was the wrong one. But Wrighty wasn't wrong. He was right. So right, he was eventually voted the best sweeper in the whole tournament.

The severe concrete bowl of the Stadio San Paolo in Naples is not a very pretty stadium*, but when the crowds come in, it catches fire like no other arena in the world. Come quarter-final day, we intended to toast the Cameroons on that fire. Bring it on!

They had Roger "King of The Road" Milla, Francois O'Mam "my How I Love Ya" Biyik, Cyrille "Car" Makanaky and they had other superb players. And they would need them if they were going to beat us. As it turned out, they almost did. The first half went by in a flash. They probably shaded it and we were really happy to go into the break with a goal lead courtesy of a Platty header. And so were our fans! What a great time they were having in Italy, by the way. Alright, they were herded around like cattle before games and left to make their own way after them – often after public transport had shut down for the night. And they were roughed up here and there and treated like war criminals by any official they came across. But hey, that's all part of the fun of being an England supporter abroad. One thing the fans don't mention is that they were often given free drinks by sympathetic journos. Buckets of booze were donated to them and to rival fans occupying bars nearby. Operation "Light The Blue Touch Paper", the Gentlemen of the Press called it, for some reason. See, that's the sort of nice thing people forget.

I went on for Barnsey – who was struggling with a knock – almost from the off in the second half and I must say, it wasn't an easy game to get into. Things weren't going our way and on 63 minutes, they equalised with a pen. Worse was to follow when Ekéké converted a Milla chip two minutes later. What happened after that was the most energy-sapping experience I'd had on a football pitch up to that point. I worked my socks off. I ran. I dribbled. I shot – hitting the bar twice with outrageous dipping benders. I even scored more or less from the corner flag with a deft outside-of-the-boot drifter that every fan and expert who witnessed it had to pinch themselves to believe. "It would have been the greatest goal ever scored in a World Cup match – no question about it," Jimmy Hill said. It was a view shared around the world. A little further down the Italian Peninsula, a gentleman by the name of Salvatore

*There are a few contenders for the honour of best looking football stadium in the world, I reckon. The Galpharm in Huddersfield and Benfica's Stadium Of Light are my faves. The new Wembley looks a bit special, too. And the shockers? There are some right shit-heaps in the lower leagues. But anywhere with a running track between the pitch and the fans gets the thumbs down from me. Take the Olympic stadia in Rome and Berlin. They generate about as much atmosphere as a wet weekend in Wakefield. No offence.

Palledure was so impressed, he decided to buy my company. But more of that later. Why didn't my wondergoal stand? A non-existent push was spotted in the box. Thanks Ref. W***er.

I kept working, working. But nothing paid off. I was practically dead on my feet when, with only seven minutes to go, I raced into the box on the end of a Mark Wright through ball and got tanked by Kunde, the guy who had slotted their pen. Now we had a pen of our own. Only one guy to take it – Gary. You'd put your wife's savings on him. He's slotted it perfect and we all breathed again. And felt renewed. Amazing what a goal will do. At ninety minutes, it was two apiece. Extra time. More military stuff amongst the usual formation talk and other tactics. To be honest, I didn't really listen. Why? How many times has a Mister Formation delivered a killer pass? Or a Mister Tactics scored a goal? Never. No, Reader, it's players that win games.

They continued to trouble us all through extra time and I started to get so tired near the end that I could actually see the pulse in my eyes beating. Then, with the whole pitch a vibrating mass of green, I watched as Gary's picked up a ball from Gazza and knifed into the box where he gets sardined by a couple of Cameroons. He goes down. It was a defo pen – a stonewall stick-on, twenty-four carater. And the Mexican referee's... given it! Yes! I fell to my knees on the pitch and knew we had won. Gary would score. Never mind that he'd just had six kinds of stuffing knocked out of him – I knew he would net. And net he did. F***ing lionheart. Rejuvenated once more, I picked myself up and got on with the game. We played out time. And finally... we were in the semi-final of the World Cup. Marshall Field's Montgomery would have been proud of us. From Shilts to Waddler, Des Walker to Gary, we'd given our all for the cause and won through. And none more so than Mark Wright. Bewitched, bothered and be-bandaged, the guy had been a giant.

Now for the hated Krauts.*

The Press fancied them. Telly and Radio fancied them. The neutral fans fancied them. And even one of our entourage – who will remain nameless – fancied them. Yes, in that way. F***ing freakshow.

Like I say, players of opposing teams have a lot more in common with each other than they do with supporters of their own team. But for reasons I hope are obvious,

---

*Whatever.*

that rule doesn't apply to the Krauts. We boys in white had come to Italy with a job to do and so far, done it we did. Now it was personal.

It has to be said that footballistically, the Germans were a great team. They'd qualified not just with the ruthless efficiency for which their nation is rightly noted – "vot dit you do in ze vor, Grendet?" – but by playing nice football. I particularly rated their skipper, Loathsome Matthäus and star striker Jürgen "High Board" Klinsmann. I've got a confession to make now. It's something I'm not proud of, but I may as well get it off my tits. I like Jürgen. Sorry, everyone. The fact is that I've played against him and met him several times since Italia 90 and I have to speak as I find. For a German, he's a really nice fellah. In fact, there's no way round it, I have to report that he's one of the nicest guys I've come across in football; full stop. For a while, I wondered if he really was a German. After all, I'd never once seen him eating curry wurst or trying to invade Poland. But the private detective I hired proved he was. Despite that, I had no alternative but to keep on bad-mouthing, ridiculing and blanking him – as you would with any Kraut. Now that I'm in a more mellow phase of my life, I would go as far as to say that I regret treating him that way. I'm pretty sure we could have become close mates – if he hadn't come from the country even their own people call the Farterland.

We were sorry to say goodbye to the sunny south as we decamped Alp-wards for the semi-final. Turin was our destination, home of The Old Lady, and the club she supports, Juventus. The Stadio Delle Alpi looked good on telly and it didn't disappoint in the concrete. We trained on the pitch and could just imagine what the atmosphere would be like with 60,000 fans in. We felt good, although the battered Wrighty was doubtful and so was Barnsey. Still, we had to remember Don Kirk. Apparently.

As the big day got closer, me, Gazza and Tony Dorigo decided to nip into the city just for a look-see. No booze. No birds. No nothing – just to "see what's going down" as my mate Spike Lee calls it. Well, we come across this tattoo parlour. Tony doesn't fancy it and goes off to do his own thing, but me and Gazza venture in. I'd been thinking about getting a tattoo for some time – now I have seven as you probably know – but I was still untouched by the artist's needle back in 1990.

After signing a couple of autographs – I added them to my mental total – and posing for about five hundred photos, we were finally shown some designs by Paolo the owner. First, Gazza's fancied an eagle flying across his shoulders. Then he's changed his mind and gone for a Ferrari coming out of his navel. Then it's a pair of love birds building a nest on his arm. Then ... you name it, Gazza wanted it. I didn't fancy any of those. The owner's taken Gazza on one side and left me with his assistant, Carlo. He suggests a few typical things, but wanting something a bit different from the norm, I didn't fancy them. A few more suggestions were made, but I didn't go for them either. I was on the verge of leaving Gazza to it when Carlo's said that if I fancied something really different, how about a "riga?" He got down a book and showed me a picture of a guy's c*** marked off in centimetres. The short and the long of it, if you catch me. Now I'm as forward thinking and as broad minded as the next man, but I'm also an old-fashioned traditionalist and I have to say that there was no way I was going to plump for centimetres. Inches for me!

It was going to cost extra – Carlo would need to make a template – but who cared. As always, I could afford it. It was a great idea to have a tattoo on your c***, I thought. For one thing, nobody but a few thousand women and my various team mates would get to see it. And for the vast majority of those, it would be on the dangle – roasting hadn't really come into football at that point.

Speaking of points, getting that tattoo was quite some experience. Before it began – Dave Green would have been proud of me – I said "no cameras". See, I was learning. A couple of years previous, I wouldn't have thought of that and my pr*** would have been splashed over every porno page and website in the world. For decency's sake, how Carlo did his work must remain a secret. I'll just say that it involved the talents of – let's call her "Maria" – who gave me a great bl** j** whilst Carlo got to work on my throbbing shaft. I wouldn't say it was an exciting experience but I blunted two of his needles.

So how many inch markers did the tattooist put on? Let's have a bit of fun, shall we? Maths time. If you take a centre forward's traditional shirt number, subtract the number of times Man United have won the European Cup, add the number of goals England scored when we won the World Cup in '66, subtract the number of defenders in a classic flat back line, then add... Are you still doing the maths? Crikey mate. Get a life!

Me and Gazza came out of Paolo's parlour well pleased with our new body artwork. In the end, Gazza's gone for a Panzer tank on his arse. With a triumphant English flag stuck right in the turret. Nice one, Gazza. Yes, we were well chuffed with our designs. Until they started smarting.

Match day was something else. We knew if we won, we'd be facing Argentina who'd put out the hosts in the first semi. On pens. We fancied beating the Argies, even though they had the genius of all geniuses in their ranks. All we needed to do was notch one more win and we were there.

Tension. Nerves. Smarting tattoos – all part of the big match experience. We had to have a re-shuffle – Wrighty moved up with Terry dropping back to sweep, and we had no Barnsey – a bitter blow. Another injury was more personally significant to me. The great Peter Beardsley, a player whose skills and whose telepathic understanding with Gary Lineker was respected and feared the world over, picked up a strange knock

A street of two halves. This is the "Poor End" of Sandringham Avenue, Crosland Moor, Huddersfield. I had to kick a lot of balls to move my parents onwards and upwards...

...to where they rightfully belonged – the "Nob End" of the street. How did Mum and Dad repay me for installing them as owners of "The Elms?" By disowning me

Spurs Ace Robbie Keane comes a cropper trying to imitate the dynamic climax to my three-stage goal celebration. He should have stuck to his usual naff forward roll and archer routine

Bound for glory! One of my childhood heroes, Skippy the Bush Kangaroo. It was his happy hopping that inspired the first stage of my goal celebration – the first to be copyrighted in football history

The calm before the storm. A minute later, Ossie Ardiles went into a hypnotic trance instigated by Yours Truly. It was one practical joke too far for Spurs Supremo David Pleat and I was shown the door. Thankfully, Mister Alex Ferguson was waiting for me on the other side

The morning after the night before. Page 3 Stunna Bobbi from Ormskirk tells all in the *Daily Scum*. Did I say Stunna? Bumma is nearer the mark

Bristol Rovers' Ian Holloway demonstrating his universal components. Or nearly.
And he wasn't the only one to wear dangerously short shorts back in the late 80's.
How did it all start? With me, of course, and a daft bet...

...I made with my three drinking amigos,
(from left) Robbo, Macca and Nasty, seen here with Sparky Hughes

My horror at scoring the infamous own goal at the start of the 1990 FA Cup
semi-final against Oldham was nothing compared to the rollocking I got from Fergie.
Straight from the kick-off my 'backpass' found the net to the incredulity of
Mike Phelan (left) and Jim Leighton (gk). That was my Old Trafford career over

But not before having to suffer the agony of missing out on a second FA Cup
Final in three years. This time it was worse as United won. Here Lee Martin
(whatever happened to him?) celebrates with the trophy. It should have been mine

The basket of shame Tarka and I found stashed away in a closet at The Elms. Our parents may as well have garrotted us with a rusty wire for all the pain it's caused over the years

The moment when England's World Cup dreams blew sky high. And I can now reveal that it was Chris Waddle's Pygobacaephobia which cost us a place in the final. That's me by the way, partially obscured by the ball

It's funny how everyone remembers Gazza's tears at the end of the semi-final – especially when you consider what he was really crying about! There's just a clue in this famous picture as you can see him clearly holding the top of his backside

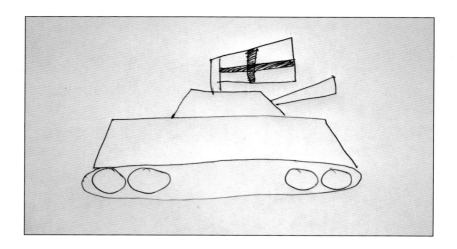

And here's an exclusive which I discovered when I was looking through all my 'shit'. Alongside my design for my c*** tattoo, I discovered the tattoo artist's original drawing of Gazza's Panzer tank. Now do you believe me?

The Grappanese went loopy over me when I signed for them in 1990. And the love affair continued. Here, a fan sports the "Burkes 36" shirt, celebrating my record haul of goals in a season. Over 20,000 of them were snapped up on the first day of sale

When Gazza and I frolicked in the Trevi fountain it was so widely reported that the next day a record number of lira were chucked in

Diego Armando Maradona certainly knew something about being a showman during his stay in Italy and I learned a lot from his stunts. And took them to the next level

A behind-the-scenes snap of me preparing to play the role of waiter in the TV Ad for Saponissima which caused so much discontent amongst the tifosi of Grappanese

| BISCUITS | WEEK 1 | WEEK 2 | WEEK 3 | |
|---|---|---|---|---|
| SUN | CAS | EELAND J | CRAIGY B | |
| MON | DIMMY | DOOBS | SHIP | |
| TUE | HOPPY | BURKSEY ~~FLETCH~~ | LE SOCKS | |
| WED | HITCH | GAU PEACOCK | WISEY | |
| THU | SINC | HOD | CAS | |
| FRI | WISEY | JOHN | | |

The Chelsea biscuit rota which caused me so many problems on my first day at the Harlington training ground. I should have realised that Hod the god wasn't joking

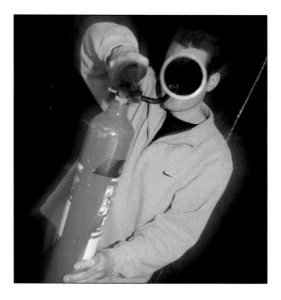

One of the photos from the infamous shoot the Police stage-managed to cover the tracks of the investigation into the whereabouts of Lord Lucan and Shergar

Football came home in 1996, but people still don't know the real stories behind the dentist's chair and Southgate's penalty miss. Until now that is

Euro '96. For laughs, German keeper Andreas Kupcake apes my heartfelt performance on Russ Morris' "Brass Knuckles" TV programme. The consequences of Kupcake's callousness were devastating – it led directly to our penalty miss that signalled our exit from the tournament

It was good to see Tony Blair in number ten as it meant a return to my valued Thatcherite principles of freedom of speech and choice. I was honoured when he invited me (just behind Mr Blair) and England manager Kevin Keegan to play head tennis with him at one of his excellent school open days

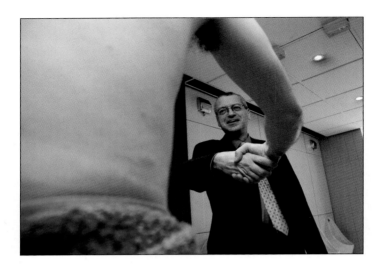

Goodfellas. Following a slump in which even Journo Giant Larry Harrison had written me off, a dazzling display against Leicester re-confirmed my status as "The Godfather of Goals." Here, I show my greatness by accepting the repentant reporter's apology

The plaintive jar of honey which symbolises the lowest point of my existence. Thankfully the story was then turned on its head by Deep Member to secure the Olympics for London in 2012

And some of the thousands of letters I received in HMP Calderton wishing me well

The only known photo of infamous recluse Mr Grady Speerman, owner of Sporting Meriden and my footballing saviour. Here he proudly stands outside the magnificent Can Gas Heart of England Stadium. I had to use the full measure of my wiles on Grady Speerman Junior's gorgeous wife Ellie, to prise this shot out of the family album!

Those British boys celebrate their boating Gold medals. But I ask you what has someone like Steve Redgrave ever really done for English sport?

He didn't for example, unlike me, contribute to bringing the 2012 Olympics to London, sparking a wave of hysteria unseen since VE day

in training – I honestly had nothing to do with it – and that meant that I was going to start just behind Gary. The King was, if not dead, at least crocked. So long live the king. And a king of England at that.

We started well and I think it surprised the enemy. We didn't let them play – not in a negative way, but by being quicker than they were in mind and body. Wrighty led the way, robbing Klinsmann several times with almost Bobby Moore-like tackles. Then we started to play a bit ourselves. After a quarter of an hour, Gazza did Brehme with a double drag back and he's pinged a ball across the box that was perfectly weighted for one of my trademark bullet headers. I got in front of "Coca" Kohler and rattled the crossbar with the goalkeeper nowhere. Other chances came and went and we thought we were unlucky to go in only level at half-time.

As soon as we hit the changing room, Gazza didn't sit down as normal, he's lay on his stomach instead.

'What's thah f***in' mattah, man?' says Waddler, never far from his mate's side.

'My f***in' arse is killin' us, like.'

Then Chrissie's clocked I'm pulling a bit of a pained expression, myself.

'And what's thah mattah with yous?'

'My c***'s sore. You see me and Gazza felt like... '

'Whoaah, what the f***in' 'ell's goin' on here!?'

'No – it's not what you think. We got tattoos done.'

'Thank f*** for that.'

I tell you, what goes on behind the scenes – you've no idea. But if you're thinking that Gazza's performance – or mine – was in anyway compromised by our smarting nether regions, think again. Gazza and me had been the best players on the park in that first half.

Mister Robson's come in and wasted no time outlining what he wanted from us in the second period. By the time he'd finished, we were confident we could do it. Why? As the Gaffer himself said:

'We'd harried them. We'd worried them. We'd stopped them. And we'd played beautifully ourselves. We could do it again in the second half. I was sure of it.'

All we needed was the rub of the green to make it through to the final.

Typical of football – just the opposite happened. On the hour, Shilts has been given no chance with a wickedly deflected free kick off Parks and we go behind. We still continue to create more than them, though. And then, with only ten minutes to exit time, a botched German clearance falls to Gary. He controls it with his thigh, sprints clear of the two screaming Stukas on his tail and shoots us level. A proper goal, not like their jammy effort. Yes! I was the first over to him. A magic moment.

At ninety, it was all-square once again. Extra time loomed.

Now, I don't know why I'm telling you this. You know it all already, don't you. Or do you? For the first time I will reveal what really happened in the two most remembered incidents in a match that has become part of all of our lives.

I'm sure you remember Herr Thomas Berthold. It was his Oscar job that earned Paul Gascoigne the booking that meant he would miss the final had we got through. Now don't get me wrong, Gazza was gutted and he did have every right to shed a few tears of disappointment. And that was the popular perception back home – that Gazza's blubbed because he was so devastated at missing out on the final. But there's more to it than that.

The simple truth is that in making the grass-burning lunge on Bertie Kraut Features, Gazza's skinned himself right on the tank turret, a sickener that would have brought tears to anybody's eyes. Yes, that was the main reason he broke down and cried. Have you never wondered how the Great Man could have played on as he did, totally committed, totally focussed, totally brilliant – if he had lost it as badly as everybody – including Gary "Have A Word With Him!" Lineker – thought? Doesn't add up, does it? No, if you want to find the real source of that torrent of tears, look no further than Gazza's arse.

Nobody except one lone amateur snapper in the crowd saw it*, but at the moment Gazza was booked, I let a few tears go myself. Why? Because my c*** was smarting? No. It was the thought of playing in the final without the man who had done so much to get us there. But do people talk about my tears? No, of course they don't. I'm not supposed to have any feelings.

The other incident I want to talk about occurred during the infamous penalty shoot-out. If you remember, Gary (powerfullly), me (cheekily), and then Platty (securely) – all scored before Pearcey's slightly scuffed his shot and their keeper, despite diving the wrong way, has somehow saved it with his legs. That made it 4-3 to them in the

*I have the photo in an album at home. Alas, it cannot be shown for legal reasons. And this brings me on to another gut-wrenching truth of my life. You will notice that none of the photos used in this book show my face. Why? Because I don't own my own image rights. It all stems from the moment when a fan asked me for an autograph some years ago and as always, I obliged. And how! By putting my moniker on that paper, I gave that "fan" complete control over all published images of my face for the duration of my football career. I wondered why he wanted me to sign in three places. Years later, Dave Green is still disputing the case in the courts, hopeful that one day I will get my face back. And the revenue that goes with it. Parasites? Tell me about them. F***ers.

shootout. We needed the great Waddler to step up and convert to put pressure on their last man. To give him a bit of encouragement as he's about to make the long walk to the spot, I've gone up to him and reminded him of a pen he'd taken that had nearly broken the net at The Lane when we were both players there.

As I said it I saw a look come into his eyes I didn't like. A look of fear. I shouldn't have mentioned the past. If I'd said the words "there's a piranha in your pants", I could hardly have done a worse thing. I know now that The Wad's walked up to the spot reciting the mantra his therapist had given him to get his life back on an upward track to try to cope with his debilitating Pygobacaephobia: "Aim high, Chris, aim high!"

Nooooooooo!!!!

So we were out. And whose fault was it? Mine. In a way. Okay, who's to say their last guy wouldn't have scored and we would have gone out anyway. We'll never know. But one thing we do know. Some have speculated that Chris's miss was caused by "the curse of the mullet". It's true that he'd had his famous style cut off immediately before the match. But since when did something as trivial as a haircut cause anything to happen in football? The idea is total bollocks.

I learned something that night. I learned that actions have, like, consequences? Who knows – Waddler may even have developed those distinctive sloping shoulders because he was always looking down to check his kecks. Whatever, I vowed never to subject a fellow human being to another practical joke as long as I lived.

Fat lot of good that did us at the time. We were the best team at Italia 90. I don't care what anybody says. We should have been World Champions. Instead, big, clinging German mitts lifted the trophy.

So that was it. Apart from a meaningless third place play-off game, England's Italian job was over.

For me personally, it was just beginning.

# CHAPTER TWELVE

# LA DODGY VITA

My wife Iona has read what's been written so far, sorry, what I've written so far, and has found the experience "fascinating, touching and funny". They don't waste words these TV presenters. Now Iona knows I've had a colourful past and that doesn't worry her – in fact if you're honest, it turns you on big style, doesn't it babe! But seriously, she reports being "appalled" by a lot of the language I've used in these pages. And she thinks it will appal a lot of the readers of this book. All I can say is – sorry, to you over-sensitive sugarplums out there, but swearing is the language of sport. I'll tell you something that we in the football community do that is amazing and is almost never commented on. When a bloke comes straight out of a changing room – or even whilst he's still walking off the pitch – and he gives an interview, how many times have you heard the guy let a swear word slip? Almost never. Even if he's been giving it the full Reidy the second before, suddenly, he's the Archbishop of Canterbury's maiden Aunt. I think that's classy. So come on you f***ers, credit where it's due.

I'd come back from Italia 90 with no medal, but I'd garnered huge kudos and interest. Because of my audacity and my technique, I'd always been a crowd pleaser. And I had long since gained entry to the most exclusive club in football – I was a player that other players love to watch. After Italy, you could add managers, chairmen and administrators in the very highest echelons of the world game to my ever growing list of admirers.

What was it The Barred* of Avon said? It's something like: "all the world's a stage and all the people are merely players." "Merely players", eh? He must have been an Elgin City fan**. But even when Huddersfield Town released me, I knew that I wasn't

---

*Just why the Prince of Playwrights was barred from using door-to-door beauty products I can't say. He certainly wasn't barred from the William Shakespeare Memorial Trophy Room at Sporting Meriden's Can Gas Heart of England Stadium. By the way, the sculpture of his bust – really just his head and shoulders – that adorns the Trophy Room was done by the multi talented former Half A Sixpence star, Julia Foster.

**I keep being told not to diss other professionals and clubs, but hey, that's all part of being in football isn't it? If it means I sell a few less copies in Elgin then I'll live with it.

just a mere player. I knew I could become one of the game's immortals. True –
I wasn't there quite yet. But I was knocking on the door. And as Dave Green told me,
"the door to success is labelled 'push'." Okay, so perhaps knocking wasn't what
I should have been doing there. But you get the idea – I'd nearly made it, but not
quite. Let's just say that I'd got as far as the door and I was about to get through it
– perhaps by a combination of knocking and pushing – and let's leave it at that. But
that's a side issue. It's not important.

What is important is to recognise how far I'd come in such a short time. And how
much I'd learned. Shit, when I first went to Tottenham, I thought Bagels was a First
World War fighter ace. Alright, I'd stuffed up here and there and done a lot of things
I shouldn't. But we're all going to die sometime, so who cares*? Seriously though,
I knew I'd learned some things, but there was still a lot left to learn out there. And I'm
not just talking about football formations and the like. I'm talking about something
that most of us participate in every day – life.

Eventually, my third wife, Brandee, would teach me the most important lesson I ever
learned – apart from never sign a pre-nuptial agreement, that is. No, she showed me how
to grow as a person by forgiving myself for the numerous problems I'd caused others.
See, she understood something fundamental about me that nobody else had. What was
my basic problem? I didn't love myself enough. That's why I, like, behaved as I did?

*Yes, we can't live for ever, can we? So may I take this opportunity to recommend
Shadygladelawn Funeral Homes to you? Two modes of service are offered; one traditional, one innovative. The 'Heritage' service is available at any of Shadygladelawn's
network of established, local family-run outlets, each one pledged to provide caring,
personal attention twenty-four hours a day. With 'The Heritage', your hour of need will
be forty-eight minutes you will cherish for ever.

The 'New Horizon' service is an entirely new concept in post-living care. Beautifully
landscaped 'Like Life Parks' will shortly be opened in which our non-living clients will not
be hidden away like treasures in so many safety deposit boxes. Instead, they will benefit
from the outdoor non-life. Yes, each will be displayed as they lived – in a variety of
personally relevant attitudes and poses. These could include gardening, windsurfing or
limbo dancing. The choice is yours. And there's more. A range of tailor-made animation
packages means that good old Grandpa could still ride his Harley, cut a rug, or even
catch that salmon! With the 'New Horizon', Shadygladelawn puts the fun into funeral.'
Note: Shadygladelawn Funeral Homes is a brand of the Stelsat Corporation of America.
All rights reserved.

I suppose I'm saying all this here because when I came back from Italia 90, I was on what astronomers call "the cups" – the division between two segments of life. Yes, as I got off the plane, I found out that I had been transfer-listed by Manchester United Football Club. Like I say, I was fancying a move, but it's one thing to jump, another to be pushed. I was gutted, but determined to put a brave face on it, I imme-diately got smashed, laid and went paintballing – it was trendy then.

But who was going to come in for me? The answer was just about everybody who needed a star striker. My performances at Italia 90 had hiked up my price and, thanks to my Guardian Angel keeping his word, my reputation as a bad boy had lessened as well.

But who to go for? Me and Dave Green surveyed the options like a couple of punters checking out the talent in a Turkish Knocking Shop – not that we've ever done that – and came up with a shortlist of exciting possibilities. Of course in those pre-Bosman days, Manchester United could sell me more or less to who they wanted, but I have to say that they were very fair about seeking a deal that was good for us both.

Whilst we're on this topic, do you remember me saying early doors that if there was a vote for Man Of The Millennium, I'd go for Pelé? Thinking about it, Jean-Marc Bosman is a stronger candidate really, isn't he? Just think what this guy has done for the most important people in the great game of football – players and agents. He's set us all free. Free from the tyranny of the bosses. Free from the shackles of pre-historic contracts that sought to bind us to clubs like mere employees. Free to enjoy playing in European competitions with unlimited numbers of foreign team-mates. Free to attract colossal signing-on fees, salaries and other monies. Actually, when you really think about it, Man Of The Millennium isn't a big enough accolade for this man. He should be sanctified. Jean-Marc Bosman – Patron Saint of the Modern Day Footballer. Pelé – I'm still your man!

But back to my transfer from United. Club Chairman Martin Edwards sent me a copy of one letter that registered the writer's interest in signing me and I'll never forget it. It came from Radcliffe Rockets FC and was signed by first team skipper, nine year-old Darren Braithwaite. The Rockets had been struggling lately he said – they'd lost their last game seven-nil against Besses O' The Barn Under Eights – adding that if I joined them, they all thought that they might at last score a goal and maybe even win a match. They couldn't pay me anything, but the goalie's Dad ran a sweet shop and free Midget Gems were a defo possibility.

The letter raised a smile. A week later, I turned out for the Rockets in a specially arranged match. As sub. With fifteen minutes to go, the boys were losing eight-nil to a Whitefield Church Lads Brigade XI when manager Kevin Braithwaite signalled for the Rockets' starting centre-forward to come off for me. An expectant buzz has gone round the crowd. All except for the departing player's dad. He's gone mental, shouting at the coach: "Eh! My Mikey's the best f***ing player on that park! Why don't you hook that spas Colin? The little f***er's useless!"

Can you believe it? Imagine having a father who cared that much about his son's football. I tell you, I envied the stripling striker as he's trotted toward me, eager to high-five his famous replacement. As Mikey Senior has entered into a free and frank exchange of punches with the outraged father of the useless Colin, I run on and for a moment or two and have a spot of bother scaling my game down. After a couple of mistimed tackles – sorry boys – I get the feel of the thing and the Rockets eventually run out 13-9 winners. It was a great afternoon out. I signed 687 autographs, had all the midget gems I could eat, posed for countless photos, kissed scores of older sisters, mothers and even grandmothers – one of whom was a right fit sort, by the way – and everybody was happy. Especially Dave Green, who had organised great press and media coverage for the game.

To bring the afternoon to a close, I gave away shed loads of kit and shit and finally, presented the secretary of the North Manchester Junior Football League with a healthy cheque. Then, just as I was paying off the lads I'd hired to keep an eye on my Jag, a reporter comes up to me from *The Daily Sick Bucket*. With two scumbag photographers aiming their cameras at me, he says:

'Too bad you don't pay more attention to your own son.'

For a split second, I didn't react. And it was a good job for that reporter that I didn't, because it gave Dave Green, who was standing a couple of paces away, time to jump on me. He's only a little bugger, but he'd worked in the Stock Exchange, so he knew how to put himself about a bit. Seeing his boss react, his minder, Errol, has followed suit and it was him that saved the reporter's bacon. Errol's a lovely lad, but at six-foot six and twenty-two stone, the former powerlifter's one serious piece of real estate. He's also got a grip like a JCB and I couldn't shake him. The Scumbags got a picture. But they didn't get the picture they were wanting. Then Dave, who was hanging on my back like a human rucksack, has grabbed my keys, Errol's bundled me into the back seat of the Jag, and seconds later, we've merged into the traffic on Ainsworth Road.

'Sorry if I hurt you', says Errol, re-waxing my hair.

'You should have those hands of yours registered as offensive weapons', I say, still feeling their impression around my torso.

'They are, man', he replies, producing a right Ray-Ban buster of a smile. As a mood lifter, it wasn't a bad thing in its own right, but accompanied by the sort of high-pitched giggle that only dogs can usually hear, the whole effect was so joyful, it really changed the atmosphere in the car. Errol Grey – the man should be available on the National Health. Just don't introduce him to any women you're hoping to impress. Then he gets on his mobile and calls for a cab to meet us at a garage just outside Farnworth. The guy is there when we pull in and he takes the boys back to Radcliffe to pick up Dave's car. Agents – they're brilliant I'm telling you. I drove home to Hale, turning over the incident in my mind like a washing machine turns over clothes. What came out in the wash?

One thing I knew already was that if you're a star, you must never stuff up in any way.

Why? Because the M.W.L.T.D (Men With Like Teensy Dingalings?) will get you. Yes, I reckon Brandee was on to something there because, believe me, muckraking journos must be compensating for something. They're certainly not normal human beings. They're not interested in the good, kind, fun, spectacular or brilliant things that we do. They are only interested in the shit. The shit that we cannot avoid producing because we are animals. Animals with elementary canals. Let me tell you something – scumbag scandal scroungers are not as good as animals. They are parasites. Parasites who eat, breathe and think shit.

It's funny what you remember. I came off the M56 that lunchtime and, desperate to get home as quickly as I could, got stuck behind an estate car on Hale Road. It was one of those stately Swedish galleons whose drivers never go a mile an hour over the speed limit even if there's nothing ahead of them on the road – you know the type. After several metres of frustration I'd had enough, so I scream up its arse flashing and air-horning. The thing doesn't shift, so I have to force it onto the pavement to get past. Then the driver flips me the bird as I pull away! Unbelievable. If the woman had wanted different treatment, she should have stuck a "Baby On Board" sticker on her tailgate. Then I would have driven at a quiet, sensible distance behind. No sense of responsibility, some people.

Speaking of which, some of you may be wondering about the remark that provocative scumbag made after the kiddies match in Radcliffe. Was I an absent father to my son? Of course I was. Although you may have read differently in Roxanna's ludicrous magazine piece on the subject, that's the way the Ginger Whinge wanted it. Wanted it from the moment Frankie was born. It wasn't until quite a bit later that I was allowed to take more of an active role in his growing up. How active? I haven't got the exact figures in front of me, but eventually I kept a good percentage of my available C.A.R.P (Charities And Related Projects) window open for the young sprog. Even when it wasn't convenient. Which was all the time, really.

As we're on this area, many journos and other commentators have dissed me over the years for not visiting more sick children in hospital, becoming directly involved in African aid projects or other similar schemes closer to home. They've spotted that

I do give money – hey, thanks guys – but also that I almost never turn up in person to places like Great Ormond Street, Burkina Faso, or Hackney. It's true that the vast majority of the game's so-called "pampered" and "selfish" stars give a lot of time and energy as well as dosh to these kind of things* – you'd be surprised – and I applaud them. So why don't I? The simple truth is that I am far too sensitive a soul to do it. I'm telling you, if I see a sick child, it upsets me for weeks. And that does nobody any good. So yes, I align myself with those few players who never do anything one-on-one to help people worse off than themselves. But think of this as well – those "worse off than myself" means just about everybody on the planet. And I couldn't help everybody out. Who am I – Superman?

Of course, I too was to fall victim to life's vicissitudes. And did anybody reach down to help me? Well, eventually they did, yes. But I'd visited Hull, Hell and Halifax first. But more of that later.

Which club to play for? I decided to follow my instincts and see if the Boggle frame had anything to reveal, I Ching-style. Don't know what Boggle is? Look it up on a website, I can't be bothered explaining it. Anyway, with such an important decision to make, I prepared myself properly and shook up the letter cubes whilst repeating the mantra, "who shall I go and play for?" As they settled into their cavities like so many false teeth, I looked down at them intently, looking for a clue, a sign, an answer. Here's how the frame fell out:

ARSENA

FORBUL

BESKRA

UYNOWR

LCEHTE

So no help there. But shortly afterwards, I got the sign I needed. Permission was granted for legendary Italian club director Salvatore Palledure to talk to me and I was sold on the idea of playing for his club, AC Grappanese, in five minutes flat. Based in

---

*For all you cynics out there, they do it when there are no cameras around as well.

129

the southern city of Grappa, the Traspareneti* were going places and lacked only one thing – a top striker. Signor Pipi – as he was known to all and Sunderland in his native Italy – thought I was that man. I was surprised that they wanted me in Italy, in a way. Not because of my football itself – I was a smash with the tifosi like I said before. The problem was the live TV interview I had done in Sardinia – the one following Pilch Fest 90 – which had left a bad smell. I still felt the Eye Ties loved me, mind you. But I suspected it was a love most of them were content to experience at a distance.

I needn't have worried. Sig. Pipi assured me that by so crudely dissing Sardinia – according to him "the land of sheep sh***ers and motherf****rs", – I'd made myself an instant hero with the Grappanese. Italians – don't you just love them?

Although I was keen on the idea, I needed to know more, so Dave Green mounted a feasibility study, sending a crack team of accountants, marketing people, style consultants – oh and a football bloke as well – to Grappa. Their findings? Yes – it was the right move for me. It would be strange to be separated from Dave, but he would always be no more than a mobile phone call away. And he could be in Grappa in less than three hours. Spooky, eh? There I was just a week or two previously thinking how cool – or hot – it would be to work, rest and play, not on Mars, but in Italy and now here was an opportunity to do just that. And if I needed an extra nudge to push me on to that plane to sunny Italy, the business with the Paparazzi at Radcliffe had provided it. Yes, I was through with England. Let the good times roll. Grappa, here I come!

But first, I had a farewell party with my United team mates. Some of them had been with me for three years at Old Trafford and I would miss them. And as for Captain Marvel, the man I'd nearly crippled in Cagliari? I would miss him most of all. I really looked forward to our future England get-togethers.

Talks with my new club took place at the Paris Hilton and the second my name went on to that contract, I doubled my weekly wages on the spot. The seven million pound transfer fee itself was subject to all the usual terms and conditions, but there was a huge surprise when the moment came to hand over the cheque. Grappanese's negotiator, the curly haired and swarthy** Punto Calbanetto opened his briefcase and took out the entire sum in cash. Edible gasps came from United's side of the table. 'There is a problem?' Sig. Calbonetto's smile faded quicker than a sliced drive.

---

*I'm told that the team's nickname is a sort of joke relating to the colourless grape brandy that shares its name with the city. Thanks to my mate Stephen Fry, for that.

**From now on, just assume that all the Italians I talk about are curly haired and swarthy. Although a surprisingly large number of them aren't.

'Erm, I don't know', says the United representative. 'No, I don't suppose there is.'

The Calbonetto gnashers are switched back on, the money is exchanged, hands are shaken all round and I am officially a Grappanese player. Gianni Calbonetto, one of Punto's sons, is appointed my personal liaison officer and so the adventure begins.

News of my impending arrival hit Grappa like a hurricane. For everybody's safety, a huge security operation was mounted. With a grin, Gianni tells me that the arrival of only one other footballer in the history of the region had created such a fuss. Polish goalkeeper Karol "Pope John Paul II" Wojtyla must have been quite some player.

The days before I was due to be presented at Grappanese's Fango Cotto Stadium are ones I'll never forget. To draw some of the Paparazzi and fans away from me, the club recruited a squad of "Burksey-alikes" from the local population to roam around the place impersonating me. To be honest, most of these laddos looked nothing like me, but a few – the 'A Team' – were really authentic. And well trained. These elite Burkseys were sent into the most popular spots around town and drew huge crowds. I even saw one of them interviewed live on telly. Subtitled for the locals, it made interesting viewing:

'Burksey, it is so wonderful having you here in Grappa. What do you think of the place so far?' asked gorgeous presenter, Lucetta Strabalone.

'By Gum, Bimba. I'm fair over t'moon wi't' job', the Eye-Tie "I" replied.

'What do you think you can bring to the team?'

'That's a brainteaser, Carissima. Come down to t'stadio and see for thissen.'

'I will. Who are you most looking forward to playing with?'

'Are you doing owt later, bella?' I tell you, this lad was getting me off to a T.

'Flirting! I think you are an honorary Italian!'

'If t'cap fits, wear it, no?'

'Seriously.'

'Seriously, I'm right made up wi' winger Florian Mirandola. Centrocampista Ivo Zaccherini's a belter, and t'skipper, Nando Corvopone's real, an' all.'

'And your fellow striker, Fennichio Zul?'

'We'll see,' "I" said, seemingly unconvinced.

Too good, this boy. My first impressions of Zul were that he was a jumped-up one-trick pony with a huge ego. However, the volatile* crowd didn't seem to share

---

*Thanks once more to that walking encyclopaedia, Stephen Fry. By the way, his rubber-faced gagster colleague – Hugh Laurie – once did the same kind of boating as Sir Steve Redgrave. See, that's the kind of people who go in for it. They'll be giving out gold medals to people who can beat Dawn French at Twister next.

"my" reservations and voiced their displeasure. But the laddo doing me hadn't finished yet.

'Yes, we'll see just how magnifico Nico is in t'flesh. I've been fair bowled over by his performances on t'box, Dolcezza.'

At that, the crowd's roared its approval and began to push forward even more. Lucetta gets a message in her earpiece and calls the interview to an end:

'Well, we're all excited at the thought of seeing you in action. Long live Burksey and long live Grappanese!'

'Si! Viva! And so long, Lucettina.'

You couldn't make it up, could you? I wondered if the lovely Lucetta knew that the "Burksey" she'd been interviewing wasn't the real one. She couldn't have been much of a football fan if she didn't. A few days later, I asked Gianni about it as we helicoptered over the city on our way to my presentation to the fans at the Fango.

'Lucetta's one of ours, don't worry.'

'She's a Calbonetto?'

'In a sense, yes. She started out as a Happy Haddock Girl at the stadium and let's just say we helped her move up.'

'Happy Haddock?'

'Si, Happy Haddock – *Merluzzo Contento* in Italian – is the club sponsor.'

'Right. Well, that could come in handy – I love fish.'

'So do we, my friend. It's handy as you call it for us to have things coming in through the docks, no?' said Gianni, tapping the side of his nose and raising one eyebrow.

'I suppose so.' Hmm. Bit of a different carry on from Old Trafford this, eh? Still, that was all part of the fun of being here. Tarka was coming over in a couple of weeks and I couldn't wait to get him up to speed with things.

I'd never flown in a helicopter before and I must admit I was a bit nervous. Italians drive like maniacs even in those little three-wheeler van jobs. Give them a chopper to play with and there could be some real excitement. I wondered if wearing a track suit over my new kit was the way to go, but my bowels held firm as we soared over the city.

I guess I was also a bit nervous about the occasion. There was still a month to go before the start of the season and so I wasn't being introduced to the crowd at half-time during a match. There might be no bugger in the stadium to greet me. We were over the bay now and it was an astonishing sight. Heat hung over the perfect ultramarine water like a diaphanous blanket of gold. I risked looking straight down. It was a f***ing long way. But then, shimmering on the horizon, I saw the giant upturned rim of the Fango Cotto, the white concrete bowl where

I would soon be strutting my fortnightly stuff. The rim seemed to be floating above the stadium somehow; shining through the mists of time like Dildo's ring, lit from within by the promise of a bright new future. One ring to bring them all. And in the Fango bind them. Soon, I too would be bound, bound indissolubly to my new team mates in a quest for our holy grail – the Scudetto, the Italian League Championship Trophy.

'How many do you think will be in?' I asked as Gianni snorted a line of coke. Hey, what the guy wanted to shove up his conk was no concern of mine.

'How many will be in ..? *Phhttt.*'

'The stadium.'

'Sixty-five thousand. *Phhttt.*'

'No, not the capacity – how many will be in today – to see me?'

'Sixty-five thousand.'

I couldn't believe my ears. And then I couldn't believe my eyes as the stadium hove into plain sight. The place was heaving. Descending into that bowl out of the serenity of a clear blue sky was like being lowered into a boiling cauldron of noise and colour. And it was all for me. To say that the crowd was excited when they saw me emerge from the chopper would be a classic bit of English understatement. The understatement we do better than anybody. What the crowd actually did was go stark raving balls-on-fire crazy.

As a brass band strikes up *On Ilkley Moor Baht 'At* – or it could have been *Sugar Sugar* by The Archies, it was a bit difficult to tell – Gianni leads me to a red carpet laid on the touchline opposite the directors' box. There, amongst others, I shake hands with some ageing ex-player or other*, a young kid**, and some guy in a suit with a chain around his neck***. Then I wave at the crowd as we head off towards a raised dais set-up in the centre circle where club director Sig. Salvatore Palledure, the other members of his Board, and a bevy of Promo Girls are waiting to formally welcome me to the club.

'He looks pleased to see me', I say to Gianni, having to shout even at close quarters.

'They were going to slit his throat and hang him from a meat hook if he hadn't signed a *giocatore bravissimo* before the start of the season. That's probably why.'

'Fancy.'

---

*Former Grappanese Great, Gianfonso "Gi-Gi" Guantocaldo.

**Grappanese Academy Player of The Year, Roberto Ingrato.

***His Most Esteemed Mayor of the City of Grappa, Ercolano Cazzata.

The casual insouciance of my remark seemed to impress Gianni. But I'd seen it all before. I reckon that the British Press were an even bigger bunch of cut-throats than their Italian colleagues. But time would tell. Back to the action.

I look toward the dais where, already, the barrel chested Padrone has got up from his throne and is standing with arms extended toward me. The crowd noise ratchets up a further couple of gears as I extend my arms to him. Well, it seemed rude not to – even though there were still a good thirty yards to walk. Then Signor Pipi does an excited little jig. I follow suit. Then he starts punching the air. I do the same. Now the stadium's exploding.

Then I have a brainwave in my head. I do sometimes. Assessing that there was about fifteen metres to go to the dais – just enough room to perform my crowd-pleasing goal celebration – I decide to go for it. The tifosi duly explode as, arms still outstretched, I bound kanga-style into the pirouette and splits. They erupt still further as I spring on to my head for the skull spin climax. But, if ever there was a time to add a variation, this was it. Still below the level of the dais, I shoulder-flip into a running forward somersault that takes me well above the level of the platform party. In mid air, I have just enough time to unzip the track suit and jettison it before I come to land in a kneeling, head-bowed posture at the feet of Signor Pipi. For the first time, the ecstatic crowd see that I'm wearing the black and orange stripes of their beloved club. It was quite a moment – a gladiator paying homage to his Caesar dressed as a humbug. Me – not the Caesar. I hold the pose as giant blowers sited either side of the dais blast a moving mountain of black and orange tickertape into the air as the club's anthem *Taglieremo Le Sue Balle* (trans: 'We'll Cut Off Your Balls' – obviously Grappanese were a side with a strong defensive tradition) rend the air at rock concert levels through the stadium's PA system. The result of all this? An outpouring of emotion never before witnessed at any football ground anywhere, any time. Amongst the falling paper, I can feel Sig. PiPi's tears raining down on my head as he bellows hysterically, "My son, my son!" Then, as he's lifted me up by the shoulders to kiss me on both cheeks, I see that behind him, the other Board members are all screaming as well; at least two of the "Happy Haddock" Promo Girls are having orgasms; and my new friend Gianni is pinching himself and casting a quizzical eye over the stuff he's just snorted.

The scene was complete. Or so I thought. At that moment, the sky suddenly went ominously dark. I look up to see a Grappanese flag the size of the Isle Of Man floating over the arena. Then seemingly from nowhere, a team of sky divers burst through it from above. Linked up to spell "Welcome Burksey" in English and Italian, they pull their ripcords and land in a perfect circle around the dais. Magically, the flag floats down after them, unerringly draping itself over the entire stadium as it finds its final landing place.

More than sixty-five thousand Grappanese gathered together under the club's battle standard – it was an awesomely uniting experience, I can tell you. Later, it was reported that the words "Merluzzo Contento" – Happy Haddock – were clearly readable from the fathomless infinity of Space.

One flag to bring them. And in the Fango bind them.

Nifty start, eh?

There's that English understatement again. Really, it's a form of lying, isn't it? So it would be wrong of me to downplay things. To state it baldly, my spectacular performance at the Fango that afternoon made me an instant hit, an instant star, an instant legend of the club. Yes indeedimo. And I hadn't even kicked a ball yet. Maybe Ian Rush should have tried something similar when he arrived at Juve. Still, I'm sure those who turned up enjoyed his riveting demonstration of keepy-uppy. It was good. Really, it was.

Dave Green was made up with me. Footage of my arrival was sold around the world and a whole new raft of sponsors began melting his mobile trying to get a piece of me. My profile had shot through the roof quicker than my Grandma back in '66 and suddenly, I was in more demand than a good-looking secretary at FA Headquarters. It was mental. My face was wanted everywhere. Dave immediately dispatched his most trusted Personal Assistant, Jehanna, to deal with the day to day running of my new life "in sit you" and I welcomed the luscious lesbo – yes, it was one of the tragedies of my life that the exotically beautiful "Jay" was a muff buff – with open arms.

I picked her up at the airport in my new Maserati – a gift from my adopted "Papa", Sig. Palledure – and drove her back to "Aston", the name I'd given to the Villa I was living in. Everybody thought that was great joke. I'd never been so popular!

Actually, it's quite an interesting story how I got the place that became my home for the next three years. Dave's Estates and Property people had tried to buy me a house in the area, but they had been told in no uncertain terms to forget it – Grappanese would find me "a little place". A little place that would cost me precisely... nothing. Jesus, I thought, what sort of cockamamie cottage were they lining up for me? But when I saw the cottage in question, a luxurious fourteen room villa overlooking the Bay of Grappa, I was beside myself. And it was another kindness on behalf of the club that I really appreciated. One thing was absolutely clear about my new friends, neighbours, colleagues and bosses – if they liked you, there was nothing they wouldn't do for you.

Jay organised so many "calls" for me that I thought fitting it all in wouldn't be easy. Pre-season training was about to start. Still, I knew that wouldn't be as demanding as the hard physical graft I'd been used to. You could tell by the skill levels of all Italian teams that the accent would be on ball work and not on running as it was back home.

I turned up at La Porta, our maximum security training facility hidden high in the hills above the city, feeling great about everything. As Sig. PiPi's adopted son – virtually – nothing was barred to me in and around the city. If I earned a speeding ticket – no mean feat in Italy – that ticket would be torn up. If I parked where I shouldn't – ditto. And if I wanted something, whatever it was – it was mine. Usually free of charge. One time I joked that I felt like a sandwich made with Cumberland Sausage from G.G. Garnham's in Penrith. It arrived six hours later. And f***ing fabbo it was, too!

And tup? Boy, did I suffer from beaver fever that first few weeks. It would have been handy to have had a turnstile installed in the bedroom doorway. The old riga was up and down like a Friday flitting and I almost wore away a couple of the markings.

Things were sweet on the drug front also. It was still early days for me, but if I fancied a smoke or a line or two, all I had to do was ring up Gianni and he would have the stuff brought round by scooter. It was just like ordering a takeaway. Except there was never an extra onion bhaji.

And speaking of food – my God. You think Leonardo Da Vinci Code was a great genius? You think Michael Angelo was a bit of an old maestro? Go down any back alley in Grappa and you will find far greater artists at work. From young girls to Grannies, these people can cook, brother. What they can do with sheep brains, bull bollocks, cow ears, pig tails – is quite indescribable. And that's on top of all the fish, pasta, pizza, garlic, peppers, onions.... On and on. Oh, and do you like ice cream? You've never had it unless you've had it in Grappa. The best way to sample it is *"Su Le Tette"*, where they dollop the stuff on to a bimbo's nipples. Believe me, there's nothing to compare with the sensation of licking a couple of chocolate coppas off a pair of big bronzed buppies. And there are other interesting variations as well. Aah, La Dodgy Vita!

Yes, I pulled into the car park at La Porta for that first day of training more completely satisfied with life than I'd ever been before. Of course my demons were still all there lurking beneath the surface. But hey, that's the way it goes.

My new team mates – ninety percent Italian interestingly enough – greeted me warmly and I felt pretty much at home from the word go. Fellow striker Nico Zull was just about the only one to remain a loofah, but that didn't worry me. It was his loss. Besides, if I got upset, I could always cry on the shoulder of the eighteen year-old beauty I'd got lined up for my evening session. This kid was so cute, she made Bambi look like Shrek, I'm telling you.

In sweltering ninety-degree heat, I jogged slowly out on to the pitches with the guys, swapping terms for the male and female anatomies in our respective languages – just the same as had happened at Spurs and Man U. Like I say, I didn't want to lose my Yorkshire identity, so I made a big effort to forget all the Italian words. With my steel trap of a mind, it wasn't easy, but I managed it straight away.

The most notable aspect of this first training session was that I would at last be meeting the Grappanese Gaffer, ex-Serie A star defender, Carlo Strozzato. He had been away on holiday and looked delighted to meet me in the flesh. We shook hands. I looked him over. He seemed relaxed. He smiled a lot. He was friendly. Good, right? Wrong. I could see it was all a front. Unlike just about everyone else I'd met in Grappa, Mister* Strozzato's one-man jury was still out on yours truly. Through Gianni, he congratulated me on my "triumphal entry into the Fango", but I could tell that it hadn't impressed him one little bit. The mouth smiled, but the eyes told a different story. They were cold as ice. And twice as sharp.

I proved to be right about Mr. Strozzato. He turned out to be just about the hardest bastard I've ever come across – before or since – in the world of football.

Any thought I had that training was going to be a ball-juggling kick around went right out of the window when we warmed up. Everything was measured, scientific. Moves were stop-watched and precisely controlled. I knew if the warm-up was like that, training proper would be equally regimented.

It was. And bugger me, there was a big accent on fitness. Ever done sprint interval training? It's a killer. After several sets of really hard reps, I was sick. There was still a full set to go and I was barked at for my pains. And of course meanwhile, my fellow striker, Nico Zul, is bombing up and down like a Scouser looking for a lost giro. The f***er.

The thing went on in the same gut-churning way until, finally, it came to what can only be described as a merciful end. I was wrecked. Through Gianni, I was told by Strozzato that he'd never witnessed such a poor session from a professional footballer. From any division. "Was this what the club had paid a record fee for?" He made it clear that I would have to shape up or I wouldn't get the opportunity to show off my famed goal celebration for real. Nico Zul particularly enjoyed that last remark as he swaggered off to the showers. I felt like doing the little c*** big style, but thought better of it.

I hadn't found my feet yet and didn't want to rock any boats or I might be skating on thin ice. Now wasn't the time to push any envelopes. Although if I did, I knew exactly where I would like to push them.

*Because their language is difficult to pronounce, Italians call managers 'Mister'. They use loads of English words, actually: Spaghetti. Incognito. Austin Allegro, etc.*

Hmm. As my dear Auntie Vi used to say, "There's always a serpent in Paradise, love. And two-to-one, it'll be a greasy little foreign job."

Here's a revelation for you. I was so knackered after training that I had to send home that little eighteen year-old I'd lined up for later. Sacrifices? You've no idea.

Training the next day had a different focus, but it was still very tightly regulated. I was really surprised by all this. At least I was only sick once this time. Whilst I was barfing, it dawned on me that burning the candle at both ends was part of the problem I was experiencing and I decided there and then to slow down in the bedroom, at the table and on the dance floor. And by the pool. In the gardens. Etcetera.

My burgeoning media career, though, was a different story. My first really important gig happened a couple of days before our opening game against despised rivals S.S.C Napoli*. Jay booked me on to the popular TV programme *Che Buffo!* (trans: "What fun!"). I tell you, you've never seen anything like this show in your life. It was unreal.

My "spot", an eight-minute interview with one of the show's presenters, Pietro Loffa, came after the following goodies: a film of a young blind girl who had used squirrel entrails to accurately predict the sex of every baby born in the seaside town of Brindisi for the previous twelve months; a man who sang *O Sole Mio* whilst writing out the lyrics on his wooden leg with a blow torch; and a competition to crown the "Worst Stripper Of The Week" from a group of housewives performing live in the studio.

This last segment was a belter. Each contestant did her act to varying volumes of abuse picked up by the "mike of dislike"** suspended high over the audience. The louder the abuse, the higher the needle rose on the "gauge of rage" set up on the

---

*Any team from a city located to the north of Grappa – most of them in the league – are despised because their citizens are regarded as prissy sophisticates. If you've ever been to Naples, you'll know that "prissy" isn't the first word that comes to mind, so you can just imagine what the Grappanese are like. The two or three clubs located to the south of Grappa are despised because their fans are considered sub-human slimeballs who eat their own shit. Anybody who has been to the gorgeously vibrant city of Palermo will know just how wrong that view is. Mark Lawrenson is just one critic to have picked up on this misplaced criticism. I may be parachuting his words, but they went something like this: "I tell you what, Manish, those Sicilians are not slimeballs. They're sublime-balls.' Wise words, Lorro. Not that I would repeat them to my mates in Grappa!*

**I tell you, they love their English, the Italians. Franglais, I think it's called.*

stage. The "winner" was the stripper whose needle had risen highest. Her prize? To be tossed into a tank of stinking gunk and then be hosed down by a posse of off-duty firemen, who had won a competition of their own for the privilege. Tasteful, eh? I cast my professional eye over the proceedings and I have to say that the lass who "won" was unlucky. She was a really tasty young sort and I think most of the noise she generated came from fly buttons hitting the mike.

My interview flew by and I can scarcely remember anything about it. I was wildly popular with the audience, I can tell you that. Oh, I remember one "beet of farn", they had in store for me. They ran a reel of Burksey Bloopers – mis-kicks, mistimed tackles, fights – you know the sort of thing. My first reaction was to get off my stool and punch Loffa's lights out – which wouldn't have taken much doing, believe me – but Gianni whispered to me to be charming and funny – so I did my best. To be fair, Gianni supplied the jokes, making it look as if it was me that had come up with them. It was a pity he had to resort to that, in a way. Anybody who knows me will tell you that I am one of the funniest people you will ever meet. But somehow, it doesn't translate on to the page. You'll just have to imagine it. Can you do that for me? Cheers.

As we were whisked away after my spot, both Jehanna and I approached the winner of the strip contest with the idea of getting her on the plane back to Grappa. Gentlemanly to the end, I said Jay could have the first go at her. But the lass still stank of gunk, so we decided to pass. I gave her my autograph – making nineteen thousand, three-hundred and two since I'd arrived from Man U – posed for a photo with her – and was gone.

The opening match of the season, with all modesty, can only be described as a total and complete triumph for me and my new team. The Fango was full. The temperature was pushing ninety at kick-off. The atmosphere was electric. The crowd was on tenterhooks. The clichés were coming thick and fast. Anything you want to say about the game was true. Why? Because it had everything. Eventually, it had three trademark goals from Steve Burkes – bullet header, bicycle kick, screaming bender; it had three trademark goals from Diego Maradona – two blatant handballs and a wonder dribble – and it had a winning last-minute penalty from our skipper, Nando Corvopone. Brilliant!

My debuts with my former clubs had been fairly low key affairs in which I'd come on as a sub, shown a few nice touches, hinted at promise to come and that was that. My debut for Grappanese will still be talked about long after I've gone to that big stadium in the sky. Have you ever had a day like that? Not on the same scale, obviously – but a day on which just everything has gone perfectly? All I can say is, you should have become a superstar footballer because your chance of experiencing such things is increased hugely.

Of course the day will also be remembered as the first ever on-pitch showdown between those two maverick megastars, Diego Armando Maradona and Tristran Stephen Burkes; footballers of no fixed ideas, limits or underpants. So, was Diego as good as people say?

No, he wasn't. He was a hundred times better. I have to hold my hand up immediately and say that Maradona had more talent in one of his nose hairs than your average international footballer has in his entire body. Glenn Hoddle and Paul Gascoigne were the best pure footballers I'd shared a pitch with up to that point. Both were geniuses – there's no other word for it. But whatever they had, Diego had that little bit more. Some have suggested that whereas some great players have a God-given talent, Diego's brilliance came from a slightly lower source. That may well be true as I've heard from a friend of a friend of a friend of a friend that he is absolute dynamite in the sack. But wherever it came from, Diego had it in spades and then some. I'm telling you, the guy could dribble a ball along a clothes line with his eyes shut. And then curl it through a half-open window. Thirty yards away. Without breaking the glass. Maybe he'd grown up doing things like that in the back streets of his native Argentina, who knows? One thing is certain, I bet the little tinker hadn't attended ballet classes like I had.

As the final whistle went at the Fango that afternoon, I found myself within a couple of yards of The Great Man and caught his eye. He looked straight through me, super-miffed that I'd bested him in the match. But I went up, tugging at the hem of my shirt and raised my eyebrows enquiringly – the internationally acknowledged sign that I wanted to swap shirts. Stony faced, he's whipped his off. As we exchange, I said one of the few Italian words I knew. And one that I knew would be appropriate.

'Grassy.'

He looks at me, not quite sure what to make of it. Then I add:

'Grassy, Maestro.'

You may have noticed that I have occasionally put my foot in it with my mouth-work. Saying the wrong thing at the wrong time has been a bit of a thing of mine through the years. Well, in saying "thank you, Master" to Diego, I couldn't have said anything better. As a result, the pint-sized Prince of Pomp hasn't exactly thrown his arms around me, Pelé and Bobby Moore-style – he was still too gutted for that – but he gave me a wink, tousled my hair – not like Ruud Gullit had – and said "well played" in perfect English.

I was made up, I can tell you. Diego was acknowledging that I was a force to be reckoned with and I valued that hugely. And of course, his Napoli shirt immediately became the most prized exhibit in my footer memorabilia. Yes, just this once, I'm not going to call it my shit.

I loved the headline in the Gazzetta Dello Sport the following week by the way. Jay, who, unusually for a lesbo, was really picking up the lingam, translated it as "Burksey Wins Battle of the Tango At The Fango." The article went on to outline how Maradona – 'Il Pibe De Oro' had been outshone by Burkes – 'Il Pube De Oro' – and I tell you, the thing couldn't have been any more complimentary if Dave Green had written it himself.

If I was popular before our four-three win against Napoli, my rating afterwards was off the scale. Right from Sig. Pipi to the little kid who carried my bag to the club bus, everybody in Grappa was in love with – and in awe of – little old me. It was magic. The night of the match, we had a great party back at Aston. Just about the whole city was invited. I sent out for: Finest French champagne, which has great erotic squirting potential and tastes wonderful; Finest Russian caviar, which has great erotic dolloping potential and tastes like shit; Finest Colombian Snort Candy, which has great erotic hardening potential and doesn't taste of anything; and G.G. Garnham's Cumberland Sausage, which is just too good to lark about with, so think on.

As I'd already discovered, nights of hot poke and coke action can take it out of you, but the morning after, I turned up for training at La Porta feeling absolutely wonderful. I felt more or less as God must have felt on the seventh day. Or as Armand Jammot did after he'd dreamed up *Countdown*. After a great bit of crack with the lads – couldn't understand a word of it, but who cared? – I jogged out slowly to where Mister Strozzato was waiting to see me, secure in the knowledge that I'd earned my stripes with him. Unbef***inglievably, he tells me that he still wasn't totally happy with my level of performance. On the whole, I'd played "effectively", he said. Effectively! I'd taken my "occasions very well", but I'd missed "several other occasions" to put the little f***er Zul through. Because of it we'd had to rely on a dubious last minute penalty to win the game. After everything I'd done, I was speechless. My previous Gaffers would have kept my feet on the ground, yes, but they would also have had an arm round, praising and encouraging me. I could hear Tarka's organ note big style at that moment. Hear it loud and strong.

And so I lose it. I can't stop myself. As the other players gasp in amazement, I go to throw a savage right hook on to the not inconsiderable chin of the man known throughout Italy as "Il Sodo di Tutti Sodi".* It lands square on the target. He shudders with the impact, but doesn't go down. And he doesn't throw a counter. Instead, he's given me the full Pearcey. Yes, he's just stared back with a "is that the best you can do?"

---

*I don't know what it means, but it's not "a big poof" I can tell you that.*

141

sort of sneer. And then he's told me to meet him by the perimeter fence in a couple of minutes. Gianni has an "eh up, what's going off here?" look on his face as I jog over there, thinking I've got away lightly.

Five minutes later, I'm running round the razor wire with a rucksack full of bricks on my back. It was nearly a hundred degrees in the shade. Except there was no shade. It made three hours of solid "fire drill" feel like a Sunday afternoon picnic. On the third circuit, I faint. Half-an-hour later, I'm in hospital. Of course, the thing is hushed up by the football club. My stay in hospital is put down to a spot of VD – more plaudits from the locals – and three days later I'm back in training. On meeting up with Mister Strozzato again, no apologies are asked for or given and I get on with things as best I can.

I could tell that he thought he'd won. He thought he'd beaten me. But nobody can ever beat me. Nobody in the world. And one day, I would show that stocky little pockmark just who the real boss was. He could count on it.

It was great having Tarka to stay. And boy, did he enjoy himself. The band didn't require its members to be physically fit, so he was able to really push the boat out.

His new thing was dropping acid (taking LSD) on top of his other veinous pleasures. There was no way I was going there. Experiencing hallucinations was all I needed.

On his last night, we're sipping drinks and petting babes on Sig. Pipi's "yacht" – actually a forty-metre mini ocean liner – when Tarka turns round to me and says:

'Course, you realise Tris that these people are all Mafiosi.'

'What are you talking about?'

'They're *Gola Infiammata*\* – the local organised crime. The lot of them.'

'What makes you think that?' I say, as a cheer goes up from the deck below. Apparently word had just come through that a rival business family had just lost a "Capo". I've lost a cap, scarf *and* gloves before now, but I doubt if it made anybody cheer.

'Just look all around you, man.'

That's acid, for you, I thought. Once you can't trust your senses, you're in trouble. When he came down, he'd see things differently. We changed the subject as a volley of gun shots rang out followed by a couple of heavy splashes as something hit the water. They know how to enjoy themselves, these Italians!

When I said goodbye to Tarka at the airport next day, he's given me a big hug as usual and said, 'Really look out for yourself with these guys, man. They're one mean machine.'

'Tark, they're the most generous people in the world. And they love me here.'

'Well, just don't do anything to cross them. Promise?'

---

*\*Trans: 'sore throat.' How could that have anything to do with the Mafia?*

Where was he at? 'I promise, I promise. Now get on that plane, you nutter.'

Worried that Tark was addling his brain with too much acid, I kissed him goodbye and drove back to Aston. For his part, he was worried that I was getting in with a bad crowd. What a pair. But we were both survivors. We would make it through. No sweat.

But I'll tell you someone a lot bigger and better than either of us who didn't make it through. In late November 1990, the woman who had changed Britain for good and for ever was no longer its Prime Minister. Yes, to their undying shame, the Conservatives ousted my all-time top heroine, Mrs Margaret Thatcher, from the leadership of the party she had served with such distinction for so long. The footage of her leaving Number Ten for the last time as Leader – the bit where her little chin wobbles – I can't watch to this day. It's right up there with footage of that little girl with the ... no I can't go on. I need to compose myself. Change of subject.

The rest of the season on the pitch continued on the same serene course on which it had started. I couldn't put a foot wrong. The fans even loved it when I got sent off in Turin for booting Juve hard man Gianozzo Cagata in the bollocks in revenge for a key shirt-pull he'd subjected me to at the Fango. At the end of the season, bad injuries to key players cost us dear and so did referees who disallowed so many good goals I began to smell a rat. We finished fourth in the Scudetto, Grappanese's highest placing for twenty years. And who won the Golden Boot as the top goal getter in Serie A? I did – and on the last day of the season too. For some reason, it really made Gianni and his brothers laugh when I came back into the dressing room after the match and shouted:

'Yes, I've f\*\*\*ing done it! I'm the top f \*\*\*ing hit man in the whole of Italy!'

'Sure you are, Burksey – sure you are!' they guffawed. 'We'll make you a made man, yet!'

I know "make you a made man" wasn't good English, but you had to admire them for trying to speak our language. And Mister Strozzato? Some of you probably know that he was still far from happy with me. I guess we just weren't *compatico*, as they say.

Over the close season, so many Italian women came forward claiming that I was the father of their new born babies that my DNA was on the Favourites Menu on the computer at the local lab. I think it even had its own website at one time. Not one of the claims turned out to be genuine, by the way. I told you I couldn't put a f\*\*\* wrong.

By the way, repeated requests to my hero Frank Worthington to come and join me out in Grappa for a spot of sun, sand and whatever else took his fancy landed on deaf ears. I think he was too busy with his church work at the time.

It's as we sail majestically into the 1991/92 season, that my memory starts getting hazy on a few things. I'm afraid that too much booze, and increasingly, too much Bogota Conk Stonker were starting to take their toll on the old bonce. But it didn't affect my form on the pitch. Goals came in a never-ending flood at the weekends, and girls came in a never ending flood the rest of the time. The Happy Haddocks had never been so happy, I'm telling you.

With me and several other players doing their stuff – skipper Nando Corvopone and new boy defender Pico Fernandez from Barcelona were outstanding and for the second year running, Ivo Zaccherini and Flo Mirandola really bossed things in the middle of the park and out wide respectively – Grappanese were third in the league heading toward Christmas. Only giants AC Milan and Juve were ahead of us.

In a welcome breath of fresh air, David Platt had started playing for Bari that season and it was great having a fellow English Lion padding around the local paddock. To be fair, we didn't see a right lot of each other. As somebody once said, "Both are brilliant footballers, but Platty's a proper, decent human being – no wonder he and Burksey don't get on." You can read between the lines on that one if you like. Know what I mean?

An interesting sidebar to our time in Italy was how much it boosted our fame back home in England. And that went for our fellow ex-pat, Des Walker as well. Even Gazza's profile was enhanced. Why? One reason for it was the *Forza Football Italia!* TV show that started up just as I moved to Grappanese. Coincidence? I don't think so.

Hugely popular with the viewing public, F.F.I. served up a great mix of news, features and live games from Serie A. Brainy young presenter Richard Jameson did stuff on me practically every week and, until he made one smart crack too many about my off the pitch activities, I enjoyed being a regular on the programme.

One interview will always stick in my mind. And his. In a book he did about the series, he devoted a whole chapter to me entitled, "Pennine Prince To Apennine King". In it, he wrote:

> The La Porta Training Ground was the backdrop to one of the most remarkable performances I've ever witnessed by a footballer. The interview with Burksey had begun in the changing rooms and the four of us – cameraman, sound recordist, production assistant and myself – continued it without a cut as we followed the Grappanese centre-forward out into the car park. Our destination was God 9 – his gleaming red Maserati parked in the far corner. As we began crabbing our way over to it, The Great Man picked up a ball on his instep and without looking, flicked it on to his left shoulder. With a shrug, he flicked it over his head on to the right one. And then flicked it back again. And carried on doing it. He never faltered. He made no compensating adjustments. He just kept flicking the ball backwards and forwards over his head as we walked and talked.

I reckon the word magic is overused. But this was magic. Under Burksey's control, the ball's unbearable lightness of being was transformed into something obedient and predictable.

He was still effortlessly pulling off this sleight of shoulder when we arrived at his car. I asked him if his Italian team-mates had been surprised that an English player could boast such supernatural skills. "Dunno", he said, glancing back at the changing rooms as Nando Corvopone emerged and turned to walk away in the opposite direction. As befits his rank of club captain, Sig. Corvopone's car – a Ferrari convertible – was parked away from the others in an area specially reserved for the club's dignitaries. Status, privilege and respect – very important phenomena in the land of the Pope, La Cicciolina, and the Mafia.

Burksey winked cheekily. "Let's ask Nan what he thinks", he said, dropping the ball off his shoulder and volleying it at Corvo's retreating back. He must have been about thirty yards away. After a moment, Burksey shouted "Nando?" turning the skipper to face us at the precise moment the ball hit him square on the top of the head. "What do you make of us skill levels then?" shouted the ex-Man United magician. "Oh and keep the ball!" he added as it ballooned high into the air before landing flush on the open passenger seat of the Ferrari. After reeling off a string of choice Sicilian swearwords that even I didn't understand, Sig. Corvopone drove off.

He still has that ball.

Not bad, eh? And for once, the sass-mouthed Mister J didn't slip in the odd snide quip to take the legs out from under his victim. By the way, a couple of million fans saw my moment of magic on TV back in the UK* and requests to Get Real! for autographed pictures and the like broke all records as a result. Cheers, Richard. But think of this – you could have done many more interviews with me over the years if you hadn't made that joke. You know the one. And you're wrong in any case. The tenth budgie doesn't have to stand on one leg.

*Don't you just hate the way ex-pats always call England 'The UK'? Sorry about that. But don't worry – it won't happen again. The guy that was responsible for it just realised he had a prior engagement and won't be helping me any more.

Two shattering things happened to me in my second season with Grappanese. The first occurred in February and it occasioned one of the biggest crises of my career. Put quite simply, I was warned by a leading trichologist that if I continued with the skull spin climax to my famed goal celebration, I was putting the life of my hair in serious danger. Yes, I could be no more than a hat-trick away from needing a weave. Obviously, the news hit me like a sledgehammer. Can *you* picture Burksey with a re-turfed roof garden? Of course not. I know they don't *all* look as if somebody's fired buckshot into the victim's skull from above, but I was having none of it. Yet there was no way I could perform my routine without its wow finish. What to do? I racked my brains long and hard for a couple of minutes before my stylist, Gianpaolo came up with the answer.

'Mind, all you have to do is wear a headband and the job she is a good 'un, no?'

Brilliant. Although it would make me look like a slight tit, I went for GP's suggestion. Of course, I had no idea what the consequences of my actions would be. Being a style god meant that players soon jumped on the bandwagon, donning a series of ever more trendy designs in an effort to outdo me. From girly Alice bands to minimalist thongy jobs, half the players on the planet were at it eventually. So to you, the long-suffering fans who have to put up with all this nonsense, I apologise unreservedly. By the way, as a little footnote to this story, who could have foreseen how getting some pink paint on my hair – I'd been touching up a bedroom wall after an unfortunate incident – would turn out? My future team-mate Freddie Ljungberg and cricket's Kevin Pietersen are just two to have followed me blindly down that path.

The second shatterment occurred in March. We were still pushing for the title, but it was then that something happened that took my mind off football for some little while. I was taking part in a magazine shoot in Milan – I was male underwear designer Silvio Robaccia's *Groin Of The Year* – and after we wrapped, I went along to a fashion show at Locatelli's. He was showing his new collection and anybody who was anybody was there. Naturally, my presence caused a huge stir, but that was nothing to the stir I felt in my insides when to the strains of *Alive* by Pearl Jam, out pads this girl onto the catwalk. She was wearing a simple sarong dress. Simple in that it had almost no back. I'd seen hundreds of photos of Supermodel Cinzia Pifferi in mags and even seen her interviewed on telly, but none of that prepared me for looking at her in the flesh. She was simply the most beautiful anything I'd ever seen in my life.

Since Roxanna, I'd vowed never to fall in love with another woman. "F*** 'em and move on" was my motto. If you're reading this, by the way Frank – or in time my other son Diego – don't follow in the old man's footsteps on this one. It'll make you go blind.

But back to Cinzia – "L'Acciuga"* as she was known. I won't say it was love at first sight. But it was f***ing close. From the moment I saw her, I felt my heart beat with a new purpose and my attitude to love and sex took on a whole new perspective.

I simply started to think about women in a different way. Just to take one thing, perhaps I hadn't respected the ladies as much as I should. For the first time, the prospect of rounding up my mates and looking for oven-ready bimbos to roast seemed almost crass. Even if I didn't go on to Bogart the Tail End Charlie position.

I left Milan without saying a word to her as I wasn't sure where I was at. As my lovely old Auntie Vi used to say, I'd "come over all unnecessary". It was a shock to the system, I can tell you. But I struggled on, trying to put it to the back of my mind with all that other stuff. Life at Aston changed a bit on the bird front after that. It didn't seem right to carry on the way I had before, so I cut my amorous needs down to just one girl a night and I decided to completely give up roasting, dogging, bagpiping, planting, plonking and slarting. Away from sex, I continued to drink, smoke and snort as before, but when I went to sleep at night, it was often Cinzia's beautiful face that floated in front of me.

I vowed – and you know what happens when I make a vow – that if I still felt the same way in six months, I would ask her to marry me.

The season ended in qualified triumphs on three fronts and unmitigated disaster on two. First, the near triumphs: we finished third in the Scudetto – our highest placing for thirty-seven years; we were losing semi-finalists in the Italian Knock-Out competition – not a patch on our FA Cup, but that's another story; and we were beaten quarter-finalists in the UEFA Cup. So what were the two disasters? They were connected. I only finished second in the Golden Boot competition – one solitary goal behind the great Milan striker Marco Van Basten. The reason? With three matches to go in the league, I suffered my first serious injury in senior football. It happened after only five minutes in our away fixture at Samp's Stadio Luigi Ferraris. Keeping my eyes only on the ball as I sprinted into the box to get on the end of a teasing Flo Mirandola cross, I ploughed straight through the back of Nico Zul, tearing my right anterior cruciate ligament. The little arse-wipe would be playing again in only eight weeks following his "extensive" leg and spinal injuries. Me? After reconstructive surgery, I would be out for three months. What a pisser. Apart from missing the end of the domestic season, it meant no Euro 92 for me. F***!!!!!!!

*Trans: 'The anchovy'. The nickname is a jokey reference to that English supermodel of a previous generation, the still very gorgeous Twiggy.*

Remember how Graham Taylor's England side performed in Scandinavia without me? And without Gazza? And without John Barnes? And with Carlton Palmer? We did nowt. We didn't win a single game. And in the 2:1 defeat against hosts Sweden, Professor Taylor saw fit to sub the great Gary Lineker. Subbed him in his last game for England. I'm not going to add to the 'Turnip' Taylor debate here. I'm saving that for a later chapter: a chapter in which I will give you the low down on our shameful failure to qualify for the '94 World Cup in The States. Hang on to your hats. It'll be a bumpy ride.

But back to my 1991/92 campaign in Italy. "Campaign": that's a real Sir Bobby Robson word – it must be thinking about World Cups that put it in my mind. Anyway, all in all, 91/92 had been another cracking season for me and, although the Grappanese fans had gotten a bit more used to me by now – and therefore not quite so excited at the jollies I was dishing out to them – my profile and popularity were still huge. My speeding tickets were still torn up. My every whim was still catered for. I was still entertaining a steady stream of babes. But true to my word, I was doing them strictly on a one per night basis with no re-admittance.

And Strozzato? He still hated my guts. Why? Because he thought I was capable of more. He kept making remarks about how Maradona was more skilful than me, about what a great team player Van Basten was, about how David Platt was the best English import to Italy since football itself. Carlo Strozzato. I was biding my time with that f***er. My middle name wasn't "The Last Laugh" for nothing. Actually, my middle name is Stephen, but you know what I mean.

My gambling habits had taken an interesting turn since I became a Grappanese. Because of the language barrier, my Frank Stapleton diet at Man U – daily Boggle and Scrabble games –– wasn't possible. But I soon took up with a couple of card schools. My playing partners were all part of Gianni's or Signore Pipi's immediate or suspended families and I believe one of them – Alfonso Coglioni di Cammello* Contolone was some sort of accountant for the family. To begin with, my losses were written off at Sig. Pipi's request. By the end of my second season though, thanks to the combination of Dave Green and Punto Calbonetto directing all comers to chuck money into the Bank Of Burksey, I had acquired so much dosh that I insisted in paying off my losses myself. Yet another act of Burksey generosity that's gone unnoticed in the Press.

My third season at the club got off to only an average start on the pitch, but with my TV work and other fashion and media commitments, I didn't have time to worry

*Trans: 'Camel knackers.' Don't ask.

about it. My Fango fan base was still strong and I was still receiving sack-fulls of mail from my adoring UK followers, but for the first time there were odd whisperings. Maybe the great Burksey was getting a little too big for his boots; maybe Burksey was spending too much of his time in hated Rome and even more hated Milan; maybe Strozzato should stick him on the bench to get his head back on his shoulders; maybe Burksey drinks, smokes and snorts too much; maybe Burksey isn't getting enough of l'altra* as he used to. Only whisperings. But they were there.

And then it happened. A photo shoot for a Turin firm who made iced tea overran and because of it, there was no way I could get to training in Grappa the next day. I was too smart to admit the reason for my absence, so still in Turin, I phoned in sick from my mobile. No problem. Except that a few hours later, I was seen having brunch with some fashion people. Seen by millions of people as it happens. How come? Because the next editions of the papers carried photos of the event. We haven't had a quiz question for a while, so how many photos do you think some of these papers carried? One? Two or three? I'll tell you. Some of them had four-page *spreads* of the "brunch of shame".

It didn't go down too well in Grappa. With anybody. And neither had shots published the previous week which showed me and my great mate Gazza – he'd signed for despised Roman rivals Lazio in the close season – embracing each other in the middle of the Trevi Fountain**. Fraternising with the enemy – especially in his own playground – was considered disloyal. And there were jokes that I was filling my shoes with water because my goals were drying up at the Fango. Comparatively speaking. In an interesting development, the club refused to pay the heavy fine I received for trespass. Lazio paid Gazza's. Hmm. Was Burksey suffering a bit of a dip in popularity here? After everything I'd given the club? Yes I was – just a little. I'll tell you what confirmed it. The little kid who always carried my bag between the changing room and the bus at the Fango suddenly switched to carrying Pico Fernandez's instead. Funny how that hurt.

But I was determined I wouldn't let anybody tell me how to live my life, so I carried on as I had been. In fact I increased my off-pitch commitments. And it wasn't as if it was hurting the team. Because of a slow-down in my rate of scoring, we weren't bagging as many as we had been. But with Nando and Pico ruling the roost at the back, we

---

*Trans: 'the other.' Surprisingly literal, eh?*

**The old guy employed to remove coins tossed in for good luck never had such a good haul as when Gazza and I were splashing around in the thing. I still think we were entitled to 15%!*

let in even less. I don't know how many games we won one – nil that season, but it was a huge number. As we headed into Spring, we were top of the league. Yes, at last, the Scudetto looked to be in reach. You've no idea what that meant to the fans of the Trasparenti. Or to me – at this stage in my career, despite my acknowledged footballing genius, despite playing for some of the world's biggest clubs, I'd never actually won anything.

I was aglow with pride. The whole city was aglow with pride. Nothing short of deification awaited Sig. Pipi, his board, Strozzato and us, the players. Surely, we wouldn't blow it now?

I was playing fine and at odd moments, I was still turning it on as only I and a handful of other players can do. In April, the home fixture against the first proper foreign team I ever played against – Udinese, remember? – I won the game with a chip from inside our own half. Even Strozzato applauded from the dugout. Grudgingly.

All this time, I'd been thinking of Cinzia. And finally, I believed the time was right to do something about it. As nervous as kittens, me and Jay flew off to the Pietro Verripotti show in Milan and took up our seats right next to the catwalk. Always one for omens and the like, I wondered what tune would be playing when L'Acciuga's turn came to slink out in front of us. Get this – it proved to be Madonna's *Deeper And Deeper*. How much more of a sign did one need? Although to be fair, if she'd come out to Ernie, The Fastest Milkman In The West, I would have still have been knocked sideways. The subsequent meeting over a magnum of champagne, caps of Berlin Bonce Bangers and lines of Colombian Nose Hoser was as romantic as any scene from a Fred Astaire and Ginger Rogers movie and we agreed to meet for dinner later. Stipulating a discreet table with an oversized cloth, I got Jay to book the sumptuous Hotel Serenazzo for nine o'clock. The trusty lesbo made the arrangements and then made some of her own with a couple of the models she'd met at the show. I tell you, these minge bingers are a right loose lot!

In the meantime, I visited Milan's most exclusive jewellery emporium and bought the biggest and therefore best engagement ring they had. Unbelievably, the jeweller even knew Cinzia's size – another brilliant omen – and I left the shop as happy as Larry Lloyd. At a time when half of Africa was starving and/or dying of Aids, some have criticised me for spending one point eight million on something as frivolous as an engagement ring. An engagement ring on spec, at that. All I can say to them is that love makes you do strange things. There, you thought I was going to tell these critics to f*** off, didn't you? Ah, you can never second guess Burksey.

Two unbelievable things happened at dinner. The first was that I hardly ate a thing. Yes – that shows you. Cinzia, on the other hand, was knocking stuff back like there was no tomorrow.

'Cinz, I was wondering...'

'Don't call me that.'

'Sorry, Cinzia...'

'Yes, Stiv, I'm sorry to like pull you up, but an ex-boyfriend of mine used to call me Cinz and now it gives me palpitations to hear it. Palpitations in my gall bladder.'

Fancy.

'Then I shall call you just Cinzia.' How's this for top chat stuff by the way? See how far I'd come since my first halting efforts with Roxanna?

I continued: 'So, Cinzia, I was wondering how you stay so slim when you eat like Mike Gatting.'

'I throw up between courses,' she breathed seductively, forking a truffle between her luscious lips.

'Throw up – of course!' I smiled, pouring her another glass of shampoo. 'High colonics and enemas are a boon, also.'

The conversation went on in this gay sophisticated way until we got to the brandy. All through the meal, my Jumbo Jet of love had been taxiing out onto the runway. Feeling the ring box in my Paolo Misero suit jacket pocket, I perceived the moment was right to go for take-off on a flight I hoped would never land. I was just on the point of reaching for Cinzia's hand under the table and guiding it toward my unbuttoned fly – a ploy much used in diplomatic circles – when she says:

'Stiv, I want to tell you something. I think your entry into the stadium at Grappa was the most exciting thing I've ever seen in my life. Even more exciting than Renato Vomito's use of turn-ups in his Fall Trouser Collection. And...'

'Well, I feel the...'

'Don't interrupt me. And now that I have met you in person, I can see that you are more than just a footballer *molto bravo.*'

'And that means...? I asked, starting to uncoil the old riga from its hiding place.

'How long have you been in Italy? Skip it. Let me just say I haven't met anyone who has turned me on as much as you for at least... the longest time, I don't know.'

'Darling, that's how I feel also,' I said. As violins played a romantic serenade in the background, I pinged my knob end out of my pants like a bell clapper. Now you see why I stipulated the table cloth.

Under the table, I found her beautiful slender hand with mine as she said:

'Stiv, I want to marry you as soon as possible.'

As my heart went bang, and the table practically lifted off its feet, I guided her hand ever nearer to my tower of power.

'For until we do, I cannot go to bed with you.'

I steered her hand on top of the table. 'What?!'

'Sex before marriage is impossible for me.'

'You mean you're a v...?'

'... Very good catholic girl, yes.'

Blimey. There was a turn up. And I don't mean one of Renato Vomito's. In between barfs, we decided to marry as soon as it was practical. As soon as it was practical turned out to be three months later. You want revelations? Here's one for you. In that three month waiting period, I abstained from sex. Shocking, but true. By sex, I mean sex with another person, of course. I must say it was weird voluntarily turning myself into a merchant. Still, it was educational. It taught me what it must be like to be a sad loser.

Now if you've ever tied the knot, I don't know how you turned up at the church or registry office on the day. I expect you hired a limo and felt like a million dollars as a result. Imagine how you would have felt turning up in a gold-plated gondola flanked by pure white swans wearing gold coronets on their heads. Oh, I forgot to mention, me and Cinzia were married at St Mark's in Venice.

Naturally, Tarka was my best man and the gondola ride to the basilica is something neither of us will ever forget.

As we neared the landing stage by the Piazza San Marco, our escort of swans put trumpets to their beaks and started playing a fanfare. 'Who needs acid, man?' said Tark. They were remote-controlled mechanical swans, you see. Didn't have those at your wedding? No expense was spared at ours thanks to Cinzia's parents being what is known as 'old money'. And boy were they 'well connected'. The guest list included people so famous, even I was impressed. Nobel Prize winners, Supermodels, Prime Ministers and Presidents, Oil and Drug Barons, Stars of Stage and Screen. Under the circumstances, Tarka's speech at the reception was a belter. Although I think me, Robbo, Gazza, Waddler, and the rest of my English mates were the only ones who got the point when in a mock Bernard Manning voice, Tark came out with the obligatory best man's line:

'And dun't t'bride look beautiful today, eh, ladies and gentlemen? Cinzia luv, you look a picture.' High Society doesn't do irony, apparently. Or maybe they'd just never been to a wedding in Gorton.

Of course Cinzia looked beautiful. The dress and shoes by Adela Straccio and Marco Morsa respectively were later exhibited at the Museum of Modern Art in New York. The make-up was subsequently copied by beauticians for thousands of weddings world-wide. The jewellery and floral arrangements ... need I go on? Everything was perfect, wildly expensive and totally exclusively wonderful. And speaking of exclusives, the photo deal that was signed with a certain magazine was the largest to that date ever struck. And did we have a live band for the evening do? No. We had live bands.

Plural. The running order looked like something Bob Geldof might have put together for some disaster or other.

Yes, it was quite some occasion. Too bad then, that the marriage only lasted a week.

The wedding night itself was interesting. Now guys, I don't know if you've ever sh***ed a lass who has regularly been voted the most beautiful woman in the world. Probably not. Although, if your current relationship is still in that early fantasy stage, I dare say that "the most beautiful girl in the world" is exactly how you see your new squeeze – even if she's got a face like a bag of spanners and a backside like a boiler end. But back to La Pifferi. Just seeing her naked was the most exciting moment I'd ever experienced. Was I up for what was to come? After three months without so much as a sniff of a woman, are you kidding? Jürgen Klinsmann could have dived off my d***, I'm telling you. Followed by all of his team mates. Standing on each other's shoulders. And that was before I rubbed coke into the thing.

After the visuals and the initial thrill of exploration, the excitement... was off for the night. More or less. The first few times, I thought the fault might have been mine. But by the fourth or fifth, I was starting to get the picture. Cinzia wasn't frigid. But she wasn't a normal hot-blooded woman either. I was devastated. Totally gutted. And after only a couple of hours, I gave it up as a bad job.

Brandee later explained Cinzia's problem. "She was incapable of giving love because the object of her love was, like, herself?" In other words, the f***er was so vain, she couldn't f*** properly as a result. My wife – the gorgeous Cinzia Pifferi – was a sex dud. Greater disappointment has never been felt by man. Except maybe by Spurs season ticket holders.

I could have stayed married to L'Acciuga of course – and just banged anything I fancied on the side – but it turned out we were not compatico in other ways. She was temperamental. She was demanding. She was shallow. And she wasn't particularly bright, funny or discerning. She couldn't stick Huddersfield, Mrs Thatcher or Cumberland Sausage.

Just trying to talk to her on everyday matters – say whether to take the black or the white Boxster to Lamerada for lunch – was impossible. Did you notice on that first evening in the restaurant that she kept interrupting me? It got worse. So I started interrupting her. She didn't like it. Shouting matches ensued. By Day Three, we weren't speaking. By Day Four she had moved back into her flat in Milan and refused to see me. By Day Five she called a press conference and announced that the marriage was over. By Day Seven, it *was* all over. Just like that. And I was well out of it, brother.

By the way, thanks to the legendary power of the potent Pifferi, I am legally forbidden to enter the city of Venice to this day. Like I'm really upset about it! I'd rather go to Birmingham any time. At least the place doesn't close down at eleven o'clock at night.

If Cinzia could do a press conference, so could I. A whole squad of people advised me to be as nice as possible about her, about her family, about the wedding, even the "marriage" itself. It would be disastrous not to, they said. Oh yeh? Particularly financially. So Lord help me – I complied. There, I've said it. For the first time in my life, I admit I wussed out. But it wasn't so much because of the money. It was mainly to bring the whole sorry Cinziagate affair to an end quicker. And so it did. Playing along with my advisors like that should have taught me a lesson, really. But hey, whatever.

Just a little postscript to the Wedding Of The Century. Surrounded by all that money, glitz, glamour and Leading Lightery, you'd think that my parents (Me and Tark still weren't talking to them) would finally have been proud of where their son had got to in life, wouldn't you? Oh no. I later learned that they found the occasion "ludicrous" and "vulgar". And that was before all the guests donned mediaeval costume to take part in the now infamous torch-lit procession around the city. A procession that will always be remembered for an incident on the Rialto Bridge in which Gazza grabbed one of the torches and ignited his own personal gas supply. Watching him vaulting over the parapet into the Grand Canal to extinguish his blazing pantaloons is something that will live with me for ever. Of all the moments in Gazza's life in which his genius for deflating solemnity raised a laugh, this may just have been the best. All my mates loved it, anyway. Even the press guys stuck it to him less than usual. *The Mirror's* Larry Harrison referred to the incident as "Rump and Circumstance!" Great wordsmith is Larry.

*The Times'* Bryan Gonville was just as witty, I'm told: "Gascoigne's antics on the Rialto pinched the as of gravitas with all the pungent economy of a latter-day George Cruikshank." I've no idea who the boy Cruikshank played for, but he must have been a helluva joker to compare with Gazza.

Apparently, my parents experienced one moment at the wedding that made their all expenses-paid trip worthwhile. A great fan of mine is opera god Luciano Pavarotti. He's a real footer man and used to play in goal, or maybe *as* goal*, for a club in his youth. Anyway, he had the good grace to greet my parents warmly and even sang a snatch of one of his hits, "Mama", to my mother. She was made up with the job. Good for her.

---

*Sorry, Lucky – cheap shot. I know you were quite a player in your day.*

After my marriage was over, I returned to my day-to-day life in Grappa with my tail well and truly between my legs. Mind you, that's where it's always been – but you catch my drift. After being mercilessly ribbed – ribbed for displeasure – by my team mates, they were actually very sweet about the fiasco* with Cinzia. Of course, every single one of them believed they would have done a better job of inflaming Cinzia's nether regions than I did. The Italians – they're a scream, aren't they!

But they sure know how to lay on the TLC. Yes, I guess I don't need to tell you how I celebrated when I got back to Aston. I can't go into detail, but let's just say that roasting, dogging, bagpiping, planting, plonking and slarting were all back on my menu. Big style. And a new treat – polecatting – look it up – completed my Night Of A Thousand Times.

I can't tell you on what rafts of drugs I sailed through into the morning, but I do know they put me in a hysterical stupor for three days. I missed training. I missed an appearance on a TV talk show. I missed the toilet. I missed my mouth with food. I was in a high old state. But it didn't matter, the league was already won. With one game to go, we had an unassailable lead. Yes, let joy be unconfined! Grappanese were the new champions of Italy. And I had finally won a title. I cried at the realisation.

Okay, the rollercoaster had been going down for a while, now it was on its way back up again. Right? Wrong. It was about to go further down than I believed possible. I'll tell you just how far. After the hurricane hit, not one girl came to Aston for a spot of hide the riga for three entire weeks.

It has to be said that what I did was terrible, but it wasn't my fault. In fact, I'm still furious with both Jay and Punto for not warning me of the likely consequences of my, like, actions? So what was my hideous crime? Some months earlier, I had agreed to star in a series of jokey telly ads for Saponissima, a leading Eye-Tie soap manufacturer. So what? I hear you cry. So plenty. In one of them, a simple raucous family of peasants from the Grappa area – recognisable by their typical colouring and traditional dress – go for a day out in Rome and turn up at a nice restaurant for dinner. They order a roast pig. When the porker is set down in their midst by a waiter (played by yours truly), the wretched animal suddenly comes alive. Wearing the sort of disgusted expression Strozzato usually reserved for me, its trotters go to its offended nose and pinch it, the apple shoots out of its mouth – the whole bit. Then the waiter takes a bar of Saponissima out of his pocket and hands it to the diners. After a cut,

*Yet another word the Italians have got from us. We should receive royalties for them really, shouldn't we? Something for you legal eagles to have a look at.*

they return looking and smelling sweet. The waiter is happy. The other diners are happy. The pig is happy. So happy that it picks up the carvers, cuts itself into pieces and serves the Grappanese with a portion each.

The ad was one of a series of four and the others took the piss out of people from other parts of Italy. For example in one, an in-demand Milanese gigolo (played by yours truly) is seen rushing from one client's apartment to another in his sports car. He doesn't have time to wash and brush up in between each session, so he utilises the car's own ablution system activated by a vast array of buttons on the instrument panel. It all works perfectly until he gets to his last appointment when the button dispensing the Saponissima jams. The buttons activating the other parts of the process – the steaming water jet, shampoo, shaving stuff, deodorant, cologne etcetera – all work fine. Pressed for time, he shrugs and runs into the apartment regardless. A moment later, his body (played by a dummy) comes flying off the penthouse balcony at the hands of the disgusted woman. After a cut, the body (played by me again) is shown spread-eagled across the sports car's bonnet. Ironically, the impact causes Saponissima to come squirting out of the dashboard – too late to save our fallen hero.

The adverts were meant to be just funny and they went over big in most of the country. But, in suggesting that the people of Grappa were basically a right dirty bunch, the copywriters (who all turned out to be tifosi of the hated Juve) had stabbed their pens into a very sensitive area. Opposition fans were always singing and chanting about how filthy the good people of Grappa were. Let's just say it wasn't appreciated by the Grappanese. That I had added my voice – however unwittingly – to those that derided my adopted people hurt them deeply. Dave Green flew in personally to help Jay in deflecting criticism away from me. And Gianni, as always, was a great corner-man in a crisis. I went onto local TV to apologise. I apologised on the radio. I apologised to the Press. I apologised to Signor Pipi and the club. You name them – I apologised to them.

I still got booed, whistled and generally jeered at as I shakily made my way off the bus and headed to the player's entrance for the last game of the season. I almost didn't make it through, but not because of the abuse. Thanks to heavy drug lag, I could see three separate doors ahead of me where there was really only one. I stumbled around a bit, but to my blessed relief, left-back Franco Zappa grabbed me from behind and steered me through safely. The state of my brain didn't bode well for the game ahead, but I knew I was starting on the bench. There was time to come round. You may be wondering how I managed to play for three seasons at Grappa without once testing positive for drugs when I was high on one thing or another – or on several things at once – most of the time. Let's just say that in Italy, most things are possible and leave it at that.

I have to report that as I slumped down on to my spot in the dressing room that Sunday afternoon, it brought tears to my eyes that I had been dissed by the fans I loved* and to whom I had given so much. I'd scored more goals for them in three seasons than their previous hit man had managed in five. More than twice as many.

And despite everything that had been going on off the pitch, I had still made a valuable contribution to Grappanese's first Scudetto in fifty-odd years. The city was going mad with celebrations. I would have liked to have been included in more of them. Particularly as my marriage had just broken up and I was suffering terrible c*** burn.

That final game of the season, of course, has gone down in history. Just in case you popped out for a decade and missed it, here's what happened.

We were playing a certain team who needed to win the match to stay in the league. We, as you know, had already won the thing. It was a perfect set-up for a deal between the two clubs and I'm sorry if this shocks you good footballing folk out there – but that is exactly what happened. The Grappanese players walked out on to a rapturous Fango that day intent on luxuriating in every moment of adulation that was raining down from the Curva Nord, the Curva Sud, both tribune – the whole stadium. They were also intent on losing the match one-nil. Then, everybody would be happy. There was only one snag. Nobody told me about the deal. In fact beforehand Gianni had insisted that I play as well as I could to claw back some much needed personal kudos.

'You are a real hero here, Burksey. *Phhttt*. End the season with a bang and your adoring fans... *Phhttt*... will forget Porkergate and all your other little misdemeanours.'

'I'll win them back. No sweat.' My reputation was especially important to the pair of us now because in a secret ceremony the previous day, the Calbonetti had made me a *Giovane D'Honore* – an associate member of their family. I was really touched by that.

'That's the ticket', said Gianni with a smile as wide as a Ferrari's front grille.

When, to a chorus of abuse, I came on as our third and final sub late in the second half, I had surfaced from my drug fug sufficiently to realise that the team were playing uncharacteristically poorly. We were a soft goal behind to a side who had won only one away game all season. It was understandable that, with the title won, we had taken our feet off the pedal – in retrospect, that would have been our ready-made excuse for losing, of course – but the quality of the display puzzled and

---

*I've been advised to say that. Actually, I only loved 4% of them.*

disgusted me. I got into the action immediately. It only took a couple of deft back-heels, a triple Cruyff and a rasping thirty-five yarder to silence my personal detractors. This was the Burksey that the crowd loved and hadn't seen enough of lately. A couple of snaky dribbles, a bullet header against the bar and a frank exchange of eye gouging with a certain hard-man defender and I was right back on top with the tifosi. Especially those scholars of the game encamped in the Curva Nord. Groups like the Semtex Jackals, the Granny Bangers and the Killing Floor Brigade.

But not with the team. After each new piece of brilliance, I draw exasperated looks and am told to "cool it". Of course, I have no idea why. And then, with eight minutes to go, I score direct from a free kick that my team mates try to stop me taking – even though my conversion rate was the highest in European football at the time. The highest until a certain genius by the name of David Robert Joseph Beckham came on the scene, in fact.

I go into my legendary and patented goal celebration, but when I emerge from the skull spin climax, I'm not engulfed by my team mates as usual. Funny, I thought.

Even funnier was how the game proceeded after that. First, our keeper, Carlo Cieco does a Gary Sprake* and throws the ball into his own net. 2-1 to them. Then I make it two apiece by climaxing a surging run from deep by pinging a cheeky bender past their keeper. Next up, nobody puts in a tackle as their centre-forward picks up the ball outside our box. With all the grace of a pantomime cow, he then jinks his way around our defence before scuffing a weak shot under a hopelessly mistimed Cieco dive. 3-2 to them. I reply by replicating Platty's winner against Belgium in Italia 90 – except that I pull it off direct from a short throw-in forty yards out. With it, I complete a fifteen-minute hat-trick that sends the Fango faithful into a frenzy of singing, chanting, lighting of black and orange flares – the whole bit. And that makes the score three-all. Now my team-mates are having a huge go at me. More than once, I hear words like "assassino", "bastardo" and so on. Blimey I thought, those ads I did seem to have given the players more grief than the fans. That sort of thing just never happens. And worse was to come. Some of my mates start engineering collisions with me and a couple of them were lucky not to get a slap. One of them spits at me. Good job for him that he missed.

With seconds to go, following a succession of blatantly obvious and needless fouls by our normally expert sleight-of-hand, foot and elbow merchants, the opposition

---

*Leeds United's finest did it at Anfield in 1967. Just to make Hudders fans even more happy, he did it smack in front of the merciless Kop. Sing: 'Careless hands...'

win a pen. Whatever happens, it will be the last kick of the match and of the whole season. As Carlo Cieco sells himself ludicrously early, their skipper, Gianozzo Buffone, steps up to the ball and... side-foots it wide.

With that miss, our unbeaten home record is preserved. And Sig. Buffone's team is relegated. I seemed to be the only player who enjoyed the moment. On either side.

The subsequent on-pitch celebrations were still the most brilliant experience. Being presented with my Championship Winner's medal by the great Roberto Bettega was something I'll never forget. Nor will the look in his eyes which hinted that there may well be trouble ahead for me and the club. But at last, I'd done it. A magic moment.

I don't know if you've ever been sent to Coventry by an Italian. It's a pretty lonely place, I can assure you. Multiply the experience by an entire workforce of people and you can imagine what the dressing room was like for me after the match. Only Gianni seemed pleased with my efforts – although for some reason, he pretended not to be so in front of the others.

And then Strozzato's come up to me swearing and calling me everything he could think of. And then some. I'd had it with this bastard from day one and coming on top of everything else, I couldn't let it go any longer. I started swinging hard and landed several crunching blows on the f***er's head and in his guts. He came back with some good pokes of his own and as our blood sprayed everywhere, it was touch and go for a while who would drop first. It was him, of course. Why? Because I'm from Huddersfield, the homeland of case-hardened foot soldiers who never take a backward step. People like Ray Wilson, Patrick Stewart and Gorden Kaye. And in any case, when I'm mad, there's nobody can take me out. Nobody in the world. Except Errol. And a couple of his mates. And then there's... Well anyway, very few can take me out.

I offered my hand to Strozzato as he's staggered to his feet, but the bastard refused it. What sort of c*** was he? And we had won the Scudetto. What was all this fuss about?

I found out the following morning when I woke up with a pig's carcass sharing my pillow. All this for doing a soap commercial? I was just wondering how many rashers the thing would yield when the door's burst open and instead of Maria with my early morning cuppa of Harriet's English Breakfast, in march a paramilitary death squad. Oh, they weren't dressed in uniforms – unless you call hand-cut three-piece suits uniforms – but that's what they were alright. I was dragged out of bed with my traditional – dare I say legendary morning stiffy in full donger mode, but that didn't worry these guys.

Throwing my Luca Pizzicanto mac around my shoulders, they then hood, bind and gag me and carry me outside like a roll of lino. A moment later, I'm tossed into the back of a waiting van and I roll about in the back of the thing as they drive out of the city. What a way to celebrate a first winner's medal. About three-quarters of an hour later, the van starts bouncing up and down over rough ground, but then it stops. I hear the front doors slam. Now I'm starting to wonder what these goons are planning to do to me. Rough hands drag me out and I'm bound too tight to stop them. I can just about hear and smell the sea. Hands tie me against a post. Oh-oh. Then one of them, obviously the leader, says:

'You have brought dishonour to the family. The penalty for that... is death.'

Note the pause – melodramatic bastard. 'Can't you just give me a red card, instead?' I quip, plucky in the face of what I was beginning to realise was a mock execution – a stunt designed to scare the crap out of me.

'Don't worry, we'll be sending you off, alright. To swim with the fishes. You're lucky we're making the hit look like somebody else did it. Because being blasted into mincemeat is so much nicer than being given our trademark sore throat.'

What was he talking about? A couple of Strepsils and the job's a good 'un. Now I hear the squad load weapons. A series of cold metallic clicks follow. Hmm. How far are they going to go with this thing? The leader shouts out some command... and the air erupts in a huge explosion of machinegun fire. I can feel bullets whiz past my hood, past my torso, past my legs. How they missed my stiffy, I'll never know. Then, all goes quiet except for footsteps I hear moving quickly away. Cars – where did they come from? – start their engines and I hear doors slam. They drive away. Time for me to beat it also. I start flexing and releasing my muscles Houdini-style until I've loosened the cords around my wrists sufficiently to pull my hands free. A couple of moments later, I'm pulling my hood off. So where was I? I was standing on a grassy knoll – they were obviously sentimentalists these lads – in a depression on a headland about five minutes from the main coast road to Naples.

Now, some of you veterans of the Old Firm game in Glasgow might be used to seeing a pile of machine-gunned bodies lying there, but it was a new one on me. Yes, the people who had brought me out here were themselves dead. The guys from the cars must have done it. And then left me there unscathed. I suddenly came over a bit queer. But then I pulled myself together and started running away from the scene as quick as my legs would carry me. Plenty of people have said that I could have been an Olympic sprinter if the dice had rolled out that way. I put the theory to the test as I shot off in the direction of the main coast road. Crikey, a bit different all this, eh? I'd realised early doors that if Italians like you, there's nothing they won't do for you. Now I'd twigged that once the boot's on the other foot, there's nothing they won't do *to* you.

Five minutes later, Adriano, a passing homosexual, picked me up and took me back to Aston. As we arrived, the place was surrounded by hordes of fans and media. It was chaos.

'Can you get me past them?'

'Sure, baby.'

'And that's not the gear lever, buster.'

'So who's a big boy, then?'

'Just drive, freakshow.'

'Sor-ree.'

I felt like belting him but he might have enjoyed it. But I'll give the poof his due – he was a top driver. Scattering the crowds by the classic Italian ploy of driving straight at them, we made it through into my courtyard without so much as a scrape. I asked one of the gardeners to pay Adriano off for his trouble and dashed into the bedroom to pick up my mobile. There were about twenty messages from Dave Green, another twenty from Jay and just one from Signor Pipi. For some reason, I took his first. In a shaky voice, he said that although following a meeting with the "caps", he had ordered my execution for disobeying a direct order to throw the match, it had since come to his notice that Gianni – he said the name with a fury-filled hiss – had "planted carrots" about having let me in on the plan.* This told Signor Pipi that Gianni's intentions were those of a viper of all vipers – he actually said "wiper of all wipers", but I think the message was clear – and that could mean only one thing. The Calbonetti were trying to take over from the Palledure. A turf war between the two families was officially on.

Yes folks, it was vendetta time in sunny Italy and I had started it. Although I stress, it wasn't my fault. Already six people were dead as a result. So all that time ago, Tarka had been right. These people were Mafiosi, by crikey.

But there was more to it. The Italian FA had already viewed a tape of our last match and concluded that the result had been fixed. Or would have been but for my efforts – and those of their useless skipper – and that therefore punishment to both sides was due. In an unprecedented show of "legal zealotry", they decided to strip us of the title. And relegate us and our opposition to Serie C for the next season. F***ing hell! The cheating bastards had robbed me of a winner's medal. I couldn't get over it. Just to make a few extra hundred million lire, the club had lost the title for which it had been striving all those years. One minute we were champions, next minute we were in the third division. Gutted? Disembowelled is closer to it.

---

*I've since learned from my mate Gianfranco Zola that "planting carrots" means telling a lie in Italian. Look it up if you don't believe me.

But then, "to cob dolly" as my Auntie Vi used to say, who should turn up at the house but Cinzia. Unbef***inglievable. She had seen my performance at the Fango the previous day and thought it the most incredible display she had ever witnessed. She was sorry she had said all those things and wanted me back. Taking her clothes off, she pushed me on to the bed. Someone had carted the pig carcass away and changed the sheets, fortunately. The result of the encounter? Exactly the same as before. The sex was about as exciting as watching *I'm A Celebrity – Get Me Out Of Here*. Less so. And Cinzia knew it. She left muttering that she never wanted to see me again as long as she lived. No problem there, sweetheart. Cinzia is the only bird I've ever had who gives the lie to great ex-Man U and England full-back Paul Parker's famous phrase: "When sex is good, it's great. When it's bad, it's still good."

And me? I rolled over and went to sleep. Finally, I was tired. Tired of Grappa. And yes, tired of La Dodgy Vita itself.

In less than a week, I was gone. Partly worried for my safety as corpses began piling up all over the shop, Dave Green worked miracles in securing a lightning fast move back to England for me. It was a quick sale and the transfer fee and wage deal weren't what they might have been. But let's face it, after Mafiagate, I was lucky to still have a pulse.

Yes, after three years of madness, normality was about to be restored. The normality of Glenn Hoddle and Chelsea. Home sweet home, here I come!

## CHAPTER THIRTEEN

# BACK HOME WITH THE BLUES

**B**efore we go on, I have to set you straight about some more porky pies that have been circulating about me and this autobiography. Further questioning the "authenticity and consistency of the authorial voice", some reviewers have suggested that, of all the places you can "see the ectoplasmic join between the book's various ghosts", the transition from the last section to the present one is the most obvious. Why do these pea brains say that? Because there are suddenly more reported bits of conversation – what we term "dialogue" – in the text.

So why the change in style? Let me tell you that the reason has nothing to do with the change of helper I undertook at this point. No – the reason for the change is actually a tragic one. And it's this. After all the madness I'd experienced in Italy, I had decided to turn over a new leaf in most areas of my life. Especially the leaf labelled "drugs". Yes, at one brutal stroke, I stopped taking them.

One of the many benefits I eventually got from the nightmare hell of doing the funky chicken was that my brain started working better. Especially in the memory department. To be frank, my recollection of everything that happened in my life before the Summer of 1993 is still a bit shaky. As soon as I gave up drugs, my grip on things improved. Yes, there's no doubt about it – all those chemicals I took have a lot to answer for.

This is an important area and I want to pause here just for a moment. To you kids out there, I want to say that, although taking drugs is obviously brilliant fun – especially if you lead a grey humdrum existence like most of you do – I want to warn you away from the pulsating, 3-D Technicolor pleasures that popping, snorting, smoking and mainlining offer. Drugs are bad news, brother. Put it this way, I don't have any memory – not one single second – of one of the best experiences of my life. It began on a perfect Spring evening in 1992. Driving my Maserati along the azure majesty of the Amalfi Coast, my destination was the most beautiful villa in the world, *Casaperfetta*, a thirty-room mansion owned by Sig. Luciago Ladrogrande, director of one of Italy's foremost aid organizations. There, a private screening of a yet-to-be-released Hollywood movie was to be the centre-piece of the evening. Anyone who was anyone was there and the party was as lavish a bash as the sort of shindigs La Pifferi's parents used to throw in Venice.

But apparently, the real fun began for me after the film was screened. Not that I can remember it. How come? Because by then I was smashed out of my skull.

Completely bonged off my trolley. That's a shame, because they tell me I spent the rest of the evening sh***ing the movie's two drop-dead gorgeous female stars. Together. The best triple-tup ever.And I can't remember so much as a pant. So think on, guys. Next time a pusher comes up to you in some piss-stained stairwell and offers you a passport to paradise – just say "No". Look at what you could be missing out on: memories to die for.

There's another myth I want to blow out of the water before we sail off into the bright new dawn of life at the Bridge. Again, it's about drugs. I gather that some have said – though sadly, not in print or in front of witnesses – that I only stopped taking them at this particular point because I realised I was much more likely to be caught by the bribe-free and more active – some say hyperactive – authorities we have in England compared to those I'd been used to in Italy. That is total bollocks. My decision to stop was motivated by factors of health, spirituality and morality. So get off my f***ing case, alright? Okay, let's go on.

With all that had happened in Italy hopefully behind me, I moved into my new London apartment in July 1993. Although Battersea didn't compare with Grappa in some ways, it felt good from the word go. Despite my success, I'd left Italy with a feeling of low self esteem in just about every area of my life. Take my finances. They were in a complete mess. It turned out that I'd been billed for all the things I thought had been given me – my Aston Villa, the Maserati, use of the family's Lear jet.... on and on. Written-off gambling losses hadn't been written off as I thought, either. And there were colossal fines, legal fees and other spurious costs that I knew nothing about. And God knows how much money had been siphoned out of my various accounts by the despicable Gianni Calbonetto. None of this showed at the time. Dave could have disputed so many things, but thought it safer not to. The result of all this was that I now had less money than before I went to Italy.

And talking of low self-esteem – sex. My last two Italian bed partners had been my 'model wife', Cinzia 'L'Acciuga' Pifferi, and a dead pig – I didn't catch its name. The pig was more fun. Yet Cinzia had spent every waking moment since our last encounter telling the world's media that I was the worst lover she had ever had.

"Lover she ever had", notice. And there's me thinking she was a virgin. Well whatever she was, her words hurt. I had never felt so humiliated.

Now what are you supposed to do if you're thrown by a horse? You get right back in the saddle. So now back in London, I went out of my way – once as far as Pinner – to pick up women. Women of all types, sizes and ages. Women on their own, women in pairs, women in groups. One heavy night in South London, I bagpiped an entire college netball team. And then, following a tip from their goal shooter, I nipped round to the village hall where I gave the local Women's Institute's Pickles

And Preserves Group a much needed polecatting. Put photos of *that* on your next calendar, girls.

My exhaustive self-help plan worked. After a couple of weeks of non-stop sh***ing, I'd said goodbye to a few quid and the odd pair of underpants – but I'd said hello to something far more important – my self respect. And once again I'd proved that what had been said and written about me was wrong. I was a man. And I had the scabs to prove it.

Vindicated, I decided to leave the pleasures of the flesh alone for a while. I know it sounds bonkers, but it shows you just how serious I was about what I saw as a whole new start for me. My novel approach to things showed in hundreds of ways. Take my introduction to the fans at the Bridge. After the Fango, I knew people would be expecting something flamboyant and extravagant from me – if not from the club.* But Dave Green and I opted for a different strategy. Because the exact opposite was expected, the purposeful, understated presentation package I finally P.I.A. (Put Into Action) made a huge impression on the fans. Yes, for the first time in my life, I'd discovered the truth that less can sometimes be more.

And what of my new team – Chelsea? At this point in their evolution, they were a long way short of my former club – Manchester United – who were sweeping all before them since the launch of the Premier League the previous season. You can imagine how I felt about that. But with new player/manager Glenn Hoddle at the helm of the Good Ship Chelsea, and me at the sharp end, things looked set to improve for the Blues. So, on that side of the bed, I felt good about things.

But I had, like, issues as well? Why? Because who should be the Assistant to my ex-Spurs team-mate but one Peter Shreeves, the man who had rewarded my faithful service at the Lane by shafting me up the arse and then spitting out the pieces.** And all because I'd hypnotised Ossie Ardiles in one solitary match. Yes, I still maintain that in showing me the door, Shreevoe's reaction had been as over the top as a Paolo Montero shin warmer. But I reasoned that all must be forgiven and forgotten now or the Tottenham Twosome wouldn't have backed my signing.

So all in all, I had a good-ish feeling about the upcoming season with Chelsea. And so, I discovered, did the man I would now have to call Boss. Our first meeting since our

---

*Couldn't see Ken Bates shelling out for the Red Arrows and stuff, could you?*

**Not in a pervy sex way, of course. Peter's only interest in my arse was that it was connected via my legs to my biggest asset – my feet. And that's as it should be in the world of top class football management.*

playing days took place in his office which was a bit different to Strozzato's gaf at the Fango, let me tell you. No marble, no exotic woods. No gallows set up in the corner.

Mister Hoddle was in an optimistic mood.

'I know things will be good here long term, Stevie. The Big Feller's given me a sign.'

'What – Ron Atkinson?'

'God.'

'Oh.'

'He reckons that because of a patchy squad and an unfortunate run of injuries, my first two league seasons in charge will be a bit sticky, but following a second major signing from Europe, the third should see a time of plenty. Yeh.'

'Fancy. And The Cup?' I was just kidding, but Boss Hod's smile in response wasn't an amused one. It was a smile of ... I don't know, you'd have to be a brainbox wordsmith to think of the right word – someone like Stelsat's superb anchor woman, Clare Tomlinson.

'The Cup? It's come to me in a dream. It's Wembley, Burksey. Cup Final day. And there I am leading the lads out. It's going to happen. This season.'

'Was I in the dream?' I asked. As you know, I believe in omens and the like. But to be honest – and I hope this doesn't offend anyone, especially Glenn who I greatly revere as a man and particularly as a man of football – I thought that a lot of the "divine sign" stuff he went in for was a right load of old Toshack. Nevertheless, this I wanted to hear.

'That's down to whether you've cleaned up your act, Stevie. I want to know that when I send you out on to that park, I'm sending out Steve Burkes the brilliant footballer, not Steve Berk, the filthy coke-sniffing scumbag low life.'

'Hope that's not my pen picture in the match day programme you're quoting there, Boss!' At least I was right about Ossiegate being forgotten.

'Just answer the question.'

'That side of things is all over. And so is my addiction to playing board games.'

'What about The Mafia?'

'Don't think they play board games. Maybe a little Pictionary after dinner.'

Hod may have been sporting his familiar innocent choirboy look – rosy cheeks, floppy quiff – but at that moment his gaze could have cut through a steel door.

'This is no time for jokes, Burksey. Talk to me about your membership of The Cosa Nostril.'

He's a walk on the wild side is our Glenn. But he was right – this was no time for laughter. 'Joining The Mafia was just a one-off blip, skip.' Besides, as I explained to him, the vendettas I'd been a key part of were now officially over. The week before I'd flown home, the whole complicated saga had come to a happy conclusion with the acid bath murder of Franco "The Ferret" Calbonetto and nineteen of his family – including the lying "wipers" Punto and Gianni – at a Grappa vs Palermo pre-season friendly. That seemed to reassure the Boss. But then, as I knew he would, he brought up The Famous Videos. Again the laser beam stare.

'Stevie, is it true that when you was in Italy, you took part in hardcore porn videos with a certain other superstar footballer?'

I shifted my weight awkwardly but kept my nerve. Just. 'Porn videos?'

'In which you was disguised as famous cartoon characters?'

'That's just tabloid trash Italian-style.'

Boss Hod looked unconvinced. 'Yeh? My spies tell me that the two of you done repeated sex scenes disguised as Wile E. Coyote and Road Runner.'

'No way.' It was actually Porky Pig and Elmer Fudd. Guess who was Porky.

'Cos if you done that, I'm telling you now – I've got no use for them sort of pervs in my team. This isn't Sodom United – it's Chelsea Football Club.'

Being a Yorkshireman, I hated lying. 'It must have been two other blokes, Boss.' And being a Yorkshireman, I knew which side my bread was buttered. With that, Hod's nodded, closed his eyes and gone into a trance. Or that's what it looked like. I was on the verge of laughing or calling the club doctor – I can't remember which – when he suddenly came out of it.

'Right, Stevie. I've asked for guidance and as you've turned over a new leaf... I'm giving you the nine shirt.'

Happiness surged through me like a speedball rush. 'Cheers, Boss.'

'But – and I'm only going to tell you this once – if I hear, see, or even smell anything more about you and booze, drugs, Scrabble or acid bath murders – you're out.'

'Fair enough.'

'And I'll tell you something else. If I ever catch you wearing foam rubber whiskers and a tail, you won't just be out – I will smite you.'

'Smite me?'

'I will smite you until you cannot be smote no more. Kiddies watch cartoons, Stevie – think of that. Right – we'll say no more about it.'

'You won't have any reason to.'

Hod seemed satisfied and showed me to the door. 'This is a big club, Stevie. And we're going to get even bigger. We've got the players; we've got the fans. And the Big Feller Upstairs is behind us.'

'What – God?'

'Ken Bates. See you at training tomorrow – you bring the biscuits.'

A joke! In our three years at Spurs, I'd never known him say anything even slightly funny. Not intentionally, anyway. The following morning, I drove to the Blues'

Harlington Training Ground near Heathrow in an upbeat mood. I was early and fizzy full-back Eddie Newton was one of the few guys to have beaten me to the changing rooms. He had *The Sun* open at page 3.

'Alright, Eddie?' I knew how to be one of the lads.

'Yo, Burksey!' he grinned. 'Check these big babies out!'

'He gets enough of that as it is – toss it over here', chirped goalkeeper Kevin Hitchcock. Suddenly, Eddie's face fell. 'Where's the bikkies?'

'Yeh, Burksey, I hope somebody told you it's your turn,' said Keeper Hitch, dropping the paper and spilling pages everywhere – not a good sign. But worse was to follow.

I was smiling, but it became obvious that neither of them was joking. So nor – true to form – was Hod the day before. Top professional sportsmen taking it in turns to bring in biscuits. What had I got myself into here – a championship chasing football team or an office typing pool?

Bikkies were only the beginning. I looked around at the 'facilities'. They were shared. With a college. The showers ran cold. There was only one phone in the place. Which didn't work. I'd left Italy for this? On my first day at training in Grappa, I'd been "given" a Maserati, a fabulous villa and the phone numbers of five of the city's classiest bimbos. My first day at Chelsea? Being told off for forgetting the Hob Nobs and finding some pimply young student's jock strap hanging on my peg. Which didn't fit. Any of us.

Well, I said I felt like dropping down a cog or two.

With a month to go before the season began in earnest, The Blues undertook a tour of the Far East. Despite my worries, the trip was to prove a highly successful one (played five, won five) and I opened my scoring account for my new club in the first game when I cheekily steered a cross from Neil Shipperley through South Korean keeper Lee Hung Wang's legs. It would have been far easier to have lobbed the onrushing Wang, but you know by now that Tristan Stephen Burkes never does anything easily.

Yes, things went well on the pitch, but I think I can speak for our whole party when I say that the real highlight of the trip was meeting that modern day saint, Mother Teresa, before taking on an Indian Select side in Calcutta.

What an incredible, inspiring woman the diminutive Albanian was. All my new team mates felt very humble – even Dennis Wise – as we arrived at the centre where she and other Sisters sacrificed their own lives in performing their selfless work for the sick and poor. Now, my experience of footballers is that (with the exception of the odd tender soul like David Beckham) they tend to be a hard-bitten bunch. But what happened that day moved those of us who were there immeasurably and it will live with us all forever. One by one we were admitted into the Nobel Peace Prize winner's living space. It was basically just a shack containing a bedroll and a bible. I've seen better appointed kennels. Suddenly, my Rolex Oyster Perpetual seemed to weigh a ton on my wrist and had not the Hand Of God himself, Diego, given it to me, I would have happily tossed it there and then to one of the lepers who'd been following us around like a bad smell ever since we'd arrived at the place. I could see that the other lads were feeling like I was and no-one knew quite where to look.

Then, with a sense that she was about to show us something that had special significance for her, the Mother pulled back a threadbare curtain to reveal three objects attached to the pockmarked whitewashed wall behind it. On the left was a personal message from the Pope; on the right, a crude sandalwood crucifix that looked as if it might have been fashioned by a child; and in the position of honour in the centre was a signed photograph of a gentleman who I was sure I'd seen somewhere before. The Sainted Lady grew misty eyed as she lovingly lifted it down to show us all more closely. I'll never forget her words:

'It's Chopper Harris', she whispered reverently. 'Taken just before he walked for nutting Alan Clarke at Elland Road in '74. His "never say die" attitude is an inspiration to us all.'

Yes, even here amongst this poverty, sickness, degradation, and hopelessness, the universal message of football, The Beautiful Game, had triumphed, shining out like a good deed in a naughty world. Some of us wept. Then tentatively at first, a lone voice began to hum the opening strains of our famous hymn, Blue Is The Colour. Another voice joined in, this time with words – then another. Soon the air was alive with Chelsea's anthem. And the loudest voice was the miniscule Mother's herself. We went on to sing for a good half hour before the sainted lady drew the service to a close with moving versions of *Stand Up If You Hate The Spurs* and her personal favourite, *My Old Man Said, 'Be An Arsenal Fan'*. Sadly, time was against us and all too soon, it was back on the team coach.

All except the deeply spiritual Mr Hoddle, that is. He had been granted a private devotional audience with the Mother and, although there is no record of it, I'm sure that she found listening to the Gaffer a deeply valuable experience.

The subsequent match between us and an Indian Select XI proved to be a one-sided affair and the crowd gave their own team the bird throughout the ninety minutes. The score – especially after what we had experienced that afternoon – isn't worth recording, although I did blast my fifth goal of the tour with what The BBC's Ron Jones described as "an impudent volley". I don't call that impudence. I call it class.

On the final whistle, we did a lap of honour of the pitch, giving a special wave to a section of the ground that had been reserved for the local "D and D" – Destitute and Dying. In a nice gesture, one of our club officials arranged for each one of them to receive a copy of our video *History Of The Blues* and a booklet of money-off vouchers for the club megastore. So at least some of the destitute went home happy.

The plane journey back to Heathrow was unlike any other I'd known following a football tour. We'd all been moved by what we'd experienced and the atmosphere contained what top soccer scribe Bryan Gonville later described as "a spiritual dimension, even a palpable sense of moral purpose". We were changed men. I decided that when we got back, I would immediately contact the nearest sanctuary and adopt a donkey.

And the changes wouldn't stop there. In a blinding flash, I realised that football and, latterly, modelling and acting had been my entire life and there had been no room for anything else. I recognised that there was a void in the centre of my very existence – an intellectual and aesthetic black hole. That hole needed filling.

Back at the Bridge, preparations for the opening game of the Premiership season were well under way. Although the team was uneven quality-wise, Glenn had us playing some nice football in training – it impressed our co-tenants, the Imperial College Hockey X1 anyway – and we were all looking forward to meeting our first opponents, Blackburn Rovers. But it would be without our rising midfield star Muzzy Izzett who was transferred to Leicester. Shallom, Muzz.

The game itself proved a bitter disappointment. Although I scored with an audacious bicycle kick which ultimately became the BBC *Match Of The Day* programme's Goal Of The Month, we lost it 2-1. Hod's preference for playing a precise passing game with a 3-5-2 formation was great in theory, but it was clear from the word go that we didn't have the players to do it effectively. I have to say right away that skipper Dennis "The Menace" Wise wasn't one of them. His skill levels had come on hugely since I last saw him play and he had developed a shrewd tactical awareness that – like me – he hasn't been given sufficient credit for. He was one of the first to realise that the squad wasn't capable of playing the mobile target golf that Hod wanted. And let's face it, target golf that eleven Hods could have carried off to perfection. Glenn knew that too, of course.

The game set the pattern for the season. Sometimes we played 3-5-2. Sometimes we played 4-4-2. But like I've said before, formations don't win matches, players do. And we just didn't have a strong enough squad to make much of an impression.

But back to that opening game. Afterwards, I was changing and sharing a joke with chunky defender Andy "His Second Touch Is A Tackle" Myers when a good natured groan from my team-mates heralded the arrival of Rovers' new full back, former (and future) Blue, Graeme Le Saux. He'd dropped in to have a few words with his old mates and to say hi to me.

Let me put my hand up right away and say that meeting the cheerful Channel Islander was to change my life. My void was about to be filled. Graeme was staying in town for the weekend and he suggested that I joined him and The Blues Brothers – "Hoppy" (Ian Hopkin), "Mints" (Scott Minto), "Dimmy" (Dmitri Kharine) and "Frank" (Frank Sinclair) for dinner at a little trattoria they all knew just off the Fulham Road. I asked Graeme what kind of place it was.

'It's a trattoria', Frank chimed in. 'You know, spaghetti, wine – stuff like that.' Pretty smart for a guy who'd complained of "altitude sickness" during training on our recent tour of the Far East. We were having a session on the beach at the time.

'I think Burksey of all people knows what a "trattoria" is, Div brain,' said Graeme. But he was wrong. Like I say, I'd made a point of not learning Italian during my stay.

'Are the people who run this place real Italians?' I asked Graeme warily.

'Definitely.'

'Where are they from?'

'Totteridge.'

I thanked God that they weren't Grappanese. Although the Mafia vendetta involving me was officially over, I knew that a lot of the *tifosi* still had something of a negative feeling about me. Better to be on the safe side where potential *assassinos* are concerned.

It proved to be a good night. The restaurant staff turned out to be AC Milan fans – the club that had benefited most by my "mistake" – and so treated me like royalty. And their "largesse" – as Telegraph man Harry Summer calls it – also spilled over to my mates as, for the first time ever, they tore up the bill. The staff, I mean.

Graeme and I hung on for a last drink after the others had gone – me a nice bottle of Barolo – I could handle it – and Graeme a mineral water. It was then that I noticed something sticking out of his pocket. The evening was about to get better. Very much better. What had caught my eye?

It was a book.

A novel. 'What're you reading? I asked, knowing what the answer would be. Or more or less. Footballers who read fiction read John Grisham. They read Robert Ludlum. A few read Stephen King. I didn't read. It wasn't that I couldn't. It's just something that I never got round to – like building a patio.

'It's called *The English Patient*.'

I lifted my glass. 'Which one of them wrote that?' I asked, spilling some Barolo on the lapel of my Armani jacket. Maybe I'd had a bit more to drink than I thought. I decided to stop for the evening. I could do that then.

'Michael Ondaatje.'

'Oh.'

'He's won the Booker Prize.'

There was another one I'd never heard of. 'What's it about?'

'I've only just started it, but it seems to be an elliptically told story about love, betrayal and politics.'

'Yeh? Right. Well, I think I'll wait for the movie.'

'Don't hold your breath, Burksey – they'll never be able to make a movie out of this.'

Well, Graeme couldn't be right about everything, could he? But he could see that I wasn't playing at home when it came to literature so he changed the subject. A little later, we called it a night. I was still on the wagon as regards women, so I went straight home. Of course, all those journos who call you a bad boy are never around when you behave responsibly like that. But mature behaviour doesn't sell papers.

Back at the flat, I was just settling down to a game of *Tutty Hump V Platinum Edition* on my Game Station, hoping to beat Wisey's best ever score of 385 straight podgers, when I felt something digging into my ribs. I took the offending object out of my pocket and got a surprise. It was the copy of *The English Patient* that Graeme had shown me in the restaurant. He must've slipped it into my pocket when I was saying "ciao" (Italian for 'food' – it was about the only word I knew) to everyone as we left the restaurant. I was on the point of tossing the book onto my scagliola table when something about the cover caught my attention. I looked at it. There seemed to be something fascinating about it. I looked at it more intently.

Although I didn't know it, one of the most remarkable events of my whole life was about to take place. At first I wondered whether it was because I was tired. Or I'd had a bit too much to drink. Or I was feeling super horny – I hadn't had so much as a J Arthur for almost a week. But then I realised that it was the book itself. I could feel a sort of energy coming from it. An energy generating from deep within its pages and then radiating out through its cover. It was as if the book were calling to me, urging me to accept its invitation to open myself up to the new possibilities it offered: the discovery of other worlds – worlds that could be uniquely powerful, sustaining and transforming. Was I experiencing some kind of epiphany here – living through a moment after which my life would never be the same again?

No. I wasn't. But I did feel strangely inspired. I threw the book aside and took up my Game Station handset with renewed confidence. Fifteen minutes later, I'd destroyed Wisey's score, setting a new high of 623. Wait until I showed the gifted little squirt that!

I went to bed on a high and couldn't sleep. I couldn't stop thinking about the experience with the book and what it had meant. Slowly, reluctantly, I got out of bed, put the light on and went to get it. About two years down the line, I got round to reading it. That's when my life really changed. But more of that later.

The highlight of the 93/94 Premiership season – especially for me – was doing the double over the otherwise rampant Man United. But it stood out like a stiffy in the bathwater. We finished in a lowly 14th place. More disappointing for me personally, was that I only joint top scored for the team with a modest 14 goals in all games.

The previous season, I had finished fourth best striker in Italy's Serie A. Two seasons before, I was robbed of top spot only by injury. And the season before that, I'd been the leading hit man in Italy scoring 36 goals, a couple ahead of the second place man, a certain Sampdoria striker by the name of Gianluca Vialli. Small world, football, isn't it? And it was about to get smaller.

Anyway, that was then. This was now. Only 14 goals. And only joint top scorer. And the guy who equalled me was only Gavin Peacock – no offence, Gav. Was I beginning to lose it? Of course not. Apart from the points I've already made, Glenn Hoddle would be the first to tell you that I was fearfully unlucky in a great many games. And luck, let me tell you, is a crucial thing in football – ask my old Boss Sir Alex Ferguson. Take our Premiership clash with Everton at Goodison in January, for example. I hit the post three times in the first half before picking up a knock and being subbed by Mark Stein. Everton wound up winning 4-2 and nicking the points.

Another factor was my A.C.L. (Anterior Cruciate Ligament) weakness following the injury I'd picked at the end of my second year in Italy. It had been fixed, but my right leg was never quite the same afterwards. It took half a yard off my pace. It took a couple of miles an hour out of my right-foot shot. And it sometimes required an injection to get me on to the park. I hate owning up to any form of weakness, but there it is.

Although my first league season at the Bridge was a disappointment, The FA Cup was a different story. Partly because of my famous back-heeled free kick winner against Wolves in the sixth round, we made it all the way through to Wembley – Chelsea's first major final in 22 years. Hod's "sign" – his dream at the start of the season – had proved prophetic after all.

And to add the kind of spice that makes The Cup the great competition it is, our opponents were to be none other than Manchester United. After our semi-final win against Luton, John Motson interviewed me (I'd laid on both Gavin Peacock goals in a comfortable 2-0 win) and made the point that up until then, the FA Cup had been something of a bittersweet competition for me. 'Bittersweet?' I said, dumbfounded. 'No – just bitter. Cheers, Motty.' With that, I then "stormed" (according to the Bun's Sam Curry) away to the dressing room where: "the ga-ga former goal grabber smashed everything – including bottles of victory bubbly – within reach of his pram."

Oh really? Let me – for the first time – tell you what really happened. I walked briskly to the dressing room, opened the door quietly and then, yes, I smashed everything I could get my hands on. Further – I had to be restrained by half the team from going back out into the interview area, tearing Motty's beloved sheepskin off his pudgy shoulders and ripping it to pieces. Do you think Keano's got a temper? Do you think Jimmy Floyd Hasselbaink looks a bit on the edge? Let me tell you something – when I lose it, I make both of them look like Mary Poppins. On valium.

Now don't get me wrong. As a player in England and Italy I've been kicked, punched, spat on and put through a mock execution. And I haven't turned a hair. But Motty really made me go spare – completely psycho balls-on-fire mental. It was just a good job that Boss Hod had repaired to a quiet corner of the stadium to commune with God and had missed my antics. Why was I in such a strop? Well – wouldn't you be? In my stints with Tottenham and Man U, I'd worked like stink to get both clubs to Wembley (in 1987 and 1990 respectively) only then to fall from favour and miss out on the Final Day Experience – and in the case of United, a winner's medal.

When kids ask me for advice, I always say the same thing: "Don't fall out with the manager." It cost me the best day out you can have as a footballer. Twice. So, if you're reading this David Pleat and Sir Alex, with the very greatest of respect – up yours.

By the way, I did make it up with Motty and I have to say that day in day out, he really is one of the nicest guys in football – as befits a "Son Of The Nance."*

After the semi-final win, most of the lads wound up at Luigi's – the trattoria I'd been to with Graeme at the start of the season and on numerous occasions since. We got our usual warm welcome, but I could sense that something was troubling Mario, the owner – why the place wasn't called Mario's, no-one could fathom – when he kissed me on only one cheek. Not long after the others had gone, I found out what the trouble was. It had arrived in a letter from the bank. Mario went into the extent of the restaurant's financial difficulties with me which, frankly, was a bit above my head. But I knew someone to whom such things were child's play. I got on the phone to my agent, Dave Green. Half an hour later, thanks to D G's advice, Mario's problems were over. And I was the new owner of Luigi's. I had big plans for the place, but I decided there and then that I would keep Mario on as manager and all the other staff. Mario wept. Maria, his wife wept. Marco and Marcello, his sons wept. I'm from

*The name given to lads who grow up in a Methodist Vicarage. Handy quiz fodder for you, there.

Huddersfield. I didn't weep. Then. But I was choked the following Monday morning when I found this letter on my doormat. In neat joined-up handwriting, it read:

Dear Dad,
Well done on getting to Wembley. Even although you didn't score, you done brilliant.
Love,
Frank xxx

What a wonderful little letter. And no request for tickets. I shuddered with emotion, knowing that my by now eight year-old son had written the letter all by himself. If the ever picky Roxanna had been supervising him, she would have corrected his grammar so that it read: "Even though you didn't score, you done brilliant". Worse, the sarky cow would have made him put "your son" in a bracket after his name to remind me of his existence. Roxie had some nerve. I'd provided very well for the pair of them since our split and had lavished presents on Frankie from the day he was born. Maybe I could've been there for him a bit more over the years, but what can you do? Nobody's perfect.

I decided to pay them a visit the following Sunday – the day after our Premiership clash with Arsenal at Highbury which we went on to lose 1-0. It didn't really matter – the Cup was our priority. I set off in the Maser to Buckhurst Hill hoping that Roxanna wouldn't throw a wobbly like the last time I showed up to take Frank out for the morning. Admittedly, I did have a couple of sorts I'd picked up in a club the night before with me – but the only reason they were still in the car was that I'd got a bit delayed taking them back to their convent school in Chingford and I didn't want to be late for Frankie. It's like Auntie Vi used to say: "I'm too nice for my own good sometimes."

As I arrived, I could hear a ball being kicked around in the back garden. I rang the bell. With no word of greeting, Rox let me in and I made straight for the kitchen which gave onto the lawn. As luck would have it, resplendent in his Chelsea kit, Frank had just dashed in for a quick drink – he'd probably been playing non stop all morning. That's my boy! I rushed up to him and threw him up almost to the ceiling in greeting – he always loved that.

'This isn't Frank", said Roxanna coldly. 'It's Paul, his mate.'

'Oh,' I said, feeling gladder than ever that me and the judgmental cow were ancient history.

'Can I have your autograph please, Mister Burkes?' said Paul.

'Sure.' Whatever else you say about me, I've never refused to sign an autograph.

Paul's made the twelve thousand, one-hundred and seventeenth special moment I'd granted since I'd returned to England. Pleased as Punch, the lad's trotted back out into the garden.

My ex-wife and I eyeball each other. 'Hello Roxanna.'

'Hello Stephen.'

I don't know why she had taken to using my full name. Even L'Acciuga used to call me "Stiv" – when she was being polite.

Roxie and Cinzia – how different these two women were – about as different as two ex-wives could be. Take their backgrounds: Roxie's dad had been a porter at Billingsgate fish market and her mother helped to run a crummy guest house in Edmonton. Cinzia's parents were Venetian socialites who lived in a palazzo on the Grand Canal. Take their jobs: Cinzia was one of the world's top supermodels; Roxie strangled chickens. It goes without saying that they were very different physically: L'Acciuga was dark, gorgeous, stood 5ft 10in and weighed just over eight stone; Rox was five foot five, weighed nine stone and was an average looking redhead.

Nevertheless, there was something about Ro-Ro.

And that something was sex. Ask anyone at Spurs. And I mean anyone. If you felt like some top tup, "Ginger Minge" was the girl.

L'Acciuga criticised my sexual performance, but as I've proved, the fault was really hers. She looked sexy, but she wasn't sexy at all when it came to it. For her, a "good seeing to" meant looking at herself in the various mirrors that surrounded our bed whilst we were doing it. For c***-crazy Rox, it meant jumping on top of me and really going for it. Like I've said before, she could move her hips like a belly dancer on fast-forward and her f**** had a grip like a garbage disposal unit. Maybe I haven't said that last bit before. Well you're hearing it now.

What it boils down to is that when it came to sex, Roxanna was Maradona to Cinzia's Carlton Palmer. And thinking about it was getting me hot. But now was neither the time nor the place to do anything about it. Still...

'Feel like tossing my caber? I said, reprising an old Ally McCoist line – one that had helped me score more often than he did.

'I've taken a vow of celibacy.'

'Since when?!'

'Since you walked in.'

Bitch. At that moment, Frank made his excited entrance from the garden. After checking with Rox that it was him, we left without further ado. It felt good to be reunited and I was looking forward to our special outing.

Although I didn't know just how special it was going to turn out to be. There was a crowd of kids and even a couple of adults around the Maser when we got outside.

I dispersed them with a little trick Jimmy Hill had taught me some years before. "F***
off!" I bellowed as loudly as I could. It worked. I think Frankie must have felt a sense
of awe at my ability to boss a potentially difficult situation because he didn't speak
for quite a while. But then I re-broke the ice by asking him how he was getting on
with the *Tutty Hump* Game Station game I'd had sent around the previous day.

'I got up to 2,496 podgers, but then I had to go to bed.'

'Liar. That's impossible!'

The little tinker went quiet again, but he perked up considerably when I swung
the Maser into the car park of the Happy Hooves Sanctuary For Neglected Donkeys
in Theydon Bois. We were going to see Hee-Haw, the animal I'd been sponsoring ever
since Chelsea's inspirational tour of the Far East. It had started to drizzle as we
arrived and the donkeys – about twenty of them – were all huddled together in one
corner of their paddock. Nevertheless, I spotted his grey old head immediately.

'Hee-Haw!' I shouted. 'Come on, my son!' He pretended not to hear me. It was a
game we played. But then Mary, one of the kindly handlers who worked at the place,
arrived on the scene and handed Frank a bag of carrots. She said she would bring
Hee-Haw over.

'Brilliant!' said Frank, displaying the sort of excitement only kids and Gazza know.

Frank had a question for Mary. 'Can we go for a ride? I want to go really fast!'

I thought of Roxanna again.

'I don't think he'd like that, lovey.'

I thought of Cinzia.

'But you can stroke his fur and give him a carrot.'

I thought of Carlton Palmer.*

Frank seemed to think that was a fun idea and spent a very happy five minutes
of quality time stroking and feeding his new friend. And then it happened. I was just
about to suggest that we call it a day, when Frank dropped his last carrot between
Hee-Haw's front legs and I bent down to pick it up.

The rest, as they say, is history. Seeing me suddenly ducking down in front of him
spooks the donkey. Before I can get out of the way, he's swivelled round, gathered
himself and let fly with his back right peg square against my already suspect right knee.
I go down quicker than a Cockney slag. Mary comes to my assistance immediately,
leading Hee-Haw away to where he could do no further damage.

*Hey, just pulling your plonker, Carlo! People who call you a donkey are just jealous.
Next time they say that, you should say, "Have you played for England?"*

'I want that f***ing animal destroyed!'

'Don't be silly, Mister Burkes. You're just in shock.'

Frank, the cry baby, starts to blub. I get on my mobile to the Boss.

'Mister Hoddle – it's Steve Burkes.'

'This is my day of rest, Stevie. It'd better be important.'

'It is.'

'Cos we've got two hundred coming for our annual Say, Sing and Sizzle in a minute.'

'Say, Sing and Sizzle?'

'Prayers, hymns and a barbecue on the lawn.'

Suddenly my knee didn't feel so terrible.

'Listen, Boss. I've just taken a bad kick on my right knee.'

'Talk about a late tackle – it was yesterday we played Arsenal.'

'Hee-Haw, the donkey did it.'

'What – Martin Keown?"

In the end, I got the message across and the Chelsea Medical Machine went into top gear. I unreservedly apologise here and now to the doctor, physio and nurse who had the task of informing me that the injury would keep me out of the 93/94 FA Cup Final against my former club. All I can say in my defence is that I didn't enjoy punching their lights out. And I did make it up to the nurse by promising to give her a good night in when she came out of hospital. Another bit of Burksey generosity that didn't make the papers. Her reconstructive nasal surgery went well, by the way.

The F.A. Cup – "bittersweet"? If I'd never received Frankie's heart-warming letter, I'd never have taken him on that fun day out as a reward. And I wouldn't have missed out on my own, as a result. That Chelsea went on to lose 4-0 was no consolation at all. You'd be forgiven for thinking that God never lets a good deed go unpunished, wouldn't you.

And as for kids? As I write this – after taking a whole raft of rescue and healing programmes in California – I regard my relationship with Frank as one of the most important and fulfilling of my life. Back in 1994, I often thought that I would have been better off with a dog. Frank – if you're reading this – I'm really comfortable around our relationship right now. I'm there for you. And you can contact my agent for a meeting, any time, son.

1993/94 was a season of two halves as far as my England activities went. Students of the game won't need telling why. In November out went old Boss Graham Taylor, and in, like a breath of fresh air, came Terry Venables.

It should have happened sooner. There is no doubt in my mind that England would have qualified for the '94 World Cup in America had Terry been in charge from "the, like, get go?" as Brandee used to say.

Now let's clear up a few things about Mister Taylor, starting with something that seems to have escaped everyone's notice. There's no doubt about it, the man was an accomplished top level club manager. Think you could have done better? Think again. And since retiring from the dugout, G.T has made a second successful career for himself as a broadcaster. And a very popular one he has become. Yes, thanks to his work for the peerless Radio Five Live*, the affable Gaffer is now a welcome guest in most of our homes. Personally, I love to hear the Worksopian's well-meaning tones coming in over the air waves. There's something reassuringly familiar about it. It's as if the family's faithful old slipper-wearing, pipe-smoking Labrador has just come padding in from the garden and ... Sorry – just had a bit of a flashback there. I realise dogs don't smoke pipes. Or wear slippers come to that. Even Labradors. Anyway, you get the point.

Graham Taylor is a very decent man. In fact, he would make an ideal next-door neighbour, wouldn't he?

But they don't give out World Cups to people for being pleasant. Otherwise, the former Liverpool and Hamburg Great, Kevin Keegan, would have walked the thing when he was in charge.

No, at world level, soccer is what the Americans call "hard ball". And perhaps in that sense, nobody had softer balls than Mister Taylor. It wasn't just the "Do I not like that?" Turnip stuff. Nor was it the substituting of Gary Lineker – along with Alan Shearer the best English striker I've ever played with – in the vital Euro 92 clash against Sweden. It was a lot of things. What it all boils down to is the man's approach, vision and ideas about the game of football.

At the top level, his approach was suspect. His vision was blurred. And his ideas were just plain weird.

The place: A corridor in The Europa Hotel, Rotterdam. The time: The 13th of October 1993 – three hours before kick off in our vital World Cup qualifier against Holland. Enter the players – scores of millions of pounds worth of talent, who line up outside Mister Taylor's suite like naughty schoolboys waiting to see the headmaster. I'm the first to be admitted. Wearing the kind of expression that could curdle milk, he hands me a sealed envelope. For a minute, I wonder if I'm getting a bung.

Just kidding.

But then he tells me that we are going to have a one-on-one "tutorial" about our "ordeal against Holland" to come. During the session, he is going to give me a "motivational tool" which I am to think about and use during the match itself.

*Naturally, if the even more peerless Stelsat did radio, it would be a different story.*

'Burksey – how well do you think you personally performed in our fateful, disastrous 2-0 defeat against Norway earlier in the competition?'

'Personally? Not too bad – I was unlucky with that clearance off the line.'

'Granted. But overall. If your performance was an object, what object would it be?'

'Eh?'

'What object, what thing, do you think would accurately represent how you played that day?'

'Still don't think I follow you, Boss.'

'For example, when you played superbly and scored four goals against San Marino at Wembley in February last year, you might say that your performance was like a grand prix racing car. Or a sharp sword. Or Mount Everest. Do you see what I'm getting at?'

'I think so.' The Gaffer was having another one of his turns.

'So what object do you think represents your performance against Norway?'

'A key.'

'Why?'

'Because I kept trying to open the door.' Good answer, I thought.

'I see. Right, now open your envelope.'

I opened it. It contained a photograph. It was of dog shit. A huge brown steaming Mister Whippy.

'That's how well I think you played, son. Yes – like a giant dollop of dog excrement!' Graham's face was a picture of righteous indignation.

He waited for the image to sink in. I felt numbed, humiliated.

'Now, because denial is the first stumbling block to recovery and improvement, I want you to repeat after me: "I played like a giant dollop of dog excrement."'

'I played like a dollop of excrement', I muttered, still in a kind of shock.

'How big a dollop?'

'Giant', I said, the word barely audible.

'And what kind of excrement was it?'

'Dog.'

'Now put it all together and shout it out as loud as you can.'

'I played like a giant dollop of dog excrement.'

'I can't hear you!'

'I played like a giant dollop of dog excrement!!!!!'

'In fact sunshine, you ARE a giant dollop of dog excrement, aren't you?'

'I suppose I am.' I hung my head.

'Not good enough, is it?'

'No,' I whimpered.

'Right – now you've owned up to what you are, you can move forward and improve. Right?'

'Yes." I blew my nose.

'But to stop you from sliding backwards, I want you to take that photograph out onto the pitch this evening rolled up in your sock. Whenever there's a stoppage, I want you to take it out, look at it and meditate on its meaning. Right – that's you finished.'

With that, an FA official began escorting me like a zombie to the door. I stumbled, unable to feel my legs.

'Play well', said Graham behind me. 'Next!'

I learned later that Graham Taylor was using something called 'reverse psychology'. A motivational tool? He certainly was. Other players took the field that day with photos of custard, Reliant Robins, and Orville The Duck stuck in their socks. Did the strategy work? Put it this way: I played like shit, we lost two nil and blew our chance of going to America.

Some weeks later I was a guest on a live radio programme hosted by the genial John Inverdale. He asked me what I thought of Graham Taylor.

'Is this a family show?

'Yes.'

'He's a c***.'

I didn't do live radio or TV after that for a while. Actually, I've met up with Graham several times since those dark days and had a laugh over the by now infamous photos. It takes a big man to do that. Me, I mean.

The 94/95 season will go down as probably the turning point in my career. But not for football reasons. Chelsea had qualified for the European Cup Winners' Cup through Man U's double-winning performance the previous term and we actually reserved some of our best football for the competition. Although I banged in almost a goal a game, there was no repeat of The Blues' triumph of 1971 and we crashed out at the semi-final stage. It was close, though. We only lost out by the odd goal in seven in forcing Real Zaragoza into extra time at the Bridge. It was easily the highlight of the season: we finished a dismal eleventh in The Premiership and suffered an early exit in the FA Cup. So how come 94/95 represented a turning point? Once again, enter the Professor – Mister Graeme Le Saux.

Unlike his prim predecessor, new England Boss El Tel encouraged the lads to go in for a spot of innocent horseplay and G.Le.S was our practical joker in chief – a role

I knew only too well, myself. One stunt that will always stick in my mind happened on 28th March 1995, the day before our clash with Uruguay at Wembley. Graeme had stowed a polaroid camera in the Bisham Abbey changing rooms and after final training used it take undercover photos of the lads' wedding tackle. Then, he stuck up the photos – in size order of the equipment in question – on the noticeboard under a sign he'd made which read: "The Pecker Order of the England Football Team". Everybody thought it was a great laugh – including the Gaffer who presented the winner (yours truly, but then you knew that, didn't you?) with a nominal prize – a BMW convertible, if memory serves. The only person who didn't seem to enjoy it was a teenage Robbie Fowler, who'd joined the squad for a bit of experience. Read into that what you will. Just kidding.

Encouraged by Terry's confidence-building management skills and newly bonded by Graeme's sense of fun, we went into the Uruguay game as a real unit bursting with self belief and camaraderie. The result? We drew 0-0 in a totally lacklustre display. Football!

Whilst we were changing after the game, Graeme said:

'Ever read that book I gave you, Burksey?'

'What book?'

'The Ondaatje.'

Of course I hadn't. 'Oh, yeh – it was great.'

'Really?'

'I couldn't put it down.' At least that bit was true. Sort of.

'In that case, you want to go to The Anville Gallery, Soho 7.30 on Monday night – they're showing work by a new young find called Damien Hirst.'

'What – art?' I said with total incredulity. Who did he think I was – David Hackney?

'Yeh. If you enjoyed *The English Patient*, you'll love his work. If you really think about it, he's exploring some of the same themes. In a way.'

Shit. 'I don't know, Graeme. Art, you know it's not really for the likes of... '

'Pat Nevin's seen the show and he says it's a knockout. So has Nobby.'

'What – Nobby Stiles!?'

'Norbert Lynton, author of *The Story Of Modern Art*.'

Thank God for that – there are some things that should never change.

At that moment, Boss Terry called for quiet. He looked unusually serious. And he was holding a stack of photos. Oh, oh!

'Okay lads – tonight – you all played like this.' Terry held them up in a fan. They were the shots Graeme had taken in The Abbey changing rooms. So there we had it. Under Graham Taylor I was shit. Under Terry Venables, I was a dick.

Terry continued. 'But next time you play, every one of you is going to play like the best footballer who ever lived. There's an envelope under each of your benches. Open 'em up.'

Feeling like I'd been down this humiliating road before, I did as I was told. I took out the photo which I guessed would be of Pelé. Or maybe Bobby Charlton. Or my old adversary, Diego. I was wrong. It was a photo of one Tristan Stephen Burkes – scoring against Man U earlier in the season. On my left, Graeme was holding a photo of himself performing a characteristically incisive tackle; and on my right, Teddy Sheringham was looking at a shot of himself delivering one of those brilliant defence splitting passes for which he is rightly celebrated. And so on throughout the team. Silence. We were all choked. Then skipper David Platt spoke up. 'Cheers, Boss,' he said, simply. But it spoke volumes. Did Michael Ondaatje's book say anything as powerfully moving as that? Or this Damien Hirst's paintings? I doubted it. What Terry had done was typical of the man. It was big, full of wit and warmth and let's face it – guaranteed to make you want to die for him out there on the pitch.

When people ask me who is the best I've ever played under, the answer I give is always the same: my ex-wife Roxanna. In terms of managers, it's Terry. He's by far the best reader of a game I've ever come across. He's positive. He's fun. He doesn't throw dinner services at you. He's got a good singing voice. He can dance. He can write scripts, hang doors, mend sinks. There's no end to the bloke's talents. Ask him sometime.

But did all this 'forward psychology' work for us – the England team? Yes. In our next Wembley game, we destroyed Japan 2-0 to prove we were heading in a completely new direction. And so was I personally. Terry Venables had opened the door.

Damien Hirst was to push me through it.

I took myself off to the "Hirst Show" at the Anville Gallery in Soho more out of curiosity than anything. What did I have to lose? What I had to lose turned out to be over a hundred grand. What I gained was ownership of some brilliant art works. They weren't paintings – that's probably what I liked about them in the first place. To be honest, quite a few of these "installations" made me laugh.

Does humour belong in art? It did for me. And apparently for Mister Hirst. There was a bicycle with dead rabbits stuffed between the spokes entitled Now That's What I Call "Startled". There was a complete toilet installation made of glass in which you could watch various items of waste (labelled "ideas") as they were flushed down the pan, circulated round the u-bend, and then pumped back up a pipe (labelled "this is not a pipe") into the cistern for the cycle to begin again. This piece was called: Superfluity, Fluidity, Futility. I howled. I couldn't help it. Tears were streaming down my face when a tasty but haughty looking young gallery assistant approached me. She was not happy.

'You obviously have no idea what PoMo is all about.'

'I f***ing do', I said, wondering what an arty farty tart like her knew about football tactics. To the uninitiated, P.O.M.O. (Point Of Maximum Opportunity) refers to a position on the pitch that offers a player the greatest chance of hurting the opposition – say the back post for a cross.

Before the thing could develop into a full scale barney, I felt a hand on my shoulder. It belonged to the wronged young maestro himself – Damien Hirst. I flexed slightly in case he tried to give me a slap – I'd been caught like that before when backstage at a Versace show in Milan, Linda Evangelista took offence at a remark I made about lapels and nutted me. I missed four vital Serie A games for Grappanese as a result. Fabien Barthez still laughs about it.

I needn't have worried about Damien. 'I can't believe it!' he said, holding out the show catalogue for me to sign. 'You're one of the greatest artists ever.'

'That makes one of us', I said. Although I was starting to like the kid, and rate his stuff, I didn't want him getting ideas above his station.

Naturally, Ms Haughty – Jemima – was now all over me. I decided that I'd whip her back to the flat afterwards to show her what a real one man show was about. But I amended my plans when I heard a familiar voice behind me.

'The great artist is a man who refuses the question: "why is a mouse when it spins?" Or not.' It was current Bolton Boss Sam Allardyce. I'm just kidding. It was – who else? – Monsieur Eric Cantona.

The arrival of a second footballing superstar was too much for Damien. Shaking, he went to lie down on one of his couch installations – or it could have just been a couch – it was difficult to tell. An intrigued Jemima looked on as Eric and I greeted each other warmly – our mutual respect was genuine – but there was a look of surprise in his eyes.

'Sometimes a zebra is a horse in the stripes of Newcastle United.'

'Eh?'

'And sometimes it is just a zebra.'

Whoosh – Eric's thoughts went over my head. Like sudden wind. 'I'm not with you, son.'

'I am not your son, *visage de merde*.' Beautiful sounding language French, isn't it?

'Alright, don't get your croissants in a twist, Monsieur Jean Paul Sarky!' I countered.

I didn't know exactly what it meant, but it had stuck in my mind ever since I heard Peter Schmeichel shouting it at Eric at The Bridge earlier in the season. The Great Dane had let a tame shot from Eddie Newton trickle through his legs for our first goal (we went on to lose 3-2) and Eric had let him know what he thought about it. I knew I was inviting trouble bringing it up but *Le Roi* (French for Eric) as they called him at Old Trafford, smiled inscrutably in response. You can never second guess me. You can second guess Eric even less.

'I mean only that I didn't expect to see you here.'

'Sometimes, the great striker aims at art stuff – not just the goal', I said. That showed him. Two could play at this clever cryptic word crap.

'Our goal is the net. And a net is patterned space – connected like the mind.'

That got Jemima going. 'With interesting Gestalt implications', she said.

More wind over my head. Eric turned to her. For one fleeting second I thought he was going to give her a kicking. But he contented himself with just spitting menacingly.

'That', he said, indicating the spittle and pausing for effect like only the French can, 'is my gestalt.'

Jemima looked impressed. Gobbing is art now, apparently.

The three of us decided to go back to my place where what the tabloids love to call a "three in a bed romp" was definitely on the cards. We took our leave almost immediately. But first I phoned D.G., my agent, instructing him to shell out for the works I'd selected and to have them delivered as soon as the exhibition "wrapped".

Back at the flat, I didn't think it would take us long to un-wrap Jemima. But I was wrong. We got talking. I didn't usually bother with foreplay, but Eric and this girl were beginning to interest me. And what they were beginning to interest me in was the modern art scene. "Fuck off Burksey!" I hear you cry. "You've been smoking Utah Puffballs again!" No, hear me out. Eric got the ball rolling with an interesting remark to Jem:

'Burksey here a couple of games ago took a free-kick against Arsenal just outside the box. You have seen such a moment?'

'Of course, it's when the defenders all form a wall with their hands in front of their c***s.'

"C***s", eh? Now this may shock you, but I'm not keen on women who talk dirty as a rule. That's my job. But being French, Eric didn't mind.

'Good, well the kicker usually tries to bend the ball up and over the wall. This man has a different mentality. He tried to drill the ball *under* it.'

'Impressive.'

'When facing the installations of Hirst, Burksey has used his mentality again. Laughing at them is the kick under the barrier of the artwork.'

Jemima purred with pleasure. 'Of course the works are supposed to be playful.'

Eric sighed and stared off into the distance as the girl caught up with his thought processes. 'Exactly', he said.

Jemima picked up the ball and ran with it: 'In fact, I think Burksey's revolutionary thinking against Arsenal means that he is fundamentally a performance artist.'

Eric raised his eyebrows.

'And you too, of course, Eric.'

Eric lowered them.

After a few more points, Jemima concluded that my "sensibility" was after all an authentic "Post Modern" one and that I was "in a sense deeply sensitive to conceptual continuity."

Still more wind. But Eric agreed and spat appreciatively. They both thought that a key aspect of modern art was that it was trying to promote "a more democratic and integrated relationship between the artist, the art work itself and the spectator." You weren't supposed to bow down in front of Damien's toilet passively, you were supposed to be an active part of the whole "dialogue". Further, Jemima said that: "the contribution made by the spectator to the work itself is totally crucial."

Now that I understood completely. My contribution had been over a hundred grand. With it, the boy Hirst could carry on with his work for a good while longer.

Eric enjoyed Jem's last point so much, he spat twice. More gestalt for me to wipe up.

'When the hawk flies only from the glove', Eric opined, 'it is because the dead hand of the bourgeois has been cut off.' And with that – he was gone. No "three in a bed romp", "triple tup", "mini-roast" or whatever you want to call it – for us tonight. And Eric's reason for leaving?

'I've got to get home to the wife.'

Jemima spat three times.

Eric's sudden departure may have pissed off Jem, but it suited me. We didn't waste much time getting stuck in. My new conquest proved to be an adventurous lay and we didn't leave the bedroom much for a couple of days. Late on the second night, she said that she fancied doing it doggy style wearing one of my football shirts. Who was I to argue with a lady? She slunk off into my trophy room and came back wearing a Notts Forest number with "Pearce" emblazoned across the shoulders. That seemed appropriate – he'd shafted me often enough on the pitch. At first, I thought I'd made the wrong decision. Taking Jem from behind, Psycho's name kept leaping up at me and I couldn't get him out of my mind, really throwing me off my stroke. But it delayed my climax so much that, for the first time ever, my partner came first. With brilliant almost Roxie-like results. For future sessions, I made a mental note to get hold of a Dean Windass shirt from somewhere.

Jem turned out to be a right pain and I soon stopped seeing her. But she helped me take my first faltering steps along a road that was to really change things for me and for that, I thank her.

I've still no idea how she knew about P.O.M.O.

CHAPTER FOURTEEN

# CULTURE VULTURE

The 1995/96 season was the one Boss Hodd had long been looking forward to. According to his lights, this was when everything was going to change. Some hopes, eh?

Well f*** me, everything did change. Thanks to the Gaffer, there wasn't an organ in the entire organization that didn't feel the spirit of renewal flushing through its innards. It was like watching one of Cinzia's enemas at work. Not that I ever did that, of course. That would have been sick.*

But back to the football club. A new dawn was on the horizon and its pulse was beating with a vital new purpose. Glenn had realised that cheap and cheerfulness off the pitch tended to produce cheap and cheerfulness on it. You put rubbish in, you get rubbish out – even from gifted players. He was not alone in that view. For years, the team had been regarded by friend and foe alike as a disaffected and flashy outfit – cheesed-off Champagne Charlies whose championship challenging chances were about the same as a bunch of chain-smoking Chavs from Chiswick. That was set to change. Even if it meant rattling cages, ruffling feathers – "pinching the gorilla's bollocks" as they say in Italy – a brave new world** was coming. In fact, it was here right now.

Yes, in an act of sacreligous brutality, Glenn tore up the bikkie rota. And brought in a top nutritionist. It didn't stop there. In came a top reflexologist to help us take a nap for half an hour whenever we felt like it – sorry to help our feet recover from running all those miles and kicking all those footballs.*** Which,

*But if you say just one more word about me, Cinzia, so help me, I'll post that bastard video on the interweb.

**Blues fan Aldous Huxley wrote a book about it. "Silas In Gaza" it's called. I'm told old Aldous was a bit of an acid head in his day. It shows. Everybody knows Gazza's spelled with two zeds. And he's never played for Chelsea anyway. And as for the boy Silas – I've no idea who he is.

***Apparently, that's not what they're for either, but hey, I'm a footballer not a foot fetishist. Actually, I am, but that's between me and a certain celebrity chef.

unlike their moth-eaten forebears, were all fully pumped-up now. I tell you – you've no idea what things were like before.

Harlington was abuzz with changes and it made us players feel as if we were actually worth something. Ground improvements were going on at the Bridge also. There was even a wild idea that the area of the stadium known affectionately as "Poland" would get roofed toilets. Blimey, don't push the boat out too far, Ken.

Unbelievable when you consider where Chelsea Football Club plc is at nowadays, isn't it? Mister Abramovich, we could have done with your money back in those days.

1995/96 was also a time of personal evolution for me. I was opening myself up to new people and to new experiences. I started going to all manner of high brow cultural events and that was despite the rigmarole of having to ring Jay so that she could sort out the tickets, post-show dinner reservations and a suitable companion for the evening. In one pulsating week, I went to see the Complicite Company's exploration of hope, love and survival in a peasant community in France in their production of *Three Lives Of Lucie Cabrol* at the Shaftesbury; Alexander's Goehr's reworking of Monteverdi's exploration of hope, love and survival in seventeenth-century Italy in his *Arianna* at the Royal Opera House; and Steve Barron's exploration of hope, love and survival in the art world of Raphael and Michelangelo in his *Teenage Mutant Ninja Turtles: The Movie,* at The Warner. Well, I needed a break after all that other stuff. I was doing my best, but there were limits.

Take experimental theatre. I'd give Beckett's *Waiting For Godot* a miss if I were you. *Waiting for Sod All,* I call it. No wonder they murdered the writer in that cathedral slaying. And don't get me started on Harold Pinter. Nobody talks.................like that. And have you ever been to a Benjamin Britten opera? Don't bother. Unless you enjoy hearing blokes with voices like belt sanders "singing" about sailors being hung and shit.

Art, though, was different. That, I enjoyed. It may be controversial – who cares? – but in going from Britten to Britart, I think you're going from the ridiculous to the sublime. There wasn't just Damien pushing the envelope. There was a really good squad of artists flying the flag across the board. Tracey "Unmade Bed" Emin; Herbert "Great Deeds Against The Reds" Chapman and his brothers; Marc "Self" Quinn;*

*How Quinny had the idea – and the balls – to produce a portrait sculpture made from eight pints of his own solidified blood is beyond me. And just imagine how well he would have led the line for Arsenal, Man City and Sunderland if he'd had a normal bodyful of the stuff? The super nice Paddy would have been frightening. Whoops, I think I may just have had another flashback...

Sam Taylor-Wood... the team sheet goes on and on and it reads like a who's who? of top cutting-edge talent.

I have to say that my new interests were starting to put me in solid with a few of the footballing fraternity and so I learned not to talk about it in front of them. The thing you must never do as a player is be seen to be getting ideas above your station. Football teams are like a very conforming community? Jesus, some will call you a poof for reading a paper. A proper one like The Guardian, I mean. I could take their barbed bullets myself, of course. But I didn't want any ricochets heading the way of my more vulnerable fellow culture vultures, ex-Blues Graeme Le Saux and Pat Nevin.

Another problem was that my celebrity made it difficult for me to get in to theatres, cinemas and galleries unnoticed. There was only one thing for it. I dusted off my wardrobe of Francis "Tanky" Smith disguises and once more pressed them into service. Very few theatre goers recognized me dressed as a South American Bishop. And fewer still as a nineteenth-century deep sea diver. Mind you, that outfit wasn't without its drawbacks. Going to the toilet in the thing was a nightmare. And getting in and out of my seat in the stalls was a production number all of its own. If anyone ever asks you why lead-weighted boots never caught on with the theatre-going public – there's your answer.

My cultural work was getting me noticed by sections of the media that normally left me alone and I gave several interviews at the time. I still tended to be a bit on the defensive side with people I thought were taking the Micky Hazard – but hey, that's the chance you take. But I would like to apologise here and now to multi-talented brainbox Sir Melvyn Bragg, who despite being a devout Gooner is also one of my biggest fans. The incident in question took place during the filming of an interview for a South Bank Show featuring footballers with unusual interests and hobbies. A South Bank Show in which my "slot" has never been shown or even acknowledged as existing. Until now.

The morning's "shoot" had gone well. Vinnie Jones had demonstrated his pride and joy – a flea circus which had been in the family for generations. Remarkably, many of the microscopic performers could actually sing. I've never heard the *Hallelujah Chorus* sound so interesting. And I'm from Huddersfield whose Choral Society's *Messiah* is the stuff of legend.

Then former Liverpool Great, Phil Thompson, brought in a few of his collection of nearly five-thousand doilies and antimacassars. The following exchange was typical:

MB:     'So why do you collect doilies, Phil?'

PT:     'I don't know. I just do.'

Then came my turn. I was nervous, pressured, like, really stressed? I was going to talk about my theatre-going and had brought along several match day programmes to illustrate my remarks. Which, by the way, had not been written for me by a special consultant employed by Dave Green as some back room boffins at ITV have suggested.

MB: 'Burksey, I see you're a devotee of Edward Bond.'

B: 'So?'

MB: 'I was wondering what turns you on about his work?'

B: 'Ah. I know that one. I find his exploration of human alienation and submerged anger in many plays resonant. But surely his major achievement is to have reformulated the terms of the debate on the role of drama in relation to the social and historical contexts his work seeks both to define and be defined by.'

MB: 'You mean his work has rendered redundant the notion that drama can serve either as a passive mirror of society or as an active instrument of change?'

B: 'I suppose you think you're clever.'

MB: 'Sorry?'

B: 'You will be, sunshine.'

With that, I've got out of my chair and nutted the presenter square on the conk.

Anybody who has seen – or more importantly heard – the show since will know what the consequences of "by boment of badness" were. Sorry, Belvyn. I know you could have taken all kinds of action against me and you didn't. You're a scholar and a gentleman and I thank you. By, the way, you did right to have second thoughts about taking a swing at me at the time. It would have been the biggest mismatch since Parky and Muhammad Ali.

I fared much better with an interview I did the following week. A Ms Suzanne Steadman from *Funky Feminist Magazine* – see how I remembered names now I was more or less drug free* – had dropped in to see me basically to take the pistachio out of my "antique male opinions and attitudes".

'So, Steve, what do you look for in a woman?' she said, rolling her tape recorder.

'I wouldn't say I look for anything in particular. I take people as I find them whether male or female.' See, I was doing better here because I felt on safer ground. In both senses – my new Cheyne Walk flat was where I'd been hanging my hat for the past six months. Not that I had a hat. But if I did have, this is where it would have been hung. Well hung, if you will.

---

*Her name was actually Sarah Streddar. And she worked for FemForum Magazine. Thanks to Jay for the update.*

'There must be some quality that attracts you?'

'Well, if pressed, I would say, a calm, sensitive intelligence.'

'A calm, sensitive intelligence?'

'And a clitoris the size of a Malteser.'

Her eyes lit up at that. As well they might. 'So now we come to the truth.'

'Well, you asked.'

'It's been said that you've "made love" to over six-thousand women.'

'Yes, but not all at once,' I said, essaying my sweetest smile.

'So why do you think you need so much sex?'

'Well, a Doberman needs a lot more meat than a Jack Russell, doesn't it?' I said momentarily adjusting the bulge in my Lorenzo Scivoloso swimming trunks.

At that, Suzanne's let out what could only be termed a snort of disgust. With a squirt of disdain on the side. And a dollop of derision to follow.

Five minutes later, we were in bed. Three days later, she left to take up a missionary position in Africa. It gets them like that sometimes. Oh and just for the record, she was more of a marrowfat pea than a Malteser.

But back to the football. Yeh, the wind of change blowing through the whole infrastructure of Chelsea Football Club was most welcome. But bikkie rotas are one thing. Playing staff rotas are another. And this is where we really scored. Scored big time. Boss Hod's "second major signing from Europe" turned out to be none other than Judge Dread himself, the incomparable Ruud Gullit. He was a former World Player of the Year, European Player of The Year, European Cup Winner... To sum up, the powerful midfielder was the best thing in shorts since Wallace and Gromit. Animated shorts at that.

Yet to begin with, I wasn't sure what to make of his signing. It wasn't because I feared he might steal my limelight – nobody could do that. No, it was because – to sound like my first Boss, Mick Buxton, for a moment – I just didn't know what to make of him. The only time we'd talked previously – despite numerous subsequent encounters in Serie A – had been back at Italia 90 when we had had a bit of a ... I don't know what it was really, but it involved the business with the hair stroking, if you remember.

I needn't have worried.

'Burkshey. I can't tell you how glad I am that we'll be playing alongshide each other', he said at our first meeting at Harlington.

'Me too, Ruud', I said, extending my hand. The subsequent handshake was so knuckle-crunchingly powerful – on both sides – that lesser men would have suffered injury. He was tough, this guy. I immediately challenged him to a game of keepy uppy.

**191**

'No thanksh. You're bound to beat me',* he smiled modestly. 'But hey, we're going to play shome shexy football together, yeh? Winning football alsho.'

As Glenn blew his whistle to begin our first training session of the season, I felt great. In the head, at least. In the legs, and especially the F.R.K. (F***ing Right Knee), I wasn't so happy. But nevertheless, I thought the term ahead was going to go with a bang. It was certainly going to start with a spark. A spark in the form of the Welsh Wizard, my former United team-mate, Mark "Sparky" Hughes. It would be brilliant having "Calf Boy" operating in the hole behind me once more. On the pitch I mean, you sleazeballs.

For the benefit of young kids, the uninitiated or the just plain thick, I'll tell you something about Mister Mark Hughes. If Sparky had had anything like my pace, he would have been one of the game's All-Time International Greats. He was still one helluva player, brother. Another genius to have been spat out by the Old Trafford mincing machine. If you think that's harsh – ask the incomparable Roy Keane.

Any students of the game out there? Any students of Chelsea football club in particular? Then maybe you can explain why, with everything we had going for us, CFC didn't hammer everybody out of sight in the season that followed. Actually, don't bother, I'll tell you why. We were still uneven as a squad. In fact, you could argue that we were more uneven than we were before. The gap between our good and our great just got bigger. Ruud Gullit and Andy Myers anyone? What about Steve Burkes and David Lee?

The result? Mid-table mediocrity in the Premiership and a second round exit in the Cola Cola Cup. What a let down. After all that had been planned, sweated over and carried out, we were back more or less where we had been two seasons before. At least our diet was good and our feet felt nice.

The FA Cup, though, was a different story. Once again, it proved to be our saving grace, the only competition in which we did anything significant. We went out at the semi-final stage eventually. And just to apply that final twist of the knife into our guts – into me and Sparky's guts especially – the victors were .... Torquay United.

Just kidding. It was Manchester United who did us 2-1. Nobody seems to remember now that after only five minutes, I netted with a perfectly legitimate header that nearly ripped Peter Schmeichel's right hand off. I was judged to have pushed the said

---

*He wasn't a bad judge wasn't The Dread, mind you. My record – seven hours, thirty-seven minutes and fourteen seconds still stands as a club best today. By over seven and a half hours. Some have said that nobody else could simply be bothered breaking it. Yeh, right!

Keano in the box as I've got on the end of a fizzing Ruud banana. I wanted that goal and that win bad. I still can't think of it now without wanting to chuck something... say Old Trafford into the River Orwell. Brandee later gave me the low-down on my feelings:

'It's like Man United was your lover and she wanted out? So then it's over, but in your heart you still love her? Then you, like, internalise the hurting? And the only way the suppressed pain can express itself is through an eruption of, like, sudden anger? And so when the ...'

'Look, hurry up and come, willya? My jaw's going to sleep, here...'

One fascinating aspect of playing in that semi was watching the young David Beckham in action up close. There had been such a lot of hype about him and I must say you could see why. Talk about a sweet right foot. It was obvious to me that Becks could bong a ball into a bucket from fifty yards if he'd wanted to. I was impressed. Big style. And I've continued to be impressed right up to the present moment.

Now I know with everything that has happened since those early, carefree days, that some have come to love Becks and some have come to feel slightly less positive about him. The detractors* point to the super extravagant lifestyle he enjoys with his lovely and talented wife, Victoria. They point to the couple's seemingly insatiable thirst for publicity and media attention when it suits them – and their contempt for the very same process when it becomes "intrusive". Critics point to the tattoos, the wardrobe, the estuary English, the fact that Becks may not be the brightest slice in the loaf.... On and on. You know what? These people are jealous. It's as simple as that.

English Heroes? There's no such thing is there? Why? Because we build people up only to knock them down in this country.

I'm telling you, if Lord Admiral Nelson, William Shakespeare, and Winston Churchill were playing today – they'd cop some right stick from the fans. Just a final note on Becks. I reckon he's the nicest, kindest guy in football. Even if he were just a really good player instead of the genius he is, that should be enough for you fans. You ungrateful f***ers. Right, sermon over. Amen.

For once, I'm not going to tell you how many goals I scored at the end of the season. You stat nerds out there will know anyway. But think of this – a striker is only as effective as the service he receives. True, we had the drive of Wisey, the brilliance of Rudi, and the sharpness of Sparky. But we had the combined efforts

---

*So called because his first critics were fans of Ipswich Town.*

of Dopey, Sleepy, Grumpy, Happy and Bashful as well. No wonder my tally wasn't the greatest of all time. The problems surfaced early. After the first six games, I'd netted only once – and that was a bundled-over-the-line effort off my groin. Hence the chant that opposition fans cottoned-on to for the next few games. To the tune of *Colonel Bogey*, it went:

> *Burksey*
> *Has only got one goal*
> *And that one*
> *Came off his f\*\*\*ing pole*

I'm not sure how the thing continued, but I remember the advice given to me at the end was an anatomical impossibility.

Yes, I ended the club season on all sorts of footballing lows. My knee required a jab before every game. And frankly – I'm sorry if this shocks you – after mid-season, a sense was starting to creep in that if I reined back a bit here and there – did it really matter? Don't forget that I'd run around like a mad thing for every second I was on the pitch for the past ten seasons. Maybe now I was just getting a bit more Saviola. Yes, there was no doubt about it, for the first time in my career, the daily diet of bread and butter football I was eating was beginning to taste like its real life nutritional counterpart to me. It was simple fare necessary only for sustaining physical life, not the exciting "soul food" – as my close friend, Jazz Great Wynton Marsala calls it – that nourished the mind and spirit as well. In a nutshell, I was getting stale. Only a bit, mind you. But it was there.

Before we get on the feast of footer soul food that was Euro 96 – the first major football tournament to be played in England since we destroyed the hated Germans\* thirty years earlier – I had a sad experience to go through. Orange Microdot, the band my brother Tarka had started with some school mates as long ago as 1977, played its farewell concert that Summer. They went out in style, headlining at the Purple Onion Ring, the legendary rock venue on the outskirts – the "burbs" as they call them – of Hackensack, New Jersey, USA. Ever mindful of his players' needs, Terry Venables let me fly over for the event en-route to the Far East where England had a few drinks lined up at a lap dancing club – sorry, where we had a couple of vital warm-up games to play before the tournament.

---

\**Yeh, yeh.*

I flew off with mixed feelings. I was proud of all my brother had achieved in music and it wouldn't be easy watching him bow out. The gig turned out to be huge from start to finish. The punters exploded as Tark's famous riff led the band into their opening number – *Penistone* – and they went even more mental as he climaxed the final encore with my fave from Brighton days, *Serving Number Seven*. And then... it was all over.

It was an emotional night all round. Particularly as I met my third wife-to-be, Brandee Ebelficker (as she was then), at the post-gig party. The vibrant Californian was blonde, had a radiant smile and the cutest mazongas since Pammie Anderson. And they turned out be real as well. In short, I went for her in a big way.

'Are you like Tark's brother?'

How's that for sweet? She didn't realise I was the more famous one of the two.

'Guilty.'

'Bitchen!'

I was just about to give her a slap\*, but Tarka told me that it was American for "awesome", so I let it go. I didn't see Brandee again for a few years after that night. But the groundwork had been laid. And so had she, let me tell you – I raised the old Union Jack over her Twin Peaks good and proper that night. And thanks mainly to a few tabs of Sun Valley Brain Marinade, my right knee felt as right as ninepence all through the doggie-style section. Yes, my injury had got to the point where just kneeling on it sometimes gave me a problem. Thanks to Nico Zul. Thanks to Hee-Haw. Thanks to countless other donkeys.

But let's rewind a moment. Why were The Dots giving up? Because they'd basically had enough. Twenty years of touring had left its mark on each and every one of them. Now new horizons beckoned. Three of them, bass player Dave Lightowler, keyboardist Ben Sykes and drummer Mike Schofield decided to stay in music. Tark and the other guitarist, Dilip Choudhary were leaving the scene altogether.

Now me and Tark are a couple of hairy beasts\*\* so the following day we decided to pop out for a Back, Crack, and Sack at Mack, Zack and Jack's Hackensack Wax

---

\*Here's a tip for you guys – and especially for Frank and, in time, my other son, Diego. Never take abuse from a bird if you want her to respect you. Burksey's Law, Page One. Paragraph One. Point One.

Point Two – wear a knob box at all times.

\*\*We get it from mother. "Old Chimpy", she was known at school. The kids had a pretty bad name for her as well.

Shack. As our shorn locks piled up all around us, Tark expanded on his decision to quit the rock scene. It made interesting – and relevant – listening.

'It's just not the same any more, man.'

'But you love it. It's what you were made to do. Eh! Careful with that tadger!' That last remark was made to the said Zack, who was enjoying his work a little too much for my liking. But I soon forgot about at it as Tark's continued with his thoughts.

'I think I've just been doing it for too long. I've got stale. Have been ever since the *Fire In The Shire* album.'

'What're you going to do? Yes it *is* marked like a ruler, Perve Features.'

'I don't know. But I do know I need a new challenge. Maybe more than one. I might even go to college. Learn how to be or do something completely different. And if it goes wrong and I ever did want to re-enter the music scene – I dare say there would be a way.'

'Bitchen!' But then I had to turn back to Zack. 'Mate, it's a back, crack, and sack, not an end, tend and bend, alright?'

I tell you, I'm as open-minded as they come. But ladyboys? I don't know about you, but I could live without them. Mind, I have to say that the plaster model I let him cast from my hard-on\* does look impressive. So impressive, I eventually had it made into a table lamp. "Turn the light on would you, love? Switch is just on the top there. No, the bottom, sorry. No, it's the top, I keep forgetting. Just under the rim." Works every time!

I thought about what Tarka had said all through the ten-hour flight to China. Except for when I went to the toilet, of course. I hate using the onboard WCs and always give it maximum concentration. I read in the National Requirer once that a guy flying from Washington to Chicago was sucked completely out of his plane when the toilet he was using flushed unexpectedly. Talk about an internal flight. See, these are the things they don't tell you.

Anyway, back to Tarka's words: "not the same...", "stale...", "need a new challenge...", "I dare say there would be a way...", "This tea's crap...", "Seen my plectrum?"

Those last two weren't particularly relevant. But the rest? Hmmm.

---

\*Don't get any ideas, matey boy. The first part of the task was accomplished with the – let's just call it "help" – of Shack spa and waterbed consultant, Maria Fonguapez. Yes, that Maria Fonguapez. If you've never heard of this remarkable young lady, she later became Chief Personal Assistant to the – let's just call him "George." And by the way, don't worry about Zack cashing in on the plaster cast thing. After he had made me, he broke the mould. Just as God himself had done, twenty-nine years previously.

Despite a nasty plaster rash, I scored twice in our three-nil destruction of China in the opening game of the mini-tour. Who got the other? Charlie Chan's Adopted Son, Gazza. His goal celebration was typical of him. As were most of the things he did, come to that. In fact, all of them were. But then, that's what behaviour is, isn't it?* Anyway, what he did was to pull his eyes into slits and go round shouting "Me velly solly for scoring honourable goal!" It was hilarious and I must say the Chinks looked to take it in good part. Ah, what a brilliant thing it is to be part of the E.W.F.M. (Expanding World Football Markets) business. You can get away with owt, I'm telling you. More or less.

We didn't have to get out of second gear to beat China, but it was a nice warm-up for the lads and it reinforced my feeling that the squad was a pretty strong one. Man United's remarkable Neville Brothers showed that they could play football as well as sing; skipper Tony Adams — we were now on a more friendly footing — was a towering Rock of Gibraltar at the back; Jamie Redknapp had a bit of something about him**; Incey "The Guv'nor" Wincey, was more of a tiger than a spider; Precision passer Teddy Sheringham had a slide-rule in his head where normal people have a brain; and of course, in Psycho, we had simply the most dependable full-back in world football. And there was a young striker by the name of Alan Shearer who wasn't too shabby.

As Euro 96 got ever closer, I felt that the squad didn't enjoy quite the same degree of unity as the Italia 90 brigade. There was a real pedigree chumminess in that camp. And the playing standard, despite El Tel's brilliant input, wasn't quite as high, either. Still, come the tournament itself, I had a feeling that we might just do something on the pitch.

But before all that, we had another appointment to keep. A dentist's appointment in Hong Kong. The chair was already waiting...

*Perceptive, eh? Can there be any wonder that with my new philosophy and culture-filled bonce, I later went on to address the Oxford University Union? My talk, "Shin Pads And Sh***ing", is still fondly remembered today.

**That something is sex appeal according to most of the seventeen-thousand, six-hundred and eighty three women I know. Can't see it myself. He was a good player, that's all that should concern any football fan.

## CHAPTER FIFTEEN

# RINSE AND SPIN

The last time I'd arrived in the pulsating city of Hong Kong, I was a raw kid of eighteen. And just when I was beginning to question my present and my future, my past came back to prompt some interesting thoughts. It was in this very place, eleven years ago almost to the day, that my career as a professional footballer got rolling. And now?

Looking around me as I changed into my England kit, I felt as if I was drifting back in time. Perhaps I was trying to trace a causal link between the then and the now. Trying to account for the sense of "been there, done that" that was starting to infect my game. The ever vigilant Tony Adams must have clocked that I looked a bit out of it and, being the conscientious captain that he was, came quietly across to me.

'Wanna step into my office, Burksey?'

'What – you've got an office here? Oh, I see what you mean. No, I'm fine, thanks, Tone.'

'Sure?'

Despite everything that had gone before, I felt I could open up to this guy. He had a bearing. A kind of dignity, I suppose is the word. And I knew he was dead straight and whatever I said would go no further. It was quite a moment as I'd never levelled with anyone but my brother before. 'I want to tell you something.'

'I'm listening.'

'Right, deep breath. At the start of my career, when I changed into proper kit, I used to get so excited, I got a hard-on.'

'Okay.'

"Okay" – just like that. No, "You f***ing mento, how sad are you?" Or anything like that. I was right to trust him. Maybe there was a lesson for me right there.

'Then I used to get one when I scored. Well not a full stiffy – just a dingle, you know.'

'We've all been there, son.'

'Right. Well now, the thing is – I'm wondering if I'd get even so much as an uncoiler if I won us Euro 96. With the best goal ever scored.'

'That's what you wanted to talk to me about?'

'Yeh.'

Tone's knotted his brow as he thinks about what I said. He doesn't reply for a second. Suddenly I'm aware of all the things going on around us in the changing room. The soundtrack to the scene is our stirring unofficial new anthem, *Three Lions*, blasting out from Incey's boom box. What was everyone up to? Steve Stone's larking about with Gazza's kitbag, putting what looks like a rubber turd in it; Platty's stretching out his hamstrings and nattering to Jamie about the locals' habit of eating dogs; Les Ferdinand is swapping hairy biker stories with Gareth Southgate and getting a laugh by predicting that one day, he'll be flying his own helicopter; the Neville brothers, usually busy little bees, are trying to blot out what's going on around them, staring into space as they repeatedly bounce balls in front of them. Gary's focus face, a stern iron mask that could land him a role as a hit man in any Bond movie, contrasts with Phil's, who just looks a bit vacant; the Gaffer's his usual ebullient, smiling self as he goes round giving last minute tips to the starters – until he gets to Teddy who gives *him* one: "Slagheap" in the eight-thirty at Happy Valley, I think it was; Gazza's singing along with Three Lions at the top of his voice, but suddenly stops as he's asked Pearcey: "Who's this Jill Rimmer f***ah then, like?" Psycho tells him who and what Jules Rimet was and Gazza looks impressed as he's carried on even louder than before.

I turn my attention back to Tony as, brow unknotting, he responds to my remarks.

'I reckon all you're saying is that you're growing up, Burksey. That's all. And I'll be honest with you, it's about time in my opinion. But better late than never, eh?'

I'd never thought of it like that. Maybe TA was right. Although...

At that moment, we had to take the field in what turned out to be the worst England performance most witnesses remember seeing. This was before the Northern Ireland v England World Cup Qualifier in 2005, of course. I scored from a brilliant Alan Shearer pass – he can when he wants to – but apart from that, the game stank.

Never mind, there was the evening to look forward to.

It began weirdly when Robbie Fowler talked to me on our way to the nightclub – Fat Sloppy's Bar, Grill and Lap Dancerama on the Kowloon waterfront. What was so weird about that? Because me and Robbie didn't get on. Nothing against the player. He's given full value wherever he's gone and in his first spell with Liverpool, he was one of the best strikers around. But ever since he'd taken the Micky Quinn out of me by aping my goal celebration – not close enough to warrant a lawsuit – we hadn't exactly been Becks and Posh. So how come I got up his nose? He'd heard I'd once read a novel.

Anyway, there we were in the stretch on the way to the club and chalk Robbie has asked cheese Burksey how he was.

'Fine, mate. No worries. Yourself?'

'Sound, yeh. Just bought a few more blocks of flats this morning, you know.'

'Sweet.' Good old Man Of The People is Scouser Rob.

'Not bad, yeh.'

Alright, the conversation was, like, forced? But we were on the same team now – briefly – so the entente cordiale* was the important thing. We would have to wait until we were back with our clubs before we carried on knocking lumps out of each other. Those of you with the attention span of a gnat may be wondering why I didn't choose to poyse** Robbie in training. It was because I'd given a vow never to crock another squad member after the unfortunate incident with Bryan Robson at Italia 90. Remember now? Especially if the player in question was a rival for a starting spot. Not that that applied to Scouse Boy.

It was Gazza's 29th birthday and he was in fine form at Fat Sloppy's, endearing himself to everyone with a range of top class antics and jokes. Even after he'd got laid out – just in fun – from a right hook by Wisey, who'd found a pair of knuckle dusters in his fortune cookie, he had the whole place eating out of the palm of his hand. As always.

Now, I'm sure you all know about the famous Dentist's Chair Incident. Or thought you did. For the first time anywhere, I'll tell you what really happened in that nightclub. Ready for this? What happened was....... nothing. Nothing at all. "F*** off Burksey, you've been chewing Moggin's Carpet Foam again", I hear you cry. "We've seen all the pictures in the papers. And read all the accounts. It must have happened." Must it? Have you never heard of Diplomatic Expedience and Photo Editing Software?

Yes, the whole story was a lie from start to finish. A cover story. A cover story designed to deflect attention away from the truth. And what was the truth? I'll tell you.

Into Fat Sloppy's club that night walked the two most sought after fugitives on the planet. Yes, in plain sight for the first time in years, Lord Lucan was seen dining, drinking and dancing with Shergar. Now we players are experienced clubbers and had clocked the man/horse duo earlier in the evening. We thought nothing of it. Why? Because we'd seen more exotic combinations taking the floor on numerous occasions in Docklands and the West End. I tell you, when you've seen Kelly Brook doing the Charleston with a giraffe, a bloke vogueing with a horse doesn't look particularly noteworthy.

*Trans from French: A close drinking partner. Literally, "an Aunt who likes the juice".
**Trans from Huddersfield: To kick. Especially up in the air. Educational this book, isn't it!

It wasn't until throwing out time that we realised something was up. Apart from a bit of fun with a fire extinguisher – they expect it – we'd done absolutely nothing wrong all night. Then as we were leaving, a fusillade of shrill whistle blasts told us that either David Elleray was in town or there was a police raid going on. It turned out to be the latter. We were all questioned, but no-one had noticed where "the bloke on horseback had gone". Even the Neville Brothers hadn't logged their exit and they seem to notice most things.

Then, in march a couple of lorry loads of British Army soldiers – Hong Kong was still ours then – whose commanding officer, a Colonel X, gave us a run down on what was going on. He finished by stressing that the international operation, of which the army and police formed just a part, must remain a secret.

'To that end, I want all of you chaps to play dumb', said the Colonel, an upper crust, rugged-looking Jack Hawkins-y, Trevor Howard-y* sort of type.

'Playing dumb? That should be easy enough', quipped the Gaffer, all eyes turning to me and Gazza. Cheek.

'It's clear that The Lone Ranger and Tonto** are chancing their arms and legs a little more at the moment thanks to the false sense of security our initiative has created. So at this very sensitive time, it's crucial that the pair don't get wind of anything.'

All eyes turn to me and Gazza again. Double cheek.

'So I have a favour to ask', continued the Colonel. 'To throw the fugitives orf the scent, I want you chaps to take the blame for this little show. As far as anyone is concerned, the only horse that was spotted in here tonight was a spot of over-the-top horseplay by your good selves. This is a matter of the utmost international importance so I expect your co-operation.'

El Tel's a tough cookie and he wasn't taking this thing up the arse. 'And if we don't give it?'

---

*Ever wonder who that face on the screen belongs to? Then allow me to recommend Fred's Film Fans Face Finder to you. Comprehensible, cross-referenceable and never reprehensible, this user-friendly guide will banish your movie-watching blues at a stroke. With Fred's Film Fans Face Finder at your elbow, you'll never confuse Burt with Debbie Reynolds again! Just one of a range of Face Finder Guides by Fred.
Note: Fred's Film Fans Face Finder is a brand of the Stelsat Corporation of America.
All rights reserved.
**The authorities' codenames for Lucan and Shergar.

'Then it would probably be just a case of working out how many conjugal visits a year you'd all be entitled to', said the Colonel with a smile that reminded me of Strozzato. The cold smile of an alligator eyeing up lunch.

'Jungle visits? I'm not going off to no f***in' jungle', says Gazza in my ear. I was with him. I hate snakes and things like that.

'Alright then, we'll have to co-operate. So what are we supposed to have done here?' I can see the Gaffer's got the needle. But what could he do but go along with this thing?

'Oh, nothing too terrible. In fact didn't someone let orf a far extinguisher? We'll base the thing around that. Our lab boys will rig a few pictures. And we'll sort out the Press. And then tomorrow morning, I'll get my liaison officer to pop over to your hotel with the details. In the meantime, Mum's the word. That's all.'

With that, he and his staff turned on their heels and were gone. After we'd signed autographs* and posed for photos, the police followed them.

As we've filed out after them, the theories about what the Lone Ranger and Tonto were wanted for came thick and fast.

'Whatever it is, it must be something big', opined Dave Seaman.

'You think?' quips the Gaffer, watching the cast of Platoon pull away from the club.

Then everybody's favourite ton-up boy, Les Ferdinand, comes up with an interesting angle.

'Hey – do you reckon it was Lord Wassisname and the horse what trashed the Blue Peter Garden?'

'Don't be stupid. How could Shergar get over the wall?' says Wisey.

'Yeh', agreed Ted. 'He was a flat horse, wasn't he? Derby winner.'

'What's that fellah's Mum, gorra do wi' it, like?' asks Gazza.

'Eh?' says Incey, genuinely perspexed.

'Well, he's said "Mum's the word", hasn't he?'

'You know, Gazza, the only difference between you and an idiot savant, is that you're not a f***ing savant', said another one of the party, who will remain nameless. After Gazza's given him a slap, he's almost remained lifeless as well. Rightly so.

'So what's his Mum gorra do with it?'

'To keep Mum means to keep schtum, Gaz', says Gaffer Terry. 'And that's what we'd better do.'

*Another ninety-seven for my total.

We went back to the hotel and kept ourselves to ourselves for the rest of the night. We didn't have to wait to be briefed by Colonel X's man the following morning. Stories of "The Dentist's Chair" incident were all over the papers. Backed-up by life-like photos. The Police had worked their usual magic and spread the forged story across the planet.

Here's a tip for you good people out there and it's gospel. You cannot believe a single word or picture that you see in print. It was worth you putting your money down and buying this book just to read that. If I hadn't been there myself, I would have believed the story completely. So we were "plastered" were we? Let me tell you something. The only things that were plastered were pix of the "event" all over the papers. They were amazingly convincing, I have to say. I reckon somebody must have taken a snap of me firing off the extinguisher at Gazza and Ted in Fat Sloppy's and the Lab Boys used it to form the booze-pouring centrepiece to the shots that you all saw over your toast and tea.

Makes you think, doesn't it?

At the meeting with Colonel X's Liaison, he's made us all sign a document in which we swore that any reference we ever made to that evening would support the party line. So that was that. We were bad boys. It was official. And we never did a f***ing thing.

As a postscript, I have to report that we were ultimately recognised for our sacrifice. Yes, for keeping Mum so brilliantly – even to the extent that we aped the infamous Chair Photos after Gazza scored that goal against Scotland – we were all invited to – let's just call it a big house – to be awarded gongs. It was a nice ceremony, although carrying the thing out of the room whilst walking backwards wasn't easy. I dropped the gong bonger – the mallet thing – several times and had to keep stopping to pick it up. Of course, every time I bent down, I dropped the gong itself. Then the various parts of the stand. By the time I got it through the door, it was more of a gong kit really. The lads called me Clouseau for a while after that. I don't know why. Today, the gong and its secret inscription has pride of place in my loft. Well, at dinner time I have a Swedish maid who says "dinner is served" and that's that. I think most of the guys do.

By the way, one of my helpers, in a rare moment of help, has suggested that I shouldn't have given you the real low down on Dentistgate. He thinks I might get into trouble. "Big f***ing trouble" was the phrase he used. But he's forgetting that me and Tony Blair are like that. Remember the moment after his election win in 1997 when he and I engaged in a spot of head tennis along with the new England boss Kevin Keegan? That was a great occasion for Tony. And for me actually. As you all know, I'd long been an ardent supporter of Conservative policies, so it was a thrill to meet a Prime Minister who was making the pips squeak louder than anyone since the great Mrs T herself.

As a final footnote, some have suggested that Mr B used a heading double for the aerial ping pong we three wowed the world's Press with. That's bollocks. You can see it's him and anyway, you've got my word for it. As a final, final footnote, the ball wasn't remote-controlled either. And, sorry to further disappoint you doubting Thomas Brolins out there, but we did the thing in one take as well.

As a final, final, final footnote, I've always been sorry that Tarka politely but firmly* rejected Number Ten's offer to take part in a televised jam with the PM at Chequers**. I love my brother to bits, but he can be as rigid as a riga on coke in his views, sometimes. I tell you one thing, if Tony's skills on the guitar are as silky as his footballing ones, Tark missed out on a treat, there.

But back to our physical, mental and tactical preparations for Euro 96. After a lively flight back to Heathrow from Hong Kong – to be honest, I spent most of it lit up like a Christmas tree formation*** – we came down to earth with our expectations sky high.

England's footballers were coming home. And so was football itself.

---

*If you can call "F*** off, I'd rather play with Vlad The Impaler" polite. Defo firm though, wasn't it?

**Some have seen such fun initiatives as a form of free advertising, a shameless exercise in brand promotion to win votes. It upsets me that people are so cynical in this country. Rory Bremner, John Bird and John Fortune – you should be ashamed of yourselves. We should cherish Top Man Tony. Ever wondered why he carries a tea mug into his Press Briefings? Or why he always has his jacket off? It's because he's working like stink for us all.

***Brand a man a drunk and he'll behave like one. Thanks, Colonel X.

## CHAPTER SIXTEEN

# THIRTY YEARS OF HURT

We knew the FA meant business when we tried on our suits for the campaign ahead. They were good schmutter. As Englishmen, we already felt we were representatives of the greatest country on the planet. Now we looked as if we were as well. Whilst the old saw that "clothes maketh the man" may not be strictly true, they cometh pretty damn closeth in my book.

Footballistically, our opening Group A match against Switzerland at Wembley would set the tone for the whole competition and everything was geared to ensuring that we got it right. Or would it set the tone? In my experience, the opener hardly ever acts as a pointer to what follows – after all Cameroon had beaten Argentina in the opening match of the 1990 World Cup, but the Argies had still made it to the Final*. But the idea serves as a convenient tool to motivate the more impressionable players. Players like me, it has to be said. Preparations went well and, wearing my superb new white Avatak Bulletcap boots, I was as ready as I'd ever been.

Yes, no-one needed to worry about my motivation for the tournament. This wasn't bread and butter stuff. It was roast beef and Yorkshire pudding. Washed down with a pint of Timothy Taylor's. When it finally arrived, the atmosphere for that first game was magic. As we walked out, I could feel the eyes of the world focussing on that seven-thousand square yards of prime English turf. That sort of thing gets your attention, believe me. And then there was the capacity crowd. When they began singing the brilliant Three Lions, I tell you – it makes the hairs on the back of my neck stand up just thinking about it now. David Baddiel and Frank Skinner – you're true Lions of England, yourselves. You should have been given squad numbers, we all thought.

So what went wrong in the game? We started lively enough, and I sensed that there would soon be as many holes appearing in the Swiss defence as in a slab of Andy Hessenthaler. You probably remember the simple, but effective goal I scored

---

*Mind you, Diana Ross's missed spot kick during the opening ceremony of USA 94 was spookily prescient, wasn't it? Buddhist hair enthusiast Roberto Baggio was one of four players to reprise her comically bodged effort in the penalty shoot-out that saw Brazil win the Final.

half-way through the first half. It was a bit untypical of me, but it was a goal and it got the ball rolling. We went into the interval with nothing to worry about. Everything was fine.

I was especially happy with the way we looked at the back. The great David Seaman was probably at his peak. Then complementing the peerless Psycho at left back, young Gary Neville was proving just what a brilliant talent he was on the right. In the centre, the power, passion and precision of skipper Tony Adams combined superbly with the astute and athletic Gareth Southgate. They looked set to boss anything that came their way.

On the midfield flanks, I'll hold my hand up and say I wasn't completely convinced by the talented and likeable duo of Darren Anderton and Steve McManaman. Why? Because they weren't John Barnes and Chris Waddle. Unfair I know. But there it is. In Incey though, we had a guy who had top quality shining through everything he did. And remember that he played most of his career with that potentially crippling post-hypnotic suggestion injury hanging over him. Yet he always managed to overcome it and get his shirt on eventually. Good going, Guv'nor. But coming back to the side, we then had Gazza. Genius. 'Nuff said. And up front me and Teddy had a bit of something going. That boy could deliver a killer pass, brother. Still can.

So the second half should have been a foregone conclusion, right? It should, but it wasn't. We slowly fell apart. Why? I'm not sure. One suggestion I can scotch is that some of us got a bit confused about which of Gaffer Terry's many tactical systems we were supposed to adopt in the situation. Bollocks. We were one-nil up in the second half against weak defensive-minded opposition who had to come out and score – so that meant we stuck to number Twenty Seven in our Field Guide – Mature English Larch With A Couple Of Bits Sticking Up At The Top. Or 4-4-1-1 to you. No problem. And in any case, true to my maverick instincts, I always wandered around like a tart at a tea party whatever system we played. Terry knew that and allowed for it. He also knew about my right knee so after an hour, he thought it safest to prune me. Did I not like that. Even though it was in my best interests, I hated going off. Always did. Yes, Rejection City Arizona is a pretty forlorn burg.

In my place, on trotted Blackburn Rovers starlet Alan Shearer. It pains me to say this, but he looked the part from the word go. Brave, bright, sneaky, sharp. A bit low on pace and magic. But high in everything else. Especially in his opinion of his own talents, it has to be said. But I like that in a player just as I like it in a bird. A bird who doesn't fancy herself isn't worth sh***ing, in my view. Of course it can go too far – look at Cinzia, Fabrizio or Robbie. But back to Shearer. He looked good. Very good. A classic English centre-forward.

We haven't had a brainteaser in ages so here's one. How many times when I've been subbed in a tight game has my team gone on to win it? I'm talking my whole career – league, cup, internationals, friendlies – the lot. Guess as a percentage. Eighty percent? Seventy percent? Sixty? I'll tell you. It's diddly squat percent. Blind zero. Yes, not on one single occasion when I've been subbed in a tight game – a game that has no more than one goal in it – has my team gone on to win.

Cognisant of this remarkable stat, Dave Green tried to get it written into my contracts that once I was selected in a game, I would be squibbsy from the hook. Understand this – we weren't thinking of me. We were only thinking of the well-being of the team. The Gaffers tended not to see it that way.

DG:    'So Alex, it would mean that Burksey couldn't be subbed except for injury.'

AF:    'What?! F*** off, yous f***ing f***er! Who the f*** do yous think y'are? F*** off oot of my f***ing office and dinna come f***ing back! F***ing c***! (turning to Martin Edwards) Have yous ever heard anything rike that in your f***ing rife?! The World's gone f***ing mad! Mad! And I will tell you this, boy, I will tell yous this – these f***ing agents are just the thin f***ing end of a very thick f***ing wedge. They're going to ruin our f***ing game if we ret the f***ers. Mark my words!'

So that was a no, then. Do you notice that Alex tends to go a bit Glaswegian when he gets angry? But the crucial thing to note was his refusal even to consider the idea.

England Boss Terry was just as blind to the truth. So, post-Burksey, what happened on this occasion? The Swiss equalised with a pen eight minutes from time and the game finished one-apiece. Not a disaster. But not what we'd hoped for either.

After everything calmed down, we settled back in to Gazza Manor – Burnham Beeches as it's usually known – where everything was done to preserve the mood of optimism we'd generated going into the tournament. The Jocks lay in wait just a week down the line and we were determined to do them. Do them large. Bragging rights for the season ahead were at stake for one thing.

There's no doubt about it, the country went a bit quiet after the Swiss game and the need for a restorative boost was apparent – for the people and for the players. In a nice gesture, telekineticist Uri Geller, he of the bent prong, offered to come over and put us through some mumbo-jumbo – sorry, some motivational drills – designed to get us back on winning ways. His main idea was that if we all touched some famous balls,* our confidence would come flooding back. Mister Venables declined to extend an invitation.

Instead, we got stuck in on the training pitches and in the classroom. Over the next seven days, I knuckled down to some hard work, only rarely escaping for fun and frolics.

Yes, it was tournament time again, so you know what that means. Sponsors were setting out their stalls all over the shop and there was a whole new crop of promo girls out there to cherry pick from. And I filled my basket, believe me. But didn't all that plucking take it out of my legs? Not at all. Just the opposite. "Snatches in batches win matches" was my motto.

Talking of sponsors, Dave Green had sorted me out a cracking series of ads, endorsements and PA work since coming back from Italy. I'd become as familiar a face, groin and legs on billboards and on telly as I was on the pitch. When it came to shows, I'd guest on anything, really. Except things that put you on the spot. I'd never go in for Mastermind, for example. True, I could answer questions all day on specialist subjects like the singles of Belinda Carlisle, the life and career of Michelle Pfeiffer, and the rise of Britart.** But I'd feel, like, too exposed? to take part in the general knowledge round at the end. And that would lead to a punch-up so it was best avoided. Same with Question Of Sport. I've appeared as the Mystery Guest a record five times, but the quiz part is a no-no for me. If I got something wrong, I'd go mental and do something stupid. Like Coisty.

I've been asked to appear on *Have I Got News For You* and *They Think It's All Over* countless times. I might do the former if my mate Boris Johnson's asking the questions. But Angus Deayton? He's just got one of those faces you want to smack, hasn't he? I have to say Shaka Hislop and Paul Merson are funny people, but both dislike me for different reasons so there could be trouble there. As for *They Think*, Gary Lineker told me that the hilarious Misters Hancock and McGrath have worked out a lot of funny stuff to rib me with. That's fine – so long as the boys wouldn't mind

---

*I told the lads they could forget mine in double quick time. But just when we were deciding whose balls we would touch if we had to – we plumped for Nelson Mandela's – word came that Mr Geller meant footballs from famous England triumphs. The orb from the 1966 World Cup Final being the top choice.

**Sniggers again, eh? Well let me tell you that there isn't much I don't know about it. I could name every single thing on and around Tracey Emin's bed, for instance. A complete inventory. And I could tell you all the stuff Damien cut in half. Could you do that?

taking a nutting in return. Still want me on, guys? The pain and the double vision go eventually. It's up to you.

But back to what matters. The game against Scotland – our first encounter for seven years – will live long in the memory. Two key moments, weren't there? Big David's penalty save from Gary McAllister. And that genius goal from you know who. Mind you, I always reckon Gazza was lucky to still be on the pitch to score it. Not because of falling foul of the trigger-happy refs who were doing their best to bugger the tournament,* but for what he shouted at David after Key Moment One. Yes, for reasons known only to himself, Gazza's come running up to the Arsenal Ace and come out with:

'F***in' brilliant, Beaver Face!'

As much as I love Gazza, if he'd called me that, he'd have spent the rest of the tournament in traction. I don't think Dave can have heard him because he let it go.

A few minutes later, I've put Gaz through from out wide and he's worked some real magic before volleying his own flick up past Andy Goram. My favourite goal ever.

By another player, I mean. And I was so glad I was on hand to supply that final ball. Not enough credit has been given to it over the years. It took a special player to deliver that pass. Someone like Darren Anderton, for example, would never have had the composure, the vision or the touch to bring it off.

There was an interesting programme on telly a couple of days after the Scotland game.

And I was in it. I've mentioned before that I'm far too soft and sentimental to do personal appearance stuff for disabled, disadvantaged, differently abled, or even just double-jointed kids. But when I took a call from a researcher for the BBC's *Brass Knuckles* programme, what she told me made me break the habits of a lifetime. I got permission from Terry and a couple of hours later, I drove myself to the studio to record a P.T.C. (Piece To Camera) and an interview with the programme's producer, Russ Morris. What had stirred me so? It was this...

A crazy cocktail of radioactive contaminants feeding into the outfall stream of a nuclear power station in Cumbria had helped spawn a species of giant underwater

---

*Twenty-two cards issued after the first three games. I could have understood it if they'd carried the sponsor's logos, but this was mindless madness.*

bees – Beeus Bigus Underwaterus – that were threatening the seaside holidays of thousands of English kiddies. The bees, some of them six-foot long, but capable of attacking children in only two inches of water, were terrorising beaches from the Solway Firth to Southport.

Because of Government Reporting Restrictions on Potentially Panic-Inducing Stories, nothing was being done about it. I saw pictures of children being carried from the water with two-foot long stings sticking out of their heads, their legs, and even their little backsides. Those pictures made me mad. On camera, a stern-faced Russ asked me what I would do if I came face to face with one of the bees. To help me visualise such a moment, curtains open and an inflatable life-sized model of one of the bastards appears on a plinth between us.

Me: 'What would I do? I'd f***ing tear the f***er's wings off.'

Russ Morris: 'Would you give it some right pastie?'

M: 'I certainly would.'

RM: 'Would you marmalise it?'

M: 'Believe it.'

RM: 'Squeeze the life out of it?'

M: 'Just give me a chance.'

With that, Russ hands me an iron bar which is connected by an electrical cable to the bee's air supply. He tells me that the more I can bend that bar, the more the bastard will deflate in front of me. I get stuck in. It's hard going, but with each yark, the striped assassin lolls ever more limply toward the floor. With all sinews straining, I lower the killer insect to within about a foot of death. But then I falter.

KM: 'Come on, Burksey – kiddies are being stung all over the North West!'

I let out a roar of raw power as, turning red, I knot my muscles into greater effort. I close my eyes with the pain, but that was no problem – a bell was set to ring when the bugger was finally downed. And I wouldn't stop until I'd heard that "ding of death".

RM: (listening to his earpiece) 'Oh no! I've just heard that little Bryony and Ben, paddling at Blackpool, are being eaten by the biggest f***er yet!'

B: (redoubling my effort) 'Aaaaargh!'

Still no bell. Realising I'm not going to make it, I leap out of my chair and in a frenzy of blows, smash the insect to bits with the iron bar. The plinth goes west along with it.

FX: 'Ding!'

Later, dressed in special anti-sting goggles and wetsuit – way too small for me, but it was in a good cause – I record a piece in which I tell viewers about what their children were facing and what they could do about it: money was needed to supply these suits and "Neptune's Tridents" – specially adapted cattle prods – to every child in the country; Paddle Patrols needed to be set up, staffed by experienced underwater bee hunters; and finally, the Underwater Bee Research Establishment at Imbeinghad Bay in Cornwall, desperately needed money to continue with its crucial work.

There, and they say I never do anything for children. Others giving heartfelt pleas on the programme included Anne Robinson, Gordon Ramsay and Jeremy Clarkson.

The lads watched the show open-mouthed. Afterwards, Terry had tears in his eyes when he came over and put his arm around me. His words were simple but profound:

'You poor f***er.'

Solidarity means a lot to me. Thanks Tel. And thanks, viewers. Russ later rang to tell me that an overwhelming public response to the appeal spelled the end of the bee attacks for good and all. So next time your little ones are safely paddling at Blackpoool, Fleetwood or Morecambe, you'll know who to thank.

Most fans have great memories of the game against Holland. Those fans don't include me. Why? Because I missed playing in what was arguably England's best performance in years, thanks to a knee knock I'd picked up in training. "Knee Knock Powell" as quipster Terry called it, for some reason.

Big joke. Teddy and Shearer nabbed a brace each as we took Ruud's boys apart. Only one thing cheered me. Kluivert's consolation goal near the end meant that Scotland were going home. As ever, Psycho had the mot juste when he's led the singing on the bus back to Burnham:

> *Who put The Jocks Out?*
> *Who? Who?*
> *Who put the Jocks out?*
> *Hol – land – that's who!*

Could catch on that ditty, couldn't it?

Missing the Dutch match had been a real pisser. But worse was to come. I would miss the quarter-final against Spain as well. Despite a strict diet of R.I.C.E (Rest, Ice, Compression, Elevation), the inflammation wasn't going down quickly enough. And there was no time to fit in another operation. Injections would only take me so far. The only thing for it was to carry on knocking back the RICE and hope for the best.

And of course, it meant that I had to send out for talent. They came in dressed as maids, women journos, masseuses, that sort of thing. I tell you, I got sick of that broom cupboard after a while.

Watching the quarter-final game unfold was murder. Particularly when it went into the newly devised "golden goal"-governed extra time. Who dreamed that exquisite little torture up? Adolf Hitler? I tell you, I don't know how you punters sit on your backsides watching matches week after week. You must come away feeling impotent every time. That might be okay for you. But not for Burksey. But back to the action. I believe that if I'd been playing, the game wouldn't have needed to go to golden goals or pens.

Two heroes stood out in the game for me. "Beaver Face" Seaman for his all-round display and for saving Nadal's spot kick in the shootout. And Pearcey. Again, the all-round performance was top drawer. And what about that pen? Talk about balls. His mind must have gone every which way when he's trotted up. But he never looked like missing.

And then the reaction. "Like an enraged Norman Wisdom" as one of the journos put it – Larry Harrison I think it was, but I stand to be corrected on that.

So we'd reached the semi-final. And it was going to be against – who else – the hated You Know Whos. An all-party forum consisting of Des Lynam, Alan Hansen, Martin O'Neill, Johan Cruyff, and Bobby Robson discussed the game on telly a couple of days before. The question of the likelihood of my involvement in the game came up early doors.

Des Lynam: 'And what about Burksey, Martin? Think he'll play?'

Martin O'Neill: 'I've been shot down on this one so many times before – it's nothing new – it goes with the territory – I expect that – so to be perfectly honest if you're asking me if he will play – I've no idea – I can't answer that.'

DL: 'Johan?'

Johan Cruyff: 'If he'sh fit, he'll play, but with problem coming from shin she many yearsh behind with shtrikersh kneesh then itsh could be move of difficulty. Shpringing from back comesh problem with motion. And then shit creek without paddle up alsho.'

DL: (thinks about it for a moment) 'Right.'

Ron Atkinson: 'I think Johan's got a point there. I know he'll want to play, will Burksey, no messing. But to be fair, he's not been in the best of form, lately, you know. He might not get a start even if he is fit.'

DL: 'What's been the problem? If there is one. (smiling archly, one eyebrow raised to camera) Don't want Dave Green ringing in, there.'

LAUGHTER

RA:     'To be fair, he's always been in the Wide Awake Club has the lad, but you practically need a spotter's badge to clock his goals at the minute.'

Alan Hansen: 'Well, a niggle can do that to you. If you're carrying a knock – right? – It gets to you. And when you talk about knocks, there's nothing worse than a knocked knee. You can't go all out. And that'll hurt a player like Burksey.'

Bobby Robson: 'He'll be there.'

DL:     'No doubts?'

BR:     'No doubts. He's young, he's scoring goals. He's playing in a good Blackburn side...'

DL:     'Burksey, Bobby. Not Alan Shearer.'

BR:     'Burksey? No chance.'

They droned on in the same vein for a while, finally coming to the conclusion that I had a fifty-fifty chance of being fit. And a fifty-fifty chance of starting if I was fit. Top telly, eh?

To say I was desperate to play in the match would be to undersell it hugely. I did everything I was told to do to get fit. I even prayed. And I said goodbye to the broom cupboard. You name it – I did or didn't do it, depending.

Terry's come to me on the eve of the match.

'Alright, Burksey?'

'Never better, Boss', I said, pluckily performing a series of extravagant moves with my suspect knee.

But Terry didn't fall for that. Instead, he's looked me square in the eyes. I've looked back. For what seemed an age. A real Mexican stand-up. Then he's smiled, patted me on the shoulder and nodded. I cried. I couldn't help it. For the first time in ages, I felt enough to let a few drops go. It felt good, actually. I guess things had been bottling up for a while. And now – "at last" I hear some of you cry – I didn't go straight out and celebrate with a few pints, lines, pills, and a spot of hide the riga. Instead, I retired to bed with *Tutty Hump VI Mega Platinum Edition* and prepared to do battle against The Hun the following day.

I was fit. And I was starting. Alan Shearer was on the bench. His time would come.

I don't recall ever being so hyped as we walked out at Wembley for that game. Three Lions was nearly giving me a hard-on, I'm not kidding. It made me feel seventeen again. In the heart and head, that is. I looked across at Berti Vogts' men. I was glad my mate Jürgen Klinsmann had failed a fitness test on his suspect right calf. It made it easier for me to blank them. They were a mean bunch, alright. Just looking at the cocky and ruthless Matthias Sammer made me want to stick one on him. And that also went for Reuter. Helmer. Scholl. Kuntz. The lot of them.

But there were two things I hated about our line-up as well. The first was that one of the stars of the tournament so far, our right-back Gary Neville, was suspended for the game. And that was a huge loss to us. The other thing sounds trivial, but it isn't. Any ideas what it might be? I'll tell you. It was our shirts. Shirts of finest dish rag grey. That, let me state unequiveringly, is not a colour likely to inspire an England player on the verge of waging war. It did about as much for my morale as Mister Taylor's photo of dog shit had done in '93. Whoever was responsible for Raggate should've been shot.

Typical FA. They rev you up with Baddiel and Skinner only to... No, let's leave it there. It's making me too mad to think about it.

The match got off to a flyer. After only three minutes, Kraut Keeper Andreas Kupcake is forced to punch a great Incey drive away for a corner. Gazza takes it. TA heads it on at the near post. It looks as if it might fall to me. I control the dive. I guide the header downwards instead of going for power. Get in! Yeeeeeeeeeeeees! One-nil! One-nil to us. Take that you f***ing Deutsche Bankers! My goal celebration was the most joyous I'd performed in a while. But I know what you're thinking. With a trick knee, was such an explosive gymnastic demonstration a good idea? Listen, if I'm fit to play, I'm fit for anything.

My goal was only the second the Germans had conceded in the tournament. How would they react? How do Germans always react? They fought back. And which of our defensive sectors did they target? Our right-back area, the zone normally bossed by the missing Gary Nev. In raid after raid, left-back Tommy "The Bat From" Helmer got behind our lines and caused trouble. About twenty minutes in, he caused trouble big time. Picking up a pass from Andreas Moeller, he once more found space on our soft right flank and fired in a dangerous low cross. That ball had goal written all over it and watching it scud across our box was like watching the preamble to an accident you know is going to happen. An accident in slow-mo. And so it proved. A slide and a toe poke from the slippery Kuntz just beat Psycho's lunge and left David with no chance. One-all.

Here we go again. It was a brilliant game to play in. Especially for me, Pearcey, Platty and Gazza, the four survivors from Italia 90. At times, it felt as if our wrecking ball-like attacks would do it for us, but then they would seize the initiative back and we were forced to hang on for a while. A real heavyweight contest.

And that's the way it continued right through the second half, into extra time and finally, the nightmare hell of penalties. Proper fans won't need telling that by that stage I was sitting on the bench with an icepack round my knee. And of course, as soon as I went off, our chances of going through to the final against the Czech Republic went with it. I'm not blowing my own trumpet here, I'm just reminding you of a statistical fact.

But for the first time, I will reveal just how we bowed out. You've already heard my thoughts on the crucial loss of Gary Neville and the appalling disgrace of the shirts. And don't forget Darren Anderton's near golden goal when he hit the woodwork with Kupcake well beaten. And of course, there was Gazza's goal-bound lunge missing Shearer's perfect cross by a whisker. All of these played their part in our eventual downfall. But here I'm talking about the actual moment when we crashed out. I'm talking about poor Gareth Southgate's miss in the penalty shootout. The tame shot that, famously, his Mum reckons he should have belted.

Remember that Brass Knuckles programme I'd taken part in a couple of weeks before the semi? It turns out the Germans had watched it at their team hotel and thought it the funniest thing they had ever seen. That's how sick these people are. When it came to our match, the callous bastards were reminding me of the show all the way through. There was nothing obvious – they just made little buzzing noises after tackles and stuff like that. The ref, Mister Puhl of Hungary, didn't pick up on it. And neither did the rest of our guys. It was classic velvet glove stuff. But there was an iron fist in that glove, make no mistake.

The pens stood at five apiece when Gareth stepped up to take his. It was then that Kraut Keeper Kupcake had his wicked inspiration. His impersonation of me busting a gut to bend that iron bar is barely perceptible on the video. But it's there alright. That bit of gamesmanship got to Gareth. What an image to put in the mind of a sensitive and caring person like him at such a crucial moment. It was no wonder he scuffed his effort. Some barmpots have alleged that GS was stifling an energy and focus-sapping giggle just before he took the kick. Bollocks. That parting of the lips was a grimace of sympathy for the sting-studded sprogs of Southport, Blackpool and Morecambe.

I've taken a lot of flak over the years for my – let's just call it "reaction" – to Herr Kupcake after the game. Talk about apportioning blame wrongly. Why do I say that? Because after his despicable act of cheating, it was me who got it in the neck for unsportsmanlike behaviour. Unbelievable. And do you want to know what I did to the Kraut that was meant to be so terrible? Reader, I harried him. That's all. Harried him up the tunnel.

So there you have it. Although it wasn't my fault, once again, I was responsible – indirectly – for our failing to get through a penalty shootout in a major tournament. And this time I wasn't even on the pitch.

Well, there has to be some reason for it, doesn't there?

Gutted? Hung, drawn and quartered says it better.

So Euro 96 was over. Football had come home. And gone straight out again. To Germany. Brilliant. And do you know what it feels like to win the Fair Play Award after a tournament? You feel like the F.U.S. (Fat Useless Spanner) who wins Pass The Parcel at a kid's party only because the host's caring parents rig the game. Patronising f***ers.

In the aftermath of the competition – Euro 96, not Pass The Parcel – Terry Venables stood down as England Boss and I was really sad to see him go. There's just nobody like this guy in football. Or in anything else, come to that. Adios, El Tel.

His successor? None other than Mister Glenn Hoddle. Hang on, wasn't he managing my club, Chelsea? He was. But now we had a new man in charge; a man who in his prime as a player was almost as gifted as the great Glenn himself. Yes, it was time for the Sultan of Sexy Football to shake his dreads under two hats: "Player/Manager Ruud Gullit – come on down!" Just on this point for a moment longer – here's another brainteaser for you. Can you think of another football club in history who have been managed by two such brilliant players one after the other? I can't. I know Mick Halsall and Barry Fry come close at The Posh. But seriously – Hoddle followed by Gullit? Beat that if you can.

As a healing postscript to Euro 96, I took solace wherever I could find it. If it hadn't been for drink, dolls, drugs and my ever growing art collection, I would have been miserable beyond belief. A happy moment occurred, though, when Dave Green got me a seat in the Royal Box at Wimbledon to watch some guys and a couple of birds playing tennis. The crowd on Centre Court went ballistic with appreciation when they saw me. And so did another group of fans encamped on a big grassy mound elsewhere in the complex. "Burksey's Bulge", they named it. I'm kind of proud of that.

I'm always asked who I saw playing that day. The great Pete Pampas was one, I think. And some guy who had copied my headband. Anyway, it was a fun day out nevertheless.

Following a much needed three-week break in The Seychelles, I got into pre-season training and, although my knee was still a cause for concern, I was really looking forward to the new Premiership campaign.

I'd been doing some hard thinking. I had to admit that in the term just gone, something was not quite right with me and my game. Big Ron, as always, had been spot on when he'd voiced his reservations about my form in that telly debate with Des and the boys. He was not alone in his assessment. In print, scumbag muckraking journos had had their knives out for me since, like, forever? and now they could attack my game as well as my perceived weaknesses of character and behaviour, they wasted no time in doing so.

I didn't give a stuff about them. But the proper sportswriters, the Paul Waywards, the Bryan Gonvilles, the Larry Harrisons, the Iain Didleys, the Barry Wooldoughs, the Richard Williamsons, the Hugh Tacklepennys – and not forgetting my Guardian Angel (bet you thought it was one of the aforementioned, didn't you) – these guys' opinions were worth taking seriously. Almost as seriously as they take them.

But "f*** off, Burksey!" I hear you cry. "Taking notice of journos? "You've been licking toads again!" No guys, hear me out. Although I've had a love/hate relationship with all members of the press and media over the years, I have to say that proper print journos have usually been very fair to me as a footballer. I realised early doors that to claim the attention of hard-bitten seen-it-all sportswriters, all you had to do was play well. But to grab their tired imaginations, to excite them, to remind them of why they became football mad in the first place – you had to do far more. You had to be a football genius. You had to be a George Best. You had to be a Michel Platini. A Pelé. A Maradona. A Hoddle. A Gascoigne. A Zinedine Zidane. Or, with all due modesty, you had to be a Steve Burkes.

Why did they rate me so highly? Because pro journos, like hard-working pros in any walk of life, get sick of the same fare every day. Even if it's good tucker. After a while, they crave something different. With me, they got something about as different as it was possible to get. And to them, it didn't matter – within reason – how I behaved off the pitch. The likes of Barry Wooldough knew I was no choirboy. *The Mail's* Paul Wayward once called me "deeply unpleasant." Iain Didley wrote, "every atom of intelligence and imagination in Burksey's being is concentrated in just three parts of his body: his feet, his forehead and there are no prizes for guessing the third." Okay. But ask these guys if they would pay good money to watch me play. Well, that might be going a bit far but you get my point. As a footballer, these journos love me.

That's why it hurt to read these remarks in Larry Harrison's column in *The Mirror.*

"Newsflash: Hurricane Burksey has officially been downgraded to a tropical breeze. Defenders – go back to your positions, you have nothing more to worry about!"

Bryan Gonville did nothing to restore my confidence, either:

"Burksey's kingdom – the attacking third of the pitch – has become disputed territory. The striker's always unconventional approach to space and movement has suddenly begun to look merely eccentric, the product of a possibly ailing body and mind. On Saturday, his wanderings put one in mind of a latter day Lear tramping the blasted heath. And with no Gascoigne, The Wise Fool, at his back as he is for England, the once regal striker cut an increasingly isolated and forlorn figure. 'Is Burksey no more than this?'"

F*** me, those words would have hurt as well – if I'd understood them. I got their gist, though. And that gist tasted bitter. Sam Curry was easier to follow. Though no easier to swallow:

"Lately, Burksey's been more garbage truck than bulldozer."

Ouch. Of course, the journos had a point. But they had no idea what I was up against. They were all up to speed with my knee, but there was a lot of other stuff they knew nothing about. I was still getting the occasional pig's head through the post from Italy. And paternity suits were still being chucked at me like confetti. Not one bastard proved to be mine, by the way. And worst of all, my most recent tattoo had become badly infected. Yes, the scene – a Viking helmet-wearing Mrs T driving a flaming chariot through a massed phalanx of poll tax rioters – had turned my scrotum into a weeping, multicoloured mess of pain. You try playing six Premiership games with septic balls and see how well you do. And there were other things as well. But don't get me started, Tim. My low mood inspired me to write another poem:

> A bitter gist
> Can make you feel pissed
> Quicker than a shot from a rifle.
> But what of he
> With blancmange for a knee
> And bollocks that look like a trifle?*

Yet despite all this, I sensed that my crazy rollercoaster of a life was about to zoom upwards again. Just because I'd suffered a crisis of confidence, or a conflict of interests, or a confederacy of dunces – whatever – in 1995/96, that didn't mean the trend was set to continue. Far from it.

As August approached, I felt raring to go again. Yes, I was sure that great things lay ahead for me. It's funny isn't it? Sometimes you just know.

*Thanks to Wisey for coming up with that last line.

## CHAPTER SEVENTEEN

# DECLINE AND FALL

The time: 4th September 1996. The place: my Cheyne Walk apartment. The mood: upbeat.

'Yeh, it should be a lot better now. Look at my hat-trick against Leeds last April,' I said, flicking the ball off my heel over my shoulder on to my instep, then back off my instep over my shoulder on to my heel. By the way, in all my years in the game, I've never known another player who could do that more than a dozen times without spilling the pill. It's the backheel part that's tricky. Yet, I'd been doing it for the last twenty minutes whilst holding an interesting conversation. Still not missing a beat, I continued:

'Yeh, I played a full ninety in that game more or less on one leg. It wasn't so much the pain, it was the restriction to my movement that got me.'

'Yeh, listen...'

'Take the draw against Spurs a couple of games later. The f***er actually gave way a couple of times in that one. And it's seized-up solid before now as well. But anyway, that's all behind me now. Hopefully.'

'Right. Do you think...?'

'Oh – sure, yeh. I'll have... a seventeen with pilau rice and a... Bombay Aloo. Half an hour? Right. Bye.'

I put the phone down and finished my routine in the usual way – by booting the ball off the balcony into the street below. There were always a couple of kids camped outside the flat and they loved collecting these free gifts. I was really impressed when I later heard that one of the little sprogs was selling the balls on. He'll make a good agent one of these days.

So why my optimistic mood? Because following an operation just before the season was about to begin, my knee had never felt better. A scan overseen by Top Professor Hans Bumpfinkle from Berne had convinced him that if I went under the knife back at his clinic in Switzerland, a complete recovery was probable. Without it, I would continue to struggle. So – to have or have not the op? It was what some misguided people call a Gallagher Brothers – a no brainer. In less than an hour, my bags were packed and off I flew to the land of cheese, Toblerone and... Well cheese and Toblerone's good enough.

Now most of you will have been hospitalised at one time or another. You know what it's like. You worry about going in, but once you give yourself up to the experience, it usually turns out to be nowhere near as bad as you were anticipating. On this occasion, the twenty grand a day Matterhorn Suite at the Schwarzbein Clinic up in the Alps was a bit short on jollies. But a couple of cracking nurses – Inge and Lisel – made up for it big time.

Here's another dollop of disillusionment for you Daily Shithead readers out there. It's totally untrue that these dedicated girls were fatally late for an emergency call to another suite because they were having "a full-on sex session" with me at the time. They were not having a full-on sex session with me. They were adjusting my drip when their beepers went. Alright? Good. Let's move on.

I flew back to London in high good humour even though I knew I wouldn't figure in any games until October. But the fully restored state of my knee would make the wait worthwhile. And that wasn't my only cause for optimism.

Gaffer Dread Head had made some killer signings in the close season and I was excited that, finally, the team looked strong all over the park. An obsessive thought, dormant for a week or two, returned with all the vengeance of an Italian vendetta. Could this be the one? Could this be the season when Steve Burkes finally won something? And got to keep his medal? I was sure it could be. I was determined to make Mister Gonville et Al Hansen eat their words. The King wasn't dead. He'd just gone for a piss.

Things were definitely cooking at the Bridge. Into our melting pot came two top drawer ingredients – my old anniversaries from Grappa days, Gianluca Vialli and Gianfranco Zola. To those two world-beating Italians, add a lesser, but still very good one – Roberto Di Matteo. And then put Frenchman Frank LeBoeuf into the mix. Stir in the top quality stock that we already had in the kitchen cupboard and you had something tasty. Something f***ing delicious, in fact.

With me sidelined, our new team actually started a bit quietly. A nil-nil draw at The Dell was followed by a slender home win against Middlesbrough. But that was alright. Wait until I hit the pitch running. Running at my top pace for the first time in years.

Despite a five–one tanking at Anfield in late September, the signs were still promising for the team. I came back for the reserves the following week, bagging a hat-trick against Spurs with consummated ease. And how did my knee hold up? Perfectly. Herr Bumpfinkle? Thank you from the bottom of my heart. You done brilliant.

Time for a Burksey-style celebration!

One of the great things about playing in London is that you have a bigger pool of mates to mess about with. And that night, me and players from several clubs got together for the biggest roast since Vesuvius. "The Wrecking Crew," as we called ourselves, were a great bunch of lads and it's just a shame that, for obvious reasons, I can't name them. To be fair, there is one guy I'm glad I'm not having to name. This lad is the only player I know who's got a bigger Graham* than I have. And that's bad for business! I went back to Cheyne Walk feeling on top of the world that night.

A week later, I made my long awaited comeback – away at Leicester. I didn't exactly get a warm Filbert Street welcome as I trotted on for Gianfranco Zola after he'd taken a knock from Neil Lennon. But I'll never forget hearing the crowd gasp as I sprinted at top pace on to the first pass I received – a superbly weighted through ball from Wisey – and without taking a touch, cracked a vicious screamer past a hopelessly beaten Kasey Keller. I'd been on the pitch twenty seconds. I was ecstatic as I kanga'd into my goal celebration. My team mates were ecstatic. Our fans were ecstatic. And even the Filbert Faithful had to applaud. My former champion – Larry Harrison – was ecstatic also: "Brilliant one-smash football" he called it in the paper. We went on to win 3-1. After the game, Larry sought me out. Wisey was the first to smell journo and he was on guard duty double quick.

He's a bloody good mate to have is Dennis, I'm telling you. He's one of those who'll put his hand into fire for you behind the scenes and not even tell you he's done it. But he needn't have jumped in between us on this occasion. Despite everything I'd been through, I wasn't in the mood for giving the Mirror Man a slap – a move that would have had disastrous consequences for us both. I don't think I even told him to f*** off.

Larry proceeded to make a little speech and then offered his hand in reconciliation. The gesture silenced the lads immediately and all eyes were on me as I stared at the extended mitt, considering my options. It was like one of those charged confrontation scenes in *The Godfather* or *Goodfellas* or something. We had a history me and Larry.

For years, we'd bossed our adjoining turf in an atmosphere of mutual respect and trust. But the line had been crossed when he had written me off in the paper. The tension was really getting to the lads as I still made no move. At the back of the group, I could just about hear Steve Clarke whispering to Gianluca Vialli:

*This nickname for the angry male d*** was inspired by the lads' favourite ref, Graham Poll. Just so there are no misunderstandings, I want to state that the Humdinger from Tring is not now, nor ever was, a member of The Crew, The P***y Posse, or any other outfit. Nor ever thought of being. And rightly so.*

'A ton says Burksey'll still put his lights out.'

Gianluca thought about it for a moment.

'Nah, Burkasey 'e's an 'appy chap an' I theenk 'e will be spot-on with the geezer.'

The Italian Goal Gorgon was right. I took Larry's hand and shook it. And do you know – I think I saw the soccer scribe's eyes mist over as a result. I know mine did. Or maybe it was down to Freddie Grodas' after-shave. Either way, it was a good moment.

Wouldn't you know it, we lost our next game – a simple-looking home match against Wimbledon. But if ever there was a telling moment in a season – especially for me personally – it was provided by the next two fixtures: Spurs at home, followed by Man United at Old Trafford. F\*\*\* me, we won them both, five-two on aggregate, as it were. And I scored three of those goals. I was so happy, I could have bagpiped for England\*.

My life was just brilliant again. And you were glad for me at the time, weren't you? I had everything. And what I didn't have, Dave Green could get for me. Take my hi-fi system. It consisted of an Audio First And Last handmade pre-amp, two Gargantuatron 500 watt monobloc power amps, Moetsu six-box CD player, McAndrew DAT recorder, Kryptonite Grand Central Multi Room Sound Router, and Michelozzo Navelli Sistine electrostatic/horn hybrid speakers. That little lot was voted Hi-Fi Nutcase Magazine's System of the Millennium. I forgot to mention the cables. The Sylost Ultimo Plus wires that connected it all together were made of pure platinum filaments. And as clean mains current is essential for good sound, I commissioned the electricity company to build a sub-station for my own personal power needs on land I owned just outside the apartment block. The results were sensational. Let me tell you something, you've never heard *Blue Heaven Is A Place On Earth* until you've heard it on a £385,000 system.

Remember what you were doing on the evening of 17th November 1996? I'll tell you what I was up to. I'd just kissed a well known TV personality goodbye at my door – no, it wasn't my pal Eamonn Holmes – and decided to have a little nightcap. So I padded into the kitchen, poured myself a Tequila Slam Dunk and went back into

---

*\*Actually, I did just that back in the 1992/93 season. Yes, I know it will make all right-minded Englishmen proud that on a Gola Infiammata-sponsored Sex Olympics Weekend in Grappa, I took the gold in six of the seven disciplines against players from Italy, France, Germany, Spain, Brazil and Argentina. Only my plonking let me down. Although I still think I was unlucky to be disqualified for an illegal hold. In my book, there's no such thing as an illegal hold in plonking. If it had been slarting, I could have understood it.*

the lounge, intending to play back the video of my amorous adventures of the evening on my prototype Plasmacotronic 42 inch flat screen TV. I started watching it, but the tape only confirmed what I'd just experienced in the flesh. A bird with a bad boob job isn't worth b\*\*\*ing.

So I went to my sleeping bed a little disappointed on that score. But everything else in my garden of delights was wonderful. A riot of glorious blooming colour.

I woke up the next morning with no inkling that all hell was about to break wind.

Remember what you were doing on the morning of 18th November 1996? I'll tell you what I was up to. I was being shafted up the arse by an FA Committee. Now I've been totally honest about all the drug taking I've gone in for over the years, haven't I? I've told you that at Grappa, for example, I snorted, popped, smoked and mainlined with the best of them. The result? For practically three entire years, I was as high as space probe on acid. I admit that.

But I want to make a very important point. Never once did taking drugs enhance my performance on the pitch. Enhance it? Shit, I could hardly stand up before some games. On returning to England, I cut back a huge amount as I'd promised Hod, but I've said that I still went in for the odd thing here and there. Again, I admit it. And again, I'm telling you that it did nothing to boost my on-pitch efforts. Now let's talk about the results of the random dope test that was the reason for my appearance before the committee on that cold November morning. I cannot dispute that the sample taken three months previously contained more than a hundred times the permitted level of a banned substance. But I swear on my life that I didn't even know I had taken a drug. Of any sort. When I obtained the stuff, I thought I was getting Dandrolone, a treatment for dandruff.

The clowns at the FA conceded that my hair had looked flake-free for the last couple of months, but it did no good. I was fined £30,000. Big deal, I hear you say. But you know the real shocker. I was banned from playing in any and all matches for six months. Some say I was lucky it was such a short ban. Yeh? Really? Want to give me your names and addresses? I'll see you later, scuzzballs. As soon as the sentence was pronounced, Dave Green was out with his calculator. He went white. Jay went white – quite a trick for a lass from Antigua. Ruud Gullit didn't go white. But he looked sick.

'When does that mean I can play again?' I said anxiously.

The three of them put their arms around me. It was Ruud that spoke first.

'May 18th, Burkshey', he said simply. 'The day after the Cup Final.'

'Noooooooooooooooooooo!'

Blood drained from my head and I felt my knees give way. Suddenly, it was like I was looking at the room through the wrong end of a telescope. Voices echoed distantly as I disappeared into a black hole that opened up at my feet.

When I came round moments later, Jay was patting my face and saying, 'Maybe there'll be a replay, sweetie!'

Dave added: 'Yeh, and who's to say Chelsea will even make the final, anyway? Sorry Rudi. But it's no gimme for any team at this stage.'

It was true that the FA Cup hadn't even begun for the top teams yet. But do you know something? I knew that The Blues would make it through to Wembley. Knew it. And more than that, I knew we would win.

And of course, win it we eventually did. 2-0 against Middlesbrough. Chelsea's first trophy for a quarter of a century. And I missed it. Missed it because those c***s didn't believe my story. Note the cruelty of the timing. Despite numerous appeals, they refused to bring my return forward a lousy twenty-four hours. I will never forgive those "people" for that.

Nor will I forgive *The Daily Shitbucket's* Darren Garbstock for writing:

"You wouldn't think Burksey would fail a random dope test, would you?

There isn't a more random dope in football."

If I ever come across you in your miserable spotty little flesh Darren, I will kill you.*

My brother, my team-mates, former colleagues, Dave and everyone at 'Get Real!' – you name them – all gave me great moral, spiritual and physical support through the nightmare hell of my enforced lay off. Do you know what it's like to be paid fifty grand a week for doing nothing? It saps you, I can tell you. And another thing was being invited by Mister Bates and Ruud to share in the on-pitch victory celebrations at Wembley. I appreciated the gesture hugely, but I didn't accept. As I've always said, charity is for losers. Not for champions.

When it came to press and media coverage, opinion was divided about whether I was guilty of deliberately trying to boost my performances by artificial means. I will always be grateful to those who stated in print or on telly that they believed my version of events.

---

*One of my helpers has advised me not to make such a threat in print. Okay, I don't make it. It's just a joke intended to make you laugh, Daz. So when you're sitting there at 17 Clayport Rd, London W13 or in your weekend place, "Wits End Cottage" Green Ley Lane, Fowey, you have absolutely nothing to worry about.

In fact, loads of football's Great and Good spoke up on my behalf. I'll never forget what Terry Venables came out with on a live TV interview with Jim Rosenthal:

JR:     'Well Terry, you've been right at the top of the game for a long time now. And you know Stevie better than most people...'

TV:     'That's true.'

JR:     'So what about this Nandrolone business and Burksey, then? Do you believe the big fellah really thought he was buying a dandruff remedy?'

TV:     'I do, yeh. Let me tell you something. Burksey is by far the most gullible person – not just footballer – person, that I have ever met in my life.'

Thanks Terry. Those words meant a huge amount to me. 'Nuff said.

After Nandrolonegate, I drowned my sorrows in all the ways you would expect. But I also took up brass rubbing, a traditional English pastime I'd overlooked before. It sounds daft, but rolling around in bed with some old slapper – instead of the fit young beauties I was used to – was strangely exciting to me.

But back to football. Thanks largely to an explosion of TV money, The Premiership was going from strength to strength. By 1996/97, it was probably the best league in the world. Matches were exciting, gates were up, football was on everybody's lips. But for me, the season was a total drag. Don't get me wrong – I wished the lads well and everything. It's just that I'm a poor spectator at the best of times – most footballers are, you'll find. And this wasn't one of the best of times.

We finished sixth in the Premiership eventually, the best result for donkey's years. You can imagine where we might have finished with me playing regularly. Especially as I was now completely over my knee problem. In fact, it's true to say that I had never been fitter in my life than I was during this period of inactivity. Talk about life's little ironing boards.

If I couldn't fill my boots with goals, I could at least fill my flat with art works. I went to a lot of exhibitions with Graeme, Pat and the Great Eric all through the year. At one show at the White Sphere Gallery, Eric saw another Damien Hirst installation – the boy is a genius, no doubt about it – that really caught his imagination. *Le Roi* was so moved by it that he began singing the *Marseillaise* at top volume on the spot. It was just like that scene in *Casablanca* – you know the one.

What did the installation consist of? It was a trademark tank of water with a replica trawler "sailing" across it. A flock of seagulls was massing behind the boat as fishermen cast unwanted sardines – what a waste! – into the water. The title of the piece? *Premonition Seascape*. It meant a lot to Eric for some reason. I admired it also. It had a certain... I don't know. I just liked it, alright?

A week after the show closed, *Premonition Seascape* was sitting in my lounge at Cheyne Walk. Eric had bought it for me as a present. Why? Kindness. He knew a thing or two about enforced lay offs from the game and he had thought it would help me through it. How do you like that? Class or what? I tell you, second guess this guy? You've no chance.

At last, after six months of waiting, my final twenty-four hours of exile – Cup Final Day – arrived. It was a double-edged experience for me as you can imagine. Was I praying for a draw beforehand? Of course I was. And for the first time I can reveal that I promised the lads I would buy each of them a belting bit of Britart if they played it that way. Result? Di Matteo scored after forty seconds. Good call, Burksey. Of course, part of me still celebrated the triumph. I was especially glad for dear old Eddie Newton who scored our decisive second goal. Top stuff from a top pro and a top lad. But it didn't help me much.

I went home after the game, took solace in some fairly routine tup with a lapsed nun and a pair of twin Inuit fire dancers, and then got round to thinking about preparing myself for bed.

But I never got that far. For a reason I shall never understand, the book Graeme Le Saux had leant me all those years ago – *The English Patient* – came back into my mind.

Maybe now was the time to actually read the thing. It was easy enough to find it on the shelf. I sat down and opened it. But I couldn't get into it. Every few words I would look up, distracted. But I persevered, hoping for the best. It was during one of my periodic coming up for air moments that I suddenly noticed that *Premonition Seascape* was really situated in the wrong place in the lounge.

Why I thought that for the first time then, I've no idea. I can't help you there. Anyway, I figured that it would look much better facing the patio doors rather than being at right-angles to them. So I decided to move it. By myself. Duh. The biggest duh of all time.

Now Ruud Gullit is a nice, laid back sort of guy. But ringing to tell him that I would be out for at least another six months – and maybe beyond – was a tester. I was so low with gutment as I broke the news from the hospital that I could barely speak.

'So I need a double hernia operation. And there are more serious complications.'

'How did thish happen?'

'I was moving one of my art works and ...'

'Art worksh? Burkshey, if I wanted an art critic to lead the line, I'd have gone for Brian Shewell.'

'I think Robert Hughes* would have been more your man. He's a lot harder in the box.' I was falling back on the old FA ploy of going for humour in a crisis. Look at some of the appointments they've made over the years. But it didn't work with Mister Gullit.

And it didn't work with me either, to be honest. Low doesn't get anywhere near how I felt.

But I hadn't even begun. I'd always been susceptible to the temptations of the Three Ds and the Two Gs and The Three Fs quickly followed. A whole alphabet soup of depravity and degradation was warming up for me on the stove. And I was ready to dive in head first. Well, let's face it. I had nothing else to do, did I?

*Big footer fan is the Aussie Art Buff. You may have read his book "The Shock Of The Newcastle Back Four". And his book on Barcelona's a belter as well.

## CHAPTER EIGHTEEN

# PORRIDGE

E ven though it had its occasional funny, heart-warming and fascinating moments, it's just too painful for me to trace every step of my gradual descent into hell. Maybe I'll do that in another book some time. Let's just cut to the chase and say that less than two years after the installation-moving accident, I'd become clinically obese, I was addicted to everything, and I was living back on the dole in Brighton. If you can call it living. Still, I was grateful for my crummy bedsit in the Moulsecoomb area of the town. Compared with living rough on the streets, it was a palace. As I had reason to know later.

But my nightmare didn't stop there. Oh yes, worse was to come. In the game of so many halves that is the Life of Burksey, there was a Go To Jail card waiting for me in the deck. I'll never forget 11th June 2000, the day I began my detention at Her Majesty's pleasure. Why my being incarcerated pleased Her Majesty so much, I don't know. I had done nothing but represent her with great distinction everywhere I had gone. Despite my problems with her anthem. But back to the plot. You wanted revelations? For the first time, I'll tell you a bit about how I fared during three months of hard porridge at HMP Calderton.

So why was I sent down? Taking A Vehicle Without Consent, Criminal Damage To An Off License Window and Actual Bodily Harm were the charges. Was I guilty? Yes. Did I deserve to be sent to prison? Of course not. To start with, I hated the experience. Not because being banged up in itself was bad. I really enjoyed the camaraderie, the three square meals a day and the ping pong*. It wasn't much different from being in a training camp with England. No, the problem was that being sent to prison meant the whole f***ing world now knew where I was. Why was that so bad? Because I'd spent the last two of the three years since Damiengate incognito, incommunicado – in short, in a right old state. Yes, I'd "gone missing". Nobody knew where I was.**

*I won 343 straight matches – a prison record.

**To cover my tracks, I changed my name repeatedly. Here's a partial list: Richard Kimble, Diego Charlton, Edmund Pond, Joey Pilates, Dave Trotter, Armstrong Sidley, Jock LePox, Kevin Mate, Zoot Horn Pangbourne, Stan Pants.

I want to stay on this a second to scotch a bunch of stories that has yanked my chain so many times. Many have asked where Tarka, Dave Green, Jay, my team mates, managers, lovers, wives, friends and associates were during my "missing years". People have pointed out that I had no shortage of support when I was living high on the hog during my drug ban. So where were all these people when I really needed them? I'll tell you where they were. They were busting a gut to try and get in contact with me so that they could wade in with all kinds of help. It was me that kept them at arm's length.

Why? Because I couldn't bear them to see what I was becoming. And eventually became. I knew I was letting everybody down. Especially Mrs Thatcher and Frank Worthington. And I couldn't face it. I couldn't handle it. The simple truth is that it was easier for me to hide. Hide from myself. And hide from the world. I let the people I cared about know I was okay, but told them to forget about me. It would be best for everybody. They didn't let it go at that, of course. Dave Green mounted a "Where's Burksey?" campaign immediately I'd moved to Moulsecoomb and dropped out of sight – a campaign that my enemies wasted no time in dubbing "Where's Wally?" by the way. That didn't stop Dave of course and he actually got close to finding me on a couple of occasions. As did poor Tarka.

Despite my totally changed appearance, people occasionally clocked who I was and reported the sighting to the press. Some sadist on the *Sunday Shit Shoveller* wrote:

"Once famous for his naff disguises, Burksey was spotted at a New
Cross council estate on Saturday wearing his most convincing outfit yet
– that of a fat useless bonged-out wino with nothing in his pocket but
fluff and memories."

You know what? The bastard was right. I'll tell you how low I got. I don't like admitting it, but all human life is here, right? Here goes. Month after miserable month, I spent every afternoon watching daytime TV. There, it's out. For hours on end, I watched shows like *When Lobotomies Go Wrong, The Window Box Detectives,* and *The World's Cleverest Gerbils*. In between, adverts for "easy" loans and accident insurance – what a laugh *that* was – made me even more depressed. I thanked F*** when they repo'ed the telly.

I suppose I realised I'd reached the bottom dead centre of my life when I was forced to sign back on the dole, thereby renewing my acquaintanceship with one Ms Y Killmartin of the S.S. She had the nerve to ask me what I'd been doing since I signed on the last time. My "unrealistic" dream had become a reality, bitch. Alright, it had turned into a bit of a nightmare, but that didn't alter the fact that I was one of the most gifted footballers ever to have played the game. At least this time round she dropped the idea of sending me off to the nearest building site for a job. Why? She didn't think I looked fit enough.

And of course, she of the elephantine memory remembered the packet of poo I'd sent her through the post. Although I'm still unsure how she knew it was from me.

Our fortnightly meetings were at least a point of contact for me and the relationship began to take on a sort of weird sadomasochistic vibe. At my lowest ebb, I think I asked her to marry me. She turned me down. Another first. Thank f*** again.

And then – Prison. It's got a ring to it, hasn't it, that word? Or should I say "clang". The clang of the cell door as it closes behind you. The first thing I did as Prisoner 459125 Burkes, T.S. was to carry out a tip given me by a guy who had been incarcerated countless times – leading Italian Industrialist Pietozzano Lumazonto. I went up to a Trusty and asked him who the Lags' Leader was, the King Krim who nobody dare cross. One Jack Sprout turned out to be the kiddie. I found him in a corner of the exercise yard and nutted him. He went down quicker than a whore's drawers and as he was lying there, I threatened to kick his teeth in if he dobbed me in to the screws. Out for the count, he couldn't hear me. But everybody else did and that was part of the point. Doing time at HMP Calderton was going to be hard enough for me as it was. Now I figured none of the inmates would think of making it harder. Even if I bent over in the showers.

My cell mate, Ronald Edward Cooper was a good old lad. An eight-time loser, he was an expert on crime, prison, chartered accountancy – life in general really. As we lay on our bunks during lights out on that first night, he filled me in on a few things:

Ronald Cooper: 'That business with Sprouty – that was shocking, that you know.'

Me: 'I was just putting down a marker, that's all.'

RC: 'Oh, putting down a marker, was it? I see.'

M: 'Why – don't you think it was the right thing to do?'

RC: 'Well if this was Sing Sing or even The Scrubs in the old days, it might have been, yeh. And if Sprouty had been Roy 'Mad Dog' Earl.'

M: 'He is the hardest man in the place, isn't he?'

RC: 'Hardest of hearing, maybe. He's only a Blue Collar Criminal, you know.'

M: 'Shit, I didn't realise. Blue collar? What did he do?'

RC: 'He stole a police uniform and held up a Securicor van.'

M: 'How did it go?'

RC: (giving me a quizzical look) 'Oh brilliantly, yeh. We all thought it was the crime of the century in here. I think you must've headed too many of them footballs, son.'

M: 'So you know who I am, then?'

RC:     'Only by your name. What's happened to you? I know what you're in here for – but the last time you ram-raided your way into my consciousness, you were holding down a place in the England team, holding down forty grand a week and holding down any birds that happened to be passing.'

M:      'You know who Damien Hirst is?'

RC:     'What, Geoff's brother, is he?'

M:      'Who?'

RC:     (disbelieving) 'Strike a light. No go on – Damien Hirst, the pickled shark man. Yeh, go on, I'm listening.'

M:      'Let me tell you something. There's more to Damien Hirst than pickled sharks. There's a marvellous conceptual continuity to his work.'

RC:     (Unimpressed) 'Oh yeh?'

M:      'Yeh. Well the long and the short of it is that I tried to lift one of his installations. Bad move. It stayed where it was – my insides shifted about a foot. My spleen...'

RC:     'Steady on son, steady on. I can feel that semolina we had coming up, you know what I mean?'

M:      'Sorry Coop. Anyway, I was badly injured and a lot of people loved it. Loved it that I'd hurt myself moving one of my Britart works. They thought I'd bitten off more than I could chew with my interest in Damien's art – and it had just bitten me back.'

RC:     'Hirsted on your own petard, eh?'

M:      'What?'

RC:     'Skip it, son. He'd suffered for his art – now it was your turn, yeh?'

M:      'Something like that.'

RC:     'But you're leaving something out, ain'cha? That all happened three years ago.'

M:      'It all happened gradually. It was the lay off coming so soon after the other one, you see. That's what started it. And there was the uncertainty. First they thought six months. Then nine. Then it was going to be a year. Then – who knows? So I just went to pieces. And nookie was out of the question for a good few months as well – because of my injuries. So I went for anything else I could get my hands on. Painkillers. Junk food. Booze. Drugs. More painkillers. More junk food. More everything. My weight built up and up. I got more into this and that. Then eventually, my willpower went.'

RC:     'That must have been hard for you.'

M:      'And I had the worry of being out of contract at the football club as well. I was holding out for a new one when I had the accident, you see. Once I was injured, it was put on hold. Permanently.'

RC:     'Alright, your wages was stopped. But what about all that other dosh you were earning? What about all the ad campaigns and the endorsements?'

M:      'They continued for a bit. But (indicating my florid flab) would you put this on a billboard? Or on telly?'

RC:     (sitting up on his bunk for emphasis) 'Now stop right there, Burksey. You're getting dangerously close to self-pity there, my son. You don't want to become a martyr to that. It's a one-way street, that is.'

M:      'I think I've already gone down it.'

RC:     'Well come out the other end! (shifting his bulk back on to his bunk) Alright, you lost your wages and your PA work. But what about all your bank accounts? What about your portfolio of stocks and shares? What about the houses, the cars, the yachts, the watches, the state of the art... everything?'

M:      'Let's just say that things cooled off for me in the asset department.'

RC:     '"Cooled off", did they, yeh? Listen, I've had my assets frozen completely off before now, son. And that was after they installed central heating in this place. But I never sunk as low as you. So one more time from the top – that famous solid gold, blue chip megastar jet- setting lifestyle of yours – where's it gone?'

M:      'Ever heard of Boggle?'

RC:     'No.'

M:      'It's a word game. I used to play it for money.'

RC:     'Say no more.'

We wound up talking all night. Coop made a lot of sense, but there was no way I felt I could act on his advice at the time. Knuckling down to anything but food – the fare in prison was the best I'd eaten in a long time – was all I could manage. I eased his mind about one thing, though. Playing word games for money was a no-no for me for now on. Losing over eight million pounds at Boggle will do that to you. Curse that Robbie Fowler.

Enjoy sad stories? The day after I arrived at Calderton, us prisoners were allowed to watch England's opening match of the Euro 2000 tournament being held in Belgium and Holland. Sad enough for you? Thanks to Damiengate, I'd missed playing in the sensational France 98 World Cup as well. I would have been a star in both tournaments.

So it was no wonder I could barely watch as we took the field against Portugal. But I cheered like everyone else – except Sprouty who was still in the hospital wing – when Paul Scholes headed in a cross from David Beckham after only three minutes. If I'd stayed at United, I would probably have played a couple of hundred games with these two masterful footballers. And with Giggsy. And with the Nevs. And with... On and on. And look how many medals I would have won. The previous season, the now Sir Alex Ferguson had masterminded a brilliant campaign on three fronts. Result? Three trophies. Three winner's medals for the players in one season! The tally for my illustrious career? None.

Then we went 2-0 up with Macca smashing in from close range. Game over. Sorted. Surely?

But I looked on helplessly as Kevin Keegan's side gradually lost control of the middle of the park to the great Luis Figo and his men. Lost control? Gave it away is closer to the truth. I could watch no further. Not because of England's increasingly inept tactical display. But because it was just too much for me. I couldn't handle it. I felt Tarka's low organ note humming away in the back, then the middle and then the forefront of my mind, like a constant reminder of how my life had sunk from its highs to its present low. After the Portuguese's third and winning goal, I went back to lie on my bunk. And cried.

But the following day I had a couple of visitors. I'm sure I don't need to tell you who they were. It was Tarka and Dave Green, my two best friends in the world, neither of whom had seen hide nor hair of me for nearly two years. I almost turned round and disappeared back into the bowels of the prison when I saw them. They looked tanned, fit, prosperous. I looked like a huge sack of shit. Mister Graham Taylor, how right were you all those years ago? Yes, I so nearly turned round... but I didn't. Neither of them could speak as I lumbered across the meeting room towards them. For those of you who want to picture the scene, I'll describe it for you. Forget that glass screen and intercom telephone combo you've seen in the movies. The visiting room was a bright open space with tables and chairs arranged in regimented ranks. It looked like a mini version of the canteen at Harlington. But there were potted plants and other homely touches – like a mural made out of tea cosies. It could almost have been a bit of Britart. I resisted the temptation to straighten it.

The guys stood as I came over and the screw in charge allowed us to hug. That didn't last long. Only about five solid minutes.

When intelligible words were finally uttered, it was me who managed to get them out.

'So, Tark. You're still living in The States, then?'

'Yeh.'

'What you up to now?'

'I'm a lawyer. Music Bizz stuff. There was an opening over at the Musimondo Corporation and I took it.'

Tark a corporate lawyer? This just goes to prove that LSD really is the most dangerous drug of all time. Kids, take note.

'That's... great', I said, trying to look positive.

'No, it was okay for a while. But now I'm thinking of putting another band together. With Dill.'

Panic over. Kids – get popping!*

'But the main thing is, how are you, man?' he said, reaching out and holding my hand.

'Yeh, Burksey. You've no idea how many people want to know how you're doing. I've brought some notes and things for you', added Dave, looking enquiringly over at the screw. He's nodded in response and with that, the door opens. A post guy comes in carrying a mailbag. And then another one. And then.... you get the picture.

I suppose I'd got a bit cynical over the years and when I looked into that first bag, I expected to see eight different types of envelope filled-in in eight different laser-printed "handwriting" styles. I had seen Dave's "public support" machine going into action too many times, I guess. But this was nothing of the sort.

Okay, there's no point in beating about the bush. I'm blubbing as this is being written.

So do you know how many notes, cards and letters I received that day? Apart from people telling me I'd already won a holiday or a new Ford Focus, I mean. I'll tell you how many I got. Forty-five thousand. Forty-five thousand goodwill messages. The vast majority of them were from fans, of course. And I thank them from the bottom of my heart for sending them. But – and I hope this doesn't upset you – the ones that mattered to me most were the messages from people in the game.

Frank Worthington sent me a moving note. And I was touched that stars like Tony Adams, Gazza, Gary Lineker, Psycho, Bryan Robson, Paul McGrath, Gary Mabbutt and Dennis Wise had taken the trouble to pen me a good few words – and in the case of Gazza, add a couple of hilariously filthy cartoons as well. I suppose I could have expected that the guys I'd gone into battle with so many times would have stepped

---

*Actually don't. Taking drugs is very bad news as I've said elsewhere.*

up like that. Every manager I'd worked under also wrote very inspiring notes to me – especially Sir Alex Ferguson, whose great depth of feeling most people only see the negative side of. And there was a ton of stuff from Italy. Including instructions on how to garrotte a warder without making a sound. Thanks to Mgr. Marcantonio Storto, chaplain to AC Grappanese for that one.

And I wasn't surprised that good guys like David Beckham, Niall Quinn, Ian Wright, Carlton Palmer, Graeme Souness and Roy Keane – yes, those two have surprised you, haven't they? – took time out of their busy schedules to give me a verbal boost. Nor was I particularly taken aback that I got a nice response from many of the opponents I've faced over the years. I've already said that we players have more in common with each other than we do with fans of our own clubs. So messages from the likes of Ronald Koeman, Stan Collymore, Enzo Scifo and Steve Claridge weren't that surprising. I was particularly delighted that the great Diego Maradona sent me a brilliant – and funny – note.

But the thing that really floored me was how many great messages I got from opponents I'd had big clashes with. Opponents I'd skinned, humiliated, late tackled and tried to injure. People like Vinnie Jones, Romario, Colin Hendry and Andreas Kupcake.

And who could have foreseen that people from my very early days in the game would have been moved to write a few words. Brian Stonehouse, striker at Huddersfield when I was just a young shaver, sent me a three-page letter of support. That sort of thing moves you. As did all the stuff from journos and the other media. My Guardian Angel wasn't the only one to bring a tear to my eye as I read through them. To this day, I can't hear Radio Five Live's Alan Green coming keening through the airwaves at me without thinking of the kind words he put in his note: "I've heard some people who ought to know better say you belong in prison. That's rubbish. Absolute rubbish. A total joke. You've lit up my life and you've lit up the lives of millions of others. I send you my very best wishes and Jimmy sends his as well." And Lorro? I won't embarrass you by reprinting the nice things you wrote. Thanks, pal.

And then there were things from celebrities. People that I had no idea I had touched – and I'm not talking about the many TV birds I've bedded and so on. Stars like Michael Parkinson, Barbara Windsor, John McEnroe, Julie Walters, Tim Robbins, James Earl Jones, Giles Brandreth, Michael Fish, and Kate Winslett. Amazingly, the great Chelsea fan Sir Richard Attenborough somehow opened a window in his hectic film-directing and impersonating Ken Bates* schedule to

---

*At that time, Sir Dickie used to stand in for the look-alike chairman at functions where projecting charisma and compassion are essential. Such as the P.F.A Annual Dinner.

make me an hour-long movie. Touched? He must have been. It's become one of my most treasured possessions.

And best of all, I got top messages from some of the Greatest Gods of our Game. Let me tell you something, when you receive notes from Pelé, Michel Platini, Johan Cruyff Bobby Charlton, Denis Law and the now tragically late George Best, on the same day – you know you mean something in this world.

At that moment, I knew it like I'd never known it before.

I turned to Tarka.

'Anything from Mum and Dad?' I asked.

He glanced away for a second before looking back. 'No, mate,' he said softly.

## CHAPTER NINETEEN

# CALIFORNIA DREAMIN'

E ver been to prison? Ever been to Santa Monica? Not very similar, are they? When Dave Green checked me into the Om Pom Pom, Rehab, Meditation and Friction Therapy Centre in April 2001, I weighed eighteen stone, I had, like, issues? you wouldn't believe and I had all but lost interest in everything except food, booze and drugs. I hadn't had sex in nearly a year – not even with myself – and on my first "power prowl" along the prom, prom, prom, the sight of scores of bikini-clad Californian beauties did nothing for me.

But every journey of a thousand miles starts with one step, right? I was here, that was the main thing. Yes, thanks to the huge groundswell of support I had received in pokey, I had decided after my release to allow Dave to send me to the Centre for as long as it took to get me back on track.* And by back on track, I mean just becoming a human being again. That was my goal. Anything else would be a bonus.

Enter Brandee Wavedance-Ebelficker, the babe I'd seen to at Tarka's farewell gig in Hackensack some years back. Yes, f*** me with a six-foot barge pole if the former interior designer wasn't the therapist assigned me. How was that for an omen? Even though I was basically depressed, I felt a deal of chuffment at seeing her again. She was a woman unlike any I'd known in my life. Not that she recognised me at first. Yes, that's how bad I looked, folks. Without letting on who I was, I gave her chapter and verse on our encounter that night in New Jersey.

'And then the third time, you gave the guy a tit f*** whilst singing Hare Krishna.'

She shook her head with a mixture of disbelief and awe. 'That is like so amazing? It's exactly what happened. So spiritual. You have the gift!'

'Do I?'

---

*Dave paid for my first two years in Santa Monica – living expenses, therapy, the lot –completely out of his own pocket. Would your agent do that for you? Sure, he was hoping I would make a miraculous recovery and start earning again eventually. But there was absolutely no guarantee I would. Dave Green – a Prince among men. By the way, it was a good job he wasn't banged up in prison with me. He can wipe the floor with me at ping pong.

'Sure!' she said peppily. She was the original California babe, this one – bronzed, blonde and busty. Her only drawback was that voice. The way she said "sure" sounded like a power saw slicing through a plank. But never mind. Nobody's perfect, right?

It was clear we were talking at cross porpoises, so I decided to set her straight about the non-supernatural nature of my story.

'Brandee, love – I don't think you're with me. I'm not seeing into the past. I was there. I am that guy. I am Tarka's brother.'

A rare occurrence followed the revelation. Brandee stopped talking. But she picked it up again after a couple of moments.

'Stephen, I am, like, so sorry? Of course it's you. You're looking great!'

I gave her the sort of look everyone from Mick Buxton to Terry Venables had given me at one time or another. "Frank Incredulity"* Bryan Gonville calls it.

'Stephen', she said, taking my hand. 'You're sceptical only because you're looking at your, like, outer shell? Inside that shell – way, way inside – I can see that you are still a beautiful being; a strong, virile spirit whose inner flame has just been dimmed. But with the correct guidance, your flame can light the world again. Light it even brighter than it has in the past. There is a long journey of discovery and rediscovery ahead of you. But in the fullness of time, I know that you will like reignite that flame once more? Now Stephen, will you allow me to take you on that journey? Will you allow me to be your guide?'

'Righto.'

'Fabulous!'

'So when's lunch?'

According to Brandee, I needed help in just three areas – mind, body and spirit – and I was signed up for every course the Centre provided. This made me a "Platinum Voyager" and it was great because it cut out the need to read brochures, menus and stuff. As so often in the past, with Dave Green at the helm – albeit distantly – I didn't have to think. I just had to do. As a "Plat" I could have anything I wanted – when I wanted it.

Some of my fellow Om Pom Pom-ers weren't so fortunate. Day visitors – "Silver Voyagers" – for example, were much more limited in what they could have.

It was quite a place. Take Mantra Beach, the Centre's purpose built 'Astral Golf Course'. Naturally, players didn't negotiate their way around the beautiful parkland facility by hitting shots with clubs. Oh no. They "cosmically projected" their way

---

*Sam Allardyce once tried to sign him for Bolton, my mate Harry Redknapp tells me.

around the seven non-holes of the course non-competitively. And non-enjoyably from what I could see. Anyway, after I'd been at the Centre for about a month, I found myself heading over to the course one morning, not to play a non-round, but to pick up where I'd left off with a bottle of Scotch I'd hidden behind a chakra ball washer.

It wasn't there. In its place I found an improving message addressed to me. It made interesting reading. Amongst other things, it said that the only spirit I needed on my voyage of discovery was Brandee* and that if I persisted in hiding things, I would never find my true self. Et-corny-cetera. I waddled back to my bungalow as miffed as a miff enthusiast in Miffment Month. But after a while, a different emotion began to seep into my vexed brain. Strangely, that emotion had something like a smidgeon of relief in it. Even a trace element of hope. Where had that come from? I'll tell you. It was beginning to dawn on my resistant bonce that, for all their dubious claptrap, these people really were looking out for me. For the first time, I gave credence to the notion that if I went along with them, I might just get somewhere. Somewhere worthwhile.

That was the moment my rehab really began, I think. The moment I turned the corner and started heading back toward myself. Now here's a bit of free advice for you. If you're feeling hopelessly down and out of it – say you're living in Scunthorpe or something – I really recommend a visit to Om Pom Pom. And you don't have to be an alcoholic, drug addict or depressive to use the facilities. No, some of the world's fittest, brightest and best people nip in to Om Pom Pom to sample a range of treatments and stuff. I've no idea how much it costs, but time spent here will put a wad into your well-being bank like few other places can.

I never made it back to my place. Passing Stimulation Zone 'Tang,' a treatment area laid out around one of the Centre's palm-lined pools, I suddenly saw a familiar face. One of the most familiar faces in the world, in fact. Now it's not every day you get to share adjacent treatment tables with one of the greatest actors who's ever lived, so I sidled over and introduced myself. I can't name him for reasons of client confidentiality, but let's just say that he was one of the Fittest, Brightest and Best I was telling you about. It was a tickle to meet someone I felt I'd known all my life. And he didn't disappoint.

But wait a minute. Me – having to introduce myself? Being a superstar footballer usually does away with the need for such things. As you know, footballers are at the centre of absolutely everything in this world. But we're in America, don't forget. The

---

*Shoot that pun and have it stuffed – jokes in New Age Land are rare beasts, believe me.

land where people don't know what's going on in the next county, let alone in the next country. The land where about half the population think that London and England are the same place. And all this despite the ready availability of – and ease of access to – one of the finest Distance Learning Programmes available on the planet*.

But back to my Oscar-winning chum. I've no doubt that this man – a self-confessed sports nut – would have recognised me instantly but for one small thing. I was still five stone overweight. Anyway, as he was waiting for his "Guide" to show up – he wasn't staying at the Centre, he'd just popped in for a pamper – we get talking about this and that. Then, clocking his Therapy Menu, I enquire about what he's having done.

Arching one eyebrow above his trademark sunglasses, he grins cheekily as he points to his choice. In hushed and silky tones, he drawls:

'Just called in for a Tired Testicle Tone 'N' Tingle. With bananas. Know what I mean?'

'Sounds great.'

'You?'

'Nothing for an hour or so. But then I'm having an eye test. A Third Eye Test to be exact. Couldn't see a thing through it yesterday so I'm hoping for better today.'

'Hope springs eternal, my friend.'

I tell you, I could listen to this guy talk all day, but our conversation is interrupted by the arrival of his therapist. She says hi, keys the star's Day Visitor status into her PDA, and then asks him what he would like to experience "this lovely morning". Sighing slightly, he places his order.

---

*Are you dumb? Then allow me to take this opportunity of introducing Harvale University of The Air to you. For a small additional subscription to your current satellite TV package, you can enjoy all the benefits of college days without ever leaving the comfort of your own home. You will read no books. You will take no notes. You will write no essays. You will take no examinations. Yet with Harvale's faculty of top professors just a button punch away, you will never be left floundering in a fog of befuddlement again. Worried about mastering a learning process that utilises your TV set as the primary provider? Don't be. With our on-screen instructional tour, you'll know a hawk from a handset in seconds.

Harvale University of the Air – if you're pig ignorant, pig out on facts with us.

You'll never go hungry for knowledge again.

Note: Harvale University Of The Air is a brand of the Stelsat Corporation of America. All rights reserved.

'I'd like a Tee Tee Tone 'N' Tingle, no guava, bananas instead, a peach juice foamer and an ice scrub.'

The Guide looks unimpressed.

'No substitutions, I'm sorry.'

'What do you mean – you don't have bananas and peaches?'

'On the Silver Voyager Menu, the Tee Tee Tone 'N' Tingle is a Number Six', she says, pointing to it. 'It comes with guava pips, pomegranate splash, and an oil rub.'

'I can see what it says – but that's not what I want.'

'I'll return when you've made up your mind.'

'Hold it, Sweets. I have made up my mind. I'd like a Tee Tee Tone 'N' Tingle, no guava or pomegranates on the balls, a peach juice foamer and an ice scrub.'

'I'm sorry, there's no way you can't have an ice scrub with a Number Six.'

I have to say, our Movie Megastar was being incredibly patient with the Menu Nazi. I'm glad I didn't have any problems like this with Brandee. Still keeping his temper, he continues:

'You don't have any ice? You make drinks, don't you?'

'Shall I bring over the Manager – Guru Satayajit Sun Zoom Spark – to talk through the problem with you?'

'Look, you've got water and an ice maker of some kind?'

'I don't make the rules, sir.'

'Then I'll make some...' he says with a coldly manic smile that brought Strozzato scything back into my mind. I tell you, the confrontation between Star and Guide was like a scene from a movie – one that looked like running and running – so I decided to split to another part of the Centre. Brandee would find me. By some sixth sense, she always knew where I was.*

We met up by Serenity Zone 'Surf', where Brandee wasted no time in putting my third eye through its paces. It was, like, still cloudy? so she recommended I wore a "cosmic monocle", a lens specially designed to clear the "opto-mystical pathway". Now, here's a tip for you, if you want to look like a total spanner, stick a monocle in the middle of your forehead. I know I said I was going to go along with these people, but there were limits.

'You're f***ing "opto-mystical" if you think I'm going to wear that bugger', I said.

The "Cosmonocle" made me think of the last time I encountered specialist eyewear – the anti-sting goggles I wore on Russ Morris' *Brass Knuckles* pro-

---

*It turned out my Platinum Voyager wristband had a miniature G.P.S. transmitter in it. Very Psychic, eh?*

gramme – but that was for a good cause. No, when it came to vision, being able to see straight through my two ordinary eyes was my priority. Brandee could see something herself – that I wouldn't be budged on this one – so she let it go.

Punishing sessions of reiki, pongo-pongo and karmic tap-dancing followed. Unsurprisingly, I still didn't feel like renewing my acquaintance with sex after that lot so I went back to my bungalow to have a rest before lunch – or the rabbit food extravaganza that passed for lunch at Om Pom Pom. Still, I'm not knocking the nutritional side of things at the Centre. I'd lost six pounds since I'd arrived and if I kept that up – as they promised me I would – I would be back to my proper weight in just over a year. And I would get there without resorting to the "Frankenstein's Monster methods" of stomach stapling, mouth sewing or gut sumping favoured by certain rival establishments. That was alright with me. I'll take lettuce munching over ten minutes on the Lipo Vortex-A-Tron any time.

So did I make it twelve months down the line? I'm Burksey – of course I did. I was still having trouble seeing with my third eye; my aura was in constant need of balancing and polishing; my kundalini release was pitiful and my chakras were blocked to buggery. But I did get back to my fighting weight of 175 pounds. And by then I was back to something like my supercharged sex best of 25 times a month, as well.

Why so few, I hear you cry?

Because one way-out wackiness I had got into big-style was tantric sex. My record? Eleven hours, seventeen minutes and six seconds. Uncoked. Beat that, Mister Sting! By the way, eleven hours was about the same length of time it took my Hollywood buddie to successfully order a Tee Tee Tone 'N' Tingle, no guava, banana instead, a peach foamer and an ice scrub, the previous year. We laugh about that now. But the message is a serious one. Perseverance pays – a good lesson for you kids, there.

As my time at the Centre went on and I got more and more fit, Dave started making subtle suggestions that I consider returning to the game. He did it gradually; first just by talking about important matches that were going on at the time. And players that were making the headlines.

'Waddya make of Thierry Henry, then Steve?'

Great things, mobile phones, aren't they?

'Henry? If he could head the ball, he'd be just about the best forward there's ever been, I reckon. He's special. And what with Bergkamp, Pires, Ljungberg and Vieira, the whole team are playing special. Beautiful football. Weird for The Arse.'*

'Yeh. They deserve all those winners' medals – don't you think?'

'Hmm.'

"Subtle suggestions" did I say? And it didn't stop there. One particular conversation I remember happened back in the Summer of 2002. Me and Brandee were down at what we called her Pacific Phallusades beach house, sampling all the natural delights that another perfect day in Paradise had to offer when the phone rang. It was fine. Multi-tasking was one of my newly acquired skills.

'See the England game?' said Dave.

'Yeh.'

'Waddya think?'

'I don't know about that Sven', I said as a big roller gathered itself and broke massively on the shore in front of us. Always in tune with the rhythm of the waves, Brandee experienced a similar effect on my lap at precisely the same moment.

'Down to him, then?'

'Got to be. Especially when Brazil went down to ten. We were f***ing unlucky, mind.'

'That Ronaldinho goal was a killer.'

'Never meant it in a million years.'

'Seen you do it enough times.'

'Yeh, well. Anyway, we're out – that's all that matters. I reckon they'll go on to win it, don't you? Can't see the Krauts doing anything.'

'Yeh, it's Brazil for me as well. So who's your Man of the Tournament?'

As Brandee powered out to sea on my tantric speedboat once more, I considered Dave's question. 'Cafu. Definitely. Different class, isn't he? And what an engine.'

'Love to see you pitting your wits against him.'

'Hmm.'

Then there were the visits from my old team-mates, and quite a few opponents as well. Jürgen Klinsmann loved the scene so much, he decided to stay in So Cal** permanently.

*In my days at North London rivals, Spurs, the only precision move 'Boring, Boring' Arsenal seemed to have perfected was the synchornised arm raising for offside of their flat pack back foor.

**trans from the Southern Californian: 'So Calculated'. You'd know that if you subscribed to Harvale, The University of the Air.

I really enjoyed these visits. It was great seeing people like Gary Mabbs again. By the way, I discovered he wasn't a drug addict at all! Yes, the gunk he'd been taking is actually a prescribed drug called "insulin," a treatment for a condition known as "dire beaties." Amazing, eh? The guy had a seriously irregular heartbeat and he played like a trouper all those years. Big respect, Mabbs. If only he'd told me, I wouldn't have spread all those rumours. These people who keep things close to their chest bring problems on themselves.

Others who came out to see me included my old United partner in crime Brian McClair; those two old Italian war horses Ivo Zaccherini and Flo Mirandola (now at Juve and Fiorentina respectively); Top Man Mark Wright; and the incomparable Glenn Hoddle again. Guys sometimes came out on their own, but mostly with their partners. Sometimes, a whole bunch of people would come over together. However they turned up, I was always delighted to see them. And they were always delighted to see I'd made such a miraculous recovery. And they always asked me if I was thinking of going back into the game.

Bryan Robson wasn't the only one who believed I could make it as a manager. He said I didn't know anything about tactics, but that hadn't stopped plenty of others. I could leave the technical stuff to a coach. Someone like Sammy Lee, for example. I had four things going for me, Robbo reckoned: my huge reputation as a player, my huge desire to win, the huge force of my personality and the fact that I'd recently overcome such huge adversity. England's finest made a pretty convincing case. I was flattered and touched. Hugely. But did I really want to become a football club manager? Did I not.

I was still only in my mid thirties, remember – so making a comeback as a player wasn't out of the question. Quite a few of my footballing mates suggested I have another crack at it.

"Yah've got nah f***in'choice. It's ahll yah can f***in' do", said Gazza in one of his famously tactful moments. Teddy Sheringham was more considered. He wasn't sure that I would be able to pick it up again after such a long lay off. But he added:

'I'm almost exactly a year older than you. And I'm playing nearly as well as ever.'

Then, with a perfectly straight face, he went on: 'All I've lost is a yard of top pace, maybe.' At that, Barnsey, Gazza, Tony Adams, Robbo, Gary Lineker and Wisey all had a big laugh. As they were meant to. He's a good lad is Ted.

Yes, just about everyone who came out to see me seemed keen that I got back into football in one capacity or other. And most thought I could play again at some level. "You're retired a long time remember," they said. But you know what? I hadn't so much as touched a football in years. And I hadn't missed it, really.

Then there was pressure from fans and the media. Dave mounted a big "Come Back Burksey" campaign and it garnered a huge amount of support.\* From Bill Bloggs to Bryan Gonville, everybody in Britain seemed to want me back.

In terms of journo interest in what I'd been through, I granted only one interview out of the thousands requested. Yes, you've guessed it – my Guardian Angel got the scoop. And he could retire on it if he wanted to, I understand. Good on him. But for him, I might have sunk without trace years before I did. And see – I am capable of doing nice things.

Then there were the film people. Dave lined up a major Hollywood producer, Bucky Geldfarb, and after meeting him at the Beverley Hills Hotel, I agreed to his securing the rights to *Burksey: The Movie*. I think the guy must have intuited that my story had another glorious chapter still to be written because, after buying the rights, he did nothing for a while. Except secure the services of Denzel Washington to play me in the film.

In the Summer of 2003 – still with no plans of ever going back to playing football – I accepted Dave's offer of a job with his Agency, 'Get Real!' Yes, I became a consultant to the firm. What were my duties? What are the duties of any consultant? None, really. But it was great to be pulling in a nice salary again. Of course, it was nothing like it had been, but it kept the wolf from our various doors. Doors. Plural? Oh yes, quite the little property queen was my space cadet guide, Brandee. In fact, the ditzy blonde omshell was quite the little businesswoman, period. And if I didn't know it before, I certainly knew it after she became Brandee Wavedance-Ebelficker-Burkes. My third wife.

They say you should never marry your doctor, nurse, dentist, therapist or personal trainer, don't they? They also say you should never marry a big fat ugly bitch with no personality – but that's another story. But in any case – marriage – hey, who knows anything about it, really? A lot of twaddle – of course – has been written about ours.

Let's clear up a couple of things. Yes, the wedding ceremony was performed in the surf off Malibu. Yes, Best Man Tarka dropped the ring and had to snorkel for it. Yes, his new band played so loud, that there have been no sightings of whales in the area since. But no, the ceremony was not performed by 'Chi', Brandee's German Shepherd dog. Being a fully ordained minister of the Church of Cosmic Possibility, he

---

*\*Demonstrations outside football grounds was one thing. But there were also a rally outside the Houses of Parliament, Buckingham Palace and a march down Whitehall and into Trafalgar Square. Thanks for organising those, Dave.*

could have done it, of course. But he was attending the Burning Dog Festival in Nevada at the time.

And the marriage itself? This is going to surprise you. It was great. For a year or two. Despite Brandee's numerous irritating qualities – her professed wisdom on every topic under the suntan, her far-outer-than-thou-ness, her unbelievable pickiness with food and above all, that voice – I thoroughly enjoyed being around her. Quite simply, we really hit it off and experienced some great – if strange – times together. Maybe I'll write about them all sometime.

In non-financial terms, I owe Brandee a lot. Her devotion to me was very genuine and although her efforts at understanding and analysing me were often laughably off the wall, floor and ceiling – her cosmic scatter gun approach did hit the target sometimes. As a result, I understand myself far better now than I ever did before. And I'm a more mellow person for it. That's down to her. It's also thanks to her that one of my great interests in life – sex – returned. You don't need me to add "big style" to that, do you? And crucially, it's thanks to her putting in literally thousands of hours of effort that I am now booze and drug free. Summing up, I wouldn't be where I am today if it weren't for Brandee Crazy Names. Together with Dave Green and Tarka, she saved my life.

So what went wrong? I'll tell you what went wrong. Feng-Shui – that's what went wrong. Or that was what applied the coup de grass. To cut an incredibly long story short – I left the toilet lid up too many times in our various homes. Doesn't sound serious to you? You've never been married to a Devotee of the Daft Arts, have you? Yes, leaving that lid up caused so much "energy" to go down the pan – literally – that it threw Brandee into a complete decline. And "if you, like, felt anything for me, Stephen, you would, like, so remember to do it!"

This only confirmed to her that I was not after all, the right man for her. We were not as cosmically in synch as she had first imagined. I had already committed the single greatest crime against Brandee that you can commit against any American. What – I had tried to murder her? Oh no, my crime was far more serious than that. What was it? Hang on to your hatstands.

I attempted to lower her self-esteem. Lower it to dangerous, melt-down levels.

How? By describing her singing voice as "about as tuneful as a foghorn on helium." Just once, I said that. Once was enough.

And then there was Brandee's growing conviction that I had once been a soldier in General Miles' army. And I had taken part in the massacre of Native Indians at Wounded Knee. I've kept that quiet, haven't I, eh? It happened in one of my past lives, you see.

To Brandee, the proof of my crime against humanity back in the nineteenth century was obvious. It was the reason I had suffered so many knee injuries in my life as a footballer. Wounded Knee – knee injuries – get the connection? It was so Karma.

I hear what you're thinking – what kind of knob end would believe such incredible garbage? A New Age knob end, that's who.

So Brandee sued for divorce on grounds of mental cruelty. With the hearing taking place in California, she naturally won the day. Won it without even having to cite the self-esteem lowering scandal or my past life as a war criminal. The open toilet lid did the business for her.

Many people have asked me what Brandee is up to nowadays. Because of the terms of our pre-nuptial agreement – or licence to rob blind as I call it – she has done very well, thank you. Since I made it big all over again, Dave Green rightly gets fifteen percent of everything I make. Brandee? She gets fifty. Yes, because I used to leave the toilet lid up, that lady gets half of everything I earn now.

Unbe-f***ing-lievable, isn't it? Remember my earlier advice to young players: "never fall out with your manager?" Here's an even more important tip: "never sign a pre-nuptial agreement without showing it to your agent first." Brandee opened a therapy centre of her own – La Tra La – more or less on the strength of it. And do *I* get half of everything *she* earns from the place? Oh no. But good luck to her. And I mean that.

A lot has been said and written on how I actually got back playing football again. For the first time anywhere, I can tell you exactly how it happened. I'd just started living apart from Brandee – brother did I enjoy leaving the toilet lid *and* seat up in my new gaff – in the period before the divorce went through and I was getting to grips with the changes. One glorious Summer morning, I was rollerblading along the speedway in Santa Monica when I felt a sudden urge to go for a bonce-clearing paddle in the ocean.

A few moments later, I was treading distractedly across the sand with my blades tied round my neck – and my concerns tied on right along with them – when my attention was taken by something lively happening away to my left. I looked across and saw a group of young college kid-types playing beach soccer. The cool, cool water was calling me, but I didn't go in straight away. Instead, I stood and watched their game. And as I did, something stirred deep within me. Something that transported me back in time to a rainy afternoon in Huddersfield thirty years before and street kids playing three-and-in with a Space Hopper. I couldn't just see the scene – I could hear, taste and smell it as well. Then a streaking flash of images later and I was back on the sand of Santa Monica, watching the bronzed young dudes strutting their stuff.

For reasons I understood only too well, kicking a ball, even an uncontrollable plastic one, suddenly looked like the most wonderful thing in the world.

I spat out the lace of my rollerblade.

The Beautiful Game had regained one of its own.

## CHAPTER TWENTY

# THE RETURN OF THE KING

I t has been described as the Goal Of The Century, the Greatest Goal Ever Scored, and probably The Most Incredible Moment in Sport's History. And not just by me. What did I do to earn these accolades? I'll tell you.

The match was only ten minutes old when I've gone back to defend a corner, tracking their big centre-half who's a bit useful with his head. He hangs around on the edge of the D, obviously intending to attack the ball when it comes over. The corner taker goes to clip it, the big number five charges in – but it drifts well behind him straight towards yours truly. I glance behind me and clock that their keeper – understandably – is standing way off his line. Is it on? Just maybe. Arms wide, I perform a variation of my age old head trick, and by making as if to head the cross out for another corner, I get the space I need. As the ball homes unerringly in on my Z.O.C. (Zone Of Control) I launch myself off the deck, whiplash my body backwards and bicycle kick the thing eighty yards upfield, over their keeper's head...and straight into the centre of the goal. On the full.

The crowd erupt with as much noise as sixty-odd people can muster. Then the players of both sides – to a man – come over and shake my hand. It was these lads who thought the goal was the best ever. And I thank them for it.

The time: Sunday 3rd April 2005. The place: The windswept South Road Ground, home of my old mate from school Keith Nunn's Brightlingsea Town FC. The opposition: Locomotive Langenhoe, current leaders of the North East Essex Newspapers League Division Two. The Occasion: My unadvertised, incognito (Rasputin beard, Edgar Davids-style glasses) comeback to football in a specially arranged friendly. The outcome: total, unequivering triumph. Number of autographs signed: Ninety two – spookily, one for each club in the four top divisions, note.

Alright, the game was no real test of my abilities. But it defo tested my fitness. I played at top lung-stretching pace for ninety minutes. I completed scores of tight, joint-straining turns without a twinge in my knee. My feet were quick and neat. My brain was sharp and clear – far clearer than it had been for the last ten years of my career. In short, the game convinced me the impossible was possible. I might just be able to cut it at the highest level once again. Thanks for helping me out with the game, Keith. You're a star.

So it was a case of "today Brightlingsea – tomorrow the world," was it? Why not? Stranger things have happened. Burksey was certainly back. And in most ways, he was better than ever. And do you know how he knew it? Because he'd started talking about himself in the third person again.

In Hollywood, I hear Mister Gelfarb turned handsprings when he took the call that told him I had come through my comeback match in style. Now I understood what that bronzed dude at the Bateman's Tower End of the ground had been up to. And why he'd gabbled so excitedly into his mobile at the final whistle.

The first thing Mister Gee did to celebrate was cast some more roles for *Burksey: The Movie*. I was delighted when I heard my faithful supporter from HMP Calderton days, Kate Winslett, had nailed the part of Roxanna. Although she is far too bright and beautiful for it, it has to be said. Sorry, Rox. At their auditions, I hear that Charlize Theron and Sarah Jessica Parker walked the roles of Cinzia and Brandee, respectively. And in the small but crucial roles of my parents, Jim Broadbent and Whoopi Goldberg won the day. Hooray for Hollywood, eh?

For the real Tristan Stephen Burkes, some big decisions lay ahead also. Which club would I choose to grace with my favour? Initially, I didn't think any of my former employers would want to take a risk on me given my record, but Arsenal, Liverpool* and even northern giants Wigan were interested in signing me to boost their remote chances of silverware. Dave Green had other ideas. He'd been keeping me abreast of the exciting developments at new kids on the block, Sporting Meriden, all through my stay in California. And in any case, you'd have needed to be a visually impaired, differently abled person in the bonce department** not to have clocked the inexorable rise of the club owned by Canadian Gas Billionaire, Grady Speerman. So when the invitation came to meet with his Chief Executive, Grady Speerman Jnr, my immediate reaction was to jump at it with open legs. Even though he secretly wanted it also, Dave Green nevertheless urged caution. "Options are like bowels" was his motto. "Best to keep 'em open."

*Don't forget at this point I was still eligible for the Champions League.

**See how much more sensitive I've become as a result of my California Dreaming experience? Inside I might still think of these people as blind mentos, but that's no reason to rub their little noses in it. Bless 'em.

The set-up looked brilliant though. Even Errol was impressed as we drew up in the 'As You Like It' Players Car Park at The Can Gas Heart of England Stadium. And there were some motors on view, let me tell you.

It was Dave Green who saw it first. A red Maserati. A Maserati V8 Biturbo Shamal. Registration GOD 9. It was my Maserati. The one I'd lost in a Sudden Death Scrabble-Off six years before. And had missed something rotten ever since. Silently, reverently, we walked across to her and peered into that fabulous interior like a trio of kerb crawlers out on a Saturday night. It was like looking back through all the best times of my life. Can you believe that her current owner had left the keys in? Twat. But then I noticed an inscription engraved on the key fob. I peered in a little closer. It read: "Welcome home, Burksey!" Well, you all know what an emotional guy I am. My beloved Maserati – the finest car in the world – was mine again. And she looked more gorgeous than ever. For one thing, those troublesome seat stains had gone.

'Thanks Dave', I said, swallowing hard. It was so like him to have gone to all the trouble of tracking her down, buying her back, and then having her refurbed and sprayed.

'I never done it', he said. 'Don't know nothing about it.'

'You'd better sign for this Speerman dude', boomed Errol. 'If you want these wheels back.'

But the Big Man was wrong. The Maser turned out to be a "welcome back to football" gift to me from the club – whatever I chose to do. In retrospect, what a genius soft sell ploy it was. Look at what it said about S.M.'s limitless financial resources. Look at what it said about their player pamperment policies. It was an almost Grappanese-style gesture. But without the craziness.

Talks went well and two weeks later, Sunday 24th April 2005, I signed for Sporting Meriden. I'll never forget it. World Poverty Day it was – a significant point in the excellent Make Poverty History campaign calendar. By the way – did you catch any of the Live 8 concert from Philadelphia? Watching Orange Microdot playing together for the first time in years was a real tear jerker for me. What a performance Tarka and the boys put on. Just as a postscript, the coverage did wonders for sales of their old albums. To say nothing of boosting the numbers of their current bands' products as well. It's an ill wind, isn't it!

But back to that afternoon in Mister Speerman's office. My signing-on fee and benefit package must remain a secret, but most of you know how much they agreed to pay me a week. Being there as Dave and their negotiator, Chad J. Sitface, went at it was brilliant. It was like watching a couple of chess Grandmasters trading moves. By the time Dave suggested what turned out to be the agreed figure, the atmosphere was electric. You could have heard a pin number drop. And then the handshake. And £110,000+ a week was mine. Sounds a lot? By the time you take off Dave's commission, Brandee's whack, tax and everything else, there's hardly anything left. You try living a megastar lifestyle on thirty grand a week basic and see how you fare. Still, it wasn't a bad deal for a thirty-eight year-old outfield player, was it! Being out of the game for six years was the key to that, though. It had been hugely difficult getting my fitness back – some didn't think I would – but once I'd done it, my legs really felt the benefit of the rest.

I'm often asked why I didn't want to sign for my old club, Chelsea, who it turned out weren't as wary of The New Me as I thought they might have been. They certainly had a lot going for them. Just like Meriden, they had a great owner, mega bucks to burn and a great squad of players – especially at the back and in the middle of the park which was ideal from my point of view. Above all, they had the best current manager in football anywhere. And one that my new girlfriend, TV presenter Iona McHardie, fancied a bit too much for my liking! But that wasn't the reason I felt I just couldn't go back to The Bridge. There was too much baggage. I needed a new start, a clean slate, a fresh carry on. Besides, Sporting had proved they cared about me. Hadn't they got my best girl, my Maser, back?

Some bright spark wrote at the time:

"The club dangled that set of wheels in front of Burksey with all the cold-eyed cynicism of a buyer from a burger conglomerate dangling a string of beads in front of a rainforest share cropper."

If the guy who penned that is reading this – I'm not going to give you any free publicity by quoting your name – my message to you is: go forth and multiply yourself. Yes, you sunshine. Alright, it's true that I am M.M.M. (Much More Mellow) these days, but that doesn't mean I've become a walking doormat. Just for your information, I am far more intelligent than your average rainforest share cropper. And the state of the art burgers on sale at the Can Gas Heart of England Stadium are locally sauced.

I'd joined the club at the sharp end of the season and couldn't wait to get out there again. The ovation I received when I filed out at – of all places – Old Trafford for my first match back was something that sends shivers down my spine when I think of it even now. Once a Red, always a Red, I guess. But there was more to it than that. I think everybody realised what they had been missing. And what I had been through. I was going to tell you what Sir Alex Ferguson, the greatest manager in the history of this or any other game, said to me when I arrived at the ground, but I just can't get it out, Ray. I'll short out your tape recorder with my tears if I try. Let's just say that they were the most generous, positive and warm-hearted words you could imagine.

Then there was glancing up at the broadcast box as we came out to see the likes of Martin Tyler and Andy Gray standing to applaud me. You don't forget things like that. And there was that other bloke as well.

We knew what we had to do in the five Premiership games that were left and we had no involvement in any other competition to distract us. It was us or Chelsea for the title. If we won those five games and The Blues, just a point ahead of us, slipped up in one, the title would be ours.

As it turned out, I scored in each of the first four matches, which all resulted in narrow victories for us. Naturally, my incredible return to top flight footy rocketed me right to the top of the charts in terms of print media column inches, photo ops, interviews, TV appearances, endorsements – and just general tongue-wagging around the country. And you couldn't drive anywhere without seeing billboards of me advertising Stelsat's new hourly messaging service that delivers pulsating 3G pictures direct to your mobile.*

But Chelsea won their games also and retained their point lead. Going into the last Saturday of the season, José Mourinho's men were away at Newcastle, while we were away at already relegated Norwich. That meant they had nothing to lose. And it made them a dangerous side. You all know what happened at St James' Park. Chelsea stumbled to a surprising one-all draw. And with seconds to go at Carrow Road, home of Psychedelia Smith's** Day-Glo Canaries, we were faring no better. But then, just as Big Ron could see our title chances fading faster than a fake tan, Ashley's bombed up the left wing for one final sortie. Then he finds Figs on the far flank with a fabulous floater, pulling their defence apart in the process. The Portuguese Prince traps it on his chest and sets off on a jinking run into the box.

Vision. You either have it or you haven't. But if you've got it, you still have to have the skill and nerve to execute what you're envisaging. Figs has all three. As he draws all the heat toward him, he suddenly flicks the ball off the outside of his right foot into a square yard of space nobody's covering. A yard of space that I'm bearing down on like a train. I'm on it. I smash it. The net bulges. Yeeeeeeeeeeeeeeeeeeeeeeeeeeeeeees!

---

*Exclusive glimpses of players arriving at the stadium, going in, and then coming out again are just some of the fascinating moments you will be able to share with your heroes for a subscription of only £10 per month plus £1 per message.*

**Now don't go getting the hump, Delia. You know I love you and your tasty hot-pots. And as for that succulent ginger sponge of yours – don't forget, my offer still stands!*

The moment gave rise to one of the most asked pub quiz questions of all time: "When did Burksey score and not perform his famous goal celebration?" The answer is known to all, but not the reason for it. I'll tell you. I fainted. Yes, for the first time I'll admit that it wasn't my team mates engulfing me instantly that stopped me from doing my stuff. I actually blacked out with the emotion of it all. What a moment. What a comeback to the big time. The Premiership title had been secured by Meriden just seven seasons after the club's foundation. Seven seasons after it took its first hopeful hacks in the Conference North. And they say football fairytales don't happen any more because of all the money in the game!

Naturally, I didn't receive a Premiership Winner's medal for my efforts. I hadn't played enough games to warrant it. But I knew what I'd done had helped win the title. And so did everybody else in the game. And there was another bonus. As champions, we qualified for the following season's inaugural playing of the European Champions Champions Cup – the richest prize in club football. Chelsea would have to be content with the workaday pleasures of the old Champions League. I gather Mister Abramovich decided the moment we won the title to make another five hundred million available for the new campaign. Fat lot of good it did him as anyone who has looked at this year's final Premiership table knows. It was us again for the title. With Chelsea second. Maybe an extra thousand million will do it for him next time around. We'll see.

The world of football wasn't the only one to rejoice at my success. In Hollywood, an overjoyed Mister Geldfarb resumed casting the movie of my life story. Mike Myers was a perfect choice for the role of Tarka; Woody Allen landed Peter Shreeves; Kevin Spacey got Glenn Hoddle. And Al Pacino fought off stiff competition from Robert De Niro, Joe Pesci and others to secure the plum role of Sir Alex Ferguson. Interestingly, Vinnie Jones missed out in his bid to play himself – the part going to Pete Postlethwaite. No surprise though that Eric Cantona had himself down pat. Yes, Eric will play *Le Roi* in the movie.

The summer of 2005 turned out to be an amazing one. The highlight? Freddie and the lads winning back the Ashes? Yeh, that was great. But I have to say that for me, two other events beat it into a cocked hat. The first was getting married to Iona – quite quietly – at McFalk Castle in Scotland. There were no gondolas, no trumpeting swans, no choir on surfboards, no Mingegate revelations on the morning of the wedding.

It was just, as I wrote in a poem at the time, a hugely enjoyable "Highland Fling kind of thing"* for eight hundred people:

*Thanks to Tarks for the phrase.*

*My heart went ping!*
*On that Highland Fling kind of thing*
*When I first put the ring on your finger*

*You looked a treat*
*From your bonce to your feet*
*But the best thing of all was the singer\**

I'd never worn a kilt before and neither had Best Man, Tarka. Now don't think we'd suddenly become a pair of filthy old crack packers, but we enjoyed it. I amaze myself sometimes with the stuff I try. It must be the new man in me. You don't half get some air around the old riga wearing a skirt and it's amazingly handy for quickies and such. You do have to watch it, though. Involuntary boing-outs are a bit of an occupational hazard and I'd like to take this opportunity to apologise to the brides-maids for frightening them at the reception. Sorry, Abi and Cat.

A lot of rubbish has been written about Iona's entry into the kirk. Arriving side-saddle on a stag was most definitely not a cheap publicity stunt designed to promote her father's venison business as has been suggested. For one thing, the practice of ceremonial deer entry is an old Highland tradition and not only that, the animal in question, Four Hundred and Sixty-Eight as he is affectionately known, is a treasured family pet.

Anyone who has bought Stelsat's excellent DVD of the ceremony will know that another story that has got around the tabloids is a gross exaggeration. The be-antlered beast did not subsequently run amok, scattering and spearing guests at will. Poor old Four Hundred. I tell you, one eye gouge and a punctured lung and they call you a spearer.

All my football mates really enjoyed the day with Gazza, inevitably, once more to the fore. But there was no jumping off ancient bridges to extinguish flaming mediaeval pantaloons this time. Skippering a two-man submarine around the castle moat was about as far as his high jinks went on this occasion. Those shouts of "Dive, dive, dive!" (Jürgen hit the deck immediately) and "Here comes anothah f\*\*\*ah over the drawbridge! Fire One!" will live with me forever.

Quiz question – who was Gazza's "first officah" on this jaunt? Answer – Sir Bobby Robson. You don't believe me? I tell you, it's true. Mild-mannered old Bobby is a right

---

*\*Thanks to Madonna for coming up with the last line.*

dare-devil.* He was a pretty good shot as well. And I'm sorry Jeremy, but anybody who drives a 4 x 4 to a wedding deserves to get a torpedo up his chuff.

Other highlights of the low-key day included Damien's special wedding cake installation (no, I didn't try to move it) and Stella McCartney's sumptuous dresses.

At the evening do, there was a whole bunch of stuff to delight and enthral: the hilarious comedy stylings of Tim Henman; the inspired shadow hand puppetry of George Galloway; David Beckham and Victoria performing their almost celebrated "Who's on first?" double-talk routine and many others. But the highlight had to be Arsène Wenger.

Surprised? You shouldn't be. Anybody who has sat next to the urbane Monsieur W. at a dinner party will know what a wonderfully fascinating racoonteur he is. And it takes something special to make stories about racoons interesting, believe me. But his talents don't end there. The homme is a very fine Charles Aznavour-style balladeer, for one thing. So it was wonderful when in the wee small hours of the morning, he loosened his bowtie, picked up a Scotch on the rocks and padded over to the piano. His heartfelt rendition of *Stop Your Tickling, Jock* made everyone who heard it cry. And whilst we're on that, I'd like to thanks my old head tennis buddy, Tony Blair, for providing the moving spoons accompaniment.**

Yes, it was a lovely, simple wedding. A tad extravagant? Possibly. But all the monies raised from the various photo, magazine, book and video deals came in very handy, I can assure you!

About Io? I've let you in on just a few of the superstud practices I've got up to with the various birds and brides I've had over the years, haven't I? But I don't think it's fair to pull the covers back on my sex life with Iona whilst we're still married. Let's just say that the pleasant and pretty presenter of TV Tonight is a right skanky minx in the sack and leave it at that. You don't think I would have married her otherwise, do you?

The other huge event of the close season was being called up by one of my boyhood heroes, Sebastian Coe, to help him and his crack team bring the Olympic Games back to London in 2012. Yes, no sooner had I got over the wedding than I was jetting off to Singapore. It's amazing – but I seem to have spent some time in the Far East every close season since I can remember. And shirt sales reflect that. Here's one for you: for every Beckham 23 shirt sold in the Asian market, there are one point-four Burkes number 9s. Not bad, eh?

So you can see why Lord Coe wanted me to take on those pesky Frogs, Yanks, Spaniards and Ruskies. And quite apart from my status as one of the sexiest and most famous sports stars on the planet, there was now the added interest of my miraculous recovery from obesity, multi-addiction, daytime TV and prison. Yes, my profile had never been higher. In short, I was more useful to the Committee To Bring The Olympics To London than my mates David Beckham and Tony Blair put together.

Jay handed me my official Olympic Bid blazer – not my colour, but it wasn't bad schmutter – in the limo on the way into downtown Singapore. The hype had started early and there was a huge crowd waiting for me outside the famous Snaffles Hotel as we pulled up outside. What we celebs call "pap flak" – fusillades of camera fire – exploded all around me as I cut a swathe through the ranks of fans, journos, paparazzi and electromedia on my way to the lobby.

But have no fear. This was no repeat of my infamous Paris C.D.G. Airport arrival some years back when, according to Larry Harrison, I made my way through those assembled "like a bowling ball scattering tenpins". Oh no, I was on my best behaviour for this one: I wore my bolted-on "just for you" smile as I made polite but steady progress; I signed (nineteen) name-dedicated autographs in books, on shirts, photos and odd bits of paper; and I fed tasty little sound bites into the gaping maws of half the reporters present as I did so. Afterwards, *The Telegraph's* Harry Summer wrote:

"Not even Becks can carry off a Drive-By Charm Offensive with such chilling efficiency as Burksey."

Better than Mister B. again, eh? Thanks Haz. But back to the Snaffles Hotel. For once, the mega attention my arrival had created was welcome. It was the reason I'd been piped aboard the Good Ship Olympic Bid in the first place. So far so good. One-nil to London.

In the elevator on the way up to our rooms, I asked Jay whether she liked the look of my speech. Speech? Yes, I had been entrusted with the task of addressing an influential gathering of movers and shakers the following morning.

'I don't know, I haven't read it yet', she said. 'But the writers say they'll have it ready in a couple of hours.' Now don't tell me you're disillusioned out there. The Olympic Games was far too big a deal for niceties like truth and integrity to get in the way.

I had hardly unpacked before I got a phone call the like of which I'd never received before. The caller was a man whose identity I cannot reveal to you. That's easy because to this day I have no idea who I was talking to. Tray mysterioso.

'Who's calling?' I asked.

'You need know me only as Deep Member...'

'Listen pal, if you're some kind of perv...'

'... Of The International Olympic Committee. What I have to tell you is of crucial importance to your campaign for securing London's election as the host city of the 2012 Olympiad.'

'Go on.'

'We cannot talk over the phone. Meet me in the filmically atmospheric shadows of the hotel's multi-storey parking facility in five minutes. Level Nine, Bay D. Come alone.'

'But why all the... ?' The phone went dead. Hmm. Intriguing. I thought seriously about it for a moment, but decided to keep the rendezvous. After all, what harm could it do? Putting on one of Tanky's simpler disguises – high court judge – I stole out of my room and made for the car park.

The air was hot as soup as I stepped out of the stairwell and looked around. The deck was deserted and the only sound was the decrescending tyre whine of a Merc spiralling down the exit ramp below. I let the sound fade completely before I made a move. My footsteps echoed in the reverberant space as I approached the rendezvous point. Thinking I heard someone following me, I stopped in mid-stride a couple of times but it was just a trick of the echo – the second set of steps turned out to be my own. Unsettling though. I continued on with a strong sense of foreboding. Fiveboding, even.

'Over here', a deep, throaty voice whispered. I followed the sound to the dense, noirish shadow cast by one of the roof pillars. 'That's close enough.'

I could just vaguely make out a silhouette. 'Deep Member?'

'Yes.'

'You have something for us? Something to help our Campaign?' Blimey, that sounded pukka. But inside I felt as queasy as a Man United fan after too many prawn sarnies.

'Yes. But first – ground rules. This meeting is officially unofficial and you must tell no-one about it. What you're going to hear, you're not going to hear from me. Do you understand?'

'No.'

'Never mind. Listen carefully. If you want the convoluted marathon you've undertaken to end with London's election – follow the honey.'

'Well I've just got married, so for a month or two I won't be following any honeys.'

'I'm not talking about that kind of honey.'

'Then what do you...?'

'In the speech you're making tomorrow – follow the story of the honey and you will secure the election.'

I pressed him again, but after I'd been talking for a couple of minutes, I realised he'd gone. Brilliant. I went back to my room none the wiser for the encounter. A full evening of briefing followed and boy was I tempted to tell Seb and the others about what had happened in the car park. But I had expressly been warned not to, so thought better of it.

Some of the briefing stuff went over my head, but I must say it was great meeting the other delegates. Especially the mega gorgeous Denise Lewis. Yowzer! But I couldn't allow myself to be distracted (not that she showed me any encouragement and not that I would have done anything about it if she had, lo), I had other fish to fry. Olympic-shaped fish. And I still had to work out what Deep Member had meant by his reference to honey. It looked as if London's whole bid could depend on it. Exciting, eh?!

I went to bed – alone – and got my brain into gear. But seconds later I fell asleep for eight hours and the job was a bad 'un. But in the morning – isn't it weird – I woke up and knew precisely what the honey thing was all about. I hadn't been thinking or dreaming about it, but it came right into my mind. And so I went off to the voting bash brimming with confidence.

It was just a shame that I wouldn't be delivering my piece at the climax of the proceedings – the final presentation ceremony. But nevertheless, scores of I.O.C. bods were going to be present for my address and the event was a highly significant vote-catcher in its own right. Seb didn't know it, but kicking the thing off with me was like selecting his strongest sprinter to run the first leg of a 4 x 100 metres relay. Yes, I knew that once everyone heard what I had to say, London would be way ahead going into the latter stages of the race.

Thanks, Deep Member. Thanks for the tip, hint, advice – whatever you want to call it. There was a huge throng packed into the hotel's conference facility – the Surabaya Suite – as I took the platform. It was all set up for me: a row of mikes at just the right height; a pair of those twin "invisible" autocues showing "my" carefully worded speech. There was just one tiny little difference from what I had agreed with Seb. I was going to ignore the prepared text completely and speak off the cuff.

It proved to be a speech of two halves. Three, really. As I began, I could see an increasingly agitated British camp gesturing furiously at me to read what I was supposed to off those twin screens. But I carried on regardless. Then, just as I thought somebody was going to be dispatched to give me the hook, I saw the mood change. I could see Seb starting to get what I was doing. The wisdom of my strategy was beginning to hit home. He shushed the others and let me get on with it. There is no tape of what I said, but here's a rough transcript:

"Hi everybody. And especially hi to the people that really matter – the decision makers dotted around this room. Can you all hear me? Because what I've got to say will knock your f... Sorry – knock your socks off. I want to share something with you. Something very personal. If you haven't got a strong stomach, it might be better if you left now."

Nobody moved.

"Okay? Right. Back in the year 2000, I was not the superfit, bronzed megastar athlete you see before you now. I'd fallen on hard times. Fallen? Crashed is a better word. Yes, back then my days were about as black as a bat's chuff. Drink. Drugs. You name it – I was addicted to it. I was criminally obese. I had no job. I had nowhere to live. I had no hope – no nothing. One September morning – like so many other mornings – I found myself lying in a caved-in stupor in a gutter somewhere, covered in pustules and vomit. I wasn't at death's door. I was in its very waiting room. All around me, rats were queuing up, waiting for the breath that for some time had merely ruffled the curtains of my existence to take its last meagre puff. And it didn't look as if they would have to wait long before they could sink their filthy fangs into my fat stinking carcass. At the time, all I had to my name was one flip flop, a pair of shell suit bottoms and a moth-eaten old duffel coat. But in the pocket of that coat was something that had sustained and nourished me ever since I'd nicked it from a market stall some months before. That something was a jar of honey. And so once more, I reached into my coat pocket, twisted the lid, stuck my fingers in and raised a gobbet to my lips. Friends, I was to be disappointed. Not because there was so little of the precious nectar left. But because it had gone rancid. Yes, that jar of honey, the thing that had kept me going, had turned sour. And with it, the little good that was left in my life turned sour right along with it. It was the final straw. I conceded defeat. I closed my eyes and prepared to meet my maker – God."

At this point, I glanced around the room. Reader, if I'd extended my hand, the entire audience would have climbed on to my palm and started eating off it. I had them riveted. And now for the kicker.

"But at that moment, people, God told me to open my bloodshot eyes and look to the horizon. At first, I saw nothing and once more resigned myself to the inevitability of becoming food for the rats. But then my gaze drifted above the kerbstones and alighted on the window of an adjacent television shop. All the screens in the window were tuned to the same station. I became vaguely aware of blueness, wateriness and movement. I started watching. I realised I was watching a struggle similar to my own. A struggle for life itself. What was I watching? Boating. Men's boating from the

Sydney Olympics. Surely, the sleek craft fighting to stay in front of the field couldn't hold on? Surely those four brave hearts couldn't keep their own rat pack at bay? You don't need me to tell you that that is exactly what Sir Steven Redgrave, Sir Matthew Pinsent, Mister Steve Williams and Mister James Cracknell did. They achieved the impossible. I remember sitting up slightly as the camera closed in on the faces of our heroes. Exhausted? Yes. Triumphant? Yes. Humble in victory? Yes. At that moment, I felt something I hadn't felt since my glory days on the football pitch. I felt uplifted, transformed. A moment later, I staggered up out of the gutter. And took my first faltering steps back to becoming something like a human being again. Yes, on this occasion, The Olympic Games had done more than just inspire a kid, or coax another performance from a top class athlete. The Olympic Games had saved a life."

For a moment there was dead silence. Apart from the odd bit of whimpering. But then, the place erupted into a tumult of applause. I glanced across at my Yorkshire buddie Seb.

He wiped a tear from his eye, then stood and applauded along with everyone else.

Not bad, eh? Alright, my story was a bit of an exaggeration. Actually, it was a big exaggeration. In fact, it was bollocks. But bollocks with a purpose. As most bollocks tend to be, to be fair. Oh, the rancid honey part of it is real enough. That moment represents just about the lowest point of my whole existence. But I wasn't revived by boating. However magnificent. In fact, it was two nice ladies from the Salvation Army who did the needful – a Colonel Harwell and a Major Tomms* picked me up and took me to a nearby hostel. Okay, it wasn't the Ritz, but there was good food, clean clothing and a warm bed. They were good listeners, too. It's just a shame that the Sally Army has such negative profiling implications or I would be more than happy to do Promo stuff for them now I'm back on top of the world. That's showbiz, eh!

But the thing that will always puzzle me is how Deep Member got to know about Honeygate. As far as I know, I've never mentioned it to anyone before now. Not even Tarka. And whilst it's true that the Olympic Bods have their eyes, ears and noses stuck into everything, I can't believe they have spies embedded in the Sally Army.

What next – the Government? The Stelsat Corporation of America? No, I'm getting like paranoid here? Anyway, how Deep Member got to know, I've no idea. Who cares? My tale had gone over big – that's all that mattered. Could our rival cities beat what

---

*David Bowie immortalised the Good Major in the opening line of one of his biggest hits. "Jean Genie," I think it is.

I'd come up with? No way. Madrid? "Ask a La Veesta, baby!" And Paris? "Voolay voo cooshay avec mwa suswa? Well you may as well coz you ain't gonna be hostin' no 'lympics!"

After I spoke, the subsequent question and answer period – not on the agenda – didn't go quite so well. A guy asked:

'Mister Burkes, you yourself have served a ban as a drug cheat, what would you say should be done to stamp out drug taking amongst athletes today?'

It was a good thing I was able to think of my secret word at that moment or I would have rearranged the bastard's furniture big style. Like a true pro, I smiled as I answered:

'Well, I've always said that if you want to see how far athletes can really go, let them take whatever...'

'Yes, thanks Burksey for those inspiring words!' butted in a rapidly arriving Seb as I was bundled off the podium by a combination of Jonathan Edwards and Sally Gunnell. Strong as horses, those two, I'm telling you. And that Jonathan looks to weigh only about eleven stone. Anyway, I forgave them. Nice people, by the way.

Despite my being on such a roll following my moving speech, I was strictly forbidden from doing anything but turn up and smile at all the remaining events. It was explained to me that it would be impossible to top what I'd already done for the cause, so I understood and abided by the decision. I'll never forget – I don't suppose you will either – the moment when that bloke finally got the envelope open and announced that London had won the right to host the Games. I made sure I was sitting close to Denise for the announcement. Our hug is another thing I won't forget in a hurry. By the way, I didn't pull the Divine One's shirt out of her skirt in the excitement of it all as has been suggested. It happened accidentally when she jumped about ten feet in the air on hearing the decision. Look at the video.

Okay lads and lasses, when you're sitting there in 2012 watching good old Sue Barker kowtowing to Michael Johnson as she introduces that first programme from the East End, I hope you'll raise a glass to Burksey. Because without him, it wouldn't be happening. And whatever you decide to go with for a tipple, drip a drop of honey into it.

One final thought. So some member pressed the wrong button, eh? Yeh, right...

## CHAPTER TWENTY ONE

# SWEET FA?

**B**ack from one triumph, I prepared myself for what I hoped would be another. I'd ended the previous football season by helping Sporting Meriden win the Premiership. But got no winner's medal for doing it. As you all know, in the 2005/2006 season that was to follow, the thing I'd been thirsting after all my life, finally came. Came like a fountain. And it was a multiple orgasm. Sporting Meriden's last gasp victory in the final of the European Champions Champions Cup thanks to yours truly's penalty was followed four days later by another, some would say, even greater triumph. And we didn't have to kick a ball to do it. Yes, in failing to win their last game of the season by more than six clear goals – some hopes, eh? – Chelsea conceded the Premiership to us for the second year running. Two winners medals for me – and the lads – in the same week. If you guys had no idea what it meant to me at the start of our journey together, you'll understand what it means to me now. There are people who say I have everything. And they're right, of course. But I didn't have everything until I'd won those medals. They mean everything to me.

I must say, the fastidious and brilliant Mister José Mourinho was most generous in his comments about our success in an end of season interview with Gary Lineker:

JM:    'I think at this moment, I have to congratulate Sporting. I have to congratulate Ron Atkinson. I have to congratulate my compatriot, Luis. And I have to congratulate Burksey for all that he has done. Twenty-two goals and thirty-one assists is ... amazing.'

GL:    'So you think Sporting deserved the title, Jose?'

JM:    'No. I think we were the best team. But this is football.'

Fair dos. It's all opinions, isn't it? I'm often asked about regrets. Are you kidding? My whole life has been punctuated by them. But I tell you one huge regret. No disrespect to any of the wonderful managers I've had through the years, but I would love to have played for Mister Mourinho. This man is football through and through and yet he's not like anybody else in the game. He's got something else going for him. Depth. Breadth. Width. Warmth. But enough of him. Let's turn our attention back to me.

In September 2005, we all watched a certain match aghast and agog, didn't we? I'm referring to England's defeat in the World Cup qualifier against the Northern Irish in Belfast. And barely sneaking past Austria and Poland in the next two games wasn't much better. But it meant we had made it through to the finals. And in top spot in the group. That was the good news. The bad was that we weren't playing like the Big Boys our top spot was meant to denote. A potent unit? We looked about as thrusting as a bunch of eunuchs with a bad case of brewer's droop.

So it was no surprise to me when a couple of days after the Poland match, I got a call from a certain Sven-Göran Eriksson. Nevertheless, hearing that familiar voice on the line made my eyes revolve like fruit machines. But would the reels eventually come to a stop on World Cup Trophies or lemons? Whatever, I couldn't wait to keep our meeting at FA H.Q. in Soho. So, a possible call up for England at the age of 38, eh? Like unbelievable? No, it wasn't. I was playing better than ever. You know it. They knew it. And he knew it. No way would I be grateful for the invite. The FA should have been begging me to come back. F***ers.

As soon as Errol and Jay picked me up, she could see I was on the simmer. And a heavy boil was rolling just below the surface. I hadn't been in such a state for years and even banging Iona's brains out just before I left the house hadn't stilled my bubbles. I didn't know it, but as Errol distracted me, Jay immediately called Dave to warn him of the potential volatility of the situation. Why? Because it was important I didn't blow the meeting. Get Real! (and a certain media conglomerate with whom Dave had worked out a fantastic, ground-breaking deal) had a lot riding on me at this important time – the run-up to the 2006 World Cup in the wonderf... no screw it – let's just call it Germany and leave it there. It was important for me, right?

Playing it tactfully, Jay tried to clear my reddening mist with a variety of strategies, some learned from Brandee, some of her own devising. But meditational chanting, Japanese bai chi, and even a session of Indonesian Slot Botti on the back seat failed to relax me. And then, in a gesture that I'll never forget, Jay, a life-long bird fancier, offered to give me a bl** j** to calm me down. Talk about "beyond the call of duty". How could I let the noted tit 'n' clit twitcher do that? Quite easily as it turned out. But don't worry, Io. Her inexperience showed and she was nowhere near as skilful as you at the ancient art.

Still, her plucky sacrifice worked* and I got out of the car in a much sunnier mood than when I'd got in. But one swallow doesn't make a summer – or two come to that – so I still wasn't certain how I would fare during the meeting itself.

*Naturally, I was keen to know whether the experience had finally awakened the exotic Antiguan Beauty to the joys of heterosexuality. Not that it mattered to me as a happily married man, of course. Anyway, after my meeting with Sven, I got my answer. Jehanna became the only woman in history to get the full measure of Burksey's ruler and not come back for more. I salute you, Jay. Silly, misguided girl.

If you've ever had anything to do with the FA, you'll know it's an unbelievable organisation. As top heavy as Jordan, but without the intelligence or charm, I've always had a negative feeling about it. And that was before they imposed – and rigidly enforced – my drugs ban back in '96. Moving HQ's since then hasn't changed anything, either.

The "new" Soho Square offices have a queer atmosphere, I find. If it weren't for the framed photos and stuff, you wouldn't know you were in a place that had anything to do with football. And a lot of right rum beggars work there. And the ones that aren't rum tend to be a bit on the plastic side. Can I just say one name to you? David Davies? Born in a suit, that man. And what's the pink tie and black shirt combo all about? I'm sure he's a very nice guy underneath, but he's one of those people who talk at you rather than to you. It's not that he doesn't listen – it's just that everything he says sounds like a press release or a mission statement. Even if he's asking you whether you fancy a tea or a coffee. Rum *and* plastic, if you ask me.

And then there are the financial bods. They've got a language all their own, these people. As Jay and I went up in the lift, we overheard two of them discussing some current disaster. Check this out. Apparently, the Strategic Planning Section of the Core Executive Team were desperate to ring-fence a front-loaded programme that had been through-tasked by a Regulation and Compliance Unit Sub Committee. Or there would be dire consequences for several income streams.

How about that? There must be some pretty dirty washing coming out of the FA if they're worried about polluting our rivers. And sticking a fence around the washing machine wasn't going to help, was it? You'd be amazed how much they pay these people for dreaming up crap like that.

Mister Eriksson leapt to his feet as I was shown into the Rous Suite, where our meeting was to be held "in camera". I wasn't happy about the press and media being there, but it turns out the phrase means just the opposite. Like weird? Anyway, I'd seen him sitting in the stands all over the shop, but this was the first time we'd met in the flesh. Urbane is the word they always use about him, isn't it? I looked it up and, had I still been addicted to word games, it would have been a useful addition to my lexicon.

Talking of men in grey flannel, Old Svenis is a classic case. In fact, the bloke looks all wrong in a tracksuit, don't you think? But I could immediately see why his players like and respect him. He's intelligent. He's a great listener. He's patient. He's courteous. He's supportive. What the f*** was he doing in football? I expect you've wondered the same yourselves. On several occasions.

But back to our meeting. I decided to take the bull by the horns.

'Look Mister Eriksson, if I'm to come back into the team, I'll require certain conditions to be met. I want to come and go to matches in my own vehicle with my own people.

I want to have a say in how the team approach each match. And I want a roving commission in the games themselves.' None of this had been agreed with Get Real! It was just my idea.

His Eminence seemed uncomfortable with my terms. And for the third time that day, Jay was rendered open-mouthed by the sheer size of my bravado. It's a gift I have. I sat tight as Mister Eriksson shifted awkwardly in his seat.

'Well, uh... that would be... disastrous for team morale, I must say. But it was not for this reason that I called for the meeting. Today.'

'You're not considering recalling me?'

'Well, uh... everybody can see that you're having a great season with Sporting. Absolutely fantastic.'

'But you don't want to consider me?' I looked across at Jay, who was already wondering how she could stop me nutting the suave Swede. 'It's alright, Baby,' I said.

'Well uh... that is for the future of course. If you stay as fit as you are then it is possible. Absolutely.'

'So why did you want to see me?'

'Well uh... as a senior international player – one who has known great adversity – I was hoping that you would talk to the squad before our game. Against Argentina.'

There you have it. My performance at the Olympic bid in Singapore had gone before me. My new found brilliance as a motivational speaker was the immediate reason for my "recall". I thought about it for a moment. At least it was a foot in the door, right?

The place: The William Tell Suite in Geneva's noted Hotel Alpendummer. The time: seven fifty-five pm on Friday 11th November 2005 – five minutes before I was due to address the assembled England players on what it would take from them to defeat the mighty Argentineans in the following day's friendly. As I sat there sipping a mineral water, my mind went back to a similar occasion in Cagliari in 1990. Yes, on the eve of our first game in Italia 90, the management had also made use of the crack clack of a top whack motivational speaker. I remember it clearly. As the guy went into his spiel, we were all ears. Especially Gary Lineker. In the end though, I have to report that Danny La Rue's speech* didn't really do it for us.

*Although his version of "On Graham Kelly's Doorstep" made a great sing-a-long, I have to say.

And now, fifteen years later, there I was in Mister or Miss La Rue's position.

"F\*\*\* off Burksey!" I hear you cry. "You're no Danny La Rue. You must have been having one of your Bong's Rust Remover flashbacks again!" You're right of course, but you can see where I'm coming from on this. Still, the speaking gig didn't necessarily mean that it was all over for me as an England player.

I looked around the room at the current squad. Ledders and Crouchy, of course, were playing with me at Sporting. And Ash and Stewie would have been there if they hadn't been injured. But overall, how did these lads compare with other England teams I'd known? I'll play the game of picking my best all-time England team later on, but for now, I'll just say that some of the current crop were definite possibles.

Skipper Becks got up to say a few words by way of an introduction. As he did so, I reached into my pocket for my little black book. No, not that one – it's not right portable.

Remember me saying I've always made notes on my opponents? Well I'd brought my current season's notebook along. Opening it at the Chelsea page, I looked through some of the entries:

*John Terry: Watched him applauding his brother playing for Yeovil in '04. Clapped like a woman. But plays hard as nails. Hungry. Great reader. Great leader. Great tackler. Great header.*
*Weakness: No pace, so play your football away from him.*

*Frank Lampard: Great everywhere. Bit like Scholsey with better engine and physique. Less vision and subtlety though.*
*Weakness: wears blinkers in shooting range. But shooting often lethal. Indestructible body and bonce. No point winding him up.*

I flicked through to the Liverpool entries:

*Jamie Carragher: Improving. Sound all-rounder. Hard worker.*
*Weakness: Too decent. Needs a bit of the Gianluca Sporco about him. Not quickest or strongest either. Exploit this.*

*Stephen Gerrard: Now fully grown into his strength. Got the lot. Best in world on his day. If he's in mood, his surges will kill you. Great mean streak.*
*Weakness: Great mean streak. Also can go missing when he looks troubled, depressed. Make him feel it's not worth the effort and/or kick him. Red card candidate.*

And Man U:

> *Rio Ferdinand: Total class in all defensive areas. But something's not right. Prone to his mind wandering during games – and before drug tests. Weakness: Not so hungry and he's sensitive. Maybe too sensitive. Blank him in tunnel. Make him wonder what he's done wrong.*

I was just about to get to my entry for Wayne Rooney as Becks drew his remarks to a close.

'Of course, what Burksey's had and what he's come through is unbelievable. I don't think any of us here have had anything like what he's had and what he's gone through. And, of course, we all know he's come through it with flying colours. To have the season he had last year and the season he's having again this year is unbelievable and so let's put our hands together to show our appreciation for a great footballer.'

Choked? Bet your life. Becks is the best passer of a football I've ever seen in my life. It meant a lot that he thought I was a Great. And so did the applause in the room which was warm and genuine.

I stood up, ready to deliver a load of shit about how I'd done this, that and the other thing to get back to the top. And how a little bit of the same stuff would help them. Yeh guys, the services of the Sally Army and a ditzy Californian is all you need to beat Argentina. How could I say that? This is the England football team we're talking about here. Instead, I got my notebook out of my pocket and held it up so they could all see it.

'See this notebook? Nobody's ever seen it before or any of the others I have at home. So what do you think I use them for?'

A few choice suggestions were made. None as funny as Gazza, Psycho or Butch would have come up with in their day. But there you are.

'No – in these books I make notes on every player I've come up against – or even might come up against. This one is just this season's. It pulls no punches. It says exactly what I think about you. Your strengths. Your weaknesses. What you like to do, where you like to go, and above all, what time you like to go out, so I can nip round and give your old ladies a good seeing to...'

Laughter. And a few worried looks.

'... Just kidding. John Terry?'

'Yes, mate?'

'Stand up.'

He stands up. I'd learned yonks back that people will do anything if you tell them to do it authoritatively enough. Good tip for you Beaver Patrol cadets out there.

'I'll read out what I've got about you.' An amused buzz goes around the room and the player himself has a "this is a good laugh" sort of expression on his face as I begin.

"John Terry: Hungry. Great reader. Great leader. Great tackler. Great header. Weakness: None that matter. First name on the team sheet. No better centre-back in the world."

You see I had learnt from my experience of being in their shoes and suffering the kind of rubbish that Graham Taylor had tried on me. So it doesn't take a genius simply to do the opposite. And the odd white lie never hurt anyone.

I look up from my notebook. 'Okay, John. You can sit down.' Glancing across at Sven and David Davies, I clock that they're made up with my approach. Cheshire cats, the pair of them.

'Cheers, Burksey', JT says as he sits down, looking quite emotional. I turned to Frank Lampard next and read out his entry without the bit about the blinkers. And I carried on in the same vein through the whole team – always accentuating the positive, leaving out the negative. It worked wonders. By the time I asked my final "victim" to stand up, the guys all felt like world champions. Worthy world champions at that.

'Wayne Rooney?'

He stood.

I looked hard at the lad I hadn't yet played against. Injuries and suspensions had so far kept us apart. He was trying to appear casual. But he was emotional under-neath, alright. And slightly defiant. If he didn't like what I said, he might tell me to f*** off, might this lad. Or come over and nut me. Or both. And he exuded strength. His head looked like a castle of skin and gristle set on a huge rampart of neck and torso. I gazed deep into the embrasure slits of his eyes and saw something there that I had never seen in any other player. It was an incredible moment for me. I didn't even refer to my book as I said, 'Wayne Rooney: In you, I see myself. But you... could be even greater.'

Tears welled up in his eyes and one dripped down his drawbridge. 'Tan Foof', he said. Or something like that. Reader – here's one for you. I meant every word of it. Yes, of all the things I said to the players that evening, the stuff I said to Roon was the truest. I really believe that if the boy can steer clear of the various road-blocks that have got in my way at various times, he could achieve even more than I have in the game.

But that was for the future. Nevertheless, in the Now, I knew my assessment of his talents still suggested something huge. It suggested that I would never start in any England match for which my natural successor was available. The King was dead – long live the King? Yes, possibly so. How did I feel about it? Gutted? No – I felt differently somehow. There and then, in order to clarify my position, I asked my new pal – God – for guidance:

'If it be thy will, Lord, let the World Cup pass from me?' It was quite a prayer.

And did He answereth? He didth. And what hath He answereth?

F*** off, that's between me and Him.

But I tell you one thing. That evening cemented a feeling of connection between Wayne and me – especially considering our very different backgrounds – that ran very deep. So much so that ever since, the Man U Goal Monster has seemed more like a son to me than my own actual boys. Now don't get a complex about that, Frank and Diego. Although if you do, Auntie Brandee will sort you out later if need be. And Uncle Dave will pay for it.

So, after all that, did my little team talk work? What are you – a hermit? Course it f***ing worked. We destroyed Argentina three-two the following day and looked the world beaters we always promised to be into the bargain.

So I'd begun this phase of my life in international football demanding all kinds of concessions from Sven and I'd ended it more or less expecting that I would never play for the national side again. It's a funny old game.

As a postscript to Hotel Alpendummergate, I have to say that it's a good job no-one at the News of the World asked me to give my assessment of Mister Eriksson that evening. Do I like the guy?

Yes – hugely. Do I rate him as a manager?

Ask me after 9th July 2006.

# CHAPTER TWENTY TWO

# BACK TO THE FUTURE

Football? It's in my blood. In fact, it's more than in it. It's been my life-blood itself. And I have the great Frank Worthington, Mrs Thatcher and Dave Green to thank for it.

I began our journey together by asking you a question: what am I – Saint or sinner, w***er or winner? I hope you're in a better position now to answer that question. Yes, I've done some bad things in my life. And I've done some good. Take last week. I successfully sued* stand-up comedian Django Graham for performing a "hilarious" routine in which "I" have sex with a dead woman. Let me ask you this. Do you think it's funny to make out that I, a committed member of Sexoholics Anonymous, don't care if my f*** fodder has a pulse or not? And how do you think such gags make my partners feel? Get this straight. I have never once b***ed a corpse. Not a human one anyway. Unless you count Cinzia. The only time I let myself down was with Bernie the goat. And that was just for a laugh with the lads. And I was drunk at the time. And I was only a kid.

But back to the lawsuit. In winning it, some have criticised me – an ex-vagrant – for so crippling Mister Graham financially that he and his common law "family" had to be put out onto the street. Particularly as I now own luxury homes all over the world – including one in the Caribbean paradise of Antigua** in which I haven't even set foot in a full nine months since I bought it. My answer is this: Smart Mouth should have thought of the consequences before he stated in front of witnesses that I was a necrof***iac. His defence that he was just exaggerating known characteristics to make a silly joke for entertainment purposes was laughable. You're not laughing now, are you Django?

Why am I mentioning all this? Because it's a classic case of what looks good to one looks bad to another. I'm getting shed loads of abuse for my treatment of Mister

*The damages I received were paid straight into a programme organised by the Stelsat Corporation to bring much needed TV into deprived areas of Scotland.

**Yes, Daily Scroatscratcher readers, the story is true. So what? What do you want me to do? Re-house local families in the place? How about sending Mister Graham and his bastard brood to take up residence? Get real!

Graham. But I'm also getting masses of emails and calls from harassed millionaires, public figures and yes, top sportsmen, commending me for my action. That's Life, eh?

Football is the same. It's been good to me. It's also been bad. But what would I have done with my life if I had never trodden the green and springy? Probably become an architect. I like buildings. Especially big beautiful ones like the Stelsat International Centre in gorgeous Berlin or the Oiloco International Building in Palootaville, Texas.

Becoming an architect would have helped me in another area. My parents would have much preferred it to the route to fame and fortune God actually laid out for me. Tarka – now a leading movie soundtrack composer as you know – is sitting next to me as I write this and he knows better than anyone what effect their contempt has had on us over the years. Although we send them birthday cards* and the like, we still haven't actually spoken to either of our parents since the day my glorious Auntie Vi died back in 1990.

To my wives, I say "thank you". True, most of you have tried to screw me almost as much after we parted as we did when we were together. But you know what? It was worth it. You, Roxie – you're still my sex queen. You, Cinzia – you're still my most beautiful. You, Brandee – you're still my Saviour. And you, Iona – you're still my current wife.

Girlfriends? There just isn't enough time, brother.

My children? Some have condemned me for taking almost no interest in the early life of my firstborn, Frankie. But Roxie was responsible for that as I've already explained. Since? Yes – I've been similarly distant. Why? Because the now 19 year-old threw away his early promise as a footballer and decided to become a trainee social worker instead? No, those suggestions are the biggest bollocks since Alfonso Contolone. I've always said it's up to Frank what he does with his life. And let's face it, just because a person is your son doesn't mean you share anything fundamental with him really, does it? And you all know how I feel about Wayne Rooney.

As for Young Diego, it's too early to tell which way the bonny sports-mad baby will go, but I've already signed him up for Carl Bruciatore's Tennis Academy in

---

*Now me and Tark know where to send them. What do I mean? In 1994, our parents sold the Belmont Park mansion I had bought for them and, without telling either of us, changed their name and emigrated. I got a detective agency on it and they discovered that as Mr and Mrs B Hazlitt, they now live at 1768 Laverre Avenue, Toronto ON Q1K 8Y22, Canada. Just in case you want to write to them.

Florida. You should see him staring at the miniature Avatak tennis balls that hang down over his cot. If that boy doesn't become a natural, I don't know who will.

And my life? I've been up further than you could imagine and I've been down lower as well. One thing is certain – my place in Football Heaven is a stick-on. Ultimately, my place in that other stadium in the sky is a little more on the iffy side, I suppose. But I am assured by a certain leading light on Strictly Come Dancing – I'm one of the celebrity contestants in the next series by the way – that God will forgive me if I give my life over to His works. That's great. But I'd like to live a little more first, if that's alright with Him!

I'm sure you're all delighted to hear that my immediate future is looking spectacular.

Apart from all else*, my chat and features show Words With Burksey will be hitting Stelsat TV screens in the Autumn. Did I say hitting? Setting them on fire will be more like it. The opening show will be focussed entirely on the sensational Hollywood blockbuster Burksey, The Movie which will be out in time for Christmas. Exclusive interviews with the stars, behind the scenes looks, sneaky peaks at scenes from the movie itself – you'll be able to enjoy all this and much more on Words With Burksey.

For news of other upcoming features and guests, and a behind the scenes look at Words With Burksey itself, check out our webpage at Stelsat.tv. The only things you won't find on our fabulously entertaining site are hints about the numerous surprises planned for our first season! One thing you will be able to do – for the first time anywhere – is vote to retain or evict some of my co-presenters on the show. So if you get fed up with Io – and who doesn't time from time to time?** – you can give her the hook for – say – Abi Titmus, Mariella Frostrup or Clive James. The choice will be yours.

So as one chapter of my life closes and another begins, let's go back to where it all began. Football. I revealed early doors that I have played my last ever competitive match.

As true as a Harry Redknapp press conference statement, I believed what I said at the time. But as you know, forty-eight hours – that's two days in old money – is a long time in football. So here's my final revelation for you. I am part of Mister Sven-Göran Eriksson's plans for the 2006 World Cup. Yes, you heard it here first. I will be in Germany wearing the Three Lions of England. My involvement may go no further

---

*All else includes my youth football Academies, my various clothing lines, my hair and grooming products, my property management interests, and my sports shops. Most excit-ingly of all, look out for the launch of my budget airline, Burkesair, in 2007.
**Ooh, no cocoa for me tonight. Again.

than motivating the starting elevens against Paraguay, Trinidad, Sweden and then... who knows? But I will be there, serving my country as I always have.

And might I actually get on in any of the games? Well, you never know. Players have been known to get injured...

# POSTSCRIPT

Let's finish with a spot of Fantasy Football, shall we? Like any superstar footballer, I'm often asked to rate the players I've played with and against. Here are three teams that I would pay to see. The first is a side made up of the best players in each position on the park I've known:

**PETER SCHMEICHEL**

| | | | |
|---|---|---|---|
| **STEVE BURKES** | **STEVE BURKES** | **STEVE BURKES** | **STEVE BURKES** |
| **STEVE BURKES** | **STEVE BURKES** | **STEVE BURKES** | **STEVE BURKES** |
| | **STEVE BURKES** | **STEVE BURKES** | |

The second is my best England team made up of my contemporaries, people I've played with and against in the flesh. Modesty forbids me from picking myself. Although it would strengthen the side, clearly:

**PETER SHILTON**

| | | | |
|---|---|---|---|
| **PAUL PARKER** | **MARK WRIGHT** | **TONY ADAMS** | **STUART PEARCE** |
| **DAVID BECKHAM** | **GLENN HODDLE** | **PAUL GASCOIGNE** | **JOHN BARNES** |
| | **WAYNE ROONEY** | **GARY LINEKER** | |

Blend? Positionality? Don't talk to me about blend and positionality. These lads could do the business against any national side in history.

And finally, here's my best World Eleven from my time in the game. Again, forget that "oh, he couldn't play there" drivel. These boys could take on anybody in the Universe.

**PETER SCHMEICHEL**

| | | | |
|---|---|---|---|
| **CAFU** | **ALESSANDRO NESTA** | **FABIO CANNAVARO** | **STUART PEARCE** |
| **DAVID BECKHAM** | **GLENN HODDLE** | **PAUL GASCOIGNE** | **RONALDINHO** |
| | **DIEGO MARADONA** | **THIERRY HENRY** | |

Wot, no Wayne? No Luis Figo? No Zinedine Zidane? No Ian Marshall? If you don't agree with my picks, email your suggested side to Burksey@stelsat.tv. If your entry matches the selection of our panel, you could win a supermarket trolley dash with incomparable Irish imp, Mark Lawrenson – followed by a candle-lit supper with Welsh warble wow, Katherine Jenkins. Or the other way around, if you're a complete screaming mento.

# KNOW THE SCORE BOOKS PUBLICATIONS

## CULT HEROES

| | | |
|---|---|---|
| CHELSEA | Leo Moynihan | 1-905449-00-3 |

## MATCH OF MY LIFE

| | | |
|---|---|---|
| FULHAM | Michael Heatley | 1-905449-51-8 |
| LIVERPOOL | Leo Moynihan | 1-905449-50-X |
| WOLVES | Simon Lowe | 1-905449-56-9 |

## FOOTBALL FICTION

| | | |
|---|---|---|
| BURKSEY<br>The Autobiography<br>of a Football God | Peter Morfoot | 1-905449-49-6 |

## AUTOBIOGRAPHY

| | | |
|---|---|---|
| PAUL PARKER<br>Tackling Like A Ferret | Paul Parker | 1-905449-47-X |

# FORTHCOMING PUBLICATIONS IN 2006

## CULT HEROES

| | | |
|---|---|---|
| NEWCASTLE | Dylan Younger | 1-905449-03-8 |
| PORTSMOUTH | Pat Symes | 1-905449-04-6 |
| SOUTHAMPTON | Jeremy Wilson | 1-905449-01-1 |
| WEST BROM | Simon Wright | 1-905449-02-X |

## MATCH OF MY LIFE

| | | |
|---|---|---|
| ENGLAND WORLD CUP | Louis Massarella & Leo Moynihan | 1-905449-51-8 |
| EUROPEAN CUP FINAL | Ben Lyttleton | 1-905449-57-7 |
| FA CUP FINALS (1953-1969) | David Saffer | 1-905449-53-4 |
| LEEDS | David Saffer | 1-905449-54-2 |
| STOKE CITY | Simon Lowe | 1-905449-55-0 |
| SPURS | Matt Allen & Louis Massarealla | 1-905449-58-5 |

# ABOUT THE AUTHOR

Peter Morfoot's original writing for radio and television includes the comedy drama series *Change At Oglethorpe*, set in his native West Yorkshire; and the sketch show series *TV TO GO*, both for the BBC. He has also written for Mirror Group Newspapers websites and various other media. *Burksey* is his first novel.